D1520130

GIUSEPPE VERDI

COMPOSER RESOURCE MANUALS
VOLUME 42
GARLAND REFERENCE LIBRARY OF THE HUMANITIES
VOLUME 1004

GIUSEPPE VERDI
A GUIDE TO RESEARCH

GREGORY HARWOOD

GARLAND PUBLISHING, INC.
A MEMBER OF THE TAYLOR & FRANCIS GROUP
NEW YORK AND LONDON
1998

Library of Congress Cataloging-in-Publication Data

Harwood, Gregory W.
    Giuseppe Verdi : a guide to research / by Gregory Harwood.
       p.   cm. — (Composer resource manuals ; v. 42) (Garland
reference library of the humanities ; v. 1004.)
    Includes indexes.
    ISBN 0-8240-4117-8 (alk. paper)
    1. Verdi, Giuseppe, 1813–1901—Bibliography. I. Title.
II. Series: Garland composer resource manuals ; v. 42. III. Series:
Garland reference library of the humanities ; vol. 1004.
ML134.V47H37   1998
782.1'092—dc21

                                          98-12194
                                             CIP
                                             MN

Cover photograph of Giuseppe Verdi (ca. 1850) provided
courtesy of the Bibliothèque Nationale de France.

Printed on acid-free, 250-year-life paper
Manufactured in the United States of America

Contents

COMPOSER RESOURCE MANUALS

In response to the growing need for bibliographic guidance to the vast literature on significant composers, Garland is publishing an extensive series of research guides. This ongoing series encompasses more than 50 composers; they represent Western musical tradition from the Renaissance to the present century.

Each research guide offers a selective, annotated list of writings, in all European languages, about one or more composers. There are also lists of works by the composers, unless these are available elsewhere. Biographical sketches and guides to library resources, organizations, and specialists are presented. As appropriate to the individual composer, there are maps, photographs, or other illustrative matter, glossaries, and indexes.

Preface

A SHORT HISTORY OF VERDI STUDIES

The Beginnings

Giuseppe Verdi already stood out as a distinctive and unusually significant composer by the time his career was barely underway. Only seven years after the premiere of his first opera, an article in the *Gazzetta musicale di Milano* singled out the young composer for his "exquisite taste," "untiring elegance," and "marvelous instinct for effect" (see item 123). With the death of Donizetti in 1848 and Rossini in retirement, no one doubted Verdi's position as the preeminent composer of opera on the Italian peninsula and, through the remainder of the nineteenth century, younger Italian composers remained obscured in his shadow. His death, in the early days of the twentieth century, brought a crowd of several hundred thousand people to mourn not only the passing of a great artist but also a beloved national hero.

It is not surprising that a figure such as Verdi should have inspired an enormous amount of books, articles, essays, and critical evaluations. Several early bibliographies provide some indication of the amount of secondary literature that had already accumulated. In the year of the composer's death, Luigi Torri's important bibliography (item 15) contained about 400 items; by 1913, the centenary of Verdi's birth, Carlo Vanbianchi (item 16) had expanded Torri's list to almost 900 entries, close to the number included in this Research Guide.

Materials published about Verdi before his death in 1901 are especially valuable because they shed light on the way in which his contemporaries regarded him from musical, cultural, and historical perspectives as well as his gradual rise as a cult figure in Italy. One of the most interesting developments during this period was the composer's own involvement in the creation of his public image. During his interview with Michele Lessona in the late 1860s, Verdi depicted himself as a self-made man, rising from a peasant background of economic, educational, and social disadvantage, an inaccurate image that fit well with the moralizing tone of Lessona's *Volere è potere* (item 128). A decade later, the composer reiterated this point of view when he dictated an autobiographical sketch with a similar tone to his publisher, Giulio Ricordi. This account found its way into Arthur Pougin's *Giuseppe Verdi: Vita aneddotica* (item 131) and from there into numerous other biographies. A further example of Verdi's involvement in creating his public profile comes from the last years of his life. To celebrate the premiere of *Falstaff* in 1893, Ricordi published an account of the composer's working process which—no doubt influenced by the composer's own wishes—emphasized spontaneous inspiration and downplayed the notion of what we now know was an arduous procedure, typically with many revisions and refinements at several different stages (see items 696 and 712). This coloring of events was by no means unique to Verdi; the same happened with Richard Wagner, Hector Berlioz, and others of Verdi's contemporaries. Nonetheless, it exerted a strong influence on biographical accounts and has only recently begun to be critically examined and reassessed on the basis of primary source documents.

Many of the major advances in Verdi research have involved the study of primary source material, and among the most important is the composer's correspondence with librettists, publishers, performers, and friends. The significance of Verdi's letter exchanges cannot be underestimated: Harold Powers, one of today's leading Verdi scholars, has recently called them "the most important material we have on the musical dramaturgy of Italian opera" (item 608, p. 24). Without our modern advantages (?) of telephones, fax machines, and e-mail, Verdi used his correspondence to work through many issues and problems relating to music, aesthetics, and business. The candid tone of these letters and their vivid detail about historical genesis, compositional process, performance practice, and reception provide a basic foundation for any important study of the composer or his music. Many letters exchanged between Verdi and his librettists, for example, clearly show the step-by-step genesis of his librettos in great detail from original conception to final form. And the system was amazingly efficient. Dates of letters and their responses show that correspondence frequently moved between Verdi and his correspondent in only a day's time if they were both in northern Italy, a feat often difficult to match in today's world. The composer's correspondence not only provides an incredibly useful record of his thoughts, working process, and activities but is also highly engaging to read. Verdi had a succinct but quite colorful writing style that is often full of subtle and delightful nuances. While increasingly reliable translations are now becoming available, it is well worth the effort to learn Italian just to be able to study his writings in the original language.

While several important collections of Verdi's correspondence had already appeared, Gaetano Cesare's and Alessandro Luzio's publication of his *Copialettere* (item 28) during the centenary year of his birth ranks as one of the major turning points in the history of Verdi studies. While flawed in both accuracy and organization, the *Copialettere* provided researchers for the first time with a large collection of letters (drafts or variants in many cases) addressed to many recipients and spanning a considerable portion of the composer's creative life. The next decade, much of this core collection became available to German readers in Franz Werfel's compilation *Giuseppe*

Verdi Briefe (item 41); in later years it served as the basis for other publications, such as Aldo Oberdorfer's *Autobiografia dalle lettere* (item 36) and Charles Osborne's *Letters of Giuseppe Verdi* (item 37). Alessandro Luzio's four-volume *Carteggi verdiani* (item 29), published between 1935 and 1947, provided a substantial supplement of letters and documents, as did Jacques-Gabriel Prod'homme's publication of some of the Du Locle and Escudier correspondence (items 52 and 56). Like the edition of the *Copialettere*, however, all these early collections were riddled with errors.

Material from Verdi's letters provided an important foundation for new biographies and general studies of the composer's music that appeared during the first half of the twentieth century. Franz Werfel's *Verdi: Roman der Oper*, although closer to historical fiction than true biography, stimulated much interest in the composer and his music in German circles and touched off a period sometimes called the "Verdi Renaissance." Landmark biographies by Carlo Gatti (item 147) and Franco Abbiati (item 145) set new standards, both due to the authors' privileged access to correspondence, musical autographs, and other documentary material at Sant'Agata. Although not a traditional biography, Frank Walker's *The Man Verdi* (item 152) was one of the first to challenge many long-accepted biographical "facts," by showing that they belonged in the realm of legend.

Intensive study of Verdi's autograph musical documents did not truly become a major area of research until the last decades of this century. While the composer's completed autograph scores in possession of the Ricordi firm had been accessible to scholars, this type of research has been hindered by the general unavailability of the composer's primary working manuscripts: complete continuity drafts and some isolated sketches that he made for all but his earliest operas. Verdi's heirs permitted the publication of one of these documents in facsimile for the fiftieth anniversary of the composer's death: the continuity draft for *Rigoletto* (item 878). The same year, the Ricordi firm published a facsimile reproduction of the autograph full score of *Falstaff* (item 715).

Contributions of The National Verdi Institutes

Since 1960, much of the most important work in Verdi scholarship has centered around two national institutes: the Istituto Nazionale di Studi Verdiani in Parma, Italy, and the American Institute for Verdi Studies at New York University in New York City.

L'Istituto Nazionale di Studi Verdiani
Strada della Repubblica, 56
43100 Parma, Italy
tel. 0521/28.60.44; fax 0521/28.79.49

The Istituto di Studi Verdiani was organized in 1960 with support by the City of Parma, the Ministry of Public Instruction, and UNESCO; Mario Medici became its founding director and Ildebrando Pizzetti its first president. The statutes of the Institute defined several main objectives:

to systematically study the life and works of Giuseppe Verdi; to propagate these studies through publications, as well as through opera and concert performances; to establish and transmit, with the help of these performances together with advanced training courses for performers, the traditions of Verdian style; to collect, catalogue and preserve everything concerning Verdi, his work and his times; to restore and conserve those places identified with his name; to undertake all activity pertinent to the celebration and exemplification of Verdi as a man and an artist.[1]

Other goals of the Institute included collecting copies of Verdi's musical and non-musical autographs and exploring the possibility of publishing a complete critical edition of his works. Immediately the Institute launched the publication of an ambitious series of *Bollettini*, with each multi-part volume devoted to a particular opera.

The Italian government officially recognized the new organization in 1963, placing it under the auspices of the Ministry of Public Instruction. About the same time, the Institute moved into a new office on the Strada della Repubblica, which included space for an archive, libraries of books and recordings, and a lecture hall. By its fourth year, the Institute had acquired nearly 1,700 publications for its library; copies of more than 4,000 letters and documents for its archive; published two *Bollettini* totaling 2,900 pages and two *Quaderni* to commemorate performances of two little-known works, *Il corsaro* and *Gerusalemme*; developed plans for the publication of critical editions of Verdi's music and correspondence; sponsored several lecture series; and made plans for several musical events, as well as the first International Verdi Conference, held in Venice during the summer of 1966 (see proceedings, item 224). Several additional conferences followed in quick succession: a meeting devoted to *Don Carlos* held in Verona in 1969 (see Proceedings, item 225), a third international conference in Milano in 1972 (see Proceedings, item 226), a symposium devoted to *I vespri siciliani* coinciding with the reopening of the Teatro Regio in Torino in 1973 (see abstracts, item 236), and a Fourth International Congress, co-sponsored by the Lyric Opera of Chicago, focusing on *Simon Boccanegra* in 1974 (see abstracts, item 229).

During the early 1970s, the Institute acquired two important collections of materials: about 500 nineteenth-century scores donated by Carmen Asensio Scalvini (see item 23) and about 150 autograph letters from Verdi to Boito, which permitted the publication in 1978 of the first critical edition of Verdi's correspondence, the *Carteggio Verdi-Boito* (item 46). By this time, the Institute was also planning the publication of Verdi's correspondence with the Ricordi firm, made possible, in part, by the Italian government's purchase of nearly 250 letters from Verdi to members of the Ricordi family and firm.

The 1980s saw the beginning of a new era for the Parma Institute. In May 1980, Pierluigi Petrobelli became the second director of the Institute; in 1985 Alberto Carrara Verdi, grandson of Verdi's adopted daughter, became the Institute's fourth

---

[1] *Verdi: Bollettino dell'Istituto di Studi Verdiani* 1 [No. 1] (1960): xvii–xviii.

president. Both are still serving in those positions. A change in format was announced for the *Bollettini*: new volumes devoted to a single opera would appear from time to time, but instead of each issue being trilingual, two separate volumes would appear, one in Italian and one in English. While the final issue of Vol. 3 [No. 9] dropped the German translations, the first volume to be issued entirely under this new format was Vol. 4 [No. 10], which reported the proceedings of an International Congress on *Ernani* (item 228). This Congress took place at the Teatro San Carlo in Modena in December 1984 in conjunction with a performance of the opera based on the new critical edition. Meanwhile, the Institute announced the start of an important new periodical, *Studi verdiani*. Unlike the *Bollettini*, each issue of the *Studi* contains scholarly articles on a variety of topics. *Studi verdiani*, which began publication in 1982, also initiated a comprehensive ongoing bibliography and discography of Verdi materials.

The Parma Institute began two important research initiatives during the 1980s. In 1983, the Institute, together with the Rotary Club of Parma, began a biennial international competition, the Premio Internazionale Rotary Club di Parma "Giuseppe Verdi." Winners receive a substantial cash award that allows them to conduct research on a proposed topic. The Institute publishes the resulting research in a special series; to date, two volumes have appeared (items 371 and 540). In 1987, the Consiglio Nazionale delle Ricerche (CNR) initiated an annual scholarship for a researcher to conduct work at the Institute. Work done by these scholarship recipients has led to many of the Institute's recent publications.

Another international conference, co-sponsored by the Parma Institute, Casa Ricordi, the University of Chicago Press, and the American Institute for Verdi Studies, took place at the Gesellschaft der Musikfreunde in Vienna in 1984 (item 231). Its title, "Nuove prospettive nella ricerca verdiana" ("New Trends in Verdi Research"), bore witness to the rapid growth and maturation of Verdi studies during the previous years. Many of the papers dealt with issues regarding the new complete critical edition of Verdi's works. The conference featured a performance of *Rigoletto* based on the first volume to be issued in the new edition, prepared by Martin Chusid. The Institute also organized several important exhibitions, one focusing on the composer's correspondence with members of the Ricordi firm (item 79), another featuring iconographic material from the Bibliothèque de l'Opéra in Paris relating to *Aida* (item 578), and a third dealing with Verdi's life and times (item 237). Other significant milestones of the 1980s were the publication of a new Quaderno, focusing on Verdi's contribution to the composite Mass for Rossini (see item 993), and the publication of the score for Verdi's movement in facsimile (item 994). At mid-decade, the Institute received Carl L. Bruun's donation of 3,000 recordings (see item 21 for a more detailed description of this collection). This substantial gift included most recordings that had been made of Verdi's music and established a core collection for the Institute's sound archive.

A final important event of the 1980s was legislation by the Italian government renaming the Institute as the "Istituto Nazionale di Studi Verdiani" and placing it under the Ministero per i Beni Cultural ed Ambientali. Four years later, the Italian government gave the Institute a special bequest of three billion lira to assist its development as a cultural institution of the highest significance on both the national and international levels.

Two main themes have emerged in the Institute's work during the 1990s. The first is a more intensive investigation of the scenographic aspects of Verdi's operas, as demonstrated in the exhibition with accompanying catalogue entitled *"Sorgete! Ombre serene!" L'aspetto visivo dello spettacolo verdiano* (item 545) and an International Congress at Parma in September 1994 entitled "La realizzazione scenica dello spettacolo verdiano." Its congress report is now in press (see item 233). The second major theme is continued work toward the publication of critical editions of Verdi's correspondence, of which four new volumes have been announced (see items 48, 55, 64, and 82) and, for the first time, a critical edition of a complete continuity draft for an opera, *La traviata* (item 940).

The American Institute for Verdi Studies at New York University
24 Waverly Place, Room 268
New York, New York 10003-6789
tel. (212) 998-8300 (Music Dept.); (212) 998-2587 (Archive); fax (212) 995-4147

The gathering of many scholars and Verdi enthusiasts at Chicago in September 1974 for the Fourth International Verdi Congress, co-sponsored by the Istituto di Studi Verdiani and the Lyric Opera of Chicago, led to discussions among some of the participants of the need for an American Institute that would coordinate the recent escalation of scholarly activity with performances of Verdi's music. The infectious enthusiasm of this core group, coupled with support from Mario Medici, director of the Parma Institute, and New York University, which offered to house an archive in its recently completed Bobst Library, led to the official organization of the American Institute for Verdi Studies on 1 April 1976. Martin Chusid became the founding director and still serves in that capacity. Almost immediately, the Institute began issuing a newsletter (at first called the *AIVS Newsletter*, later the *Verdi Newsletter*). The archive quickly acquired a core collection of more than 1,000 items, approximately half of these from the library of the late Professor Scott Stringham and donated to the Institute by his widow. Soon after, Casa Ricordi donated films containing about 1,500 letters by Verdi, Giuseppina Strepponi, and other important figures.

Soon after its founding, the Institute applied for outside funding and received two major grants. The first, from the National Endowment for the Humanities, allowed the filming of correspondence and other documents at the Istituto di Studi Verdiani in Parma. The Martha Baird Rockefeller Foundation provided the second grant to film Verdi materials in private collections. This was an especially important venture, since scholars typically had very little or no access to these materials. Certainly the most important of these private collections was Verdi's estate at Sant'Agata, at which the Institute filmed 25,000 frames of documents, letters, librettos, and libretto sketches. A later grant from the Rockefeller Foundation, together with a grant from the Ford

Foundation, funded the continuation of this project, while additional support from the National Endowment allowed the filming of scores, parts, and librettos that would be needed for the forthcoming complete critical edition of Verdi's works. By 1979, three years after its founding, the Verdi Archive boasted a collection, largely on microfilm, of nearly 300 scores, 500 printed librettos, nearly 300 books, complete runs of several nineteenth-century music periodicals, and all eight of the *disposizioni sceniche*. In addition, the Institute had filmed about 12,000 letters and documents, including the manuscript *copialettere* of both Verdi and Giuseppina.

By 1982, the number of musical scores on microfilm had more than doubled, including about half of the known Verdi autograph manuscripts and many manuscript copies, while the number of librettos more than tripled (there are currently about 2,200 items). Valuable material filmed at Casa Ricordi included the *libroni* (ledgers tracing the history of each numbered publication) and much valuable correspondence with important Italian musicians of Verdi's day, such as Emanuele Muzio and Angelo Mariani. Filming continued in private collections, as well as at some city, state, and national archives and the archives of some of the major opera houses such as La Fenice in Venice and the Archivio Capitolino in Rome, which holds documents relating to the Teatro Apollo and the Teatro Argentina. The filming at La Fenice was particularly fortuitous, since the opera house and its archive were destroyed by fire in 1996. The Archive's collection of nineteenth-century periodicals continues to expand as does its extensive collection of published chronicles of individual opera houses. The Archive has also acquired a significant collection of letters and documents relating to Giuseppina Strepponi.

Like the Parma Institute, the American Institute for Verdi Studies has actively promoted many projects outside of its archival operations. One of the first activities of the new Institute was to assist in preparing materials for a performance of the first version of *Macbeth* at Louisville, Kentucky, and the Center College Regional Arts Center in Danville, Kentucky. A conference devoted to *Macbeth* was organized in conjunction with this performance, resulting in the eventual publication of the *"Macbeth" Sourcebook* (item 762). The Institute sponsored an International Congress in Irvine, California, in 1980, centered around a performance of the first version of *La forza del destino*, and another, co-sponsored by Opera Northern Ireland and the Queen's University of Belfast, in Belfast, Northern Ireland in 1993. The theme of this last Congress was "Verdi's Middle Period"; it is also the title of the recently published volume primarily based on substantive revisions of the papers presented at that event (item 235). The following year, the Institute sponsored a conference at Sarasota, Florida, entitled "Verdi's French Operas" in conjunction with the first performance in the United States of the original French version of *Les vêpres siciliennes*. In 1996 a conference on "Verdi's Revisions" accompanied a performance of both versions of *La forza del destino*. Other activities have included sponsoring performances of some of Verdi's little-known music, including the first American performance of *Il corsaro* and all of the songs that Verdi wrote; symposia; exhibitions; lectures, some combined with videotaped performances; and Summer Seminars for College Teachers supported by the National Endowment for the Humanities. The most recent symposium (1997) was devoted to "Verdi and Censorship."

Recent Trends

The most crucial issue facing Verdi scholars in the 1960s and 70s was the lack of source-critical editions of both Verdi's music and his correspondence as well as a thematic catalogue. Even at this late date, orchestral scores for a half-dozen of Verdi's operas had either never been published or were available only by rental to opera houses, not the general public. Scores for several other operas existed only in extremely faulty editions. Martin Chusid's *Catalog of Verdi's Operas* (item 1), published in 1974, provides much of the crucial information typically contained in a thematic catalogue, particularly about manuscript sources. Cecil Hopkinson's two-volume bibliography of printed scores (item 2) appeared at the same time, supplementing Chusid's catalogue.

Both Institutes threw enormous effort and energy into the long and arduous process of producing critical editions of Verdi's music and correspondence. As this *Research Guide* goes to press, the Parma Institute has issued a critical edition of the Verdi-Boito correspondence as well as two volumes of the Ricordi-Verdi correspondence; more than a half-dozen additional volumes are in preparation. *The Works of Giuseppe Verdi*, co-published by the University of Chicago Press and Casa Ricordi, is well under way; editions of seven operas and the *Requiem* have already appeared. These pivotal publications have not only been important in and of themselves but also because they have led to much additional research.

One area that particularly benefited from work on these new publications is that of Verdi's compositional process, an area that was relatively unexplored before this time. In a landmark article published in 1971 (item 452), Pierluigi Petrobelli identified several major hurdles for conducting research in this area: the unavailability of most of Verdi's compositional drafts and sketches; the complexity of Verdi's composing process, which often continued even after the early performances of a work; and a lack of previous research on which to build. Some twenty-five years later, the situation has changed dramatically. There is a solid foundation of basic research dealing with Verdi's compositional process, and much more documentary material—primarily correspondence but also some of the composer's sketches and continuity drafts—has become available.

A few sample projects will show the range and scope of recent research into Verdi's compositional process. Work on the new critical edition of Verdi's music has required some deep philosophical consideration about what ought to be considered a "definitive revision" and on what occasions the autograph score ought to be overridden as the authoritative record of the composer's wishes (items 1032 and 1033). The editor of *Ernani*, Claudio Gallico, discovered that Luigi Truzzi, who prepared the opera's piano-vocal score, often changed accent marks into dynamic markings, and that these alterations had even found their way back into the full score published by Ricordi! (item 682). Kathleen Kuzmick Hansell, as a result of editing *Stiffelio*, recently made the important discovery that Verdi tended to revise the opening and closing sections of a piece more frequently than the middle section, often to change their relative weight or to make the phrase structure less regular. Scholars have produced many intriguing studies about Verdi's compositional process in works that he later revised, such as *Macbeth, Simon Boccanegra, Stiffelio,* and *Don Carlos.* In the case of the latter opera, Ursula Günther's detailed examination of archival material (items 623, 624, and 626) has further bolstered understanding of the work's genesis and of Verdi's compositional process, showing how fruitful that type of research can be. Several interesting linguistic studies of Verdi's correspondence have appeared, including two by Umberto Macinante (items 103 and 104) and Daniela Goldin Folena's useful investigation of terms Verdi himself used to describe his compositional process (item 102).

Analytical studies have also flourished in recent years. At the First International Verdi Conference in 1966, David Lawton lamented how little research had addressed real analytical issues in Verdi's music (item 8). His selective list of the most important analytical studies to date numbered only thirty-five items; analytical studies in the present bibliography, published only three decades later, number nearly five times that amount. Many scholars have begun examining Verdi's music in the context of nineteenth-century music style and theory (items 457 and 512). A pathbreaking article in this area was Harold S. Power's "'La solita forma' and 'The Uses of Convention'" (item 496), which offered a descriptive model based on Abramo Basevi's *Studio sulle opere di G. Verdi* (item 460). Many other studies, such as Marcello Conati's analysis of the Aida-Amneris duet (item 570) and his investigation of Verdi's "orchestrated prose" in *Stiffelio* (item 914), have also examined Verdi's compositions in context of the musical traditions of his time. Researchers have recently explored a wide range of analytical issues including narrative (items 413, 507, and 863), tonality (861, 864, 933, and 953), plot analysis (item 422), archetypes (item 856), sonority (955 and 959), Schenkerian analyses (items 711, 830, and 955), and semiotics (396 and 405). In this latter case, Pierluigi Petrobelli has used some of the basic premises of semiotics as a foundation for a new analytical methodology based on the interaction among the three systems of dramatic action, verbal organization, and music (items 576 and 733). David Rosen's "Meter, Character, and *Tinta* in Verdi's Operas" (item 501) and James Hepokoski's "Genre and Content in Mid-Century Verdi" (item 936) provide other examples of exciting new methodological approaches to analytical issues. Most recently, James Hepokoski (item 956) has suggested that analysts ought to turn to issues of heterogeneity and inner tension to supplement the search for unity or coherence that often serves as the fundamental goal of analytical research.

The study of Verdi's librettos has generated much significant research. In the early 1980s, Mario Lavagetto suggested thirteen areas relating to Verdi's librettos that needed to be investigated (item 418) and much still remains to be done in almost every area he described. Some recent publications have focused on the literary sources for Verdi's operas, particularly, the identification of precise versions and translations used by librettists (items 765, 770, 771, and 819), ways in which Verdi and his librettists collaborated (items 822, 887 and 945), the effect of censors and censorship (items 674, 848, and 904) and the composer's dramaturgical principles (items 411, 436, and 440).

In a thought-provoking essay (item 429), Roger Parker has recently asserted that changes in the literary style of librettos not only exercised enormous influence over Verdi's musical style but also significantly shaped the overall direction of his later career.

For the last quarter-century, studies relating to historical performance practice have flourished in all areas of music, and this trend did not leave Verdi studies untouched. Researchers have examined singing style and technique (items 520–523), size and seating arrangement of orchestras (items 257, 258 and 529), the transition from the violin-conductor to the baton-wielding conductor (items 266, 527, and 745), and the type of low brass instruments used in nineteenth-century opera orchestras (item 533). After writing several articles dealing with ballet music in Verdi's operas, Knud Arne Jürgensen has recently produced a definitive monograph on the subject (item 540). It is well known that Verdi involved himself intensively with issues regarding staging and scenography. This area has recently produced many important studies, including a forthcoming congress report (item 233) as well as some fascinating and exceptionally beautiful iconographic volumes. Pierluigi Petrobelli has suggested that the visual aspects of his operas were fundamental to Verdi's conception, even at an early stage in the compositional process (item 544). In a similar vein, Fabrizio Della Seta (item 403) has argued that Verdi constantly sought to evoke the "scenic aspect" (*scenicità*) in both the words of the libretto and his music.

Just as opera dominated Verdi's life, research about his operas has dominated the secondary literature. On occasion, however, scholars have also turned their attention to the non-operatic works. David Rosen and others have contributed many outstanding studies concerning the Requiem. Verdi's contribution to the "composite" Mass for Rossini was recently published in facsimile (item 994), and the fifth *Quaderno* of the Istituto di Studi Verdiani (item 993) provided the first detailed investigation of the entire composition. Articles in volume 9 of *Studi verdiani* largely focused on little-known early compositions, such as Roberta Montemorra Marvin's study of an early Sinfonia in D Major (item 1001) and Dino Rizzo's investigation of a *Messa di Gloria*, begun by Ferdinando Provesi but completed by Verdi after the death of his teacher (item 1004). In both cases, the examination of an early composition led to a more detailed look at biographical issues surrounding Verdi's training and his work as a young *maestro di musica* in his native town. Researchers have also offered significant studies of some of the composer's later short works. In his outstanding chronicle of the *Ave Maria su scala enigmatica* (item 996), Marcello Conati showed that the published version of the work differed from its original conception (published for the first time in his article) because Verdi had misplaced the original manuscript and had to reconstitute the piece from memory. George Martin has studied the composer's "second" *Ave Maria*, dating from 1880, showing its relationship to settings of the text in his operas and discussing reasons why it has remained relatively unknown (item 1000).

In the 1990s, Verdi research has reached a point of maturity in which scholars are re-examining and re-evaluating not only historical facts but are also challenging or refining other long-held notions and even basic methodologies. Mary Jane Phillips-Matz's new biography of the composer followed in the footsteps of Frank Walker by seeking to correct legends that had become tradition. Gilles De Van (item 441) recently challenged a popular, traditional view that the composer "zigzagged" between traditional, conservative operas and more progressive ones, proposing instead that he drew from a wide range of aesthetic procedures to support a common dramaturgical purpose. Other recent revisionist studies include Fabrizio Della Seta's examination of the term "parola scenica," which he suggests might be replaced by a broader term, such as "musica scenica" (item 403); re-evaluations by Birgit Pauls (item 300) and Philip Gossett (item 472) of Verdi's involvement with the Risorgimento movement and the contemporary interpretation of political messages in his operas; and Roger Parker's recent questioning of some of the premises of analytical research based on Abramo Basevi's *Studio sulle opere di G. Verdi* (item 491).

The avalanche of materials relating to Verdi continues to grow at an exponential rate. Comprehensive bibliographies by Marcello Conati published in each issue of *Studi verdiani* have numbered as many as two hundred or more a year. Historical facts being uncovered by recent research and the issues being discussed are constantly raising the level of discourse to a higher and more productive level. Perhaps most importantly, the burgeoning research has matched, and even fueled, interest in the music itself. Verdi's music continues to be some of the most frequently performed of the entire operatic repertory, and companies have begun to explore some of his lesser-known works and mount comprehensive cycles of his entire operatic work. There can be no doubt that as the twenty-first century dawns, marking the hundredth anniversary of the composer's death, the future is bright for Verdi's music and for Verdi studies.

PURPOSE & SCOPE OF THIS VOLUME

Today, Verdi scholars build their work on a vast foundation of earlier research. For researchers who have not spent years with the Verdi literature or who may just be starting to explore some aspect of this giant's life and works, this foundation may seem daunting indeed. It is primarily for these researchers that this guide is intended. Its purpose is to index and describe some of the most significant studies about the composer, presenting enough material in annotations that researchers may survey the many myriad directions Verdi research has gone, ascertain the relevance of individual items to their individual interests, and pursue significant patterns and threads in which they are interested.

In preparing this volume, I have consulted a wide variety of bibliographies and indexes, including *WorldCat*, an enormous on-line database based on records of the Online Computer Library Center, Inc. (OCLC); *RILM Abstracts of Music Literature*; *Humanities Index/Humanities Abstracts*; *MLA Bibliography*; *Dissertation Abstracts*; and *Doctoral Dissertations in Musicology*. I have checked the on-line catalogue of the Library of Congress as well as the printed and on-line catalogues of the New York Public Library and other major research libraries. I have also thoroughly examined many Verdi bibliographies, including the ongoing bibliographies published in each issue of

Studi verdiani and all of the items listed or cross-referenced in Chapter 1. In addition to these indexes, bibliographies, and catalogues, I have had the pleasure of personally searching the large collections of Verdi materials at the Elmer Holmes Bobst Library at New York University, home of the American Institute for Verdi Studies, the Eda Kuhn Loeb Music Library at Harvard University, and several regional research libraries.

In preparing this selective compilation, I included the most significant materials published through 1995. I have also included some important new materials from 1996 and 1997 as well as a few significant volumes whose publication has been announced, but the coverage will not be as complete as for earlier years. Two very significant congress reports are just being issued as this volume is going to press: *La realizzazione scenica dello spettacolo verdiano*, based on a conference held in Parma in 1994, and *Verdi's Middle Period*, which contains expanded versions of papers presented at a 1993 conference held in Belfast. I have been able to include abstracts for the latter thanks to the kind efforts of Kathleen Hansell at the University of Chicago Press, who provided me with page proofs.

The vast amount of secondary literature pertaining to Verdi precludes the listing of many materials in this Guide to Research. It should, however, provide a strong enough framework for a researcher to obtain a good idea of significant work Verdi scholars have produced in any one area as well as resources to locate additional materials that are not included in this volume. Readers who are interested in a comprehensive listing of virtually all newer materials relating to Verdi should consult the large bibliographies that appear in each issue of *Studi verdiani*. In general I have excluded the following types of materials:

1. Materials written in languages other than the common Western European languages of English, Italian, French, German, and Spanish. Most important research about Verdi has appeared, in the original or in translation, in these five languages most commonly read by Western researchers. Several items in Chapter 1 list materials written in Eastern European and Asian languages; researchers familiar with these languages can also locate these materials through *RILM Abstracts*, WorldCat, or the bibliographies in *Studi verdiani*.

2. Books or articles written in a popular style for a general audience and articles published in newspapers or in popular or general-readership periodicals, including house journals of opera houses (*Opera News*, *Gazzetta del Museo Teatrale alla Scala*, etc.). These materials can easily be located through a variety of printed and on-line indexes and catalogues, such as *Music Index*, *Humanities Abstracts*, *Newspaper Abstracts*, *CARL Uncover*, etc.

3. Articles from program booklets accompanying performances of Verdi's works or record jacket notes. Program booklets for productions at European opera houses often contain detailed scholarly articles by leading Verdi authorities; unfortunately, they are almost impossible to obtain in the United States and Canada. Many of these are listed in the ongoing bibliographies published in *Studi verdiani*.

4.   Articles from nineteenth-century periodicals. This significant body of material has traditionally been difficult to use because of the scarcity of the periodicals themselves and the lack of indexes. Some important articles may be found through some of the bibliographies listed in Chapter 1; articles in specialized music periodicals are also becoming more accessible through the ongoing indexing provided by *Le répertoire international de la presse musicale* (*RIPM*), whose volumes are found in most major research libraries. Researchers in North American may also consult microfilm copies of many relevant nineteenth-century periodicals at the American Institute for Verdi Studies at New York University.

5.   Textbooks, general histories of music, and general histories of opera (including histories of nineteenth-century opera and histories of Italian opera).

6.   Theater chronicles or general books about opera at specific opera houses or in specific cities. While these types of sources offer veritable gold mines for researchers interested in performance history and reception, they are too numerous to be listed here and can be easily located through traditional bibliographic means.

7.   Master's theses and unpublished European dissertations, which are difficult to obtain in this country (a few of exceptional significance and for which copies exist outside the sponsoring institution have been included). These materials are listed in indexes such as *RILM Abstracts, Doctoral Dissertations in Musicology*, which has just initiated an on-line search engine, and the ongoing bibliographies in *Studi verdiani*.

8.   Reviews of books, articles, recordings, and specific performances.

9.   Musical scores and librettos (printed or manuscript). Readers wishing to locate particular scores and librettos should consult the lists published in the *Verdi Newsletter* (items 19 and 20), which provide locations (using RISM sigla) for an enormous quantity of this material. OCLC's on-line index *WorldCat* also provides a convenient way of finding locations for published scores (and books) in virtually all research libraries in the United States and Canada, with a few locations overseas.

10. Materials from the World Wide Web. This will rapidly become a more important area in the coming years. Some of the major opera houses (La Scala and La Fenice, for example) already have web sites that include historical information about the theaters. Researchers can easily locate information from this dynamic and rapidly changing new medium through the use of standard search engines.

Materials in this *Guide to Research* are organized topically. The first three chapters list significant reference materials: bibliographies, catalogues, and descriptions of special archives and collections; correspondence and other documents; and iconographic documentaries. Chapter 4 offers a collection of the most significant biographies of the composer as well as studies that combine biography with a discussion of Verdi's works. The following chapter serves as an addendum, listing biographical publications about people closely associated with the composer. Foremost among them is Giuseppina Strepponi, who became Verdi's close friend, partner, and, eventually, his wife; also included are selected works dealing with the composer's librettists, publishers, and other associates. The next group of chapters present general studies: conference and congress reports; broad studies touching on a large number of topics; studies of Verdi's musical, cultural, political, and social milieu; performance history and the reception of his works, both as a whole as well as in specific locations; and evaluations of the composer's influence and historical position. The following chapters include materials specifically relating to Verdi's compositions. Chapter 11 presents books and articles that consider Verdi's style or *oeuvre* as a whole or across several different works. Chapter 12, by far the largest in the volume, lists research materials related to specific operas, while Chapter 13 contains information about Verdi's non-operatic works. In this section of the *Guide to Research*, I have used the term "descriptive analysis" to denote descriptive commentaries about plot and music as opposed to true analytical articles, which seek to explain reasons behind musical events. The concluding chapters of this guide present discographies and videographies, selective collections of librettos, and literature discussing the editing of Verdi's music and the establishment of editorial practices for *The Works of Giuseppe Verdi*. Appendices include a tabular chronology of Verdi's life; a catalogue of Verdi's compositions; the organizational scheme of *The Works of Giuseppe Verdi/Le opere di Giuseppe Verdi*; tables showing librettists and other collaborations, locations of premiere performances, literary sources, and alternative titles; and a short biographical dictionary of some of the composer's principal associates. The organizational scheme found in individual chapters, which typically includes several categories and subcategories, is intended to help researchers easily find material relating to broad topical areas. Because many books and articles touch on more than one subject area, however, readers should always consult the subject index to find all relevant material.

I have prepared the bibliographic entries and abstracts from a personal examination of each item except where an item is listed as forthcoming or, in a few cases, where I have not been able to obtain a copy of an important item. In these instances, the bibliographic citations appear without an abstract. ISBN numbers and Library of Congress call numbers have been supplied where they have been available from the book itself, the Library of Congress on-line catalogues, or *WorldCat*. For libraries utilizing the Library of Congress scheme, most Verdi materials will be found under call numbers beginning with ML 410 .V4. Readers should note, however, that many libraries using the Library of Congress system deviate from the official Library of Congress number, particularly in the latter part of the call number.

Special Series

From its foundation, the Istituto Nazionale di Studi Verdiani in Parma has been very active in publishing materials about Verdi. Their first series, which began almost immediately after the founding of the Institute, was the *Bollettino "Verdi."* Interpreting bibliographic references to the *Bollettino* is sometimes confusing, since some bibliographic references show volume numbers and others refer to issue numbers. While each issue has both a volume number and an issue number, the issue numbers remain cumulative rather than returning to 1 at the start of a new volume; therefore, citations in this bibliography show both volume and issue number. Each volume of the *Bollettino* emphasizes a single opera (although miscellaneous articles on other topics occasionally appear). The first three volumes each comprise three separate numbers, issued irregularly; articles appear in three languages (typically Italian, English, and German). A change of format was announced beginning with volume 4 (number 10): dual volumes would be issued, one in Italian and one in English.

Vol./No.		Date	Main Topic	Item #
Vol. 1	No. 1	April 1960	*Un ballo in maschera*	599
Vol. 1	No. 2	August 1960	"	"
Vol. 1	No. 3	December 1960	"	"
Vol. 2	No. 4	Jan.–Dec. 1961	*La forza del destino*	721
Vol. 2	No. 5	December 1962	"	"
Vol. 2	No. 6	July 1966	"	"
Vol. 3	No. 7	November 1969	*Rigoletto*	851
Vol. 3	No. 8	July 1973	"	"
Vol. 3	No. 9	January 1982	"	"
Vol. 4	No. 10	1988	*Ernani* (Italian)	228
Vol. 4	No. 10	1989	*Ernani* (English)	"

Another early enterprise of the Parma Institute was a series entitled *Quaderni*. These are commemorative booklets issued in connection with a performance of an opera, in most cases a little-performed work. These now number five:

No.	Title	Date	Item #
1	*Il corsaro*	1963	616
2	*Gerusalemme*	1963	747
3	*Stiffelio*	1968	902
4	*Genesi dell'Aida*	1971	554
5	*Messa per Rossini*	1988	993

One other series devoted to Verdi deserves special mention here: *Biblioteca '70*. Three volumes of this serial were issued in limited edition by the Biblioteca della Cassa di Risparmio di Parma e Monte di Credito su Pegno di Busseto. Articles in each volume emphasize the early years of Verdi's life. The issues are generally difficult to locate; American researchers will find a copy of each volume at the American Institute for Verdi Studies at New York University. In addition, the same organizations issued one *Quaderno* associated with the *Biblioteca '70* series: Gustavo Marchesi's *Verdi, merli e cucù* (item 31).

Opera Guides

Opera guides, providing background information about a particular work and often reproducing the libretto, abound for Verdi. As a general rule, these guides are intended for a general, rather than a scholarly audience; only the most significant series have been included in the present bibliography. By far the most scholarly of these are the

Cambridge Opera Guides, which to this date include a volume for *Otello* (item 807) and one for *Falstaff* (item 695), both by James A. Hepokoski. Both volumes include a detailed historical study of the work's compositional genesis and reception as well as an in-depth analytical study of one portion of the opera. A parallel volume on the *Requiem* by David Rosen (item 983) belongs to the Cambridge Music Handbook series.

L'avant-scène opera* has issued fifteen issues pertaining to Verdi and his works, many of which have been re-released in second editions.

Vol.	Title	Date	New ed.	Item #
3	Otello	1976	1990	808
4	Aïda	1976	1993	551
19	Simon Boccanegra	1979	1994	879
32	Un bal masqué	1981	1992	595
40	Macbeth	1982		755
51	La traviata	1983	1993	923
60	Le trouvère	1984	1990	942
75	Les vêpres sicilennes	1985		962
86	Nabucco	1986	1991, 1994	795
87/88	Falstaff	1986		693
90/91	Don Carlos	1986	1990	619
112/113	Rigoletto	1988		843
126	La force du destin	1989		716
151	Luisa Miller	1993		751

Each of the *Avant-scène* volumes contains a series of essays, followed by the libretto reproduced in Italian (if applicable) and French. Perhaps the most valuable feature of this series is the reference material. Each volume includes a bibliography containing not only secondary literature about the opera but also more general studies dealing with the opera's general subject (e.g., the historical *Don Carlos*) and with its literary sources as well as lists of major editions of the work and locations of important manuscript materials. A few of the volumes (notably *Le trouvère* and the first edition of *La traviata*) contain large general bibliographies dealing with Verdi's life and works. Each volume also contains an extensive discography of complete and partial recordings and tables showing the performance history in some of the more important theaters around the world. The *Avant-scène* volumes are also valuable for their wealth of iconographic material, including photographs of scenes from various contemporary productions. One special volume, *Les introuvables du chant verdien* (item 515), was issued in 1986 to accompany an eight-disk set of recordings released by Pathé-Marconi; it contains much useful information, textual and iconographic, about significant interpreters of Verdi's operas.

The English National Opera has issued another large series of opera guides dealing with Verdi's operas. Essays in these volumes are generally less extensive and written in a more popular tone than those found in *L'avant-scène opera*. The English

National Opera Guides feature librettos in the original language and in English laid out in parallel columns; bibliographies and other reference materials are minimal in coverage. Some readers will find valuable the relatively detailed descriptive analyses provided by most volumes in this series.

Vol.	Title	Date	Item #
5	*La traviata*	1981	924
7	*Otello*	1981	809
10	*Falstaff*	1982	694
20	*Il trovatore*	1983	943
23	*The Force of Destiny/La forza del destino*	1983	717
32	*Simon Boccanegra*	1985	880
40	*A Masked Ball/Un ballo in maschera*	1989	596
41	*Macbeth*	1990	756
46	*Don Carlos/Don Carlo*	1992	620

The Rororo Opernbücher are the most outstanding set of opera guides about Verdi in German; six volumes were issued in the early and middle 1980s.

Title	Date	Item #
Aida	1985	553
Falstaff	1986	692
Otello	1981	806
Rigoletto	1982	841
La traviata	1983	922
Der Troubadour	1986	941

Volumes in this series contain excellent essays and documentation relating to the opera's history and reception. Librettos are reproduced in the original language and in German translations. They also contain substantial discographies and selective bibliographies.

Acknowledgments

It is a pleasure to acknowledge the assistance of many people and institutions that have made this project possible. I am indebted to Martin Chusid, Director of the American Institute for Verdi Studies, for his assistance in using the Verdi Archive, for allowing me to examine some materials in his personal collection of Verdiana, and for stirring my interest in the composer and his music during my time as a graduate student at New York University. Pierluigi Petrobelli, Director of the Istituto Nazionale di Studi Verdiani, has responded to a small bombardment of questions and supplied me with material on the history of the Institute and its projects. The photographic division of the Bibliothèque de l'Opéra in Paris kindly supplied the photograph for the cover and frontispiece to this volume and gave permission for its reproduction.

While I first accepted this assignment when living in New York City, within close reach of many large research libraries, I completed the project in southeast Georgia, which lacks any large research collection. I am therefore greatly indebted to Barbara Strickland and her staff at the Interlibrary Loan Office at Georgia Southern University's Zach S. Henderson Library, who have performed a herculean task of locating more materials about Verdi than they ever thought could have existed. Kathleen Kuzmick Hansell, managing editor of *The Works of Giuseppe Verdi* at the University of Chicago Press, provided up-to-date information about the new complete critical edition and provided me with page proofs for the important conference report *Verdi's Middle Period* so that its contents could be abstracted for this *Research Guide*. The library staff at the Elmer Holmes Bobst Library at New York University, the Eda Kuhn Loeb Music Library at Harvard University, the Music and General Humanities Divisions of the New York Public Library, the University of Georgia Library, the Warren D. Allen Music Library at Florida State University, and the Harold B. Lee Library at Brigham Young University have also been of great assistance. Andreas Giger verified several references as the *Guide* was going to press. The Faculty Research Committee at Georgia Southern University, with support from the Georgia Southern Foundation, awarded me a one-half summer sabbatical during 1996 to continue work on this project. The staff at Garland Publishing has been helpful and encouraging, particularly during the final stages of preparation for publication; particular thanks to the series editor, Guy Marco, for his comments and suggestions. A special thanks also goes to Thomas J. Mathiesen, who taught the bibliography course I took as a beginning graduate student and who demonstrated that the compilation of a bibliography can be, at times, both fun and high adventure. Finally, I am deeply indebted to my wife, Kathy, for her love, support, encouragement, and patience and to my children, Martin and Elizabeth, for their enthusiasm in constantly asking, "Isn't your book done yet?"

GIUSEPPE VERDI

Giuseppe Verdi, ca. 1850
courtesy of the Bibliothèque Nationale de France

CHAPTER 1

Bibliographies, Catalogues, Descriptions of Special Archives & Collections

GENERAL BIBLIOGRAPHIES & CATALOGUES OF VERDI'S MUSIC

The following two reference works provide crucial information about autograph manuscripts and early editions of Verdi's music and together provide much of the information that would be found in a definitive thematic catalogue.

1. Chusid, Martin. *A Catalog of Verdi's Operas*. Music Indexes and Bibliographies, 5. Hackensack, N.J.: Joseph Boonin, 1974. xi, 201 p. ISBN 0–913574–05–8. ML 134 .V47 C5.

This important reference source provides for each of Verdi's operas: 1) a transcription of the title page and cast as presented in the libretto for the first performance (and in some cases, other significant early performances); 2) location and description of the autograph manuscript, including Verdi's own titles and text incipits for the individual numbers and the presence of non-definitive revisions, if any; and 3) miscellaneous information (as available for each opera) including: location and description of extant sketches, manuscript copies, selected printed editions, staging manuals, and information about playbills for first or early performances. The volume contains a number of facsimile reproductions of pages from autograph manuscripts and librettos. Appendices list the operas by date and place of first performance and show alternate titles of operas, with information about librettos and performances. The volume also includes a substantial bibliography and an index of personal names. In the absence of a definitive thematic catalogue, this reference work is the only comprehensive source for crucial information relating to Verdi's autograph manuscripts, such as the composer's own nomenclature for individual numbers in his operas, which publishers frequently altered. See item 2 for more detailed information about printed editions of Verdi's music.

2. Hopkinson, Cecil. *A Bibliography of the Works of Giuseppe Verdi, 1813–1901.* Vol. 1: Vocal and Instrumental Works. New York: Broude Bros., 1973. ix, 106 p. Vol 2: Operatic Works. New York: Broude Bros., 1978. ix, 106; xxxii, 191 p. ISBN 0–8450–7004–5. ML 134 .V47 H6.

The author refers to this set as a "bibliographical thematic catalogue." While it offers detailed bibliographic information about editions of Verdi's music, it lacks much material normally found in a true thematic catalogue. Information about manuscript material is most often omitted (for more information about manuscript documents, see item 1 above). Musical incipits are provided for the little-known songs and choral works, but are lacking for all of the operas as well as the larger non-operatic works (such as the *Quattro pezzi sacri, Requiem,* String Quartet, etc.). Most of the entries include a short historical introduction; some feature facsimile reproductions of title pages. Appendices in each volume contain much interesting information. These include: a list of manuscripts, a list of dedicatees, brief essays on Verdi's publishers (especially useful for the little-known publishers who issued some of the songs and choral works), information about Lucca's pictorial title pages, details about collected editions of songs, and tables listing librettists and alternative titles. While these volumes provide much valuable information, there are a significant number of errors and omissions noted, in part, by Maria Adelaide Bacherini Bartoli (item 3) and by J. Rigbie Turner in his description of Verdiana at the Pierpont Morgan Library (item 26).

3. Bartoli, Maria Adelaide Bacherini. "Aggiunte integrazioni e rettifiche alla *Bibliography of the Works of Giuseppe Verdi* di Cecil Hopkinson: Edizioni verdiane nella Biblioteca Nazionale Centrale di Firenze." *Studi verdiani* 4 (1986–87): 110–35.

This list of errata and additions updates Hopkinson's reference volume (item 2). The author includes editions in the Biblioteca Nazionale that are not described in Hopkinson's work as well as a separate list of items that are described in Hopkinson without mention of a copy in the Biblioteca Nazionale.

*   Lawton, David, and David Rosen. "Verdi's Non-Definitive Revisions: The Early Operas." See item 451.

GENERAL BIBLIOGRAPHIES OF SECONDARY LITERATURE ABOUT VERDI

Ongoing exhaustive bibliographies of current publications about Verdi prepared by Marcello Conati can be found in each issue of *Studi verdiani*, as listed in the following table.

Vol.	Date	Years Covered by Bibliography
1	1982	1977–79
2	1983	1980–82
3	1985	1983–84
4	1986–87	1985–86
5	1988–89	1987–88
6	1990	1988–89
7	1991	1989–91
8	1992	1991–92
9	1993	1993
10	1994–95	1993–95

These bibliographies are especially valuable for their inclusion of materials that are not easily found in standard indexes or in American libraries. These include the typically detailed and substantial essays published in program booklets for European productions of Verdi's operas as well as European theses and dissertations.

4. Alcari, Cesare. *Parma nella musica*. Parma: M. Fresching, 1931. 259 p.

   A large bibliography of over 500 entries (pp. 218–53) appended to the biographical article on Verdi updates Vanbianchi's list (item 16) through 1930. Contains useful references to many little-known articles from newspapers and periodicals.

5. Conati, Marcello. "Bibliografia verdiana: Aspetti, problemi, criteri per la sistemazione della letteratura verdiana." *Atti 3* (item 226), 546–63.

   Surveys the history of research about Verdi and assesses major bibliographic studies through the early 1970s. The author suggests that one of the biggest remaining challenges in Verdi bibliography is to facilitate access of nineteenth-century material, particularly periodical literature. A central portion of this essay considers the significance of the *Copialettere* (item 28) and the stimulus its publication provided for later Verdi studies.

6. ———. "Fonti verdiane: I giornali dell'ottocento." *Nuove prospettive nella ricerca verdiana* (item 231), 130–37.

Describes, in general terms, types of information found in nineteenth-century periodical literature that is useful for Verdi research.

7. Kämper, Dietrich. "Das deutsche Verdi-Schrifttum: Hauptlinien der Interpretation." In *Colloquium "Verdi-Wagner" Rom 1969: Bericht* (item 227), 185–99.

   Surveys significant writings about Verdi published in German, with a particularly strong focus on Verdi's contemporaries, such as Eduard Hanslick, Ferruccio Busoni, Friedrich Nietzsche, and Hugo Riemann.

8. Lawton, David. "Per una bibliografia ragionata verdiana." *Atti 1* (item 224), 437–42.

   A short, selective listing of 35 items that explore Verdi's music from an analytical point of view.

9. Lottici, Stefano. *Bio-bibliografia di Giuseppe Verdi*. Parma: Tip. S. Orsatti & C., 1913. ix, 68 p. ML 410 .V4 L7.

10. Michałowski, Kornel. *Verdi in Polonia: Saggio bibliografico*. Biblioteca di "Quadrivium": Note d'Archivio: Bibliografia, biografia e storia, 5. Bologna: Antiquae Musicae Italicae Studiosi, 1980. 69 p.

    Indexes items about Verdi published in Poland or dealing with the reception of his music in that country. The bibliography is arranged by topic, including sections devoted to individual compositions. This list is particularly valuable for its listing of items published in Polish periodicals.

 * Oberdorfer, Aldo. *Giuseppe Verdi: Autobiografia dalle lettere*. 3rd, rev. ed., with annotations and additions by Marcello Conati. See item 36 (contains an extensive bibliography of published letters).

 * Parker, Roger. "Verdi, Giuseppe (Fortunino Francesco)." In *New Grove Dictionary of Opera*. See item 177.

11. Pavarani, Marcello. "Per una bibliografia e documentazione verdiana." *Atti 1* (item 224), 446–51.

    Assesses the significance of four early bibliographies (Torri, Maglione, Vanbianchi, Alcari) and describes the efforts of the Istituto di Studi Verdiani to assemble a comprehensive listing of all material relating to Verdi.

12. Porter, Andrew. "A Select Bibliography." *The Verdi Companion* (item 5), 239–55.

A useful prose survey of the most important Verdi bibliographies through the mid-1980s, followed by a listing of materials dealing with individual works and specific topics.

13. Surian, Elvidio. "Lo stato attuale degli studi verdiani: Appunti e bibliografia ragionata (1960–1975)." *Rivista italiana di musicologia* 12 (1977): 305–29.

An overview of the state of Verdi research in the mid-1970s serves as a preface to a topically organized bibliographic essay describing material that appeared between 1960 and 1975.

14. Tintori, Giampiero. "Bibliografia verdiana in Russia." *Atti 1* (item 224), 458–63.

Reviews the history of Verdi studies in Russia and presents a bibliography of 45 items published in Russian between 1875 and 1964. The entries are organized chronologically and include some items originally published elsewhere and translated into Russian.

15. Torri, Luigi. "Saggio di bibliografia verdiana." *Rivista musicale italiana* 8 (1901): 379–407.

An important early bibliography issued in commemoration of the composer's death. The entries are arranged alphabetically by author within broad categories: life (nearly 250 items); a work list with dates and names of performers for premieres and a few other significant early performances (40 items); critical assessments of the compositions (99 items); and a list of 25 nineteenth-century periodicals containing significant reviews or discussions of Verdi's works. A few of the citations contain light annotations. This bibliography is especially useful for its listing of articles in nineteenth-century periodicals, theatrical gazettes, and special commemorative publications.

16. Vanbianchi, Carlo. *Saggio di bibliografia verdiana.* Milan: Ricordi, 1913. vii, 118 p.

Although on the surface this appears to be a new bibliography, it is in fact an update through 1913 of Torri (item 15); the author does not acknowledge that his earlier listings are lifted directly from the earlier work. The new listings, however, are considerable. Vanbianchi lists a total of 897 items alphabetically by author, with the exception of articles and books pertaining to individual works, which are grouped together under the title of the composition and interfiled with the main author listing. Some listings for individual compositions provide cross-listings to other related materials.

SPECIFIC ARCHIVES & COLLECTIONS: DESCRIPTIVE MATERIAL & CATALOGUES

American Institute for Verdi Studies, New York University

17. Chusid, Martin. "The American Institute for Verdi Studies and the Verdi Archive at New York University." *Opera Quarterly* 5 (Summer/Autumn 1987): 33–47.

    Offers a short history of the Verdi Archive at New York University, a detailed description of its holdings, and the relevance of various types of material for research about Verdi. The descriptive portion is divided into sections dealing with scores; librettos; production materials; letters, documents, and archival materials; and miscellaneous materials.

18. ———. "On the Origins of the [American] Institute [for Verdi Studies]." *AIVS Newsletter* 1 (1976): 3–4.

    A short essay describing the founding of the American Institute for Verdi Studies, the objectives of the Institute, and its initial holdings.

19. Chusid, Martin, John Nádas, and Luke Jensen. "The Verdi Archive at New York University (as of May 1979). Part I: A Brief History and Description." *Verdi Newsletter* 7 (1979): 3–23.
    Chusid, Martin, Luke Jensen, and David Day. Part II: "A List of Verdi's Music, Librettos, Production Materials, Nineteenth-Century Periodicals, and Other Research Materials." *Verdi Newsletter* 9/10 (1981–82): 3–52.

    Part I begins with a brief prose history and description of the Archive. For each of Verdi's works, the opening portion of the catalogue lists the number of scores, librettos, and other primary source materials in the Archive's collection in addition to uncatalogued manuscript scenarios and librettos of operas that Verdi considered but did not undertake. The remaining portion of Part I lists letters on microfilm or in photocopy by writer, recipient, and date. The information in Part II largely supersedes the earlier list, providing additional detailed information (including provenance) about individual scores, parts, printed librettos, and production materials. Information on manuscript librettos must still be located in Part I. Part II also lists additional letters not found in Part I, holdings of nineteenth-century Italian periodicals, and chronicles for opera houses and theaters arranged by city. See item 20 for an updated catalogue of the Archive's holdings of Verdi's music.

20. Fairtile, Linda B. "The Verdi Archive at New York University: A List of Verdi's Music." *Verdi Newsletter* 17/18 (1989–90): 1–54.

Supersedes item 19 above with respect to the Archive's holdings of musical scores. Includes autographs, manuscript copies, and printed scores, parts, and arrangements. Entries for all materials show their original source and provide call numbers to facilitate use at the Archive.

Istituto Nazionale di Studi Verdiani, Parma, Italy

21. "'Dal labbro il canto estasiato vola . . .'. " *International Opera Collector* 1/1 (Autumn 1996): 74–80.

A recent survey of the Institute's holdings, focusing on a history and description of Carl L. Bruun's bequest of more than 3,000 recordings of Verdi's music dating from as early as 1900. The nearly completed project of cataloguing the collection has shown that it contains nearly all commercial recordings of Verdi's music from the early acoustic recordings through the early 1980s; the Institute intends to fill lacunae in order to build a comprehensive library of recordings.

22. *L'Istituto di Studi Verdiani.* Parma: Istituto di Studi Verdiani, [1976]. 52 p.

A short essay by Mario Medici recounts the history of the Institute, initiatives and publications it has undertaken, and its difficulties during the mid-1970s in finding adequate financial support. The main portion of the volume presents lists of presentations made at the first four International Verdi Congresses, articles published in the Institute's *Bollettino*, newspapers and periodicals that have published articles about the Institute, and institutions that own publications by the Institute.

23. Pompilio, Angelo. "La collezione Scalvini dell'Istituto Nazionale di Studi Verdiani." *Studi verdiani* 7 (1991): 111–88; 8 (1992): 118–43.

A description and complete catalogue of the Scalvini Collection, consisting of more than 400 printed scores of complete operas (including 60 by Verdi) published between 1820 and 1950. The second part of the essay considers the historical and cultural value of the collection to music historians and to students of nineteenth-century culture in Italy.

Other Archives and Collections

24. Cohen, H. Robert. "A Survey of French Sources for the Staging of Verdi's Operas: *Livrets de mise en scène*, Annotated Scores, and Annotated Libretti in Two Parisian Collections." *Studi verdiani* 3 (1985): 11–44.

An annotated bibliography, with descriptive essay, of production materials at the Bibliothèque de l'Opéra and the Bibliothèque de l'Association de la Régie-

Théâtrale that concern nineteenth- and early twentieth-century performances of Verdi's operas in France.

* Gallini, Natale, and Guglielmo Barblan, eds. *Mostra degli autografi musicali dei Giuseppe Verdi.* See item 111.

25. Strunk, Oliver. "Verdiana in the Library of Congress." In *Essays on Music in the Western World,* 192–200. New York: Norton, 1974. ISBN 0-393-02178-5. ML 60 .S862 E8.
    Italian translation. "Verdiana alla Biblioteca del Congresso." *Atti 1* (item 224), 452–57.

    A catalogue of primary sources relating to Verdi in the Library of Congress organized into three lists: engraved full scores (14 items), manuscript scores (10 items), and Verdi librettos in the Schatz collection (92 items). The listing is preceded by a prose essay discussing the history and contents of the collection.

26. Turner, J. Rigbie. "George W. Martin's Verdi Collection at the Pierpont Morgan Library." *Verdi Newsletter* 23 (1996): 19–21.

    Provides an overview of 350 printed scores and librettos donated by George W. Martin to the Pierpont Morgan Library. The author draws special attention to a number of items that were not listed in Cecil Hopkinson's bibliography (item 2) or for which Hopkinson states that no copies were known to exist. Turner also appends a short description of other Verdi material in the Morgan Library, including printed items, several autograph manuscripts, and 39 letters, among them a set of 25 to Antonio Ghislanzoni regarding *Aida.*

27. Zecca-Laterza, Agostina, ed. *Il catalogo numerico Ricordi 1857 con date e indici.* Preface by Philip Gossett. Bibliotheca musicae VIII; Cataloghi editoriali 1. Rome: Nuovo Istituto Editoriale Italiano, 1984. xxiii, 615 p. ML 145 .R54 C37 1984.

    A facsimile reproduction of Ricordi's 1857 catalogue of publications (music and didactic works) listed chronologically by plate number. This important primary source provides significant bibliographical information about Verdi's early operas, including published arrangements of individual numbers. In addition, the publication information sheds significant light about the musical and cultural milieu in northern Italy during the first half of the nineteenth century, showing what music was in general circulation. The volume contains author and title indexes, the latter broken down by large-scale vocal works, ballets, anonymous compositions, and collaborative works.

CHAPTER 2

Correspondence & Other Documents

Listed below are published collections of Verdi's correspondence, including general collections and more specific sets that focus on a single correspondent or topic. As noted in the preface, scholarly source-critical editions of the composer's correspondence have only just begun to appear in recent years, focusing on the letter exchange with Arrigo Boito and the Ricordi family (see items 46, 80, and 81). Other publications run the entire gamut from generally trustworthy to unreliable and should be used with caution. Translations present an additional level of complexity; where possible, scholars will want to consult the documents in the original language.

GENERAL COLLECTIONS OF LETTERS & DOCUMENTS

28. Cesare, Gaetano, and Alessandro Luzio, eds. *I copialettere di Giuseppe Verdi*. Milan: n.p., 1913. Reprint. Bibliotheca musica Bononiensis, sec. 5, no. 23. Bologna: Forni, [1968]. 759 p. ML 410 .V4 1987.

An important, yet seriously flawed, compilation of some of Verdi's letters. The main portion of the volume presents a lightly annotated transcription of nearly 400 letters drawn from Verdi's *copialettere*, a set of notebooks containing drafts, copies, and summaries of some of his correspondence (often containing variants from the actual letters). Although the editors state in the preface that their intent was an integral reproduction of the documents in terms of both form and content, they go on to make an exception for "writings that are completely superfluous in illustrating the personality of the master or the world with which he was in contact," specifying receipts, bank statements, and other similar documents. In reality, this first portion omits much significant material, including letters from entire years. The sizeable appendix (nearly half of the total volume) reproduces other letters not in Verdi's *copialettere* that provide background information, cross-referenced to the letters printed in the first part of the volume. The integrity of these letters is compromised even more than the main collection by omissions, fragmentary reproductions (sometimes with pieces from the same letter reproduced in different locations), suppressed passages, and inaccurate ordering. The volume contains an index, which is helpful in finding references to particular people, places, and compositions. English translations of selected items from this publication may be found in Osborne's collection (see item 37 below), but problems and errors in the original are compounded by further inaccuracies in translation and commentary. Despite its flaws, this volume represents an important milesone in the history of Verdi research. See item 5 for a well-presented assessment of this publication's historical significance.

*   Conati, Marcello. *La bottega della musica: Verdi e La Fenice.* See item 344.

29. Luzio, Alessandro. *Carteggi verdiani.* Real Accademia d'Italia/Accademia Nazionale dei Lincei: Studi e documenti, 4. Rome: Accademia Nazionale dei Lincei, 1935–47. 4 vols. xvi, 384 + 48 p. illustrations; 370; 201; 326 p. ML 410 .V4 A42.

This monumental publication contains a variety of letters and documents, largely previously unpublished materials in possession of the Verdi heirs at Sant'Agata. The arrangement of material into sections relating to individual correspondents or topics makes the use of the collection somewhat unwieldy; researchers can make use of a comprehensive index in the final volume that includes names of people and compositions in all four volumes (in addition, volume 2 contains a partial index relating to the first two volumes). The first two volumes contain a number of illustrations and facsimile reproductions of pages from some documents. The two largest collections of letters (although not complete exchanges) are those involving Cesare and Giuseppe De Sanctis (item 51) and Giuseppe Piroli (item 77). Also of great importance is a section that summarizes and presents excerpts from the *copialettere* of Giuseppina (item 87). A large section of volume 2 is devoted to the Boito correspondence (although it is now superseded by the superior edition in item 46). Smaller letter exchanges, some intended to supplement previously published material, involve Camille Bellaigue, Léon and Marie Escudier, Franco Faccio, Francesco Florimo, Ferdinand Hiller, Angelo Mariani, Domenico Morelli, Emanuele Muzio, Romilda Pantaleoni, Francesco Maria Piave, Tito and Giulio Ricordi, Gioachino Rossini, Antonio Somma, Teresa Stolz, Francesco Tamagno, Luigi Toccagni, Vincenzo Torelli, Cesare Vigna, and Maria Waldmann in addition to a host of lesser figures (some of these are indexed separately below). A small section also reproduces letters written by Arrigo Boito to Camille Bellaigue. Other significant documentary materials in this set include a survey of the Neapolitan censors' proposed changes in the *Ballo* libretto and the composer's reaction to them (item 601) as well as reproductions of Melchiorre Delfico's caricatures of Verdi (item 113). Additional essays explore Verdi's fight to obtain the position of *maestro di cappella* in Busseto; Verdi's relationship to contemporaries, such as Berlioz, Donizetti, Wagner, Catalani, and Giuseppe Mazzini; the composer's reaction to Molière's *Tartuffe*, which he considered as a possible opera subject; and Verdi's involvement in the issue of international copyright.

30. ———. "Giuseppe Verdi e i suoi editori di Francia e d'Italia." In *Carteggi verdiani* (item 29), 4:152–210. An earlier version with slightly fewer documents was published in *Nuova antologia* 151 (1939): 138–159; 250–75.

Presents, with commentary, about 50 letters involving Léon Escudier, Giulio Ricordi, Camille Du Locle, and other figures. The Escudier and Du Locle correspondence is meant to supplement and correct material published earlier in items 52 and 56.

31. Marchesi, Gustavo. *Verdi, merli, e cucù: Cronache bussetane fra il 1819 e il 1839, ampliate su documenti ritrovati da Gaspare Nello Vetro*. Biblioteca '70. Quaderni, 1. Busseto: Biblioteca della Cassa di Risparmio di Parma e Monte di Credito su Pegno di Busseto, 1979. 428 p. ML 410 .V4 M259.

An invaluable documentary biography of Verdi's early years. Among other significant items, the volume reproduces a series of letters exchanged between Giuseppe Seletti, a citizen from Busseto with whom Verdi lived in Milan, and Antonio Barezzi. In a review of this book published in *Studi verdiani* 1 (1982): 163–75, Martin Chusid supplements this correspondence by partially quoting from nearly 20 additional items found from the Sant'Agata collection. Chusid also provides corrections for some letters Verdi wrote to Barezzi that are printed in Marchesi's volume.

32. Martinelli, Aldo. *Verdi: Raggi e penombre*. Genoa: Studio Editoriale Genovese, 1926. 56 p. + 12 plates. ML 410 .V48 A16 1926.

This volume presents, with running commentary, the text of nearly three dozen letters, mostly reproduced in their entirety. Almost all of the correspondence (written by both Verdi and Giuseppina) is addressed either to the author, who was the family lawyer, or to Giuseppina's sister, Barberina. Most of the letters date from the late 1880s through the early days of 1901.

33. Morazzoni, Giuseppe, ed. *Verdi: Lettere inedite*; Giulio Mario Ciampelli. *Le opere verdiane al Teatro alla Scala (1839–1929)*. Milan: Rivista "La Scala e il Museo Teatrale," 1929. 248 p.

The first portion of the volume reproduces 77 letters, primarily from the archives of La Fenice and La Scala and mainly addressed either to administrative officials at La Fenice or to Francesco Maria Piave concerning the operas written for Venice: *Ernani, Rigoletto, La traviata,* and *Simon Boccanegra.* The second section of the book provides information about performances of each of Verdi's operas at La Scala through 1928 and offers prose commentary on some of the more important performances. See also a supplementary group of letters to Piave published in item 29 and a more definitive version of much of the Fenice material in item 344.

34. Nello Vetro, Gaspare. "Giuseppe Verdi, maestro di musica in Busseto: Il giudizio inedito di Alinovi e altre carte dell'Archivio di Stato di Parma." *Verdi: Bollettino dell'Istituto di Studi Verdiani* 3 [No. 8] (1973): 1142–49. Italian and German translations are provided on pp. 1503–15.

Reproduces a number of documents pertaining to the search for a music master in Busseto in 1836, following the death of Ferdinando Provesi. The documents include Verdi's letter of application, the report of the examination of the candidates by Giuseppe Alinovi, and the young Verdi's contract with the city for the post of music master.

35. Nordio, Mario. "Verdi e La Fenice." In *Verdi e La Fenice* (item 346), 10–57.

This important publication presents, with running commentary, 60 letters written by the composer to members of the theater's presidency, supplemented by related correspondence involving other individuals. A large number of the documents shed light on the genesis of *Ernani* and *Rigoletto*. Researchers using this source should carefully compare the text of all documents to the versions in Marcello Conati's *La bottega della musica* (item 344) which corrects many errors in transcription; Nordio, however, includes some passages omitted by Conati.

36. Oberdorfer, Aldo. *Giuseppe Verdi: Autobiografia dalle lettere.* 3rd rev. ed., with annotations and additions by Marcello Conati. Milan: Rizzoli, 1981. 524 p. ML 410 .V4 A35 1981.
      French translation by Sibylle Zavriew. *Verdi: Autobiographie à travers la correspondance.* New ed. revised by Marcello Conati. N.p.: Éditions Jean-Claude Lattès, 1984. 398 p.

A lively documentary biography consisting of a collation of letters by the composer (some of which are only partially reproduced), preceded by a short introductory essay. This volume was originally published in 1941 under the pseudonym of Carlo Graziani to disguise the author's Jewish ancestry. A second edition appeared in 1951 under the author's true name with four additional letters that had been excised from the earlier edition by fascist censors. For his new edition, Conati compares all documents for accuracy against the original holographs, if extant, or the most trustworthy printed sources; he also replaces letters originally quoted from *I copialettere* with more careful transcriptions from the actual documents. In addition, Conati indicates the location of the original documents, if known, as well as their earlier publications. New notes provide background information about the documents themselves and correct misinformation in some of Oberdorfer's original notes. In the bibliography, Conati adds entries for 139 published books and articles containing letters by Verdi to Oberdorfer's original list of ten sources. The new edition also boasts a chronologically organized table showing the letters and documents reproduced in the volume and separate indexes for names and titles of compositions. The only reduction of material in this new edition concerns the illustrations: the 66 pages of plates and six facsimile reproductions of documents in the original have been reduced to 22 illustrations.

37. Osborne, Charles, ed. and trans. *Letters of Giuseppe Verdi.* London: Victor Gollancz, 1971. 280 p. ISBN 0–575–00743–5. ML 410 .V4 A387.

A translation of nearly 300 letters from the *I copialettere* (item 28), including material from the footnotes and appendices. Unfortunately, this collection not only replicates the weaknesses of Luzio's edition of the *copialettere* but compounds them with a substantial number of errors and imprecisions in both translation and commentary. The volume includes a brief biographical dictionary, an index of names and compositions, and a list of recipients.

38. Perrotta Gruppi, Laura, ed. [under pseudonym of Arturo Di Ascoli]. *Quartetto milanese ottocentesco: Lettere di Giuseppe Verdi, Giuseppina Strepponi, Clara Maffei, Carlo Tenca e di altri personaggi del mondo politico e artistico dell'epoca.* Rome: Archivi Edizioni, 1974. xiii, 441 p. PQ 4259 .Q2.

The nearly 500 letters in this handsomely illustrated publication date from 1837 to 1892. Most were written by or sent to Clara Maffei, and most fall within the 40-year period from the mid-1840s through the mid-1880s. For each document, the author indicates previous publication, if any, or the collection where the original may be found. A useful index lists each letter by date, place of origin, writer, and recipient. The large number of attractive illustrations, many in color, include portraits of individuals; etchings, drawings, and photographs of scenes from Milan; and facsimile reproductions of manuscripts and early editions of Verdi's music.

39. Sartori, Claudio. "La Strepponi e Verdi a Parigi nella morsa quarantottesca." *Nuova rivista musicale italiana* 8 (1974): 239–53.

Reproduces nearly a dozen letters from 1847 and early 1848, mainly written by Verdi or Strepponi, that document Giuseppina's life, Verdi's activities in London and Paris, and (mostly by implication) their deepening personal relationship. Other correspondents include: Giovannina Lucca, Clara Maffei, Carlo Tenca, Giulia Tillet Torriglioni, Francesco Piave, and Pietro Romani.

Most of the transcriptions were prepared from the original documents, and many are published here for the first time.

40. Schlitzer, Franco. *Inediti verdiani nell'archivio dell Accademia Chigiana.* Quaderni dell'Accademia Chigiana, 27. Siena: [Ticci], 1953. 24 p. ML 5 .S57 no. 27.

    A shorter version appeared in 1951 on pp. 30–36 of a special issue (vol. 8) of the *Bollettino dell'Accademia Musicale Chigiana.*

    Presents the texts of letters from the collection of the Accademia Chigiana in five groups: 1) letters from Verdi to Felice Varesi, who conducted the premiere of *Macbeth*, supplementing and restoring deletions to letters previously published in item 789; 2) a letter from Verdi to Raffaele Colucci from 1867 declining an invitation to compose occasional music; 3) a group of letters dealing with the composer's business affairs; 4) a short letter to Giuseppina Pasqua-Giacomelli, the first Mistress Quickly in *Falstaff*; and 5) letters from several performers.

*   Walker, Frank. "Verdi and Vienna: With Some Unpublished Letters." See item 325.

*   Weaver, William, comp., ed., and trans. *Verdi: A Documentary Study*. Cited below as item 121.

41. Werfel, Franz, ed. *Giuseppe Verdi Briefe*. Epilogue by Paul Stefan. Berlin: Paul Zsolnay Verlag, 1926. 391 p. ML 410 .V4 W47 1926.

    English translation by Edward Downes. *Verdi: The Man in His Letters.* New York: L.B. Fischer, 1942. Reprint. Freeport, NY: Books for Libraries Press, 1970. 469 p. ISBN 0–8369–5538–2. ML 410 .V4 A385 1970. Reprint. New York: Vienna House, 1973. ISBN 0–8443–0088–8. ML 410 .V4 A385 1973.

    This collection, based primarily on *I copialettere* (item 28) with later additions from *Carteggi verdiani* (item 29) and other early collections, has historical significance as the first compilation of the composer's letters published in a language other than Italian (see item 324 for a consideration of Werfel's contributions to Verdi scholarship). Werfel wrote a substantial preface to the volume entitled "A Portrait of Giuseppe Verdi"; Paul Stefan provided an epilogue. The volume contains a useful index by recipient and a list of works; the English translation has, in addition, an extensive general index.

42. Zanetti, Emilia. "La corrispondenza di Verdi conservata a 'S. Cecilia': Contributi all'epistolario." *Verdi: Bollettino dell'Istituto di Studi Verdiani* 3

[No. 8] (1973): 1131–41. English and German translations are provided on pp. 1485–1502.

Reproduces, with historical background, more than a dozen letters to and from Verdi. Most of the documents date from the 1890s and concern, in some way, the *Quattro pezzi sacri*.

LETTERS & DOCUMENTS ORGANIZED BY CORRESPONDENT

This section lists the major published collections of letters involving a single correspondent. Many bits and pieces of Verdi's correspondence have been published in a wide variety of other sources, so readers should also consult the index to find all materials relating to a particular individual.

Arrivabene, Opprandino

43. Alberti, Annibale. *Verdi intimo: Carteggio di Giuseppe Verdi con il Conte Opprandino Arrivabene (1861–1886)*. Verona: Mondadori, 1931. xxxv, 349 p. ML 410 .V4 A4.

This important collection reproduces in chronological order the text of more than 150 letters from Verdi to Count Opprandino Arrivabene and about 60 letters from Arrivabene to Verdi. Annotations to the letters provide crucial background information and extended citations from other important documents. Several of Verdi's letters are reproduced in facsimile. The volume lacks a comprehensive index; a short index provides a list of letters with their main topics of discussion.

Barezzi, Antonio

* Garibaldi, Luigi Agostino. *Giuseppe Verdi nelle lettere di Emanuele Muzio ad Antonio Barezzi*. See item 72.

* Petrobelli, Pierluigi, et al. *Con Verdi in Casa Barezzi*. See item 213.

Bellaigue, Camillo

44. Luzio, Alessandro. "Carteggio Verdi-Bellaigue." In *Carteggi verdiani* (item 29), 2:299–316.

Publishes nearly two dozen letters exchanged among Verdi, Giuseppina, the French music critic Camille Bellaigue and, in one case, Bellaigue's parents. The letters date from the late 1880s and 1890s and contain many references to *Otello, Falstaff,* and the *Quattro pezzi sacri*. The author provides a facsimile reproduction of Verdi's letter to Bellaigue dated 2 May 1898.

Boito, Arrigo

45. Della Corte, Andrea. "Verdi e Boito inediti nei ricordi di Edoardo Mascheroni." *Musica d'oggi* 7 (1925): 241–43.

    Reproduces in facsimile and transcription a letter from Boito to Verdi dated 15 [January 1897] in response to news that the composer had suffered a stroke. The article also contains a short letter from Boito to Mascheroni and a telegram from Verdi to Mascheroni from about the same date.

46. Medici, Mario, and Conati, Marcello, eds., assisted by Marisa Casati. *Carteggio Verdi-Boito*. Parma: Istituto di Studi Verdiani, 1978. 2 vols. xxxv, 549 p. + 7 p. plates and tables. ML 410 .V4 A4 1978.
    English translation by William Weaver, with a new Introduction by Marcello Conati. *The Verdi-Boito Correspondence*. Chicago and London: University of Chicago Press, 1994. lxiv, 321 p. ISBN 0–226–85304–7. ML 410 .V4 A4 1994.

    A critical edition of 301 letters and dispatches between Verdi and Boito, arranged in chronological order and differentiated by typeface (Verdi, normal type; Boito, italics). A useful section in the preface reproduces significant portions of letters exchanged among Verdi, Giulio Ricordi, Giuseppina Strepponi, and Boito that provide background to the exchanges between Verdi and Boito themselves. The second volume contains annotations that describe the location of the manuscript letters; earlier publications, if any; comments about difficult readings; and explanations of obscure references. Although many of the letters have been previously published by Luzio (item 29), Walker (item 152), Gatti (item 147) and others, this edition now constitutes the most authoritative source for this exchange of letters. Various indexes facilitate the use of the *Carteggio*: one lists in tabular form letters by writer, date, and incipit; separate indexes cover places and periodicals, names, and compositions. The editors also provide a list of collections in which the various documents are found and an extensive bibliography. The English translation published by the University of Chicago Press contains a long and informative new Introduction by Marcello Conati (see item 197 for its original Italian version); this volume lacks, however, the specialized indexes found in the Italian original.

Bottesini, Giovanni

47. Costantini, Teodoro. *Sei lettere inedite di Giuseppe Verdi a Giovanni Bottesini*. Trieste: C. Schmidl; Turin: S. Lattes, 1908.

    Five of the six letters reproduced here, written between December 1871 and March 1872, concern the premiere performance of *Aida*, which Bottesini conducted at Cairo. In the final letter, written in 1883, the composer explains that he was not interested in becoming part of a governmental commission on music.

Cammarano, Salvatore

48. Mossa, Carlo Matteo. *Carteggio Verdi-Cammarano*. Parma: Istituto Nazionale di Studi Verdiani, forthcoming.

This important volume will contain more than 150 letters exchanged between June 1843 and July 1852, dealing with *Alzira, La battaglia di Legnano, Luisa Miller, Il trovatore,* and several works contemplated by Verdi but never written, including *L'assedio di Firenze* and *Re Lear.*

Corticelli, Mauro

49. Chusid, Martin. "Some Biographical Notes of Mauro Corticelli and a Previously Unpublished Letter to Him from Verdi." *Verdi Newsletter* 22 (1995): 17–24.

Provides a biography of Corticelli, focusing on his relationship with Giuseppina and Giuseppe Verdi, and publishes in facsimile, transcription, and English translation a letter from Verdi to Corticelli dated 22 December 1872. The letter contains instructions regarding an apartment Verdi owned in Genoa and also provides information about the opera season at the Teatro San Carlo in Naples, where Verdi was overseeing productions of *Don Carlos* and *Aida.*

De Amicis, Giuseppe

50. Sartoris, Leonello. *Nuovi inediti verdiani: Carteggio di Giuseppe e Giuseppina Verdi con Giuseppe De Amicis (Genova, 1861–1901).* Preface by Pierluigi Petrobelli. Genoa: Lo Sprint, 1991. 289 p. + 16 p. plates.

Reproduces nearly 300 letters exchanged between Verdi and his wife with their business agent in Genoa, Giuseppe De Amicis. The author documents the location of each letter's autograph, if known, and lists previous publications, if any. He also includes informative footnotes with supplementary details about many of the people, places, and events mentioned in the letters. An appendix offers some additional letters and documentation relating to Verdi and Genoa. The letters are carefully indexed, showing date, author, recipient, and the letters' incipits. The volume also offers separate indexes for names, places, and institutions as well as a short bibliography of items relating to Verdi and Genoa.

De Sanctis, Cesare and Giuseppe

51. Luzio, Alessandro. "Carteggio inedito di Giuseppe e Giuseppina Verdi con Cesare e Giuseppe De Sanctis." In *Carteggi verdiani* (item 29), 1: 1–240.

Reproduces nearly 250 letters by Giuseppe and Giuseppina to Cesare and Giuseppe De Sanctis, with light commentary and some citations from the return correspondence. The letters cover the period from December 1849 through January 1899, with the greatest number in the decade from the mid-1860s through the mid-1870s. Many of the letters are long and discursive, ranging over a wide variety of topics; they shed particular light on the genesis and early reception of *Un ballo in maschera, Don Carlos*, and *Aida*.

Du Locle, Camille

* Busch, Hans, ed. and trans. *Verdi's "Aida": The History of an Opera in Letters and Documents*. See item 93.

* Günther, Ursula, and Gabriella Carrara Verdi. "Der Briefwechsel Verdi-Nuitter-Du Locle zur Revision des *Don Carlos*." See item 96.

52. Prod'homme, Jacques-Gabriel. "Lettres inédites de G. Verdi à Camille Du Locle." *La revue musicale* 10/5 (1929): 97–112; 10/7 (1929): 25–37. Reprinted in English translation by Theodore Baker as "Unpublished Letters from Verdi to Camille Du Locle (1866–76)." *Musical Quarterly* 7 (1921): 73–103.

A selection of approximately 50 letters and other documents from Verdi and Giuseppina Strepponi to Du Locle spanning the decade from 1866–76. Frequent topics include the reception of *Don Carlos* and the genesis and first performances of *Aida* and the Manzoni *Requiem*. As is the case with Prod'homme's publication of the Escudier correspondence, this publication contains many errors of transcription. See item 30 for some amplifications and corrections.

Escudier Family and Firm

53. Casale, Stephen. "A Catalogue of Letters from Verdi and Giuseppina Strepponi Verdi to the Escudiers." M.A. thesis, New York University, 1983. 74 p.

Catalogues 294 letters from Verdi and his wife to members of the Escudier family. For each letter, the author lists the place, date, incipit, location of the original and of copies, and published sources, if any. Casale also notes diary entries from Giuseppina's *copialettere* that indicate additional letters; these are not treated as separate entries, however, since the original documents are not known to be extant. Notes to the catalogue provide corrections to earlier publications of these letters, notably by Jacques-Gabriel Prod'homme (item 56). Casale provides an English translation of Prod'homme's Foreword and a table showing selected performances of Verdi's works in Paris during Léon Escudier's lifetime.

54. ———. "A Newly-Discovered Letter from Verdi to Léon Escudier." *Verdi Newsletter* 11 (1983): 6–15.

Reproduces in facsimile, transcription, and English translation a letter now in a private collection written by Verdi to Escudier on 12 December 1869 and the letter from Escudier dated the day before to which it was a response. The main topic of Verdi's letter concerns metronome markings for Riccardo's fisherman's ballad in Act II of *Ballo*. The composer also comments on plans for a production of *I masnadieri* at the Athénée.

*   Günther, Ursula. "The Verdi-Escudier Correspondence About *Macbeth*." See item 773.

55. Lesure, Anik Devriès, and Alessandro Di Profio. *Carteggio Verdi-Escudier*. Parma: Istituto Nazionale di Studi Verdiani, forthcoming.

This new critical edition of the correspondence with the French publishers Léon and Marie Escudier is especially important because the previously published versions are riddled with omissions and errors of transcription.

56. Prod'homme, Jacques-Gabriel. "Lettres inédites de G. Verdi à Léon Escudier." *Rivista musicale italiana* 35 (1928): 1–28, 171–97, 519–52.
An abridged version (31 letters from 1869–77) appeared earlier in the *Bulletin de la Société Union Musicologique* 5 (1925): 7–28.
An abridged English translation by L.A. Sheppard (41 letters from 1844–77) was published as "Verdi's Letters to Léon Escudier." *Music & Letters* 4 (1923): 62–70, 184–96, 375–77.

Publishes slightly more than 100 of the 233 known letters at the Bibliothèque de l'Opéra written by Verdi and Giuseppina Strepponi to Léon and Marie Escudier between 1847 and 1877. Unfortunately, Prod'homme's transcriptions contain many errors; Ursula Günther has republished corrected versions of some of these letters in item 96. Stephen Casale's catalogue (item 53) is another essential tool when working with this collection of letters: he provides corrections for many of the transcriptions, especially regarding chronology, as well as an English translation of Prod'homme's introductory essay. See also item 30 for some amplifications and corrections.

57. Walker, Frank. "Four Unpublished Verdi Letters." *Music and Letters* 29 (1948): 44–47.

Slightly enlarged republication in Italian translation. "Cinque lettere verdiane."
Rassegna musicale 21 (1951): 256–61.

Reproduces, in English translation, the texts of four letters from Verdi
addressed to either Marie Escudier or ambiguously to "Escudier," either Marie
or Léon. The letters, which date from 1847 through 1856, are in the collection
of the British Museum. The author also includes a list of previously published
letters from Verdi to Marie and other ambiguous cases in which the letter may
have been intended for either of the two brothers. The fifth letter (published
only in the Italian version) is addressed to Léon.

Faccio, Franco

58. De Rensis, Raffaello. *Franco Faccio e Verdi: Carteggi e documenti inediti.* Milan:
     Fratelli Treves, 1934. 268 p. ML 410 .F14 R4.

     A narrative biography of Faccio, focusing on his relationship with Verdi and
     Boito. The author reproduces some letters and other documents but often in
     fragmentary form and without documentation. The volume provides significant
     information on the latter part of Verdi's life, in which Faccio conducted the
     Italian premiere of *Aida*, as well as the first performances of the revised *Simon
     Boccanegra* and *Otello*. Items 93 and 99 provide better versions of many of the
     documents in English translation, although they are not without their own
     problems.

Ferrarini, Giulio Cesare

59. Damerini, Adelmo. "Sei lettere inedite di Verdi." *Il pianoforte* 7 (Aug./Sept.
     1926): 221–26.

     Five of the six letters published here are directed to Giulio Cesare Ferrarini,
     director of the orchestra at Parma from 1856–71 and later director of the
     Parma Conservatory. While most of the letters contain only general news and
     information, one from March 1869 provides instructions about the performance
     of *Don Carlos*, warning against sluggish tempos. The author provides a short
     biographical sketch of Ferrarini.

Florimo, Francesco

60. Luzio, Alessandro. "Carteggio Verdi-Florimo." In *Carteggi verdiani* (item 29),
     1:306–12.

     Publishes a half-dozen letters from Florimo to Verdi written between 1869–78
     that supplement the collection previously published in the *Copialettere* (item
     28).

61. Walker, Frank. "Verdi and Francesco Florimo: Some Unpublished Letters." *Music and Letters* 26 (1945): 201–08.

   Reproduces in translation about a dozen letters from Verdi to Florimo housed in the library of the Conservatorio di San Pietro a Maiella in Naples. The article includes several additional letters (with some corrections) previously published in the *Copialettere* (item 28), *Carteggi verdiani* (item 29), and other sources to provide historical context.

Galuzzi, Ferdinando

62. Mingardi, Corrado. "Una nuova terribile lettera di Verdi contro i Bussetani." *Biblioteca '70* 2 (1971): 27–29.

   Reproduces in facsimile and transcription a letter dated 1 December 1839 from Verdi to Ferdinando Galuzzi, in which he laments that while he had received honors in Milan, the Bussetani had only insulted him.

Ghislanzoni, Antonio

* Busch, Hans, ed. and trans. *Verdi's Aida: The History of an Opera in Letters and Documents.* See item 93.

* Conati, Marcello. "Ei mi raggiunse . . . m'insultò . . . l'uccisi: Una lettera di Verdi sul finale della *Forza del destino*." See item 727.

* Gossett, Philip. "Verdi, Ghislanzoni, and *Aida*: The Uses of Convention." See item 572.

63. "A Letter from Verdi to Antonio Ghislanzoni, With a Transcription and Translation." *Verdi Newsletter* 23 (1996): front cover (recto and verso).

   Reproduces in facsimile, transcription, and translation a short letter dated 28 September 1972 concerning revisions in the duet finale of *Don Carlos*, Act II.

64. Spada, Marco. *Carteggio Verdi-Ghislanzoni.* Parma: Istituto Nazionale di Studi Verdiani, forthcoming.

   This significant new volume will contain more than 100 documents dealing with the genesis of *Aida*.

Hiller, Ferdinand

65. Luzio, Alessandro. "Verdi e Hiller." In *Carteggi verdiani* (item 29), 2:317–45.

This letter exchange, dating from the late 1870s through the mid 1880s, contains much informative material about a wide range of topics, including the _Requiem_, the _Pezzi sacri_, and the contemporary musical scene in Germany.

Maffei, Clara

66. Luzio, Alessandro. "Il carteggio di Giuseppe Verdi con la Contessa Maffei." In _Profili biografici e bozzetti storici_, 2:505–62. Milan: Casa Editrice L.F. Cogliati, 1927. DG 551 .L83.

Offers a selection of 83 letters from Verdi to Clara Maffei written between 1845 to 1885 (the letter of 17 December 1884 is reproduced in facsimile), eight letters from Giuseppina Verdi to Clara Maffei written between 1867 and 1875, and one letter from Giuseppina to Cesare Vigna dated 9 May 1872 citing reasons Verdi would not supervise a performance of _Aida_ in Padua. Many of the letters contribute significant information about Verdi's political, cultural, and social milieu as well as the performance and reception of his operas. Unfortunately, not all letters are reproduced in their entirety. The collection is intended to supplement the earlier publication by Raffaello Barbiera (item 217).

67. ———. "Verdi e Manzoni nelle lettere della Contessa Maffei." In _Carteggi verdiani_ (item 29), 2:292–98.

Reproduces more than a dozen letters in whole or in part written by Maffei to Verdi and Giuseppina from the 1860s through the 1880s. This small collection supplements the correspondence from Verdi to the Countess published earlier by the author (item 66) and by Raffaello Barbiera (item 217).

* Perrotta Gruppi, Laura, ed. [under pseudonym of Arturo Di Ascoli]. _Quartetto milanese ottocentesco: Lettere di Giuseppe Verdi, Giuseppina Strepponi, Clara Maffei, Carlo Tenca e di altri personaggi del mondo politico e artistico dell'epoca._ See item 38.

Mariani, Angelo

68. Luzio, Alessandro. "Il carteggio Verdi-Mariani." In _Carteggi verdiani_ (item 29), 2:203–21.

A summary of correspondence between Verdi and Angelo Mariani from 1860–71, including quotations from selected documents. Includes a transcript of Verdi's annotations in the score of _Lohengrin_, which he heard in 1871 at the Teatro Comunale in Bologna in a performance conducted by Mariani.

* Potito, Amedeo. _Angelo Mariani: Autobiografia e documenti, 1821–1873._ See item 68, 218.

69. Zoppi, Umberto. *Angelo Mariani, Giuseppe Verdi, e Teresa Stolz in un carteggio inedito.* Milan: Garzanti, 1947. 399 p. + 27 plates.

This volume's main focus is Angelo Mariani. The opening section provides a biography of Mariani, while the largest portion of the book reproduces letters exchanged among Mariani, Verdi, Teresa Stolz, and Carlino Del Signore but primarily written by Mariani. Documentary material by Verdi comes solely from other secondary literature.

Mazzucato, Alberto

70. De Bellis, Frank V., and Federico Ghisi. "Alcune lettere inedite sul *Don Carlos* dal carteggio Verdi-Mazzucato." *Atti 2* (item 225), 531–41.

Reproduces five letters written by Verdi to Mazzucato dating from 1867 and 1868. The first of the group provides one of the earliest references to the beginning of a breakdown in the friendship between Verdi and Angelo Mariani. The remainder of the letters are important for the detailed instructions Verdi gives about details of performance practice for *Don Carlos* at La Scala in early 1868. In item 248, Martin Chusid provides English translations for the letters dated 17 March and 20 March.

Morelli, Domenico

* Levi, Primo. *Domenico Morelli nella vita e nell'arte: Mezzo secolo di pittura italiana.* See item 219.

71. Luzio, Alessandro. "Il carteggio Verdi-Morelli." In *Carteggi verdiani* (item 29), 1:276–98.

Reproduces more than a dozen letters from Domenico Morelli to Verdi and Giuseppina, supplementing the collection published in item 219. Includes reproductions of some drawings by Morelli and a complete facsimile of a letter to Giuseppina written in 1873.

Muzio, Emanuele

72. Garibaldi, Luigi Agostino. *Giuseppe Verdi nelle lettere di Emanuele Muzio ad Antonio Barezzi.* Milan: Fratelli Treves, 1931. viii, 382 p. + 37 p. illustrations. ML 410 .V4 M8.

This source provides insight into Verdi's life and career during the period 1844–47, when Muzio was studying composition privately with Verdi, as well as general cultural life in Milan during that period. Nearly half of the volume is devoted to a long introduction, which sets in context the ensuing letters written by Muzio to Barezzi, his benefactor and the former benefactor of Verdi. The letters are particularly valuable for their information about the genesis and reception of Verdi's operas written or performed during this period (including *Ernani, I due Foscari, Giovanna d'Arco, Alzira, Attila, Macbeth, I masnadieri,* and *Jérusalem*). Although most of the 122 letters were written between 1844–47, a few date from later years through 1867. See item 220 for some additional correspondence of Muzio.

73. Mossa, Carlo Matteo. "Le lettere di Emanuele Muzio alla Casa Ricordi." *Studi verdiani* 4 (1986–87): 167–201.

The Ricordi Archives house a collection of more than 650 letters from Muzio to various members of the firm. Most of these documents have never been published, although Abbiati published and summarized some (with numerous omissions and errors) in his biography (item 145). As the only formal student of Verdi, Muzio's correspondence sheds important light on many aspects of the composer's career. The documents also provide important information on Muzio's own career and on nineteenth-century musical culture in general. The article includes lightly annotated transcriptions of 21 letters dating from 1847 to 1889 that have not been previously published in full.

Nuitter, Charles

* Günther, Ursula, and Gabriella Carrara Verdi. "Der Briefwechsel Verdi-Nuitter-Du Locle zur Revision des *Don Carlos*." See item 96.

Perosio, Giuseppe

74. Conati, Marcello. "Le lettere di Giuseppe e Giuseppina Verdi a Giuseppe Perosio." *Nuova rassegna di studi musicali* 1 (1977): 47–67.

Reproduces 27 letters from Verdi and his wife to Perosio, a writer, music critic, and agent for the Società Italiana degli Autori, as well as the author of an early biography of the composer. The letters, dating between 1876 and 1895, are intertwined with commentary that provides background information. The article also includes a substantial biographical sketch of Perosio and a comparison of his early biography of the composer (item 130) to other early accounts.

Piave, Francesco Maria

75. Baker, Evan. "Lettere di Giuseppe Verdi a Francesco Maria Piave, 1843–1865: Documenti della Frederick R. Koch Foundation Collection e della Mary Flager Cary Collection presso la Pierpont Morgan Library di New York." *Studi verdiani* 4 (1986–87): 136–66.

The Frederick R. Koch Foundation Collection contains 75 autograph letters from Verdi to Piave, in addition to several other miscellaneous letters involving the two figures. Some of these letters were published in Abbiati's biography (item 145); however, these contain numerous omissions and errors in transcription and dating. After sketching a history of the collection and the provenance of the letters, the author provides a detailed chronological catalogue of the letters, listing place and date, incipit, citations in published literature, and miscellaneous notes. The concluding portion of the article presents full transcriptions of sixteen letters dating between 1844 and 1865 that have never previously been published. The published letters contain extensive annotations that explain obscure references or provide more detailed information about information in the letters.

* Conati, Marcello. *La bottega della musica: Verdi e La Fenice.* See item 344.

76. Luzio, Alessandro. "Lettere inedite di Verdi a F.M. Piave." In *Carteggi verdiani* (item 29), 2:349–57.

Publishes ten letters from Verdi to his librettist, intended to supplement the larger selections published in items 28 and 33 above. This section of *Carteggi verdiani* also includes three additional letters from Verdi to Luigi Toccagni, Marie Escudier, and the master of ceremonies at the Tuileries.

* Morazzoni, Giuseppe, ed. *Verdi: Lettere inedite*; Giulio Mario Ciampelli. *Le opere verdiane al Teatro alla Scala (1839–1929).* See item 33.

Piroli, Giuseppe

77. Luzio, Alessandro. "Carteggio Verdi-Piroli." *Carteggi verdiani* (item 29), vol. 3.

Reproduces all of the letters from Verdi to Piroli known to be extant, supplemented by some of Piroli's return correspondence. The letter exchange, amounting to about 400 documents, begins in 1859 and continues until Piroli's death in 1890. These letters are particularly valuable for shedding light on Verdi's feelings about politics and society in general.

Ricordi Family and Firm

78. Cella, Franca. "L'opera di Verdi nella corrispondenza col suo editore italiano." *Atti 3* (item 226), 532–45.

Discusses the significance of the Verdi-Ricordi correspondence in understanding the composer's life and activities and some of the difficulties inherent in establishing an authoritative, critical text. The author cites numerous letters from the then forthcoming critical edition of the correspondence (see item 81).

79. Cella, Franca, and Pierluigi Petrobelli. *Giuseppe Verdi, Giulio Ricordi: Corrispondenza e immagini 1881/1890.* Catalogue for an exhibition at La Scala, 14 November 1981 to 31 January 1982. Milan: Teatro alla Scala, 1982. 75 p. ML 410 .V4 A45 1982.

Excerpts from some of the letters were also published by Franca Cella as "Verdi inedito" in *Musica viva* 5 (November 1981): 42–49.

Reproduces the texts of nearly 140 letters, some of which were previously unpublished, in categories relating to personal relationships among Verdi and members of the Ricordi firm; the revision of *Simon Boccanegra* and *Don Carlos*; the composition of *Otello*; singers and orchestras; and friends. The volume contains a number of facsimile reproductions and illustrations as well as a short essay by Cella entitled "Giulio Ricordi interlocutore di Verdi tra il 1881 e il 1891."

80. Petrobelli, Pierluigi, Marisa Di Gregorio Casati, and Carlo Matteo Mossa, eds. *Carteggio Verdi-Ricordi 1880–1881.* Parma: Istituto di Studi Verdiani, 1988. xxiv, 347 p. + 18 plates. ISBN 88–85065–05–8. ML 410 .V4 A4 1988.

This volume, the first to be published in a new critical edition, contains 246 letters and telegrams exchanged between either the composer or Giuseppina Strepponi and members of the Ricordi firm. Texts of previously published documents often contain substantial corrections; other items, particularly those addressed to Verdi, are published here for the first time. The documents are arranged in chronological order and differentiated by typeface (Verdi or his wife, normal type; members of the Ricordi firm, italics). The editors have added light annotations that provide essential background information and contexts for the documents; a series of appendices reproduces longer newspaper articles and letters by other correspondents that shed light on issues raised in the correspondence. The volume is well indexed, with separate indexes for the documents themselves (showing writer, date, and incipit); names; operas (by Verdi and others); newspapers and periodicals; and places and institutions. A useful bibliography supplies many specialized and some little-known references that concern this period. The plates reproduce photographs of the principal correspondents, facsimiles of several scores and early editions (including the beautiful title pages to the first editions of the *Pater noster* and *Ave Maria*), and scenery and costume designs for the revised version of *Simon Boccanegra*, a major topic of discussion during this period.

81. Cella, Franca, Madina Ricordi, and Marisa Di Gregorio Casati, eds. *Carteggio Verdi-Ricordi 1882–1885.* Parma: Istituto Nazionale di Studi Verdiani, 1994. xxii, 540 p. + 56 plates. ISBN 88–85065–11–2. ML 410 .V4 A4 1994b.

Contains 346 documents, many of published here for the first time. Topics include, among others, continuing work on *Otello*, the revision of *Don Carlos*, and reactions to performances of the recently revised *Simon Boccanegra*. The illustrations, many in color, primarily reproduce set designs, costumes, and documents for the 1884 production of the newly revised *Don Carlo* at La Scala. Substantial appendices reproduce contemporary periodical articles relevant to the letters published in this volume and several additional letters from Emanuele Muzio to Ricordi concerning a performance of *Simon Boccanegra* at the Théâtre Italien in Paris. For the organization of indices and other referential material, see item 80 above.

82. Cella, Franca, Angelo Pompilio, Madina Ricordi, and Marisa Di Gregorio Casati, eds. *Carteggio Verdi-Ricordi (1886–1888)*. Parma: Istituto Nazionale di Studi Verdiani, forthcoming.

   This volume will contain more than 350 documents, primarily concerning the final stages of composition of *Otello* and its early performances.

* Serianni, Luca. "Spigolature linguistiche dal *Carteggio Verdi-Ricordi.*" See item 105.

Romani, Pietro

* Chusid, Martin. "A Letter by the Composer about *Giovanna d'Arco* and Some Remarks on the Division of Musical Direction in Verdi's Day." See item 745.

Rossini, Gioachino

83. Carrara Verdi, Gabriella. "Le lettere di Rossini a Verdi." *Biblioteca '70* 3 (1973): 9–16.

   Reproduces the texts of four letters from Rossini to Verdi, written in the years 1844, 1845, 1846, and 1865, together with commentary providing context to the letters. Two of the letters ask Verdi to consider writing an aria for the Russian tenor Nicolai Ivanov. Also included is a letter dating from 1845 from Rossini to Count Pompeo Belgioioso, informing him (probably at the request of Verdi) of the requirements and conditions that Parisian opera houses made of foreign composers. Two of the letters were previously published in volume 2 of *Carteggi verdiani* (item 29), together with a letter from Verdi to Léon Escudier describing his feelings on hearing of Rossini's death.

Somma, Antonio

84. Luzio, Alessandro. "Le lettere del Somma sul libretto del *Ballo in maschera.*" In *Carteggi verdiani* (item 29), 1:219–40.

Reproduces selected letters written by Somma to the composer between October 1857 and late summer the following year dealing with *Ballo*. The letters supplement item 86 with some additional material and a list of errata in the earlier publication.

85. ———. "Il *Re Lear* di Verdi." In *Carteggi verdiani* (item 29), 2:58–79.

Reprints some of the Verdi-Somma correspondence originally published in item 86 about the proposed *Re Lear* project, inserting several additional letters from Somma to Verdi to illustrate the history of the abandoned project.

86. Pascolato, Alessandro. *"Re Lear" e "Ballo in maschera": Lettere di Giuseppe Verdi ad Antonio Somma.* Città di Castello: S. Lapi, 1902. 98 p. ML 410 .V48 D28.

Reproduces, with light annotations, 28 letters written by Verdi to Somma between 1853 and 1863 concerning the abortive *Re Lear* project and *Un ballo in maschera*. These letters are essential for any study concerning the history or dramaturgy of either of these compositions. Item 84 contains additional published documents in this letter exchange as well as corrections to some of the letters published here.

Stolz, Teresa

* Luzio, Alessandro. "Il carteggio di Verdi con la Stolz e la Waldmann." See item 92.

Strepponi, Giuseppina

87. Luzio, Alessandro. "I 'copialettere' di Giuseppina Strepponi." In *Carteggi verdiani* (item 29), 2:5–52.

Following a short introduction, the author presents a year-by-year prose summary of Giuseppina's *copialettere* from 1860–94, with some citations from selected letters.

Tamberlick, Enrico

88. Martin, George. "Unpublished Letters." *Verdi: Bollettino dell'Istituto di Studi Verdiani* 3 [No. 5] (1962): 745–54. English and German translations appear on pp. 1088–1102.

Reproduces a series of letters from Verdi to Tamberlick, who created the role of Don Alvaro at the premiere performance of *Forza* in St. Petersburg and who was largely responsible for both arranging the commission of the work and convincing the composer to write it.

Torelli, Vincenzo

89. Luzio, Alessandro. "Il carteggio con Vincenzo Torelli." In *Carteggi verdiani* (item 29), 1:299–305.

Summarizes items from correspondence exchanged among Verdi, Achille Torelli, and Vincenzo Torelli that the author had previously published in the *Copialettere* (item 28), adding some material written by Torelli in the Neapolitan journal l'*Omnibus* related to troubles with the censors over *Un ballo in maschera*.

* Walker, Frank. "Unpublished Letters: A Contribution to the History of *Un ballo in maschera*." See item 94.

Vigna, Cesare

90. Bongiovanni, Giannetto. *Dal carteggio inedito Verdi-Vigna: Con 27 lettere inedite, 10 autografi e 7 illustrazioni fuori testo.* Rome: Edizioni del "Giornale d'Italia," 1941. 75 p. + 7 plates. ML 410 .V4 A43.

Reproduces, with historical background, a series of letters from Verdi to Cesare Vigna written between 1853 and 1892. The first of these letters shed light on the early reception of *La traviata*; later ones tend to be more general in content. See also item 223 for a recent study of Verdi's relationship with Vigna.

Waldmann, Maria

91. Della Corte, Andrea. "Le lettere a Maria Waldmann." *Il pianoforte* 7 (Feb. 1926): 34–46.

Presents the texts of over two dozen letters from Verdi to Maria Waldmann, who created the role of Amneris at La Scala and was one of the soloists in the first performance of the *Requiem*. The letters date from 1873 through December 1900 and cover a variety of interesting topics, particularly about the reception of *Aida* and the *Requiem*. The article contains a brief biographical sketch of Waldmann and provides background information to the letters.

92. Luzio, Alessandro. "Il carteggio di Verdi con la Stolz e la Waldmann." In *Carteggi verdiani* (item 29), 2:222–91.

Reproduces about 50 letters written by Verdi to Maria Waldmann from the early 1870s through 1900 and fourteen letters from Teresa Stolz to Verdi and/or Giuseppina from the same period. Topics include the reception of *Requiem*, in which both women frequently appeared as soloists, and all of Verdi's later operas.

LETTERS & DOCUMENTS RELATED TO SPECIFIC WORKS

Aida

* Abdoun, Saleh, ed. *Genesi dell"Aida" con documentazione inedita.* See item 554.

93. Busch, Hans, ed. and trans. *Verdi's "Aida": The History of an Opera in Letters and Documents.* Minneapolis: University of Minnesota Press, 1978. lv, 688p. ISBN 0-8166-0798-2. ML 410 .V4 V33.

     This documentary history of *Aida* reproduces correspondence to and from Verdi dating from 1868 to 1891. The section of documents includes, among other items, excerpts from Edouard Mariette's memoirs, early synopses, scenarios, and drafts for the libretto; a facsimile reproduction and transcription of Verdi's annotations in the Italian libretto (presumably for the 1872 production in Parma); Franco Faccio's production notes regarding the Italian premiere at La Scala; and the complete production book published by Ricordi for the Italian premiere. Busch includes a set of biographical notes, which provide substantial information on about 40 significant people associated with the composer in the genesis and early productions of the opera; a brief chronology of Verdi's life, a selective bibliography, and a thorough index to the letters. A preliminary table lists each letter, the date, correspondents, location of the autograph, and earlier publication in English, if any. See also Philip Gossett's article (item 572 below), which more accurately establishes the chronology of Ghislanzoni's 35 letters to Verdi. Busch's translations are generally adequate; however, some technical terms are poorly or erroneously translated and for anything beyond a cursory survey, readers are advised to check the original documents if possible.

* Günther, Ursula. "Zur Entstehung von Verdis *Aida*." See item 559.

Un ballo in maschera

94. Walker, Frank. "Unpublished Letters: A Contribution to the History of *Un ballo in maschera*." *Verdi: Bollettino dell'Istituto di Studi Verdiani* 1 [No. 1] (1960): 28–43. Italian and German translations are published on pp. 279–304.

     Publishes, in English translation, a series of letters written by Verdi to Vincenzo Torelli, secretary of the Teatro San Carlo, and Vincenzo Jacovacci, impresario at the Teatro Apollo in Rome, concerning the genesis and early history of *Un ballo in maschera*. An appendix reproduces Verdi's contract with San Carlo dated 2 May 1856 and the composer's draft for a revised contract.

Don Carlos

95. Günther, Ursula. "Documents inconnus concernant les relations de Verdi avec l'Opéra de Paris." *Atti 3* (item 226), 564–83.

   Discusses documentation regarding the production of nine Verdi operas in Paris that is now conserved as part of sub-series AJ^{XIII} at the Archives Nationales. The collection contains 37 letters from Verdi, some of which are quoted integrally or in part. Documentation regarding *Don Carlos* is particularly rich, covering the initial negotiations regarding the work, its *mise-en-scène*, and the production itself. See item 624 for related material.

96. Günther, Ursula, and Gabriella Carrara Verdi. "Der Briefwechsel Verdi-Nuitter-Du Locle zur Revision des *Don Carlos*." *Analecta musicologica* 14 (1974): 1–31; 15 (1975): 334–401.

   Reproduces, with light annotations, letters exchanged among Verdi, Giuseppina, the two librettists, and several other individuals regarding revisions in *Don Carlos*. The letters, dating from 1870 through 1883, document the reworking of the opera in remarkable detail. Günther's introduction and commentary provides historical background and other material necessary to understand the documents. Many of the letters have not been previously published; the authors also note corrections to some of the letters cited in items 52 and 145. Part II includes facsimile reproductions of three complete items.

Ernani

97. Della Corte, Andrea. *La composizione dell'"Ernani" nelle lettere di Verdi.* Turin: La Stampa, 1941.

   An account of the work's history from its genesis through the first performances as seen in excerpts from Verdi's correspondence. Much of the documentation concerns the issue of censorship and the composer's struggle to assure himself of obtaining the right singers for the major roles. Six letters are reproduced in facsimile.

La forza del destino

* Martin, George. "Unpublished Letters." See item 88.

Falstaff

98. Busch, Hans, ed. and trans. *Verdi's "Falstaff" in Letters and Contemporary Review:.* Bloomington: Indiana University Press, 1997. ISBN 0–253–32980–9 (cloth); 0–253–21034–8 (paper). ML 410 .V4 V34 1977.

Macbeth

* Rosen, David, and Andrew Porter. *Verdi's "Macbeth": A Sourcebook.* Cited below as item 762.

I masnadieri

* Marvin, Roberta Montemorra. "Verdi's *I masnadieri*: Its Genesis and Early Reception." See item 793 below.

Otello

99. Busch, Hans, ed. and trans. *Verdi's "Otello" and "Simon Boccanegra" (revised version) in Letters and Documents.* Foreword by Julian Budden. 2 vols. Oxford: Clarendon Press, 1988. lxiii, 891 p. ISBN 0–19–313207–9. ML 410 .V4 V36 1988.
A few selected letters from this collection with commentary were previously published as "Destined to Meet." *Opera Quarterly* 5 (Summer/Autumn 1987): 4–23.

A documentary history of *Otello* and the revision of *Simon Boccanegra*. Vol. 1 contains letter exchanges dealing with the two projects, primarily among Verdi, Giulio Ricordi, and Boito. It is the most accessible source for this group of letters in English translation, although the original Italian version of many letters have recently become available in critical editions (see items 46 and 80–82). Vol. 2 provides a complete English translation of production books by Giulio Ricordi for the premieres of the two works at La Scala and an in-depth study of the characters and description of the *mise-en-scène* for *Otello* written by Victor Maurel, who portrayed Iago in the first production. The remainder of the volume reproduces various contemporary reviews and other documents that illustrate the reception of the two operas. The end material includes several useful features, such as a list of letters and telegrams showing the writer, the recipient, destination, date, location of the autograph, and published source(s); separate chronologies of Verdi's and Boito's lives; a biographical dictionary of people mentioned in the letters and documents; a selective bibliography; an index of works (subdivided by act and scene for the two main operas under discussion); and a general index. As in the case of Busch's earlier compilation dealing with *Aida*, some of the translations, especially of technical terms, may be misleading.

Re Lear

100. Medici, Mario. "Lettere sul *Re Lear*." *Verdi: Bollettino dell'Istituto di Studi Verdiani* 1 [No. 2] (1960): 767–78. English and German translation appear on pp. 1037–56.

Reproduces three previously unpublished letters by Verdi discussing *Re Lear*, two addressed to Antonio Somma and one to Cesare Vigna. The two letters to Somma supplement Pascolato's published collection (see item 86).

Simon Boccanegra

* Busch, Hans, ed. and trans. *Verdi's "Otello" and "Simon Boccanegra" (revised version) in Letters and Documents.* See item 99.

Les vêpres siciliennes

101. Porter, Andrew. *"Les vêpres siciliennes:* New Letters from Verdi to Scribe." *19th Century Music* 2 (1978–79): 95–109.

    Publishes fourteen letters written by Verdi to Scribe, now located in the Bibliothèque Nationale, in both the original French and in English translation. Additional commentary provides historical background for each of the letters and includes translations of several additional letters relating to *Vêpres.* An appendix reproduces the composer's draft for the Act IV Finale. The correspondence from Verdi to Scribe clearly shows that Verdi played a strong role in shaping the libretto.

MISCELLANEOUS

102. Folena, Daniela Goldin. "Lessico melodrammatico verdiano." In *Le parole della musica, II: Studi sul lessico della letteratura critica del teatro musicale in onore di Gianfranco Folena,* 227–53. Ed. by Maria Teresa Muraro. Studi di musica veneta, 22. Florence: Olschki, 1995. ISBN 88–222–4340–4. ML 63 .P26 1994.

    This important study considers the meaning of terms frequently used by Verdi in reference to his compositional process, such as *soggetto, argomento, dramma, programma, schizzo, selva, poesia, versi,* and *situazione.* The concluding portion of the article includes a detailed discussion of the term *parola scenica,* where the author adopts a more traditional approach than does Fabrizio Della Seta in his recent study of the term (see item 403). This article provides crucial background information for anyone seriously interested in Verdi's compositional process.

103. Macinante, Umberto. *L'epistolario di Verdi: Un'analisi linguistica.* Ph.D. dissertation, Università degli Studi, Salerno. Florence: Passigli, 1995. 102, vii p. ML 410 .V4 A4 1995.

    This highly original study surveys significant aspects and trends in Verdi's language from selected correspondence: a group of 100 letters written between 1844 and 1853, published in *I copialettere* (item 28), and 113 letters from the

1880s, drawn from the *Carteggio Verdi-Ricordi 1880–81* (item 80) and *I copialettere*. Individual topics include spelling, punctuation, morphology, syntax, grammatical construction, borrowings from French, and archaicisms. The volume contains a bibliography and an index of names.

104. ———. "Francesismi d'ambito teatrale e metafore di tradizione figurativa nel carteggio Verdi-Boito." In *Le parole della musica, I: Studi sulla lingua della letteratura musicale in onore di Gianfranco Folena*, 287–309. Ed. by Fiamma Nicolodi and Paolo Trovato. Studi di musica veneta, 21. Florence: Olschki, 1994. ISBN 88–222–4284–X. ML 63 .P26 1994.

A linguistic study of figurative metaphors and French expressions in the Verdi-Boito correspondence. Of particular interest is the frequency of figurative language and metaphors involving painting and the visual arts, which the author asserts is an important dimension of Verdi's aesthetics. The article includes a series of short glossaries, listing significant words and expressions, their meanings, and examples of their use in Verdi's correspondence.

105. Serianni, Luca. "Spigolature linguistiche dal *Carteggio Verdi-Ricordi*." *Studi verdiani* 10 (1994–95): 104–17.

A linguistic survey of unusual features and idiosyncrasies characterizing the writing styles of Verdi, Giuseppina, Giulio Ricordi, Tito Ricordi, and Eugenio Tornaghi. The analysis is based on the first two published volumes of the Verdi-Ricordi correspondence in a critical edition (items 80 and 81).

CHAPTER 3

Iconographies

This chapter lists books and articles in which the author's main intention is to present pictorial documentation about the composer or his work.

106. Bavagnoli, Carlo. *Verdi e la sua terra.* Parma: Cassa di Risparmio di Parma, 1976. ML 410 .V48 B353.

    This beautiful photographic essay displays scenes from Busseto, Sant'Agata, and environs, with brief citations from some of Verdi's correspondence. Attilio Bertolucci and Gian Paolo Minardi contribute brief concluding essays.

107. Bocca, Giuseppe. "Verdi e la caricatura." *Rivista musicale italiana* 8 (1901): 326–59.

    This fascinating article, replete with illustrations, examines caricatures and drawings by the composer himself as well as scenes and costume designs from his operas.

108. Ceresa, Angelo, and Gustavo Marchesi. *Sono i posti di Verdi.* Parma: Grafiche Step Editrice, 1983. 220 p.

    A beautiful volume featuring photographs of Sant'Agata, Busseto, and surrounding areas in which Verdi spent much of his life. Includes an index of illustrations and a chronology of Verdi's life. Tucked away in the chronology is a previously unpublished letter from Verdi to the French author Adolphe Dennery dated 30 May 1879, reproduced in facsimile and in transcription.

109. Cohen, H. Robert, with the collaboration of Sylvia L'Écuyer Lacroix and Jacques Léveillé. *Les gravures musicales dans "L'Illustration" 1843–1899.* La vie musicale en France au dix-neuvième siècle: Études et documents. Quebec: Les Presses de l'Université Laval, 1982. 3 vols. xcv, 1162; li, 173p. ISBN 2-7637-6833-4. ML 270.4 .G7 1983.

This general reference work includes nearly 100 reproductions of illustrations from the Parisian periodical *L'Illustration* that concern Verdi. Most show aspects of staging, costumes, or scenery from works that were performed in Paris. Individual items can easily be accessed through the index in vol. 3.

110. Ferrari, Luigi. *La collezione Gallini: Gusto, usanze, odi del teatro musicale italiano nel secondo ottocento.* With essays by Giampiero Tintori and Mietta Corli. Milan: Electa, 1982. 207 p. ML 1733.4 .F36 1982.

The major part of this volume reproduces costume designs from the collection of Natale Gallini. The primary artist represented for the works of Verdi is Luigi Bartezago, who designed costumes for productions at La Scala during the 1870s. The final chapter contains a small group of scene designs by an unknown artist for several of Verdi's operas. The opening essays provide useful background material relating to nineteenth-century scenography. Unfortunately, the volume lacks an index.

111. Gallini, Natale, and Guglielmo Barblan, eds. *Mostra degli autografi musicali di Giuseppe Verdi.* Milan: Comitato Nazionale per le Onoranze a Giuseppe Verdi nel Cinquantenario della Morte, [1951]. 42 p. + 32 plates. ML 410 .V48 C733.

Offers facsimile reproductions of a representative page from the autograph scores of most of Verdi's operas, in addition to selections from his songs and the *Quattro pezzi sacri.* The preliminary material presents a useful catalogue of the autograph scores, including a description of their size, format, and binding.

112. Gatti, Carlo. *Verdi nelle immagini.* Milan: Garzanti, 1941. xvi, 236 p. ML 410 .V4 G25.
   German translation. *Verdi im Bilde.* [Milan]: Garzanti, [1941]. xxi, 236 p. ML 410 .V4 G254.

An important collection of iconographic material, including reproductions of selected pages from the continuity drafts of *Il trovatore, La traviata, Un ballo in maschera, Aida, Otello,* and *Falstaff* that have never been published elsewhere and have generally been unavailable to scholars for study. The volume also contains photographs of places that Verdi lived or visited; performers, impresarios, librettists, and other acquaintances; title pages of scores and librettos; posters advertising Verdi's operas; contemporary engravings and other illustrations showing staging and costumes; caricatures and cartoons; and a wide variety of photographs and paintings of Verdi himself. An index allows easy access to illustrations on any given topic.

   * Kühner, Hans. *Giuseppe Verdi in Selbstzeugnissen und Bilddokumenten.* See item 150.

113. Luzio, Alessandro. "Le caricature verdiane di Melchiorre Delfico." In *Carteggi verdiani* (item 29), 1:313–21 + 48 p. unnumbered plates.

 Reproduces, with a short introduction, 84 caricatures by Melchiorre Delfico relating to Verdi's trips to Naples in 1858, 1859, and 1888. Includes the text of a letter from 1888 from Delfico to Verdi.

114. Monaldi, Gino. *Saggio di iconografia verdiana.* Ed. by Uberto Visconti di Modrone. Bergamo: Istituto Italiano d'Arti Grafiche, [1913]. 111 p. ML 410 .V48 M7353.

 The earliest major iconographic study of the composer and his milieu. Individual sections are devoted to portraits of the composer, caricatures, the composer's first friends and associates, and librettists. The major portion of the book considers scenography, costume designs, and performers associated with specific operas. This volume is useful for finding biographical information about early interpreters of Verdi's operas. It contains an index of illustrative material; many pages, however, lack printed page numbers, making it difficult to locate some items.

115. Nataletti, Giorgio, and Antonio Pagani. "Le medaglie di Giuseppe Verdi." In *Verdi: Studi e memorie nel XL anniversario della morte* (item 245), 401–82.

 A catalogue of 134 commemorative medals issued between 1850 and 1941 with, however, notable lacunae (some of the missing items are catalogued in item 118 below). Most entries include photographs of the medal, with a prose description of each side; historical background for the item; and a list of references in other catalogues.

* Petrobelli, Pierluigi, et al. *Con Verdi in Casa Barezzi.* See item 213.

* Petrobelli, Pierluigi, Marisa Di Gregorio Casati, and Olga Jesurum, eds. *"Sorgete! Ombre serene!" L'aspetto visivo dello spettacolo verdiano.* See item 545.

* Pieri, Marzio. *Verdi: L'immaginario dell'ottocento.* See item 180.

116. Schulz, Helmut. *Giuseppe Verdi, 1813–1901: Sein Leben in Bildern.* Meyers Bild-Bändchen, 37. Leipzig: Bibliographisches Institut, 1938. 40 p. + 40 p. plates. ML 410 .V4 S38.

 Several republications after 1951 by both the Bibliographisches Institut and the VEB Verlag Enzyklopädie list the authors as Richard Petzoldt and Eduard Crass.

The illustrative portion of this iconographic study is cross-referenced to a succinct biographical essay that provides context for the pictures.

117. Strinati, Claudio. "Francesco Hayez e la pittura di storia." *Musica e dossier 2* (December 1986), special insert, 4.

Provides a short biography of Francesco Hayez (1791–1882), an Italian Romantic painter who specialized in historical depictions, many of which concern the same topics as Verdi's operas. This issue includes beautiful color reproductions of a dozen paintings by Hayez accompanying a series of articles about Verdi. Subjects of the paintings include: *I vespri siciliani, I due Foscari,* and *La battaglia di Legnano.*

118. Tintori, Giampiero. "Le medaglie verdiane nelle collezioni del Museo Teatrale alla Scala." *Atti 3* (item 226), 587–606.

A descriptive catalogue, with illustrations, of 66 medals in the collection of the Museo Teatrale alla Scala. Some medals were designed as gifts to the composer during his lifetime; others are commemorative issues. Historical information about many of the items can be found in item 115 above; this catalogue lists seventeen items not reported by Nataletti and Pagani.

119. Tintori, Giampiero, and Pierre Petit. *Giuseppe Verdi.* Vies et visages; Documents. Paris: Editions du Sud, 1966. 112 p. ML 410 .V4 P268.
    English translation by Adel Negro. *Giuseppe Verdi.* Geneva: Minerva, 1969. 110 p. ML 410 .V48 P41.
    German translation by Jutta and Theodor Knust. *Giuseppe Verdi.* Porträt des Genius, 4. Paris: Hermes; Hamburg: M. von Schroder, 1966. 111 p. ML 410 .V48 T59.

Reproduces in black-and-white more than 100 photographs, engravings, paintings, and other illustrations with commentary by Giampiero Tintori. Neither Petit's introductory biographical sketch nor the undocumented anecdotal remarks at the end of the volume should be considered trustworthy.

120. Walker, Frank. "Vincenzo Gemito and His Bust of Verdi." *Music and Letters* 30 (1949): 44–55.

Discusses the history of Gemito's well-known bust of Verdi and the personal relationship between the two artists.

121. Weaver, William, comp., ed., and trans. *Verdi: A Documentary Study.* London: Thames and Hudson, 1977. 256 p. ISBN 0–500–01184–2. ML 410 .V4 V29.

French translation by Lulu and Michael Sadler. *Verdi: D'après les documents d'époque*. Tours: Ed. Van de Velde, 1978. 262 p.

Italian translation. *Verdi: Immagini e documenti*. Florence: Becocci, 1980. 270 p.

German translation by Egon Wiszniewsky. *Verdi: Eine Dokumentation*. Berlin: Henschelverlag, 1980. 255 p.

The first portion of the volume presents a fine pictorial biography of the composer through 287 plates, some in full color. The second part consists of a documentary biography based on excerpts from letters and other documents (a few previously unpublished, but mostly from secondary sources) arranged in chronological order. The entire volume is prefaced by a reprint of Verdi's autobiographical narrative to Giulio Ricordi, first published in the Italian version of Arthur Pougin's biography (see item 131).

CHAPTER 4

Biographies; General Studies of Life & Works

This chapter lists the most significant biographical studies of the composer, including works that integrate a discussion of life and works in a fairly even proportion (see chapter 11 for studies that concentrate on Verdi's works, with relatively incidental emphasis on biographical matters). The biographies are arranged in four main sections. The first includes studies published through ca. 1900, while the composer was still alive; these are particularly valuable for shedding light on how Verdi's contemporaries thought about him. The second group contains materials published from 1901–1930. These biographies already have a new tone: Verdi's life and career are over, as is the period of nineteenth-century Romanticism. These works begin to posture a historical position for Verdi in a more decisive manner. The third group includes works published between 1931–1965. Initiating this set from a chronological perspective is Carlo Gatti's important biography (item 147), generally considered to be the first "modern" biography of the composer due to the author's use of primary source material that had been unavailable to earlier scholars. Toward the end of this period, Frank Walker's *The Man Verdi*, while not organized as a traditional biography, is among the earliest studies calling for a revisionary approach to Verdi's biography, rooting out errors, inaccuracies, and false traditions. The final group contains biographical material published since 1966, the date of the first International Verdi Congress. This period as a whole is marked by increasingly detailed and revisionary approaches that draw on both archival documents and on new and more detailed studies of every aspect of Verdi's music and career.

EARLY BIOGRAPHICAL WORKS FIRST PUBLISHED THROUGH CA. 1900

122. Barrili, Anton Giulio. *Giuseppe Verdi: Vita e opere*. 3rd ed. Genoa: A. Donath, 1892. 156 p. ML 410 .V4 B3 1892.

A concise and sympathetic early history of the composer, with biographical narrative interwoven with a discussion of the music and its reception. The volume contains a descriptive table of contents that summarizes the contents of each chapter but no index.

123. Bermani, B. *Schizzi sulla vita e sulle opere del maestro Giuseppe Verdi (estratto dalla "Gazzetta musicale di Milano")*. Milan: Ricordi, 1846. 39 p.

This short essay, originally written for Ricordi's house journal,the *Gazzetta musicale di Milano*, offers one of the very earliest published biographies of the composer, although details are often sketchy and sometimes even erroneous (for example, Bermani gives Verdi's birth year as 1814). Perhaps the most significant aspect of the essay is the assessment it provides of Verdi (who had just completed *Giovanna d'Arco* and *Alzira*) as a major composer who rises about the general level of his contemporaries through "exquisite taste, an untiring elegance, and [a] marvelous instinct . . . for effect."

124. Cavalli, Hercules. *José Verdi*. Biografias artísticas contemporaneas. Madrid: J.M. Ducazal, 1876. Pagination unknown.
    Italian translation by Riccarda Baratta, Riccardo Baratta, and Enrica Baratta in Mary Jane Phillips-Matz, *Verdi: Il grande gentleman del piacentino* (item 179), 80–121.

One of the earliest published biographies of Verdi, written by a native of Busseto who was some eleven years younger than the composer. The account is particularly interesting for its information about Verdi's early life and the contemporary reception of his works. The account does contain many factual errors and should be carefully used in tandem with recent biographical research. Unfortunately, only a single copy of the original publication is known to exist and Phillips-Matz's book containing the Italian translation is also relatively rare. For additional information about Cavalli, see items 179 and 215.

125. Checchi, Eugenio. *Verdi*. New ed. Pantheon: Vite d'illustri italiani e stranieri. Florence: G. Barbèra, 1926. 244 p. + 6 plates. ML 410 .V48 C514 1926.

This early biography, originally published in 1887, was one of the most influential early studies of the composer, although it contains numerous factual errors. The account follows a traditional organization of interweaving biographical narrative with assessments of each of the compositions. The volume includes a list of works and a brief selective bibliography. Four of the plates present a facsimile reproduction of the beginning of the fugue from the autograph score of *Falstaff*.

126. Crowest, Frederick J. *Verdi: Man and Musician. His Biography with Especial Reference to His English Experiences*. London: John Milne, 1897. Reprint.

New York: AMS Press, 1978. xiv, 306 p. ISBN 0–404–12890–4. ML 410 .V4 C9 1978.

The first book-length popular biography of the composer written in English. Much of the material, particularly relating to Verdi's early life, comes from Pougin (item 131) and in general has been superseded by later studies. One of the strongest aspects of the book, as the title points out, is its consideration of the early reception of Verdi's operas in England. Also useful for studies in reception history is the final chapter, which reviews nineteenth-century writings about Verdi, with an emphasis on English publications.

127. Demaldè, Giuseppe. "Cenni biografici del maestro di musica Giuseppe Verdi." Trans. by Mary Jane Matz and Gino Macchidani. *AIVS Newsletter* 1 (May 1976): 6–10; 2 (December 1976): 8, 10–12; 3 (June 1977): 5–9.

The first biographical sketch of Verdi, presented here in the original Italian and in English translation. Demaldè wrote the first draft of the biography in 1853 at the request of Emanuele Muzio; however, much of the material seems to date from the early 1840s. This biography is especially important because it contains little-known information about Verdi's early life and compositions (through the premiere of *Nabucco* in 1842) and because the author was a close friend of the Verdi family. Gino Macchidani prepared the transcription of the Italian text from Demaldè's holograph manuscript in the Public Library of the City of Busseto.

128. Lessona, Michele. "Parma: Giuseppe Verdi." In *Volere è potere*, 287–307. Florence: G. Barbèra, 1869. Reprint, with a chronology of Lessona's life and an introduction by Mario Miccinesi. Collezione biblioteca, 82. Pordenone: Studio Tesi, 1990. ISBN 88–7692–152–4. DG 450 .L47 1990.

One of the earliest published biographies of Verdi, running through the completion of *Don Carlos*. Much of the material comes from an interview that Lessona had with the composer at Tabiano, a spa near Busseto. Despite the moralizing tone of the narrative and Verdi's propensity to color the facts in a certain way, this account is extremely valuable for filling in details about contemporary perception of Verdi as a historical figure and for some details about his early career.

129. Monaldi, Gino. *Verdi, 1839–1898*. 4th ed. Milan: Fratelli Bocca, 1951. 334 p. ML 410 .V4 M7 1951.

This popular biography, originally issued in 1898, considers only the years in which Verdi was actively composing. Although the volume has been widely distributed through its many reprintings and several editions, the reader should exercise great caution, for it contains many factual errors and strongly biased statements.

130. Perosio, Giuseppe. *Cenni biografici su Giuseppe Verdi seguiti da brevi analisi dell'opera "Aida" e della "Messa da Requiem."* Milan: Ricordi, [1874]. 27 p.

A brief overview of Verdi's life leads to a discussion of the composer's musical style in general and to a brief examination of the history and reception of *Aida* and the *Requiem*. The volume includes an oversize table listing his works through the *Requiem*, with information about the premiere performances of each of the operas. See item 74 for additional information about Perosio and an assessment of the historical significance of his biography.

131. Pougin, Arthur. *Giuseppe Verdi: Vita aneddotica con note ed aggiunte di Folchetto [Giacomo Caponi].* Illustrations by Achille Formis. Milan: Ricordi, 1881. vii, 182 p. + 11 plates. Reprint, with Preface by Marcello Conati. Il tempo e le cose, 6. Florence: Passigli, 1989. xii + vii, 182 p. + 11 plates. ISBN 36801307. ML 410 .V4 P616 1989.

Issued in France in book form (see note below) as *Verdi: Histoire anecdotique de sa vie et de ses oeuvres.* Paris: Calmann Lévy, 1886. 331 p. ML 410 .V47 P75.

English translation by James E. Matthew. *Verdi: An Anecdotic History of His Life and Works.* London: H. Grevel & Co.; New York: Scribner & Welford, 1887. xi, 308 p. ML 410 .V4 P8.

German translation by Adolph Schulze. *Verdi: Sein Leben und seine Werke.* Leipzig: Carl Reissner, 1887. vi, 283 p. ML 410 .V48 P87221.

Considered by many to be the first important biography of the composer, although it is replete with highly colored versions of biographical episodes. The original French version was serialized in the Parisian journal *Le Ménestrel* during 1878 and shortly thereafter in Germany (*Neue Berliner Musikzeitung*) and Spain (*Cronica de la música*). The first publication in book form was in Italian translation with some additions by Caponi, primarily in the footnotes. The following year, Pougin published his material as a monograph in France in slightly expanded form, and the English translation appeared soon after. The Italian edition included Verdi's autobiographical sketch dictated to Giulio Ricordi in 1879 as an appendix to chapter 6; the English translation incorporates this into chapter 5. Marcello Conati's elegant new edition of the Italian version includes three pages of facsimile letters and six pages of manuscript facsimiles.

132. Roosevelt, Blanche. *Verdi, Milan and "Otello": Being a Short Life of Verdi, with Letters Written about Milan and the New Opera of "Othello," Represented for*

the *First Time on the Stage of La Scala Theatre, Feb. 5, 1887.* London: Ward and Downey, 1887. i, 249 p. ML 410 .V4 M2.

The first portion of this volume summarizes Verdi's life, drawing heavily on previously published sources, and then describes meeting Verdi. The second part of the volume reproduces a series of letters, written between 30 January and 11 February 1887, describing the cultural milieu in Milan and the premiere performance of *Otello.*

BIOGRAPHICAL MATERIAL FIRST PUBLISHED BETWEEN 1901–1930

133. Bellaigue, Camille. *Verdi: Biographie critique.* Les musiciens célèbres. Paris: Librairie Renouard, 1905. Reprint. Paris: Henri Laurens, 1912 and 1927. 124 p. ML 410 .V4 B26 1927.

   Italian translation. *Verdi: Biografia critica pubblicato per il centenario della sua nascita (1913).* Milan: Fratelli Treves, 1913. 115 p. + 16 plates. ML 410 .V5 B4.

   This volume, written by a well-known music critic and personal friend of the composer, presents less a biography than a general survey of Verdi's compositions, emphasizing the formation and maturation of his musical style. Rather than systematically examining each work, the author focuses on a few key compositions from the composer's middle and later career: *Rigoletto, Il trovatore, La traviata, Don Carlos, Aida, Otello,* and *Falstaff.* The volume includes a concise list of works but lacks an index.

134. Bonaventura, Arnaldo. *Verdi.* New ed. Les maîtres de la musique. Paris: Librairie Félix Alcan, 1930. 211 p. ML 410 .V4 B67 1930.

   Spanish translation by Francisco Courolle. *Verdi.* Los maestros de la música. Buenos Aires: Tor, 1943. 188 p. ML 410 .V48 B6981.

   Primarily a survey of Verdi's works, with a concluding section on the composer's place in the history of Italian music and his aesthetic ideas. Bonaventura only briefly touches on biographical aspects. The volume contains a concise list of works but no index.

135. Bonavia, Ferruccio. *Verdi.* 2nd ed. London: D. Dobson, 1947. Reprint. Westport, Conn.: Hyperion Press, 1979. 120 p. + 5 p. illustrations. ISBN 0–88355–726–6. ML 410.V4 B68.

   This short, readable biography, originally issued in 1930 by Oxford University Press, is based largely on earlier published material, especially the *Copialettere* (see item 28). In addition to a useful chronological narrative, the author includes chapters on Giuseppina Strepponi and an assessment of Verdi's "character" and "genius." The extensive quotations in the body of the text lack references to their sources, and there is no index.

136. Boni, Oreste. *Giuseppe Verdi: L'uomo, le opere, l'artista.* 3rd ed. Foreword by Gustavo Marchesi. Parma: Luigi Battei, 1980. 146 p.

This illustrated biography, originally issued in 1901, presents a concise but highly readable account of the composer's life. The first section ("L'uomo") surveys the main events in Verdi's life, while the second ("Le opere") briefly recounts the history of his compositions. A final section ("L'artista") attempts to make a historical assessment of his relationship to his contemporaries and to the musical past. The volume concludes with a work list, giving a few details about the premiere of each work. The recently issued new edition makes this study one of the most accessible of the early biographies.

137. Bragagnolo, G., and E. Bettazzi. *La vita di Giuseppe Verdi narrata al popolo.* Milan: Ricordi, 1905. vii, 350 p. ML 410 .V48 B813.

One of the best of the early biographies, featuring lively prose, numerous illustrations (including some facsimile reproductions of autograph scores), many quotations from the early published correspondence, and a modest system of footnotes and other references to secondary sources. The volume focuses on biographical narrative, integrating some information about the genesis and reception of individual compositions but providing little technical discussion about the music itself. The concluding chapters assess the historical significance of Verdi's music, discuss facets of the composer's literary and artistic thought, and examine aspects of his character and personality. The volume includes a work list, with the operas organized in three different ways (by chronology, location of premiere, and librettist), and a substantial list of works consulted.

138. Garibaldi, Franco Temistocle. *Giuseppe Verdi nella vita e nell'arte.* Florence: R. Bemporad & Figlio, 1904. 272 p. ML 410 .V4 G3.

A discursive and somewhat flowery early biography, with fairly reliable information. It is a helpful source for information about Verdi's early life.

139. Monaldi, Gino. *Il maestro della rivoluzione italiana.* Milan: Società Editoriale Italiana, 1913. 200 p. ML 410 .V48 M7352.

Focuses on Verdi's contributions to political revolution in Italy and to a revolution in musical style. Less of a biography than a study of some of the works and their place in history. Like other writings by this author, it should be used with caution.

140. Neisser, Arthur. *Giuseppe Verdi.* Leipzig: Breitkopf & Härtel, 1914. 103 p. ML 410 .V4 N35.

One of the earliest significant monographs about the composer in German. Much of the volume surveys Verdi's music and its reception, with some descriptive analysis of individual compositions. The book includes a list of works, but does not contain an index.

141. Perosio, Giuseppe. *Ricordi verdiani: Giuseppe Verdi nella vita intima.* Pinerolo: Casa Editrice Sociale, 1928. 105 p. ML 410 .V4 P3.

Reminiscences by the Genovese music critic about his acquaintance with Verdi. The volume includes anecdotes about some of the more popular operas and an entire chapter devoted to Angelo Mariani as an interpreter of Verdi's works. The author includes several letters and documents, including one facsimile reproduction.

142. Pizzi, Italo. *Ricordi verdiani inedite, con undici lettere di Giuseppe Verdi ora pubblicate per la prima volta e varie illustrazioni.* Turin: Roux e Viarengo, 1901. 128 p. ML 410 .V4 P5.

The author reports the composer's thoughts on a wide range of topics in a number of conversations between 1882 and 1900. The final chapter presents stories and anecdotes collected in and around Busseto, in large part from Verdi's brother-in-law Giovanni Barezzi. While the information is reported second-hand and therefore must be regarded with caution, this small volume provides valuable insight from the perspective of a personal acquaintance of the composer. The author includes a list of works; unfortunately, the lack of an index makes it difficult to locate references to specific people or events without scanning the entire book.

143. Sorge, Luigi. *Giuseppe Verdi: Uomo, artista, patriota.* Lanciano: F. Tommasini, 1904. 430 p.

One of the most thorough of the early biographies, written for a general audience. The author places more emphasis on biographical details and less on description or assessment of individual works.

144. Toye, Francis. *Giuseppe Verdi: His Life and Works.* Introduction by Herbert Weinstock. New York: Random House, 1930. xxx, 467 p. Reissued many times by various publishers. ML 410 .V4 T7.
    Italian translation. *Giuseppe Verdi: La sua vita e le sue opere.* Piccola biblioteca, 10–11. Milan: Longesi, 1951. 313 p. ML 410 .V5 T7.

The first portion of the book, written for the informed general reader, consists of the biography proper. At the time of its first publication, it was one of the more reliable accounts of Verdi's life: the author carefully pruned out some errors consistently repeated by many earlier biographies. The second portion of the book discusses individual compositions. For the operatic works, Toye begins with a plot summary, followed, in most cases, by a descriptive analysis of the music and a consideration of the work's genesis and reception. A concluding chapter, entitled "Verdi the Musician," assesses the composer's position in music history.

BIOGRAPHICAL MATERIAL FIRST PUBLISHED BETWEEN 1931–1965

145. Abbiati, Franco. *Giuseppe Verdi.* Milan: Ricordi, 1959. 4 vols. xii, 796; 833; 813; 737 p. ML 410 .V4 A52.

This imposing set was at one time considered the standard biography of Verdi. At its time of publication, it contained a substantial amount of new information, due to Abbiati's privileged access to archival material in possession of the Verdi heirs at Sant'Agata and the collection of Natale Gallini, which contained, among other things, many letters exchanged between Verdi and Piave. Abbiati's study therefore became a particularly important source for citations from unpublished letters. Nevertheless, this biography suffers enormously from a number of serious flaws. Abbiati rarely cites documentary material, such as letters, in full, and does not systematically indicate omissions with ellipses. Furthermore, later research has shown that his transcriptions contain many inaccuracies. Some of Abbiati's factual statements and conclusions have also been shown to be erroneous. Although the material is organized chronologically, the lack of any index (except one for illustrations) impedes systematic searching for specific topics. Although Abbiati's biography has slowly been superseded by other studies, it remains a somewhat useful, if flawed, source that should always be used with caution.

*   Alcari, Cesare. *Parma nella musica.* See item 4.

146. Botti, Ferruccio. *Giuseppe Verdi.* 4th ed. Tempi e figure, seconda serie, 47. Rome: Edizioni Paoline, 1969. 422 p. ML 410 .V5 B751 1969.

The final section of this study, entitled "Verdi and His Relationships" and comprising about a third of the total pages, offers its most distinctive contribution. Here the author considers Verdi's relationship to friends and family (his parents, Giuseppina Strepponi, Antonio Barezzi, Angelo Mariani, and Teresa Stolz) and to other important intellectual figures in Italian culture (Manzoni, Ariosto, and Correggio); his ties to Busseto, Sant'Agata, Parma, and Montecatini; his philanthropic activities, and his feelings about religion, particularly in later life. The first portion of the volume treats the composer's life through the success of *Nabucco*; the central section centers around individual compositions written after *Nabucco*. This biography was first published in 1941. Unfortunately, the volume lacks an index.

147. Gatti, Carlo. *Verdi.* Milan: Edizioni "Alpes", 1931. 2 vols. xix, 469; 638 p. ML 410 .V4 G2.
   Updated, but substantially abridged single-volume edition. Milan: Mondadori, 1951. Reprint. 1981. 913 p.
   Severely abridged English translation by Elisabeth Abbott. *Verdi: The Man and His Music.* New York: G.P. Putnam's Sons, 1955. vi, 371 p. ML 410 .V4 G199 1955.
   French translation by Pierre Barbaud. *Verdi.* Les introuvables. Plan de la Tour: Editions d'Aujourd'hui, [1978]. 2 vols. 606 p. ML 410 .V4 G214 1078.

   Most Verdi scholars consider this to be the first "modern" biography of the composer, and it remained the standard treatment of Verdi's life and works until the publication of Abbiati's four-volume set (item 145 above). It is far longer and more detailed than any previous biography, but most importantly, Gatti had access to important primary source materials at Verdi's estate that were unavailable to earlier biographers. The narrative includes extensive citations from Verdi's letters and other documentary materials. The Italian publications, both first and revised editions, contain some beautiful illustrations and facsimile reproductions; these were omitted in the English translation. The original two-volume set provides a detailed index of names and a separate index of illustrative materials; the latter is missing in the revised Italian edition, and the English translation pares the name index by eliminating the subheadings.

148. Gerigk, Herbert. *Giuseppe Verdi.* Die grossen Meister der Musik. Potsdam: Akademische Verlagsgesellschaft Athenaion, 1932. Reprint. Laaber: Laaber-Verlag, 1980. 160p. ML 410 .V4 G394.

   An important early biography of the composer in German. Most of the text is devoted to a descriptive analysis of the individual works. Numerous illustrations, including photographs and facsimile reproductions, are a special feature of this volume.

149. Hussey, Dyneley. *Verdi.* 5th ed. Rev. by Charles Osborne. The Master Musicians. London: Dent, 1974. xiii, 365 p. + 8 plates. ISBN 0–4600–3151–1 (cloth); 0–4600–2144–3 (paper). ML 410 .V4 H8 1974.

   This volume, first issued in 1940, was once considered the standard biography of Verdi in English. The volume is heavily slanted toward the period of *Aida* and afterwards (nearly half the book). Hussey's approach, especially for later operas, is to trace the compositional history through the composer's correspondence, relying heavily on *I copialettere* (item 28) and *Carteggi verdiani* (item 29). Although Hussey's treatment is sympathetic, his account is biased toward elevating "regular" drama (particularly Shakespeare) over opera. Appendices include a chronology, a list of works, and a list of people associated with Verdi. The volume also contains a short bibliography and index.

150. Kühner, Hans. *Giuseppe Verdi in Selbstzeugnissen und Bilddokumenten.* Rowohlts Monographien, 64. Reinbek bei Hamburg: Rowohlt Taschenbuch Verlag, 1961. 170 p. ISBN 3–499–50064–7 ML 410 .V4 K77.

A brief, popular-style biography, organized primarily as a series of essays describing the history of each of his operas. The material is largely derivative from other secondary sources. The volume includes a work list, index, and a bibliography that is especially useful for listing some lesser-known books and articles published in German.

151. Petit, Pierre. *Verdi.* Solfèges, 10. Bourges: Editions du Seuil, [1958]. 186 p. Reprinted several times. ML 410 .V4 P27.
English translation by Patrick Bowles. *Verdi.* Illustrated Calderbook CB.55. London: John Calder, 1962. 192 p. ML 410 .V4 P273 1962.

This short, popular-style biography does not take into account much of the scholarly research about the composer. Nevertheless, it has been widely circulated in a number of different reprintings and translations. Perhaps the volume's strongest asset is its large amount of iconographic material. It contains a brief bibliography, a highly selective discography, and a concise listening guide to *La traviata.*

152. Walker, Frank. *The Man Verdi.* London: J.M. Dent; New York: Alfred A. Knopf, 1962. Reprint, with a new introduction by Philip Gossett. Chicago: University of Chicago Press, 1982. xvii, 526 p. ISBN 0–226–87132–0 (paper). ML 410 .V4 W3.
Italian translation by Franca Mediola Cavara. *L'uomo Verdi.* Introduction by Mario Medici. Milan: Mursia, 1964. 638 p. + 22 plates. ML 410 .V4 W3 1962b.

Rather than adopting the traditional format for a biography, Walker writes a series of essays that focus on significant relationships with other people spanning the composer's entire life, including, among others: Giuseppina Strepponi, Emanuele Muzio, Angelo Mariani, Arrigo Boito, Bartolomeo Merelli, and Teresa Stolz. One of Walker's main thrusts is to correct misinformation and legends about Verdi's life that had appeared in much of the earlier secondary literature. The first chapter, which deals with Verdi's early life at Busseto and his student years in Milan, is particularly important in this respect. While this book is considered by many to be one of the more reliable discussions of the composer's life, a fair amount of new information has come to light since its publication. It should therefore be used in conjunction with later studies.

153. ———. "Verdian Forgeries." *Music Review* 19 (1958): 273–82; 20 (1959): 28–38.

Italian translation. "Un problema biografico verdiano: Lettere apocrife di Giuseppina Verdi al suo confessore." *Rassegna musicale* 30 (1960): 338–49.

Demonstrates that a series of letters by Giuseppina discussing her marital relations with Verdi, his relationship to Teresa Stolz, and the composer's religious beliefs are patently false. The letters were first published by Lorenzo Alpino and from there found their way into some of the secondary literature. Walker discusses the topics raised by these letters in greater detail in his full-length biographical study (item 152).

BIOGRAPHICAL MATERIAL FIRST PUBLISHED FROM 1966 TO THE PRESENT

154. Abert, Anna Amalie. "Verdi, Giuseppe Fortunino Francesco." In *Musik in die Geschichte und Gegenwart: Allegemeine Enzyklopädie der Musik*, 13:1426–63. Ed. by Friedrich Blume. Kassel: Bärenreiter, 1966. 17 vols. ML 100 .M92.

The opening section of this encyclopedia article surveys Verdi's life and works; a concluding section considers the composer's historical and musical milieu and provides a chronological overview of his changing musical style. The article includes a list of works and a large bibliography by Hellmut Kühn of approximately 700 items, especially rich in German-language materials. Their prose-style format, however, makes both the bibliography and the work list difficult to use.

155. Baldini, Gabriele. *Abitare la battaglia: La storia di Giuseppe Verdi.* Ed. by Fedele D'Amico. Milan: Garzanti, 1970. xii, 336 p. ML 410 .V48 B136.

English translation by Roger Parker. *The Story of Giuseppe Verdi: "Oberto" to "Un ballo in maschera."* Ed. by Roger Parker. Foreword by Julian Budden. Cambridge: Cambridge University Press, 1980. xx, 296 p. ISBN 0–521–22911–1 (cloth); 0–521–29712–5 (paper). ML 410 .V48 B1363.

While the biographical portion of Baldini's volume is almost totally derived from secondary literature (primarily Gatti, Toye, Abbiati, and Walker), his discussion of the individual compositions is highly original, albeit at times controversial. A short introductory section surveys the composer's early life through the death of his first wife and two children. The main portion of the book interweaves biographical narrative with a relatively detailed discussion of individual operas through *Un ballo in maschera.* The section on *La forza del destino* is incomplete; the author died before finishing the complete study. In general, Baldini views Verdi's more "conventional" middle-period works as superior to his later ones. His emphasis on dramaturgy rather than musical style *per se* reflects his training and professional work as a literary critic. Roger Parker's English translation contains his own preface assessing the contribution of Baldini to Verdi scholarship and his own additional footnotes.

* Budden, Julian. *The Operas of Verdi.* See item 365.

156. Budden, Julian. *Verdi.* Rev. ed. The Dent Master Musicians. London: J.M. Dent, 1993. Reprint. New York: Schirmer, 1996. xi, 404 p. + 8 p. illustrations. ISBN 0–460–86111–5 (Dent); 0–02–864616–9 (Schirmer). ML 410 .V4 B9 1996.
German translation of first edition by Ingrid Rein and Dietrich Klose. Stuttgart: Reclam, 1987. 487 p.

This recent biography, originally issued in 1985, provides a more succinct and somewhat differently organized account of Verdi's life and works than the author's three-volume set (item 365). The first half of the volume considers biographical matters, while the second half examines Verdi's music. The writing is directed toward the general reader rather than the Verdi specialist: the treatment of biographical data is not nearly as detailed or massive as the recent biography by Phillips-Matz (item 178), while the discussion of the music is more general than in item 365. One of the most useful features of this volume is a series of appendices that provide a chronology of Verdi's life; a list of works; a short biographical dictionary of the composer's friends and associates; a selective bibliography (based largely on item 181); and a glossary of nineteenth-century operatic terms. The book includes a index of names, with subheadings for individual musical compositions. The 1996 reprinting contains a few minor corrections and additions to the bibliography.

157. Cafasi, Francesco. *Giuseppe Verdi: Fattore di Sant'Agata.* Parma: Edizioni Zara, 1994. 245 p. + 20 p. plates. ML 410 .V4 C28 1994.

A study of Verdi as a farmer and the agricultural activities on his estate at Sant'Agata. The volume contains background information on farming in Italy at the time of Verdi, Verdi's agricultural contracts and correspondence (some of which were previously unpublished), and a description of agricultural items in Verdi's library at Sant'Agata.

158. Casini, Claudio. *Verdi.* 2nd ed. La musica. Milan: Rusconi, 1982. 465 p. ML 410 .V4 C335.

A general discussion of Verdi's life and works for the non-specialist. The treatment of biographical matters is relatively trustworthy, although there are no footnotes or other references to specific sources. Descriptions of individual musical works are sketchy. An appendix provides a plot summary for each opera, along with a list of characters and information about premiere performances. The volume contains a short bibliography.

159. Cenzato, Giovanni. *Itinerari verdiani.* 2nd ed. Milan: Ceschina, 1955. 225 p. + 14 plates. ML 410 .V4 C4 1955.

An illustrated, anecdotal biography organized around general topics: Verdi's "culture," Verdi the patriot, Verdi and Domenico Morelli, Verdi and Teresa Stolz, the abandoned *Re Lear* project, and Verdi's eating habits. The volume provides engaging reading, although some of the information has been superseded by later publications.

160. Della Seta, Fabrizio. "Verdi, Giuseppe Fortunino Francesco." In *Dizionario enciclopedico universale della musica e dei musicisti. Le biografie*, 8:194–209. Ed. by Alberto Basso. Turin: Unione Tipografico-Editrice Torinese, 1985–88. 8 vols. ISBN 88–02–04228–4 (vol. 8). ML 105 .D65 1985.

This fine encyclopedia article is divided into five sections: a brief biographical profile, a survey of Verdi's musical and cultural milieu, examinations of his dramaturgical principles and musical style, and an assessment of reception and place in music history. An appendix contains a list of works, an overview of the new critical edition, and an essential bibliography of more than 100 significant items, organized by general category.

161. Ellis, Stephen D. "Father-Son Relationships in the Life and Operas of Giuseppe Verdi." Ph.D. dissertation, Union for Experimenting Colleges and Universities, 1987. v, 279 p.

A psychobiographical study focusing on Verdi's relationship with his father, Carlo. The author proposes that Carlo expected his son to provide self-esteem and success—material and emotional—to compensate for his own lack of these qualities. Accumulated hate and rage, brought on by the composer's passive compliance, led to feelings of rebellion and eventually the threat of disowning his father. The author examines Verdi's treatment of father-son relationships in *I lombardi, I due Foscari, Alzira, Macbeth, I masnadieri, Luisa Miller, La traviata, Les vêpres siciliennes, La forza del destino,* and *Don Carlos*, concluding that these operas show evidence that the composer, through his music, continued to vent rage over the loss of his mother to a jealous and demanding father. See item 173 for a similar study that reaches somewhat different conclusions.

162. Kimbell, David R.B. *Verdi in the Age of Italian Romanticism.* Cambridge: Cambridge University Press, 1981. ix, 703 p. ISBN 0–521–23052–7; 0–521–31678–2 (1985 paperback reprint). ML 410 .V4 K5.

This important study focuses on Verdi's early years (through the early 1850s and the trilogy of *Rigoletto, Il trovatore,* and *La traviata).* The first of its four major sections provides an extremely useful overview of Verdi's political, social, and cultural milieu, together with an examination of general dramatic and formal principles governing early ottocento opera. The second part focuses on the compositional history of the early operas, while the third furnishes a complementary appraisal of the development of Verdi's musical language. The final section presents a critical study of selected (including some of the more neglected) operas from this period: *Nabucco, Ernani, I due Foscari, Il corsaro, Macbeth, La battaglia di Legnano, I masnadieri, Luisa Miller, Rigoletto,* and *La traviata.* Throughout the book, the author emphasizes Verdi's relationship to literary, social, and political aspects of the Romantic movement, providing a different focus than is most often found in studies of the composer's life and works. It therefore constitutes an excellent foundation for any detailed study of this part of Verdi's career. The volume includes a modest bibliography (especially useful for its inclusion of broader studies dealing with Verdi's literary, cultural, and musical milieu) and an index of names, places, and compositions.

163. Marchesi, Gustavo. *Giuseppe Verdi.* La vita sociale della nuova Italia, 18. Turin: Unione Tipografico-Editrice Torinese, 1970. xvi, 534 + 30 plates. ML 410 .V48 M255.

This biography has a more scholarly tone to it than the author's other biographical studies listed below. It includes a short bibliography and an index. As is typical with Marchesi's other writings, the volume concentrates on biographical rather than musical aspects.

164. ———. *Giuseppe Verdi: L'uomo, il genio, l'artista.* Gli dei della musica. N.p.: International Music of Italy, 1981. 567 p. ML 410 .V4 M2575 1981.

A densely illustrated popular biography featuring numerous historical photographs, facsimile reproductions, and other pictorial material. The volume lacks an index proper but provides a summary of the contents of each chapter.

165. ———. *Verdi.* With Contributions by Giuliana Ricci, Rodolfo Celletti, and Eduardo Rescigno. I grandi della musica. Milan: Fabbri Editori, 1979. 144 p. ML 410 .V4 M258 1979.

A beautifully illustrated popular biography. This volume contains a discography of recordings available at the time of its publication; a work list, with information about premiere performances of works; a short, selective bibliography; and an index.

166. ———. *Verdi: Anni, Opere.* N.p.: Azzali, 1991. 417 p. + 64 p. illustrations. ML 410 .V4 M2585 1991.

This biography is written for the general reader rather than a Verdi specialist. As opposed to Budden's three-volume study of life and works (item 365), Marchesi emphasizes the biographical aspect and focuses less on the description or analysis of individual works. The volume contains separate indexes for names and compositions and a substantial selective bibliography.

167. Marchesi, Gustavo, and Mario Pasi. *Verdi: La vita, i viaggi.* Biblioteca della Pilotta. Parma: Ugo Guanda, 1993. 196 p. + 36 p. plates. ISBN 88-7746-704-5. ML 410 .V4 M2587 1993.

A handsomely illustrated popular-style biography divided into two main sections. The first section, by Marchesi, is titled "Verdi and His Travels." It presents a narration of the composer's life, with each short chapter devoted to his activities in one or two geographical locations. The text itself emphasizes the Verdi's reactions to the particular place and to his trips. The author includes quotations from many of the composer's letters without, however, any reference to their source. The concluding portion of the volume by Pasi, substantially shorter than the first, is entitled "The Century of Verdi." It contains a series of short, colorful, and at times whimsical vignettes describing means of travel in the nineteenth century and the various cities, countries, and regions to which Verdi traveled. Pasi also contributes a short introduction. Unfortunately, the volume lacks an index, but it does contain a short "essential bibliography."

168. Matz, Mary Jane. "Verdi: The Roots of the Tree." *Verdi: Bollettino dell'Istituto di Studi Verdiani* 3 [No. 7] (1969): 333–64. Italian and German versions of the article are printed on pp. 790–844.

This relatively detailed study of Verdi's ancestry and early life documents several important facts that have long been disputed in the Verdi literature. The Verdi family can be traced back to the mid-1600s in the vicinity of Sant'Agata; the composer's parents and grandparents on both sides were reasonably well-to-do tavern keepers, not poor farmers. Verdi was not, as he often claimed, raised as a poor farmer, devoid of culture. The author also concludes that the composer's birthdate was 8 October 1813, not 11 October, as reported in church records.

169. Mendelssohn, Gerald A. "Verdi the Man and Verdi the Dramatist." *19th Century Music* 2 (1978–79): 110–42, 214–30.

A concise psychobiography of the composer, followed by a consideration of how Verdi's personal experiences influenced his operatic treatment of sexual love and parent-child relationships.

170. Martin, George. *Verdi: His Music, Life, and Times.* New York: Dodd, Mead
      & Co., 1963. xxi, 633 p. ISBN 0–396–08196–7 (paper). ML 410 .V4 M266.
      Several different publishers have issued reprints, including Limelight
      Editions, which contains a new preface (New York, 1992). xviii, 522 p. ISBN
      0–87910–160–1. ML 410 .V4 M266 1992.
      Spanish translation by Anibal Leal. *Verdi.* Biografia e historia. Mexico: Javier
      Vergara, 1984. 470 p. + 8 p. plates. ISBN 968–497–038–2.

      This study, written for a general rather than a scholarly audience, places the
      composer's life and works within the context of the cultural and political milieu
      in which he lived. There is no attempt to describe or analyze his music.
      Appendices list family trees of the Hapsburg rulers, the Dukes of Parma and
      the House of Savoy; Verdi's works, with librettist and information about the
      first performance; and a concise annotated bibliography that includes both
      Verdi studies as well as studies about general politics, history, and literature.

171. Mila, Massimo. *La giovinezza di Verdi.* 2nd, rev. ed. Musica e musicisti, 1.
      Turin: ERI, 1978. 541 p. ML 410 .V48 M59.

      A masterful study of Verdi's early life and works through *La traviata* conceived,
      in part, as a revision and expansion of earlier studies entitled *Il melodramma di
      Verdi* (Bari: Laterza, 1933; 2nd ed., Milan: Feltrinelli, 1960) and *Giuseppe
      Verdi* (Bari: Laterza, 1958). The author interweaves biographical narrative with
      descriptions, analyses, and assessments of the operas. The volume includes a
      complete work list with information about first editions; dates, places, and
      performers for their premieres; and a substantial bibliography (see item 375 for
      an updated version of the bibliography). The second edition unfortunately
      omits the 44 plates interspersed in the original publication, many of which
      reproduce historic photographs or show facsimile reproductions of documents
      or manuscripts. It provides, however, separate indexes of names and
      compositions, which the first edition lacks.

172. ———. "Verdi, Giuseppe." In *Rizzoli-Ricordi enciclopedia della musica,*
      6:296–306. 6 vols. Ed. by Angelo Solmi. Milan: Rizzoli, 1974.

      This relatively brief but richly illustrated article contains two main sections: a
      biography and a discussion of the works. An appendix includes a work list and
      a bibliography of nearly 100 items.

173. Nello Vetro, Gaspare. "Un padre e figlio: Carlo e Giuseppe Verdi." *Archivio
      storico per le province parmensi,* 4th series 39–40 (1987): 453–63.

      After carefully reviewing the literature discussing the rapport of Verdi with his
      father, the author takes issue with extreme conclusions reached by many
      writers: one group proposing that they lived in a constantly hateful relationship,

the father envious of his talented son and the son resentful toward his father; others arguing that there was no conflict between father and son. Nello Vetro also suggests that secondary literature has stereotypically portrayed Verdi's mother, underscoring qualities such as tenderness and courage and depicting her as an exemplary mother and wife. Considerable evidence now available shows that Carlo Verdi was a loving but pragmatic father who did all that he could for his young son, yet tensions did arise, particularly in Carlo's later years as his son became wealthy. The author uses as a basis for some of his comments the civil statues of the Duchy of Parma. See item 161 for a related article.

174. Osborne, Charles. *Verdi.* London: Macmillan, 1978. 152 p. ISBN 0–333–21483–8. ML 410 .V4 O65 1978.
Spanish translation. *Verdi.* Biblioteca Salvat de grandes biografías, 27. Barcelona: Salvat, 1985. 197 p. ISBN 84–345–8172–8.

A concise, well-illustrated biography written for the generalist reader rather than the Verdi specialist. The volume emphasizes the history surrounding the genesis and reception of Verdi's individual works but makes no attempt at descriptive analysis of the music. This biography includes a one-page overview of Verdi's life, a list of works, a brief bibliography, and an index.

175. ———. *Verdi: A Life in the Theater.* London: Weidenfeld and Nicolson; New York: Alfred A. Knopf, 1987. xii, 360 p. + 16 p. illustrations. ISBN 0–297–79117–6 (British); 0–394–54110–3 (American). ML 410 .V4 O66. Reprinted several times by various publishers.

A more expansive treatment than the author's earlier biography (item 174), integrating it with material from Osborne's study of the operas (item 376) and his edition of the letters (item 37). The incorporation of many citations from the letters gives the volume a tone that is more detailed and academic than item 174; however, the problems inherent in Osborne's edition of the letters remain. The volume includes a useful index.

176. Parker, Roger. "Verdi and the *Gazzetta privilegiata di Milano.*" In *Studies in Early Verdi* (item 377), 9–38.
Previously published as "Verdi and the *Gazzetta privilegiata di Milano: An 'Official' View Seen in Its Cultural Context.*" *Research Chronicle of the Royal Musical Association* 18 (1982): 51–65.

Reports published in the *Appendice* to the *Gazzetta privilegiata di Milano* reveal important information about little-known aspects of Verdi's early career. The author discusses Verdi's participation as *maestro al cembalo* in performances of Haydn's *Creation* and Rossini's *Cenerentola*, the commissioning of a cantata to a text by Renato Borromeo celebrating the wedding of Austrian Emperor

Ferdinand I, the celebration of a Mass in Busseto with music by Verdi, and a review of the young composer's Nocturne "Guarda che bianca luna."

177. ———. "Verdi, Giuseppe (Fortunino Francesco)." In *New Grove Dictionary of Opera*, 4:932–53. Ed. by Stanley Sadie. London: Macmillan, 1992. 4 vols. ISBN 0–333–48522–1. ML 102 .O6 N5 1992.

The most accurate and up-to-date encyclopedia biography of the composer available in English. The author first considers Verdi's early years (1813–39), then divides his discussion to the composer's life and works into three periods: 1839–53 (a gradual maturation within the traditions of Italian opera covering 19 operas from *Oberto* to *La traviata*), 1853–1871 (in which compositions from *Les vêpres siciliennes* to *Aida* were strongly influenced by the French tradition), and 1871–1901 (revisions of *Simon Boccanegra* and *Don Carlos* and the final operas, *Otello* and *Falstaff*). The sections dealing with musical compositions provide excellent summaries of dramatic and musical forms; harmony, *tinta*, and local color; and reception and political commentary. The concluding portion of the article analyzes posthumous reputation, the history of Verdi scholarship, and principal editions. A table provides information about each work (including "genre," number of acts, details about the libretto and first performance, and location of the autograph score). Separate articles by the same author on each individual opera elsewhere in the encyclopedia substantially augment this main article. The large bibliography contains over 400 citations of materials pertaining to Verdi's life, operatic works, and research published through approximately 1992. This article is an especially useful starting point for someone just beginning research on the composer.

 *   Petrobelli, Pierluigi, et al. *Con Verdi in Casa Barezzi*. See item 213.

178. Phillips-Matz, Mary Jane. *Verdi: A Biography*. Foreword by Andrew Porter. Oxford: Oxford University Press, 1993. xxx, 941 p. ISBN 0–19–313204–4. ML 410 .V4 P43.
      French translation with a new Preface by Gérard Gefen. Bibliothèque des grands musiciens. Paris: Fayard, 1996. 1034 p.

This massive biography incorporates many new details about Verdi's life from archives or little-known sources. The narrative is especially strong in the area of Verdi's family background, his early years, and details of his business affairs; new information also emerges about his relationships with Giuseppina Strepponi and Teresa Stolz. Verdi's compositions and musical development receive relatively scant attention; compared to other biographies, it is weak in assessing Verdi's rich and complex relationship to his musical and cultural milieu and in establishing a sense of his historical position. The volume includes a sizable bibliography and an appendix that traces the history of the Verdi family property.

179. ———. *Verdi: Il grande gentleman del piacentino*. Piacenza: Banca di Piacenza, 1992. 302 p.

This richly illustrated volume focuses on Verdi's family and ancestors, his early life before moving permanently to Milan, and his domestic life at Sant'Agata. An important feature of this volume is an Italian translation of an extremely rare early biography of the composer by Ercole Cavalli (described more fully in item 215). Other sections of the book deal with a variety of topics, such as Verdi's early *Messa solenne*, his political activities, his travels on the railroad, and his relationship to people and institutions in the province of Piacenza. The volume contains some previously unpublished documents.

180. Pieri, Marzio. *Verdi: L'immaginario dell'ottocento*. Preface by Gianandrea Gavazzeni. Pictorial commentary by Luigi Ferrari. Milan: Electa Editrice, 1981. ML 410 .V4 P54x.

This sumptuously illustrated biography places special emphasis on Verdi's relationship to his cultural milieu and to visual imagery; a final section surveys the performance tradition of Verdi's works at La Scala from the beginning of the Toscanini era (1920s) to the present. The lavish illustrative material includes pictures of the composer and his contemporaries, nineteenth-century playbills, scene designs, costume sketches, art work related to the subjects of Verdi's operas, and facsimile reproductions of pages from his scores and staging manuals. The volume includes an index of names and works by Verdi and a chart showing a chronology of Verdi's operas in the context of works by some of his best-known contemporaries.

181. Porter, Andrew. "Verdi, Giuseppe (Fortunino Francesco)." In *New Grove Dictionary of Music and Musicians*, 19:635–65. Ed. by Stanley Sadie. London: Macmillan, 1980. 20 vols. ISBN 0–333–23111–2. ML 100 .N48. Slightly updated article and bibliography in *The New Grove Masters of Italian Opera: Rossini, Donizetti, Bellini, Verdi, Puccini*, 191–308. The Composer Biography Series. London: Macmillan, 1983. ISBN 0–333–35823–6. ML 390 .N466 1983.

Offers a fine survey of Verdi's life and works. After an opening section devoted to the composer's life through 1843, the author takes up a number of general topics including: the patriotic element in his early operas; categorization of his works into style periods (Porter discusses Abramo Basevi's division into four groups, then proposes a modification of that scheme to account for the operas written after Basevi's *Studio* was published); elements of Verdi's compositional process (selection of the subject material, development of the libretto, and composing procedure); and aspects of his musical style. Later sections of the article examine Verdi's life from 1843–80, the "grand" operas (from *Vêpres* to *Aida*), the composer's last years and final works, and his posthumous reputation. A table provides information about each work similar to that in the *New Grove Dictionary of Opera* (item 177), although it lacks consistent information about the location of the autograph manuscripts. The bibliography includes nearly 300 citations of materials published through approximately 1979.

182. Pugliese, Giuseppe. "Verdi: Da *Nabucco* ai *Vespri siciliani*." *Musica e dossier* No. 35 (December 1989): 23–62.

A richly illustrated account of the first portion of Verdi's career written in a popular style. Includes a list of works, with information about the librettist and the premiere performance, a selected discography, a short chronology, and a listening guide to the String Quartet.

183. Rinaldi, Mario. *Gli "anni di galera" di Giuseppe Verdi*. Rome: Giovanni Volpe, 1969. 268 p. ML 410 .V4 R54.

Examines Verdi's development during the years 1844 through 1849, which the composer called his "years in prison." Topics include: Verdi's musical and cultural milieu and influences of other composers, the composer's working conditions, and the significance of works composed during this era for Verdi's future stylistic development. The author includes a short bibliography. The volume is not the strongest treatment of these years and should be used with caution, comparing data and conclusions to later and more trustworthy accounts. For a discussion of some of its problematic features, see Massimo Mila's review in *Nuova rivista musicale italiana* 3 (1969): 1000–02.

 * Sartori, Claudio. "La Strepponi e Verdi a Parigi nella morsa quarantottesca." See item 39.

184. Sartori, Claudio. "Giuseppe Verdi." In *La musica. Parte prima: Enciclopedia storico*, 4:728–53. Ed. by Guido M. Gatti. Turin: Unione Tipografico-Editrice Torinese, 1966. 4 vols. ML 100 .M895.

Although this is older than other encyclopedia articles cited in this bibliography, it offers a splendid overview of the composer's life. The article integrates a discussion of life and works in two parts (divided at about 1850), but the primary emphasis is biographical. A concluding section considers Verdi's historical position. The article includes illustrations, many of them facsimiles of manuscripts. An appendix contains a work list and a short bibliography of about 50 items.

185. Southwell-Sander, Peter. *Verdi: His Life and Times.* Tunbridge Wells: Midas, 1978. 160 p. ISBN 0–85936–096–2. ML 410 .V4568. This volume has been reprinted several times by various publishers.

     A short biography written for a general audience. While the text itself would be useful to only a novice in Verdi studies, the volume contains a wealth of interesting illustrative material.

186. Stinchelli, Enrico. *Verdi: La vita e l'opera.* I grandi musicisti. Rome: Newton Compton, 1986. 232 p.

     A short, popular treatment of the composer's life and works. Includes a list of works, showing librettists and literary sources, information about the first performance, and pages in this volume relating to the work; a selective bibliography, discography, and filmography; a chronological table of events in Verdi's life; and an index of names.

* Tintori, Giampiero. *Invito all'ascolto di Giuseppe Verdi.* See item 384.

187. Wechsberg, Joseph. *Verdi.* London: George Weidenfeld and Nicolson; New York: G.P. Putnam's Sons, 1974. 255 p. ISBN 0–297–76818–2 (British); 0–399–11409–2 (American). ML 410 .V4 W37.
     German translation. *Verdi.* Munich: List, 1975. 353 p. ISBN 3–4717–9121–3. ML 410 .V4 W3715.

     A brief, but beautifully illustrated popular biography. Much of the material derives from the work of Carlo Gatti, Wechsberg's mentor, updated with material from the writings of Frank Walker, George Martin, and others. The volume contains a useful detailed index of names, places, and compositions.

CHAPTER 5

Studies of People Associated With Verdi

This chapter provides an "appendix" to the biographical studies listed in the previous chapter by listing studies about close associates of the composer. Readers should consult the index for a complete listing of references to these individuals.

GIUSEPPINA STREPPONI

188. Cazzulani, Elena. *Giuseppina Strepponi: Biografia.* Lodi: Edizioni Lodigraf, 1990. 165 p. ISBN 88–7121–097–2. ML 420 .S917 C39 1990.

    A concise and sympathetic portrayal of Strepponi's life, written for a general audience, rather than Verdi specialists. The volume contains a number of photographs and facsimile reproductions; appendices discuss Giuseppina's children and provide a chronological listing of operas in which she performed. The author includes a bibliography, but the volume lacks an index.

189. Conati, Marcello. "La Strepponi insegnante di canto a Parigi e un giudizio sconosciuto di Berlioz." *Rassegna musicale Curci* 32/2 (1979): 25–28. English translation. "Giuseppina Strepponi in Paris, with a Review by Berlioz." *AIVS Newsletter* 6 (March 1979): 7, 9–13.

    Published accounts of Giuseppina's performances in Paris are more numerous than have been previously noted. They show that she clearly intended to be a champion of the "new Italian school" represented by the late works of Donizetti and Mercadante and, in particular, the young Verdi. Giuseppina received favorable reviews from many writers, including Hector Berlioz. The author also reproduces Giuseppina's advertisement for singing lessons published in *La France musicale* in 1846.

190. De Amicis, Edmondo. "Giuseppina Strepponi-Verdi." In *Nuovi ritratti letterari ed artistici*, 223–38. Milan: Fratelli Treves, 1902.

Reprinted in *Verdi: Bollettino dell'Istituto di Studi Verdiani* 1 [No. 2] (1960): 779–84; English and German translations may be found on pp. 1057–68.

A short tribute to Giuseppina, emphasizing positive qualities of her character.

* De Angelis, Marcello. *Le carte dell'impresario: Melodrama e costume teatrale nell'ottocento.* See item 263.

191. Matz, Mary Jane. "Traces." *AIVS Newsletter* 6 (March 1979): 5–7.

Discusses the four children of Giuseppina Strepponi. The author concludes that it is impossible to settle conclusively the issue of their paternity, although recently discovered evidence suggests the father was the tenor Francesco Luigi Morini. Verdi's and Strepponi's decision to delay marriage until 1859 may be linked to her son Camillo attaining legal adulthood that year, since after this point he would not be able to lay legal claim to any of Verdi's estate.

192. Mundula, Mercede. *La moglie di Verdi: Giuseppina Strepponi.* Milan: Fratelli Treves, 1938. 317 p. + 12 plates. Reprint. Milan: Garzanti, 1941. ML 410 .V4 M75.

An important early book-length biography of Strepponi. Much information, particularly about her children and her relationship to other women in Verdi's life, must be considered in the light of more recent research by Walker (item 152), Phillips-Matz (item 178), and others.

* Sartori, Claudio. "La Strepponi e Verdi a Parigi nella morsa quarantottesca." See item 39.

193. Servadio, Gaia. *The Real Traviata: The Biography of Giuseppina Strepponi, Wife of Giuseppe Verdi.* A John Curtis Book. London: Hodder & Stoughton, 1994. x, 290 p. + 16 p. illustrations. ISBN 0–340–57948–X. ML 410 .S93 S47x 1994.

Another biography of Giuseppina written for a general audience. The volume excels at placing Strepponi's life within the context of the political, cultural, and social milieu in which she lived. The narrative has a slightly sensationalist tone, especially with respect to Strepponi's early love affairs and Verdi's relationship with Teresa Stolz. Although the author does not include footnotes, she does provide a short bibliographical narrative for each chapter describing her principal sources. The volume contains a detailed and useful index.

194. Valente, Mario. "Giuseppina Strepponi Verdi." *Opera Quarterly* 5/2–3 (Summer/Autumn 1987): 81–90.

A concise survey of Strepponi's life, with particular emphasis on her involvement in Verdi's work.

LIBRETTISTS

General

195. Rolandi, Ulderico. *Libretti e librettisti verdiani dal punto di vista storico-bibliografico.* Rome: Istituto Grafico Tiberino, 1941. 54 p. ML 410 .V58 R6.

This short monograph provides short histories of Verdi's librettists and briefly surveys the genesis of the librettos to each of the individual operas. The essay was originally published as an article in item 245.

196. Weaver, William. "Verdi and His Italian Librettists." *The Verdi Companion* (item 5), 121–30.

A brief overview of Verdi's collaboration with Temistocle Solera, Francesco Maria Piave, Salvatore Cammarano, Andrea Maffei, Antonio Somma, Antonio Ghislanzoni, and Arrigo Boito.

Boito, Arrigo

197. Conati, Marcello. "'Il valore del tempo.' Verdi e Boito: Preistoria di una collaborazione." In *Arrigo Boito: Atti del Convegno Internazionale di Studi* (item 199), 297–354.
    English translation by William Weaver. "The Value of Time." In *The Verdi-Boito Correspondence* (item 46), xii–lxiv.

Surveys the careers, mutual friends and interests, and the development and growth of a personal and business relationship between the two men through 1879, just as they begin corresponding about *Otello.* This richly documented essay was conceived as an Introduction to the English edition of the Verdi-Boito letters (item 46).

198. Magnolfi, Alberto. "Per una ricognizione bibliografica delle prime edizioni delle opere di Arrigo Boito." In *Arrigo Boito: Atti del Convegno Internazionale di Studi* (item 199), 565–83.

A bibliographic study listing Boito's musical works, librettos, literary works, translations of other authors' librettos, translations of his librettos by others, arias set by other authors, and works elaborated by other authors.

199. Morelli, Giovanni. *Arrigo Boito: Atti del Convegno Internazionale di Studi dedicato al centocinquantesimo della nascita di Arrigo Boito.* Linea veneta, 11. Florence: Olschki, 1994. vi, 598 p. ISBN 88-222-4288-2. PQ 4684 .B23 A77 1994.

This outstanding volume contains nearly two dozen articles dealing with Boito's life and works. A number of articles that concern Verdi are abstracted separately as items 197, 198, 200, 201, 699, 713, and 822. The volume contains an index of names.

200. Petrobelli, Pierluigi. "Boito e Verdi." In *Arrigo Boito: Atti del Convegno Internazionale di Studi* (item 199), 261–73.

Correspondence between Verdi and Boito clearly shows that both relished and profited from their ongoing mutual exchange of ideas. The author reviews the strengths of Verdi's earlier librettists, both professional and amateur, and asserts that Boito's talents and experience were much broader and all-encompassing than these earlier librettists. Boito possessed extraordinary abilities in the areas of poetic meter, verbal rhymes, and dramaturgical techniques in addition to an unusually rich experience with linguistics and literature. Petrobelli suggests that Verdi at first was not able to take in fully the rich complexities of Boito's literary style but reached that point by the time he had finished work on *Falstaff.*

201. Pieri, Marzio. "Le faville dell'opera: Boito traduce Shakespeare." In *Arrigo Boito: Atti del Convegno Internazionale di Studi* (item 199), 145–211.

A brief overview of Boito's activities as a translator of Shakespeare. Of special interest are the appendices, which reproduce a complete translation by Boito of *Macbeth* and partial translations of *Romeo and Juliet* and *Antony and Cleopatra.*

   * Powers, Harold S. "Boito rimatore per musica." See item 822.

202. Rensis, Raffaello De. *Arrigo Boito: Capitoli biografici.* Florence: Sansoni, 1942. 224 p. + 5 plates

The most significant early biography of Boito. It lacks, unfortunately, footnotes and critical references.

203. Tintori, Giampiero, ed. *Arrigo Boito: Musicista e letterato.* N.p.: Nuove Edizioni, 1986. 199 p. ML 410 .B694 A85 1986.

This beautifully illustrated collection of essays treats various aspects of Boito's life and works. Of particular interest to Verdi scholars is a chapter by Michele Girardi entitled "Verdi e Boito: Due artisti fra tradizione e rinnovamento." Giampiero Tintori presents an annotated edition of the complete correspondence between Boito and Camille Bellaigue in the collection of the Museo Teatrale alla Scala. The volume also includes a catalogue of Boito's musical and literary works by Luigi Inzaghi.

Cammarano, Salvatore

204. Black, John. *The Italian Romantic Libretto: A Study of Salvadore Cammarano.* Edinburgh: Edinburgh University Press, 1984. ix, 325 p. ISBN 0-85224-463-0. ML 429 .C16 B6 1984.

The definitive study of Cammarano, who served as Verdi's collaborator on *Alzira, Luisa Miller, La battaglia di Legnano* and *Il trovatore* and who also prepared librettos for many operas by Verdi's contemporaries. The first portion of the volume offers the most detailed biographical study of Cammarano available. The latter portion of the book examines topics such as Cammarano's working methods; his sources and choices of subject material; his approach toward formal organization, language, and versification; and his role in the production of operas for which he prepared the libretto. Appendices provide a chronological list of Cammarano's opera librettos and the titles for individual acts (where present) in his librettos. The volume also includes a selective bibliography and a detailed index.

Ghislanzoni, Antonio

205. Benini, Aroldo, ed. *L'operosa dimensione scapigliata di Antonio Ghislanzoni: Atti del Convegno di Studio svoltosi a Milano, a Lecco, a Caprino Bergamasco nell'autunno 1993.* Milan: Istituto per la Storia del Risorgimento Italiano; Lecco: Associazione Giuseppe Bovara, 1995. 277 p. DG 552.8 G44 O637 1995.

This conference report contains articles dealing with all aspects of Ghislanzoni's life and career, including his activities as a librettist and music critic.

Piave, Francesco Maria

206. Cagli, Bruno. "'. . . Questo povero poeta esordiente': Piave a Roma, un carteggio con Ferretti, la genesi di *Ernani.*" In *"Ernani" ieri e oggi* (item 228), 1-18.

Examines the early life and literary milieu of Francesco Maria Piave, particularly his friendship with literary mentors Giuseppe Gioachino Belli and Jacopo Ferretti. The author focuses on Piave's letters to Ferretti that shed light on the history of *Ernani.*

PUBLISHERS

207. Jensen, Luke. *Giuseppe Verdi & Giovanni Ricordi with Notes on Francesco Lucca: From "Oberto" to "La Traviata."* Garland Reference Library of the Humanities, 896. New York & London: Garland, 1989. ix, 456 p. ISBN 0-8240-5616-7. ML 410 .V4 J46.

Examines the developing relationship between Verdi and the Ricordi publishing firm during the formative years of the composer's career through the death of Giulio Ricordi, the founder of the firm. Specific topics include Ricordi's role in preparing material for early performances, negotiations about performance and publication rights, and early publication history. The author also discusses Verdi's brief rift with Ricordi and the events surrounding the publication of three operas that the composer assigned to Francesco Lucca, Ricordi's chief competitor: *Attila, I masnadieri,* and *Il corsaro.* This examination brings to light many interesting details about Verdi's working habits, including methods of orchestration, his role in the preparation of piano-vocal scores, and ways of dealing with censors. One appendix lists early nineteenth-century opera scores published by Ricordi. A series of longer appendices provide detailed information about the publication of Verdi's music by Ricordi and Lucca (including individual parts, instrumental arrangements, potpourris and similar pieces based on themes from the operas, etc.) through *La traviata.*

208. Mompellio, Federico. "Verdi e gli editori italiani e francesi." In *Verdi: Studi e memorie nel XL anniversario della morte* (item 245), 289–304.

An illustrated survey of the composer's relationship to his publishers. The study focuses on the publishing houses of Ricordi and Lucca and briefly considers the French firm of Escudier.

209. Pasquinelli, Anna. "Contributo per la storia di Casa Lucca." *Nuova rivista musicale italiana* 16 (1982): 568–81.

A concise history of this publishing firm that provides general background information. There is little detail about the firm's relationship with Verdi. (Lucca published only three works of Verdi: *Attila, Il corsaro,* and *I masnadieri*; the firm held joint rights, with Ricordi, for *Nabucco*). Pasquinelli concludes that Lucca's most significant contribution to music publishing was probably the firm's acquisition of distribution rights for works by foreign composers little known in Italy. Information for this article comes from the author's Ph.D. dissertation (Università degli Studi di Milano, 1980–81) entitled "Francesco e Giovannina Lucca: Editori musicali a Milano (1825–1888)."

210. Pestalozza, Luciana, coordinating ed. *Musica, musicisti, editoria: 175 anni di Casa Ricordi, 1808–1983.* Milan: Ricordi, 1983. ML 112 .M88 1983. English translation by Gabriele Dotto, Anna Herklotz, and Kate Singleton. *Music, Musicians, Publishing. 175 Years of Casa Ricordi: 1808–1983.* Milan: Ricordi, 1983. 268 p. ML 427 .R53 M913.

This elegant commemorative volume provides a documentary iconography of the firm's history, including historical photographs, engravings, reproductions of manuscript and printed music, posters and playbills, set designs, and correspondence. Also valuable to Verdi scholars are Francesco Degrada's overview of the firm's history, particularly its origins and development through the nineteenth century, and a brief essay by Giorgio Fioravanti about the technical evolution of music printing at the firm.

211. Sartori, Claudio, ed. *Casa Ricordi 1808–1958*. Milan: Ricordi, 1958. 93 p. + 48 plates. ML 427 .R53 S3.

This commemorative edition provides a lively history of the publishing firm. The illustrations include 16 facsimile reproductions of autograph manuscripts (including the opening chorus of *Il trovatore*, Act III) and 32 color reproductions of title pages and other materials. The volume includes a short bibliography.

212. Vergani, Orio. *Piccolo viaggio in un archivio*. Milan: Ricordi, 1953. Reprint, with a new preface by Francesco Degrada. Milan: Ricordi, 1994. 62 p. ISBN 88-7592-418-X. ML 427 .R53 V4 1994.

A short commemorative booklet originally issued to commemorate the 100th anniversary of the death of Giovanni Ricordi, the founder of the firm. Contains some very nice iconographic material.

OTHER ASSOCIATES

Barezzi, Antonio

213. Petrobelli, Pierluigi, et al. *Con Verdi in Casa Barezzi*. Photographs by Angelo Ceresa. Busseto: Associazione Culturale Amici di Verdi, [1985]. 89 p.

This beautifully illustrated volume contains essays by Corrado Mingardi and Mary Jane Phillips-Matz that consider Antonio Barezzi's family background, his life in Busseto and activities as an amateur musician and patron of the arts, and his relationship to Verdi. Color photographs show scenes from Barezzi's house and and the general environs of Busseto. An appendix reproduces more than three dozen letters and documents, including some correspondence between Barezzi and Verdi and documents relating to the composer's early life and career in Busseto.

Bottesini, Giovanni

214. Santi, Piero. "Bottesini e Verdi." In *Giovanni Bottesini e la civiltà musicale cremasca: Atti del Convegno di Studi, Crema, 25 ottobre 1989*, 7–14. Ed. by Flavio Arpini and Elena Mariani. Quaderni del Centro Culturale S. Agostino 10. Crema: Centro Culturale S. Agostino, 1991. ML 290.8 C74 G5 1991.

A brief survey of Verdi's feelings about Bottesini as a conductor and as a composer. Much of the essay centers on the circumstances surrounding the choice of Bottesini to conduct the premiere performance of *Aida* in Cairo.

Cavalli, Hercules

215. Phillips-Matz, Mary Jane. *"José Verdi*, Hercules Cavalli, and the Florence *Macbeth."* In *"Macbeth" Sourcebook* (item 762), 129–36.

    Discusses the life of Hercules Cavalli, his relationship to Verdi, and his early biography of the composer, *José Verdi* (Madrid: J.M. Ducazal, 1867). See item 179 for an Italian translation of Cavalli's rare biography.

Corticelli, Mauro

216. Azzaroni, Giovanni, and Paola Bignami. *Corticelli Mauro, impresario*. Materiali di teatro, 3. Bologna: Nuova Alfa, 1990. 187 p. ISBN 88–7779–136–5. PN 2688 .C67 A98 1990.

    Not a traditional biography but a series of essays dealing with various facets of Corticelli's career. An entire chapter examines Corticelli's tenure as an administrator at Sant'Agata, based largely on correspondence (much of it yet unpublished) with Giuseppina Strepponi and Verdi. The volume includes a bibliography but lacks an index.

Maffei, Clara

217. Barbiera, Raffaello. *Il salotto della Contessa Maffei con lettere inedite di G. Verdi e ritratti.* 13th rev. ed. Florence: A. Salani, 1919. 409 p. Reprint. Milan: Garzanti, 1943. 358 p. DG 658.7 M3 B3 1919.

    A fine discussion of the Milanese cultural circle surrounding Countess Clara Maffei of which Verdi was a member. A chapter devoted to Alessandro Manzoni recounts the story of the famous author meeting the composer and examines Manzoni's influence on Verdi. The volume also provides some background information about the composition of *Macbeth*.

Mariani, Angelo

218. Potito, Amedeo. *Angelo Mariani: Autobiografia e documenti, 1821–1873.* Rimini: Bruno Ghigi, 1985. 96 + xvi p. ML 422 .M166 P7 1985.

    The first section of the volume reproduces Mariani's autobiography, written for Giulio Ricordi at his request in November 1866. The remainder of the monograph reproduces more than 50 letters and documents, including eight letters from Verdi, all written in 1863, a funeral eulogy by Giuseppe Celli, a substantial obituary that appeared in *Nelle nuvole: Giornale umoristico*, ten pictures of places associated with Mariani, and a reproduction of the playbill for the opening season of the Nuovo Teatro Comunale in Rimini in 1857 (which featured, among other works, *Il trovatore* and *Aroldo*). The volume contains an index of people and places and a short bibliography.

Morelli, Domenico

219. Levi, Primo. *Domenico Morelli nella vita e nell'arte: Mezzo secolo di pittura italiana.* Rome: Casa Editrice Nazionale, 1906. viii, 390 p. + 28 plates. ND 623 .M6 L4.

Documents the life and works of Verdi's contemporary, the artist Domenico Morelli. One of the most valuable features of the volume for Verdi researchers is the publication of correspondence between the two artists (several of Verdi's letters are reproduced in facsimile). In addition, the author discusses the influence of Morelli's sketches of scenes from *Othello* and *King Lear* on Verdi's conception of operas on those subjects and the history of Morelli's portrait of the composer, now hanging in the Casa di Riposo dei Musicisti in Milan. Also of significance are paintings by Morelli dealing with some of the same subjects as Verdi's operas. The volume contains a useful index of names and a separate index of illustrations.

Muzio, Emanuele

220. Nello Vetro, Gaspare. *L'allievo di Verdi: Emanuele Muzio.* Revised, enlarged, and corrected from a study by Almerindo Napolitano. Chronology by Thomas Kaufman. Parma: Edizioni Zara, [1993]. 347 p. + 16 p. illustrations. ML 422 .M95 V48 1993.

An outstanding biography of Verdi's only formal student, Emanuele Muzio, with particular emphasis on his career as a conductor. The author draws heavily on letters written by Muzio to Verdi, Muzio's friend Giovanni Boldini, and the Ricordi firm. Some of these documents are reproduced here in part or in whole for the first time. The appended chronology provides a list of repertory conducted by Muzio, presented first in brief format by composer and subsequently in chronological order, with information about dates, theaters, and casts. The volume contains two name indexes: one pertaining to the biography proper, and another relating to the chronology; it also includes a bibliography and index of illustrations. Unfortunately, the author provides no footnotes or other references to individual sources.

Provesi, Ferdinando

221. Moroni, Antonio. "Ferdinando Provesi: Maestro di Giuseppe Verdi." *Biblioteca '70* 2 (1971): 107–16.

A short biography of Verdi's first teacher. Reproduces several sonnets written by Provesi and provides a listing of more than 120 of his compositions.

Tamagno, Francesco

222. Corsi, Mario. *Tamagno: Il più grande fenomeno canoro dell'ottocento.* Milan: Ceschina, 1938. Reprint. New York: Arno, 1977. 218 p. ISBN 0–405–09673–9. ML 420 .T14 C7 1977.

A biography of Francesco Tamagno, who created the title role in *Otello* and sang in many other operas by Verdi. Includes considerable information on the premiere performance of *Otello* and its subsequent reception in major opera centers. The volume lacks an index but does contain a list of recordings by Tamagno, including excerpts from *Otello* and *Il trovatore*.

Vigna, Cesare

223. Flisi, Giuseppe, ed. *Cesare Vigna: Psichiatra e musicologo nel primo centenario della morte.* Viadana: Editrice Castello, 1992. 111 p.

A number of essays in this commemorative volume deal with topics relating to Verdi, including an overview of their correspondence (published many years earlier as item 90) and Vigna's articles relating to music and medicine written for the *Gazzetta musicale di Milano.* The volume includes a catalog of Vigna's writings and a bibliography of secondary sources.

CHAPTER 6
Conference & Congress Reports

The first Congresso Internazionale di Studi Verdiani, held in Venice in 1966, marked a major turning point in both quality and quantity of Verdi studies. It initiated a substantial series of conferences devoted to the composer during the next three decades.

224. *Atti del I° Congresso Internazionale di Studi Verdiani, 31 luglio — 2 agosto 1966.*
Ed. by Marcello Pavarani and Pierluigi Petrobelli. Parma: Istituto di Studi Verdiani, 1969. 469 p. ML 36 .C769.

The first Congresso Internazionale di Studi Verdiani included 59 papers covering a broad range of themes including biography, analysis, compositional process, and reception. Some of the more important articles are abstracted separately as items 8, 11, 14, 264, 268, 360, 409, 463, 478, 530, 574, 703, 766, 796, 804, 868, 889, 979, 997, and 998. Massimo Mila provides a complete table of contents in *La giovinezza di Verdi* (item 171), 519–20 and in *L'arte di Verdi* (item 375), 374–75.

225. *Atti del II° Congresso Internazionale di Studi Verdiani, 30 luglio — 5 agosto 1969.* Ed. by Marcello Pavarani. Parma: Istituto di Studi Verdiani, 1971. xvi, 611 p. + 24 p. plates, 1 chart. ML 36 .C769 1969.

The 58 studies in this Congress Report are an important point of departure for any study of *Don Carlos*. Individual articles cover topics that include the relationship between Schiller's drama and Verdi's opera, the characterization of leading figures in the opera, analyses of various portions of the opera, the composer's later revisions of the work, the opera's place among Verdi's compositions and its relationship to other operas from the period, and its reception. Some of the more significant studies are listed separately as items 70, 260, 315, 328, 339, 437, 627, 628, 631–33, 636–39, 641, 643, 644, 650, 651, 653–55, 658, 660–66, and 1010. Massimo Mila provides a complete table of contents in *La giovinezza di Verdi* (item 171), 520–21 and in *L'arte di Verdi* (item 375), 375–76.

226. *Atti del III° Congresso Internazionale di Studi Verdiani, 12–17 giugno 1972.* Ed. by Mario Medici and Marcello Pavarani. Parma: Istituto di Studi Verdiani, 1974. xvii, 617 p. + 41 plates. ML 36 .C769 1972.

The theme of this conference was "The Theater and Music of Giuseppe Verdi." Some of the most significant of the 44 items presented at this conference are abstracted separately as items 5, 78, 95, 118, 270, 272, 273, 280, 305, 316, 394, 410, 419, 424, 425, 446, 451, 455, 462, 466, 481, 489, 509, 585, 615, 710, 797, 816, 871, 933, 946, 948, and 959. Massimo Mila provides a complete table of contents in *La giovinezza di Verdi* (item 171), 521–22 and in *L'arte di Verdi* (item 375), 376–77.

227. *Colloquium "Verdi-Wagner" Rom 1969: Bericht.* Ed. by Friedrich Lippmann. *Analecta musicologica*, 11. Cologne: Böhlau, 1972. 342 p. ML 55 .L766.

Topics related to Verdi discussed at this colloquium center on the influence of Germanic culture on Verdi's life and works, the reception of Verdi's works in German-speaking countries, and secondary literature about Verdi in German. Some individual items are abstracted as numbers 7, 294, 323, 347, and 401.

228. *"Ernani" ieri e oggi: Atti del Convegno Internazionale di Studi, Modena, Teatro San Carlo, 9–10 dicembre 1984.* Ed. by Pierluigi Petrobelli. In *Verdi: Bollettino dell'Istituto di Studi Verdiani*, vol. 4 [No. 10]. Parma: Istituto di Studi Verdiani, 1987. xxii, 327 p. + 19 p. plates. ISBN 88–85065–04–X.

Also published in English. *"Ernani" Yesterday and Today: Proceedings of the International Congress, Modena, Teatro San Carlo, 9/10 December 1984.* *Verdi: Bulletin of the Istituto di Studi Verdiani*, vol. 4 [No. 10]. Parma: Istituto di Studi Verdiani, 1989. xxiv, 328 p. + 19 p. plates. ISBN 88–85065–06–6.

This conference contains papers dealing with almost every aspect of *Ernani*, including its genesis and compositional history, history of the libretto and the intervention of censors, stylistic evaluations of the music, and performance practice. Individual papers are cited as numbers 206, 673, 676, 680, 685, 686, 688, 690, 691, and 1016.

229. *Fourth International Verdi Congress (Chicago — Lyric Opera 1974): Résumés of the Reports.* Ed. by the Istituto di Studi Verdiani. N.p.: n.p., [1976]. 83 p. (unnumbered)

This informal publication provides short abstracts in English of papers presented at the Congress with concise biographies of the presenters. No formal congress report was issued; however, some of the papers later appeared in the first issue of *Studi verdiani*. Main themes of the congress were: Verdi in America, *Simon Boccanegra*, and Verdi in the World.

230. *Giuseppe Verdi nel cinquantenario della morte: Celebrazione commemorativa promossa dall'Accademia Nazionale dei Lincei, dall'insigne Accademia di S. Luca e dall'Accademia di S. Cecilia, ottobre — novembre 1951*. Problemi attuali di scienza e di cultura, Quaderno 26. Roma: Accademia Nazionale dei Lincei, 1952. 37 p. AS 222 .R53 n. 26.

This conference report contains three articles, one dealing with Verdi's scenography (item 543) and two dealing with Verdi's legacy (items 348 and 360).

231. *Nuove prospettive nella ricerca verdiana: Atti del Convegno Internazionale in Occasione della Prima del "Rigoletto" in Edizione Critica, Vienna, 12–13 marzo, 1983*. Ed. by Marisa Di Gregorio Casati and Marcello Pavarani. Parma: Istituto di Studi Verdiani; Milan: Ricordi, 1987. xii, 137 p. ISBN 88–85065–03–1; 88–7592–039–7. ML 410 .V4 C68 1983.

A publication of most of the papers presented at the special international conference on the occasion of the first performance based on the new critical edition. Individual items are abstracted separately as numbers 6, 461, 496, 587, 667, 682, 867, 1026, 1030, and 1034.

232. *Per un "progetto Verdi" anni '80: Seminario Internazionale di Studi, Parma— Bussetto 3–4 aprile 1980*. [Bologna]: Regione Emilia-Romagna, n.d. 147 p.

At this conference, leading Verdi scholars presented ideas concerning their vision of Verdi research in the coming years. Topics included the preparation of a critical edition of Verdi's works, performance practice, bibliographic control of printed and archival documents, musical and cultural milieu, and the role of Italian cultural and political entities in promoting the study and performance of Verdi's music. Several individual papers from this conference are listed separately; see items 289, 418, 516, and 519.

233. *La realizzazione scenica dello spettacolo verdiano: Atti del Congresso Internazionale di Studi, Parma, 28–30 settembre 1994*. Ed. by Pierluigi Petrobelli and Fabrizio Della Seta. Parma: Istituto Nazionale di Studi Verdiani, forthcoming.

This important publication will contain nearly two dozen articles covering all aspects of staging.

* Rosen, David, and Andrew Porter, eds. *Verdi's "Macbeth": A Sourcebook.* See item 762.

234. *Tornando a "Stiffelio": Popolarità, rifacimenti, messinscena, effettismo e altre "cure" nella drammaturgia del Verdi romantico.* Atti del Convegno Internazionale di Studi, Venezia, 17–20 dicembre 1985. Ed. by Giovanni Morelli. *Quaderni della Rivista italiana di musicologia,* 14. Firenze: Leo S. Olschki, 1987. xv, 380 p. ISBN 88–22–23484–7. ML 410 .V4 T62.

The *Stiffelio* conference report contains papers dealing with almost every aspect of the opera, including its genesis and compositional history, history of the libretto (including the significant intervention of the censors), stylistic evaluations of the music, and the opera's later reworking as *Aroldo.* Appendices include reports on a round table discussion devoted to the problem of contemporary performance practice, a voluntary after-school seminar dealing with *Stiffelio* and *Aroldo* for secondary school students in Venice, and transcriptions of discussions by participants after the presentation of individual papers. Some of the more significant items are abstracted separately as numbers 469, 499, 907, 904, 908, 909, 912, 914, 915, 917, and 919. The volume contains an index of proper names but no subject index.

235. *Verdi's Middle Period, 1849–1859: Source Studies, Analysis, and Performance Practice.* Ed. by Martin Chusid. Chicago and London: University of Chicago Press, 1997. xii, 436 p. ISBN 0–226–10658–6 (cloth); 0–226–10659–4 (paper). ML 410 .V4 V354 1997.

A selective publication of papers presented at the International Verdi Congress in Belfast, Northern Ireland, in March 1993, all of them revised or expanded for publication. Martin Chusid contributes an important prefatory article surveying the activities and significance of this decade in Verdi's career (item 367). The remaining thirteen essays include are divided into three groups: source studies (items 910, 911, and 977), analytical examinations dealing with individual or groups of operas (items 491, 604, 607, 754, 952, 956, and 973), and performance practice (items 501, 527, and 531). The volume includes an index.

236. *"I vespri siciliani." Convegno di Studi Verdiani, Torino, 7–10 aprile 1973: Sunte delle relazioni.* N.p.: n.p., n.d. 43 p.

This informal publication provides short abstracts (mainly in Italian) of papers that were presented at the Congress. No formal report was ever published; however, some of the papers appeared in the premiere issue of *Studi verdiani.*

CHAPTER 7

General Studies

This chapter includes studies that are so broad in their scope that they do not easily fit into a more specific grouping. This category also includes books with collected essays and studies covering a broad range of topics as well as some exhibition catalogues.

237. Benedetti, Franko, and Marzio Dall'Acqua, eds. *Giuseppe Verdi: Vicende, problemi e mito di un artista e del suo tempo.* Colorno: Edizioni "Una Città Costruisce una Mostra," 1985. 217 p. + 108 plates. ML 141 .C66 V43 1985.

A catalogue issued in limited edition in connection with an exhibition at the Palazzo Ducale in Colorno, 31 August to 8 December 1985. The plates include, among other things, handsome reproductions of paintings, caricatures, photographs, costume designs, engravings, and facsimiles of scores, sketches, and titles pages that were part of the exhibit. The full scope of the exhibition, which drew upon the resources of 30 libraries, archives, museums, and private collections, is evident from the accompanying commentary. A series of accompanying essays consider several specialized topics, including theaters and orchestras at the time of Verdi (item 258) and the composer's involvement with the staging of his operas (item 539). The volume also contains a short biographical essay and tabular biography by Gustavo Marchesi.

238. Conati, Marcello, ed. *Interviste e incontri con Verdi.* 2nd ed. Milan: Emme Edizioni, 1981. 399 p. ML 410 .V4 I75 1980.
    English translation by Richard Stokes. *Interviews and Encounters with Verdi.* Foreword by Julian Budden. London: Victor Gollancz, 1984. 417 p. ISBN 0–575–03349–5. American printing under title *Encounters with Verdi.* Ithaca: Cornell University Press, 1984. xxvii, 417 p. ISBN 0–8014–1717–1. ML 410 .V4 I753 1984.

An anthology of selected, short articles describing interviews or meetings with the composer that were originally published in periodicals between 1845 and 1900. A short preface precedes each individual article, and all items contain annotations that clarify and fill out details as well as cross-references to other literature. The list of sources and works consulted contains about 250 items, many of which are relatively little known.

239. Decujos, Leonardo. "La Casa di Riposo pei Musicisti." *Rivista musicale italiana* 8 (1901): 368–78.

A short history of Verdi's project to build a rest home for musicians in Milan. Includes drawings, architectural plans, and the institution's statutory regulations.

240. De Filippis, Felice. "Verdi e gli amici di Napoli." *Verdi: Bollettino dell'Istituto di Studi Verdiani* 1 [No. 3] (1960): 1365–72. English and German translations are printed on pp. 1754–66.

Surveys Verdi's relationship with musicians and artists in Naples including Salvatore Cammarano, Melchiorre Delfico, Cesare De Sanctis, Domenico Morelli, and Vincenzo Torelli. The article includes a brief note from Verdi and a long letter from Giuseppina, both written to Torelli in 1858.

241. Gatti, Carlo. *Revisioni e rivalutazioni verdiani*. Saggi, 2. Turin: Edizioni Radio Italiana, 1952. 129 p. + 6 plates. ML 410 .V48 G2633.

A series of 20 short essays, originally presented as radio broadcasts commemorating the 50th anniversary of the composer's death. The writing is in a somewhat more popular style than the author's magisterial biography (item 147), which at the time of this publication had recently been reissued in a revised edition; these essays often expand on ideas developed less fully in the biography. Topics discussed include: Verdi's moral, social, political, and religious thought; Verdi and the public; the composer's juvenilia; his keyboard skills; Verdi's relationship to La Scala; his "counter-reformation" of the musical drama; various essays on individual compositions; and a short biography compiled from the composer's own words.

242. *Giuseppe Verdi nel primo cinquantenario della morte*. Special issue (Vol. 1) of *La regione Emilia-Romagna*. Bologna: Cappelli, 1950. 114 p.

This commemorative volume contains essays on a wide range of subjects, including Verdi's relationship to nineteenth-century Italian opera, his significance as a political figure, the evolution of his musical style, his humanity, the significance of his correspondence as a body of documents, his relationship to Trieste, caricatures of the composer, and medals featuring Verdi's image.

243. *Giuseppe Verdi: Scritti raccolti in occasione delle "Celebrazioni Verdiani" dell'VIII Settimana Musicale dell'Accademia Musicale Chigiana.* Siena: Ticci, 1951. 119 p.

This collection contains studies about Verdi's activities and the reception of his works in various European countries as well as a short discussion of versions and translations of Verdi librettos. Some of the individual articles are abstracted later in this volume as items 309, 312, 313, 318, 322, 325, 326, 333, and 992.

244. Martin, George. *Aspects of Verdi.* New York: Dodd, Mead & Company, 1988. xiv, 304 p. ISBN 0–396–08843–0. ML 410 .V4 M264 1988.

An important collection of essays, some expansions of earlier articles, on a variety of biographical and musical topics. Most of the essays are abstracted individually (see items 297, 324, 642, 726, 821, 859, 937, 957, 984, 999, and 1000). Appendices include the text and an English translation of Manzoni's "Il Cinque Maggio" and Verdi's *Messa da Requiem*; nine previously unpublished letters of Verdi; a list of Verdi's compositions including, for operatic works, literary sources, first casts, theaters, and dates of premieres; and a selective bibliography, focusing on items written in English. The volume contains an excellent index.

245. Mulè, Giuseppe, and Giorgio Nataletti, eds. *Verdi: Studi e memorie nel XL anniversario della morte.* Issued by the Sindicato Nazionale Fascista Musicisti. Rome: Istituto Grafico Tiberino, 1941. 532 p. ML 410 .V4 S45.

This large, handsomely illustrated commemorative volume contains 40 essays on all aspects of Verdi's life and works. Several chapters survey his compositions, discuss characteristics of his musical style, and examine various aspects of his historical and cultural milieu. Some of the most useful essays in this collection explore Verdi's relationship to librettists, singers, orchestral directors, scenery and costume designers, publishers, and political figures—all with profuse illustrations. The volume also contains an unusually detailed tabular chronology of the composer's life and a selective bibliography. Ulderico Rolandi's survey of librettos and librettists (pp. 183–232) was simultaneously issued as a separate monograph (see item 195). See also separately indexed articles on Verdi's publishers (item 208) and an interesting iconographic study of commemorative Verdi medals (item 115).

246. *Natura ed arte.* Special issue. 15 February 1901. Milan: Vallardi. 112 p. ML 410 .V48 V482.

This handsomely illustrated issue offers a series of articles on a wide range of topics, including biographical issues, librettos, performers, and Verdi's relationship to culture, society, and politics.

247. Pizzi, Italo. *Per il I° centenario della nascita di Giuseppe Verdi: Memorie—aneddoti—considerazioni.* Turin: S. Lattes, 1913. 213 p.

     The author divides his presentation into three sections. The first, entitled "Il paese e i tempi," provides useful background on Verdi's cultural and social milieu. The central portion of the volume surveys the composer's operas primarily from the standpoint of drama and dramaturgy. The short final section, entitled "The Man," assesses Verdi's place among his contemporaries (with respect to Wagner, in particular) and in history.

248. Weaver, William, and Martin Chusid, eds. *The Verdi Companion.* New York: Norton; Toronto: George J. McLeod, 1979. 366 p. ISBN 0–393–01215–8. ML 410 .V4 V295. Reprint. London: Gollancz, 1980. ISBN 0–575–02223–X. Reprint. New York: Norton, 1988. xvi, 366 p. ISBN 0–393–30443–4. ML 410 .V4 V35 1988.

     An invaluable collection of general essays covering Verdi's musical and cultural milieu, relationships with librettists and publishers, performance practice and musical style. Particularly useful features include a substantial name dictionary of people associated with Verdi; a list of the composer's major works by date of first performance; a chronology of Verdi's life, with references to secondary literature; and (in the hardbound edition) a reproduction of Verdi's family tree. See items 12, 196, 255, 256, 262, 297, 329, 349, 445, 462, and 524.

CHAPTER 8

Verdi's Milieu

This chapter includes only a sampling of the most significant studies dealing with musical, cultural, social, and political background to Verdi's life and works. Almost any item will provide a significant point of departure to additional related studies.

MUSICAL & CULTURAL MILIEU

249. Balthazar, Scott L. "Aspects of Form in the Ottocento Libretto." *Cambridge Opera Journal* 7 (1995): 23–35.

   Illustrates trends in the structure of librettos from the era of Metastasio through Verdi, using as central focus the ideas presented by Alessandro Manzoni in his *Lettre à M. C*** sur l'unité de temps et de lieu dans la tragédie* (1823). By the time of Verdi, emphasis on a balanced, systematic exposition of conflicts, emphasizing unity of time, had given way to a more linear structure, based on causually interlocking events that emphasize unity of action. The author briefly probes some of the implications of this change on Verdi's approach to musical form and suggests several broad areas in need of future investigation.

250. ———. "Evolving Conventions in Italian Serious Opera: Scene Structure in the Works of Rossini, Bellini, Donizetti, and Verdi, 1810–1850." Ph.D. dissertation, University of Pennsylvania, 1985. xvii, 595 p.

   This useful study places Verdi's approach to form in the context of his immediate predecessors. The author focuses not only on changes in musical style but also on developments in the literary style of librettos during this period and its effect on musical form.

251. ———. "The *Primo Ottocento* Duet and the Transformation of Rossinian Code." *Journal of Musicology* 7 (1989): 471–97.

Asserts that while Donizetti, Bellini, and Verdi continued to use the main structural framework of the four-part duet design established by Rossini, they made substantial changes including, at times, a weakening of connections between sections, omission of one or more sections, and open key schemes rather than closed tonal structures. The author illustrates these new tendencies in an analysis of the Odabella-Foresto duet from Act I of *Attila*.

252. ———. "Rossini and the Development of the Mid-Century Lyric Form." *Journal of the American Musicological Society* 41 (1988): 102–25.

An extensive discussion of the genesis and development of the lyric form A A' B A' in the works of Rossini that dominates the early works of Verdi and his contemporaries.

253. Beghelli, Marco. "Il contributo dei trattati di canto ottocenteschi al lessico dell'opera." In *Le parole della musica, I: Studi sulla lingua della letteratura musicale in onore di Gianfranco Folena*, 177–223. Ed. by Fiamma Nicolodi and Paolo Trovato. Studi di musica veneta, 21. Florence: Olschki, 1994. ISBN 88–222–4284–X. ML 63 .P26 1994.

A detailed discussion of general trends found in the usage of terms related to singing in nineteenth-century treatises. The article includes an annotated bibliography of more than 50 nineteenth-century treatises on singing; an appendix provides a glossary of more than 80 unusual or ambiguous terms found in the treatises.

254. Bernardoni, Virgilio. "La teoria della melodia vocale nella trattistica italiana (1790–1870)." *Acta musicologica* 62 (1990): 29–61.

A thorough overview of the way in which Italian theorists from the ottocento and late settecento treated the topic of melody, its construction, and its analysis. Much of the discussion centers around the writings of Carlo Gervasoni, Francesco Galeazzi, and Bonifazio Asioli, although a large number of lesser-known figures are also examined. See item 512 for a larger study of this topic that focuses specifically on its application to Verdi.

255. Budden, Julian. "Verdi and the Contemporary Italian Operatic Scene." *The Verdi Companion* (item 5), 67–105.

Discusses innovations in Verdi's compositions and their influence on the mechanics of producing an opera in light of the traditions established by Rossini and developed by Donizetti and Bellini.

256. Cagli, Bruno. "Verdi and the Business of Writing Operas." *The Verdi Companion* (item 5), 106–120.

Revised version, published in Italian. "Organizzazione economica e gestione teatrale nell'"800." In *Per un "progetto Verdi" anni '80* (item 232), 63–85.

Examines the changing relationship of composer, performer, publisher, and impresario in nineteenth-century Italy. Documents Verdi's increasing intervention throughout his career in all aspects of performing and publishing his works.

257. Conati, Marcello. "Cenni su orchestre, teatri, strumenti, e diapason in Italia nell'ottocento." *Musica/realtà* 40 (April 1993): 111–27.

A brief but excellent overview of issues regarding the orchestra in nineteenth-century Italy including: the formation of philharmonic societies, the relationship of military bands to local orchestras, the growth of theater orchestras and the gradual transformation of their makeup and seating arrangement, the eventual acceptance of baton-wielding conductors, and the adoption of a relatively uniform standard for pitch.

258. ———. "Teatri e orchestre al tempo di Verdi." In *Giuseppe Verdi: Vicende, problemi e mito di un artista e del suo tempo* (item 237), 47–78.

Surveys the theatrical boom in Italy during the nineteenth century and discusses the arrangement of main theatrical seasons. Some of the most interesting material in this article concerns the size and arrangement of orchestras in nineteenth–century theaters and issues surrounding the lack of a uniform standard pitch throughout Europe during most of Verdi's lifetime.

259. ———. "Il tempo del giovane Verdi." *Musica e dossier* 2 (December 1986), special insert, 7–30.

An outstanding essay dealing with the state of Italian opera at the beginning of Verdi's career and the gradual change in Italian operatic style that took place during the 1830s. The author pays particular attention to the relationship of Verdi's earliest operas—*Oberto, Un giorno di regno,* and *Nabucco*—to contemporary musical trends. The article includes two extremely useful tables. The first lists by year new theaters erected in Italy between 1821 and 1847. The second presents an overview of operatic seasons in Italy from 1841 to 1846. For each season it lists, by composer, the total number of operas performed as well as the the number of opera houses performing each composer's works.

260. ———. "Verdi, il *grand opéra* e il *Don Carlos.*" *Atti 2* (item 225), 242–79.

An important study of Verdi's relationship to both the genre of French *grand opéra* and to the Paris Opéra as an institution. The article provides much interesting information on the aesthetic background of Verdi's operas written in the style of French *grand opéra*, particularly *Don Carlos* and *Aida*. Conati argues that the composer's negative comments about French *grand opéra* were directed against institutional and administrative aspects and not against the musical and dramaturgical features of the genre. The author devotes a substantial part of the article to the question of Meyerbeer's influence on *Don Carlos*, concluding that the French composer's works may have affected Verdi's approach to orchestration, but probably did not have much effect on his vocal writing.

261. Conati, Marcello, and Marcello Pavarani, eds. *Orchestre in Emilia-Romagna nell'ottocento e novecento.* Parma: Orchestra Sinfonica dell'Emilia-Romagna "Arturo Toscanini," 1982. xix, 525 p.

This volume contains a series of essays by Italian scholars, each dealing with the orchestra in a particular city or sponsored by a particular institution in the Emilia-Romagna region. The locations include not only the large cultural centers, such as Parma and Bologna, but also smaller cities and towns that had opera houses or other institutions requiring an orchestra. Most of the information concerns the early and middle nineteenth century and therefore provides valuable material concerning orchestral performance practices in a wide variety of settings during the initial stages of Verdi's career. The book contains maps showing the locations of operatic performances in the region as well as a master table that illustrates the changing number and balance of instruments in various orchestras throughout the nineteenth century. Among the most valuable features of this volume are reproductions of documents such as contracts, regulations, and letters, many of which are published here for the first time. The documents (excluding letters) are indexed by location in the back of the volume. There is also a name index but, unfortunately, no subject index.

262. Dallapiccola, Luigi. *Words and Music in Italian 19th Century Opera: Lecture Given at the Italian Institute in Dublin.* Quaderni dell'Istituto Italiano di Cultura in Dublino, 3. Dublin: Italian Institute, 1964. 16 p. ML 1733 .D16.
       Italian version published in a set of collected essays entitled *Appunti, incontri, meditazioni.* This collective volume has been reprinted under the title *Parole e musica* and has been translated into several languages, including English (see item 368).
       English translation by Alvary E. Grazebrook of the Italian version listed above. "Words and Music in Italian Nineteenth-Century Opera." *The Verdi Companion* (item 5), 193–215.
       German translation. "Wort und Musik im Melodramma." In *Musik-Konzepte* 10 (see item 423).

This frequently reprinted essay discusses difficulties presented by the highly stylized language and conventions of nineteenth-century Italian opera librettos and illustrates ways in which Verdi overcame them.

263. De Angelis, Marcello. *Le carte dell'impresario: Melodrama e costume teatrale nell'ottocento.* Florence: Sansoni, 1982. 283 p. + 46 p. plates. ML 1733.4 D4 1982.

A study of the role of the impresario in the production of operas in nineteenth-century Italy, focusing on the career of Alessandro Lanari. A major portion of the book (nearly 60 pages) reproduces letters and documents either written by or pertaining to Giuseppina Strepponi who, as a singer, was under contract with Lanari.

264. Dunning, Albert. "Verdi e lo storicismo musicale." *Atti 1* (item 224), 93–96.

Surveys Verdi's knowledge of early music, particularly Palestrina, and its influence on his own compositions.

265. Gerhard, Anselm. *Die Verstädterung der Oper: Paris und das Musiktheater des 19. Jahrhunderts.* Stuttgart: J.B. Metzler, 1992. 491 p. ISBN 3–476–00850–9. ML 1727.8 P2 G38 1992.
English translation by Mary Whitall. *The Urbanization of Opera: Music Theater in Paris in the Nineteenth Century.* Chicago: University of Chicago Press, forthcoming.

This impressive study of opera in Paris contains valuable background information relating to the influence of the French operatic tradition on Verdi. Two chapters focus exclusively on the composer. "Verdi und die Krise der Institutionen" (pp. 303–42) examines the composer's merging of French and Italian aesthetics in his treatment of *Les vêpres siciliennes*, while "Verdi und das Intérieur" (pp. 363–409) explores the influence of French *grand opéra* on a work not directly associated with the French tradition, *Un ballo in maschera*. The volume contains other interesting material relating to Verdi in addition to these two chapters, including the suggestion of a possible connection between Meyerbeer's *Le prophète* and *La forza del destino* in their mutual relationship to Schiller's *Wallensteins Lager*. The volume is a revised and enlarged version of the author's Ph.D. dissertation, "Großstadt und Großoper: Motive der *Grand Opéra* in Verdis *Les vêpres siciliennes* und ausgewählten Parisen Oper von Rossini und Meyerbeer" (Berlin: Technische Universität, 1985).

* Günther, Ursula. "Documents inconnus concernant les relations de Verdi avec l'Opéra de Paris." See item 95.

266. Jensen, Luke. "The Emergence of the Modern Conductor in 19th-Century
      Italian Opera." *Performance Practice Review* 4 (1991): 34–63.

      Offers a wide variety of documentation—including citations from treatises,
      articles from nineteenth-century periodicals, letters, and contemporary
      engravings of opera scenes—to trace the gradual shift in Italian opera from
      dividing the conducting responsibilities between the *violino principale* and the
      maestro al cembalo to the modern practice of a single baton-wielding conductor.
      Some of the principal conductors discussed in the article include Angelo
      Mariani, Emanuele Muzio, and Federico Ricci. For related articles about
      conducting practices and the *violino principale*, see items 745 and 960.

267. Kimbell, David. "The Young Verdi and Shakespeare." *Proceedings of the Royal
      Music Association* 101 (1974–75): 59–73.

      Surveys translations of Shakespeare available in the *primo ottocento* and
      Shakespeare reception in Italy during the same period. Examines ways in which
      Verdi's *Macbeth* departs from Shakespeare's play, as well as Shakespeare's
      influence on Verdi's shaping of the Grand Duet from Act I and the
      Sleepwalking Scene from Act IV. See item 765 for a more detailed examination
      of Shakespeare translations and their effect on the genesis of the libretto for
      Macbeth.

 *   ———. *Verdi in the Age of Italian Romanticism.* See item 162.

268. Lippmann, Friedrich. "Verdi und Bellini." In *Beiträge zur Geschichte der Oper*,
      77–88. Ed. by Heinz Becker. Studien zur Musikgeschichte des 19.
      Jahrhunderts, 15. Regensburg: Gustav Bosse, 1969. ML 1700.1 .B43.
      Abridged version published in *Atti 1* (item 224), 184–96.

      Proposes that Bellini's influence on Verdi is most clearly seen in the realm of
      melodic style. Some passages of Verdi even suggest specific models from the
      works of Bellini. A further connection is that Verdi followed Bellini's path of
      attempting to meld music more closely with the meaning of the text. In
      contrast, Verdi does not seem to have been especially influenced by any
      particular composer, including Bellini, in his ideas about the ideal opera libretto
      or operatic form but instead draws many ideas from the same general milieu as
      his contemporaries.

269. Longyear, R.M. "The 'banda sul palco': Wind Bands in Nineteenth-Century
      Opera." *Journal of Band Research* 13 (Spring 1978): 25–40.

      Provides general background information on the history of the wind band in
      nineteenth-century opera, discussing specific examples ranging from Meyerbeer
      to Mascagni. The author devotes a significant part of his essay to Verdi's use

of the wind band, noting a tendency over time for the composer to integrate it musically and dramatically into his operas rather than treating it as an independent ensemble.

* Luzio, Alessandro. *Carteggi verdiani.* See item 29.

270. Magnani, Luigi. "L'ignoranza musicale' di Verdi e la biblioteca di Sant'Agata." *Atti 3* (item 226), 250–57.

   Reprinted in *Quadrivium: Studi di filologia e musicologia* 14 (1973): 273–82.

   Although at times Verdi claimed to have little knowledge of music by other composers, the collection of scores in his library at Sant'Agata suggests that he had extensive knowledge of works by his European contemporaries and, to some extent, earlier composers. Verdi also owned a large collection of literature ranging from Shakespeare to contemporary continental writers.

271. Marchesi, Gustavo. *Giuseppe Verdi e il Conservatorio di Parma (1836–1901).* Musica a Parma. Parma: Editrice Tipolito La Ducale, 1976. 227 p. ML 410 .V4 M257.

   The title of this volume is somewhat misleading: the real focus of the work is not Verdi but the history of the Scuola del Carmine in Parma, which later became the Regia Scuola di Musica, and finally the Conservatorio di Parma. The volume contains some interesting information about performance practice relating to some of Verdi's works.

272. ———. "Verdi e Manzoni." *Atti 3* (item 226), 274–84.

   A broad study in aesthetics, suggesting some stylistic affinities between Manzoni's writings (primarily the tragedies *Il conte di Carmagnola* and *Adelchi* and the novel *I promessi sposi*) and Verdi's approach to composition.

* Martin, George. "Verdi, Manzoni, and the *Requiem.*" See item 984.

273. Martinotti, Sergio. "Verdi e lo strumentalismo italiano." *Atti 3* (item 226), 285–97.

   Opens with a brief survey of nineteenth-century Italian instrumental music and the reception of German instrumental music in Italy during this period. The author provides examples from *Un ballo in maschera* and *La forza del destino* that bear strong affinities to the music of Schubert and Mendelssohn. The closing section of the article assesses the place of Verdi's String Quartet among his compositions, proposing that its conception and style point toward later developments in the *Requiem, Falstaff,* and some of the *Quattro pezzi sacri.*

274. Mingardi, Corrado. "Verdi e Berlioz: In margine al viaggio della rappresentanza bussetana alle feste centenarie die la Côte Sainte-Andre." *Biblioteca '70* 1 (1970): 45–49.

Reproduces two documents relating to Verdi and Berlioz. The first is a brief invitation from Berlioz inviting Verdi to dinner; the other a letter from Berlioz to Gaëtano Belloni, Liszt's personal secretary, with favorable comments about Verdi's works. The author also cites portions of four letters from Verdi to various individuals that mention his opinion of Berlioz.

275. Nicastro, Aldo. "Il ruolo dell'intelletuale e del musicista tra Rivoluzione e Restaurazione." *Chigiana* 33/13 (1976): 199–210.

Examines the relationship of the Italian opera composer to the philosophical and political milieu in early nineteenth-century Italy.

276. Osthoff, Wolfgang. "Oper und Opernvers: Zur Funktion des Verses in der italienischen Oper." *Neue Zürcher Zeitung*, 8 October 1972, 51–52.

Expanded version in Italian translation by Leonardo Cavari: "Musica e versificazione: Funzioni del verso poetico nell'opera italiana." In *La drammaturgia musicale*, 125–41. Ed. by Lorenzo Bianconi. Bologna: Società Editrice il Mulino, 1986. ISBN 88–15–01127–7. ML 1700 .D72 1986.

Illustrates how powerfully the rhythmic shape of a particular operatic text can influence the composer's creative process. The author draws many of his examples from Verdi's *Aida*, in which the composer requested the librettist to provide certain passages with particular verse structure to support his intended musical effect. This article is an excellent, non-technical introduction to versification in Italian opera. See item 485 for a more detailed discussion of Italian versification and its application to Verdi.

277. Parker, Roger. "'Classical' Music in Milan During Verdi's Formative Years." In *Studies in Early Verdi* (item 377), 39–61.
Republished in *Studi musicali* 13 (1984): 259–74.

Public performances of Viennese Classical music in Milan seem to have been rare during Verdi's early years there. Verdi's use of music from Viennese Classic composers in his training of Emanuele Muzio suggests that the composer may have studied scores from this repertory during his tutelage with Vincenzo Lavigna.

278. Pestelli, Giorgio. "Verdi come compositore nazionale ed europeo." In *Atti del XIV Congresso della Società Internazionale di Musicologia: Trasmissione e recezione delle forme di cultura musicale*, 1: 721–26. Ed. by Angelo Pompilio,

Donatella Restani, Lorenzo Bianconi, and F. Alberto Gallo. 3 vols. Turin: Edizioni di Torino, 1990. ISBN 88–7063–084–6.

Discusses various ways in which Verdi's artistic production is, at the same time, Italian and European. While it is commonplace to think of Verdi's early works as being more Italian and nationalistic and his later ones as more European and cosmopolitan, the author argues that the situation is more complex. Already in his early years, Verdi had absorbed and internalized much foreign culture, primarily through social circles in Milan, and even in his later years the composer continued to emphasize Italian customs and ways of thinking. Pestelli also proposes that "European" culture—in the context of ottocento Italy— meant in large measure "French" culture, either through the original contributions of French writers, artists, and musicians or as the channel through which German, English, and Russian culture, ideas, and literature most commonly entered the Italian peninsula.

*   Pizzi, Italo. *Per il I° centenario della nascita di Giuseppe Verdi: Memorie— aneddoti—considerazioni.* See item 247.

279. Petrobelli, Pierluigi. "Verdi e la musica tedesca." In *Colloquium "Italien und Deutschland: Wechselbeziehungen in der Musik seit 1850" (Rom 1988),* 83–98. Ed. by Friedrich Lippmann. *Analecta musicologica,* 28. Laaber: Laaber-Verlag, 1993. ISBN 3–89007–272–0. ML 290.4 .C65 1988.

After a brief examination of Verdi's musical training with Vincenzo Lavigna and an overview of music by German composers in Verdi's personal library, the author focuses on the composer's attitude toward the music of Johann Sebastian Bach. Verdi had a lively interest in Bach's keyboard music, particularly as a consummate example of contrapuntal technique. In this regard, the author proposes that Bach was the most significant German composer for Verdi. Verdi was less enthusiastic about the non-keyboard works by Bach with which he was familiar; nevertheless, he returned to study some of them repeatedly through the last years of his life. Appendices to the article list pocket scores by Haydn, Mozart, and Beethoven and all scores by J.S. Bach in Verdi's library. A short discussion by conference participants follows on pp. 99–104 touching on, among other subjects, Verdi's String Quartet.

280. Qvamme, Börre. "Verdi e il realismo." *Atti 3* (item 226), 408–414.

Discusses the flowering of the "realism" movement in Paris during the mid-nineteenth century, centering around the composer-singer Pierre Dupont, the writers Champfleury and Baudelaire, and the painters Daumier, Millet, and Courbet. Verdi's trips to Paris brought him into contact with the realists, and the composer's choice of *Luisa Miller* and *La traviata* bears witness to his interest in the movement. Particularly in the case of *Luisa Miller*, Verdi treats his subject in a more direct and realistic manner than in earlier operas.

281. Reynolds, Barbara. "Verdi and Manzoni: An Attempted Explanation." *Music and Letters* 29 (1948): 31–43.

Compares and contrasts the lives and careers of Verdi and Alessandro Manzoni and discusses topics such as Manzoni's attitude toward music and the cult of veneration surrounding the famous author. Some of the author's conclusions have been refined in more recent research by George Martin and David Rosen (see items 984 and 986).

282. Roccatagliati, Alessandro. "Le forme dell'opera ottocentesca: Il caso Basevi." In *Le parole della musica, I: Studi sulla lingua della letteratura musicale in onore di Gianfranco Folena*, 311–34. Ed. by Fiamma Nicolodi and Paolo Trovato. Studi di musica veneta, 21. Florence: Olschki, 1994. ISBN 88–222–4284–X. ML 63 .P26 1994.

Examines Abramo Basevi's use of musical terminology in his critical writings, which often have different meanings (or nuances of meaning) than they do today. Many examples come from his writings about Verdi's operas. An appendix provides a complete catalogue of Basevi's writings about music for the *Gazzetta musicale di Firenze* and *L'armonia*.

283. ———. "Opera, opera-ballo, e *grand opéra*: Commistioni stilistiche e recezione critica nell'Italia teatrale di secondo ottocento." In *Opera & Libretto II*, 283–349. Studi di musica veneta. Florence: Olschki, 1993. ISBN 88–222–4064–2. ML 1700 .O655 1993.

Examines the differences among these three "types" of opera and their reception in Italy during the second half of the nineteenth century, focusing on the writings of critics such as Abramo Basevi, Filippo Filippi, Antonio Ghislanzoni, and Alberto Mazzucato. The article sheds particularly interesting light on the reception of *Don Carlo* in Italy but touches on other Verdi operas as well.

284. Rosselli, John. *Music and Musicians in Nineteenth-Century Italy*. London: B.T. Batsford; Portland, Ore.: Amadeus, 1991. 160 p. ISBN 0–7134–6153–5 (British); 0–931340–40–3 (American). ML 290.4 .R65 1991.
      Italian Translation by Paolo Russo. *Sull'ali dorate: Il mondo musicale italiano dell'ottocento*. Intersezioni, 98. Bologna: Società Editrice il Mulino, 1992. 176 p. ISBN 88–15–03250–9. ML 290.4 .R68 1992.

Surveys the musical and cultural milieu in nineteenth-century Italy. Two particularly interesting chapters, entitled "The Roots of Musical Life" and "The Musician's Life," provide a sociological perspective. Other chapters consider the influence of the *Risorgimento* movement, political unification, and Europeanization on musical life in Italy. The index in the Italian translation is limited to names of people.

285. ———. *The Opera Industry in Italy from Cimarosa to Verdi: The Role of the Impresario.* Cambridge: Cambridge University Press, 1984. viii, 214 p. ISBN 0–521–25732–8 (cloth); 0–521–27867–8 (paper). ML 1733 .R78 1984.

Expanded Italian version. *L'impresario d'opera: Arte e affari nel teatro musicale italiano dell'ottocento.* Biblioteca di cultura musicale: Documenti. Turin: Edizioni di Torino, 1985. ix, 279 p. ISBN 88–7063–037–4. ML 1733 .R7813 1985.

Provides valuable background material concerning the business and economic side of operatic production in Italy during Verdi's time. Although the text focuses on the role of the impresarios, it also touches on related subjects, such as musical journalism and the increasingly significant role played by music publishers. In place of a traditional bibliography, the volume offers a two-page prose summary of suggestions for further reading and research. The volume includes an index. In addition to this material, the Italian translation provides a biographical dictionary of impresarios and about 60 pages of excerpts from both previously published and unpublished documents.

286. ———. *Singers of Italian Opera: The History of a Profession.* Cambridge: Cambridge University Press, 1992. xiv, 272 p. ISBN 0–521–41683–3 (cloth); 0–521–42697–9 (paper). ML 1460 .R68 1992.

Italian translation by Paolo Russo. *Il cantante d'opera: Storia di una professione (1600–1900).* Bologna: Società Editrice il Mulino, 1993. 305 p. ISBN 88–15–0–4175–3. ML 1460 .R6816 1993.

Charts the sociological, economic, and cultural dynamics of Italian opera singers from the early seventeenth century to the present. Chapters discussing the training of singers and day-to-day aspects of their professional careers are particularly informative. The author's "Note on Further Reading" contains a concise bibliographic essay that includes suggestions about locating primary source material.

287. ———. "Verdi e la storia della retribuzione del compositore italiano." *Studi verdiani* 2 (1983): 11–28.

A study of Verdi's earnings, contracts with his publishers, and attempts to firmly establish copyright set against the background of his contemporaries, most notably Bellini and Donizetti.

288. Sala, Emilio. "Verdi and the Parisian Boulevard Theatre, 1847–9." *Cambridge Opera Journal* 7 (1995): 185–205.

Examines Parisian boulevard theater during Verdi's first stay in Paris (summer of 1847 through summer of 1849) and its possible influence on the composer's dramaturgical ideas. The article focuses on Félix Pyat's *Le chiffonnier de Paris* (with music composed by Auguste Pilati), *Le chevalier de maison-rouge* by Alexandre Dumas and Auguste Maquet (with music by Alphonse Varney), Dumas' *Monte-Cristo* (with music by Maquet); Frédérick Lemaître's *Robert Macaire*, and *Le pasteur ou l'évangile et le foyer* by Emile Souvestre and Eugène Bourgeois (the source of the story for *Stiffelio*). The author discusses the musical accompaniment to *Le pasteur* in some detail, drawing some parallels from both the play and the music to Verdi's later adaptation of the work. Sala also establishes that several items from Verdi's list of potential operatic subjects correspond to plays on the Parisian stage during these years: Adolphe Dennery's *Marie Jeanne, ou la femme du peuple*; Chateaubriand's *Atala*, adapted for the stage by Dumas; Shakespeare's *Hamlet*; and *Intrigue et amour*, Dumas' adaptation of Schiller's *Kabale und Liebe*, which became the basis for *Luisa Miller*.

289.   Santi, Piero. "Contenuti e motivazioni storico-culturali nel teatro di Verdi." *Per un "progetto Verdi" anni '80* (item 232), 109–18.

Discusses the operas of Donizetti and rapidly changing cultural norms as principal elements in the formation of Verdi's aesthetics.

290.   Tomlinson, Gary. "Italian Romanticism and Italian Opera: An Essay in Their Affinities." *19th Century Music* 10 (1986–87): 43–60.

An excellent concise introduction to the musical and cultural milieu in which Verdi began his work. The author draws attention to two important philosophical essays: "Sulla maniera e la utilità delle traduzioni" by Anne-Louise-Germaine Necker, Madame de Staël-Holstein (1816), which urged Italians to renew their theatrical tradition through acquaintance with foreign plays, and Giuseppe Mazzini's *Filosofia della musica* (1835–36), which called for operatic reform through a new kind of *tinta* in music and a more sophisticated individuality of characterization. The article illustrates how these ideals of a new Italian romanticism took root in opera from the works of Rossini, gradually began to put forth new shoots in the operas of Bellini and Donizetti, and finally blossomed in the works of Verdi. The author singles out *I due Foscari* as exemplifying the principles for the "opera of the future" outlined in Mazzini's *Filosofia*.

291.   Walker, Frank. "Mercadante and Verdi." *Music and Letters* 33 (1952): 311–21; 34 (1953): 33–38.

The first part of the article is largely a refutation of uncomplimentary assertions about Verdi and his relationship to Neapolitan musical life made by Biagio

Notarnicola's *Saverio Mercadante nella gloria e nella luce* (1949). The second part of the article considers the influence of Mercadante's music on the development of Verdi's musical style. Walker argues that Verdi quickly rose above the ability of his contemporary and that Mercadante's influence was probably minimal. He allows an exception, however, for *La vestale*. Walker proposes that Verdi subconsciously assimilated many features of this work, which later rose to the surface as he was working on *Aida*.

292. Weaver, William. "Verdi the Playgoer." *Musical Newsletter* 6/1 (1976): 3–8, 24.

Examines the relationship and interaction between spoken theater and opera in ottocento Italy. Verdi's choice of authors (only one of his texts—*I lombardi*—was based on an Italian work) shows that he was both an avid playgoer and play-reader and that he was familiar with the international repertory of his period. The plays of Vittorio Alfieri and Eugène Scribe were especially popular in Italy during Verdi's formative years and undoubtedly influenced the composer's ideas about dramaturgy. The plays of Shakespeare were not performed in Italy until the mid-nineteenth century, and then often received a hostile reception. While the taste of Italian theater-going audiences was generally quite conservative, opera audiences were quicker to accept more sophisticated and avant-garde repertory.

293. Weiss, Piero. "'Sacred Bronzes': Paralipomena to an Essay by Dallapiccola." *19th Century Music* 9 (1985–86): 42–49.
    Italian translation. "'Sacri bronzi': Note in calce a un noto saggio di Luigi Dallapiccola." In *Opera & Libretto I*, 149–63. Studi di musica veneta. Florence: Olschki, 1990. ISBN 88–222–3825–7. ML 1700 .O655 1990.

Responds to Dallapiccola's widely reproduced essay about the language of nineteenth-century opera librettos (item 262). Weiss discusses the long legacy of language found in opera librettos in various types of Italian poetry and proposes that this elevated poetic style reached a high point in the Romantic poetry of the Risorgimento period.

294. Zanetti, Emilia. "Palestrina e Verdi: I motivi di una rettifica." In *Colloquium "Verdi-Wagner" Rom 1969: Bericht* (item 227), 250–54.

Examines the growing interest in the music of Palestrina and his contemporaries during the second quarter of the nineteenth century and suggests that Verdi may well have been familiar with some music by Palestrina as early as the 1840s.

POLITICAL & SOCIAL MILIEU

295. Di Stefano, Carlo. *La censura teatrale in Italia (1600–1962)*. Documenti di teatro, 29. Rocca San Casciano: Cappelli, [1964]. 152 p. + 16 p. illustrations. PN 2044 .I8257.

Offers a broad survey of censorship in Italian theaters over a span of nearly four centuries. While not restricted to opera, this volume provides useful and interesting background for any study of Verdi that involves the issue of censorship. The study includes a useful bibliography of more specialized sources listed according to time period.

296. Luzio, Alessandro. "Verdi e Mazzini." In *Carteggi verdiani* (item 29), 2:52–57.

Criticizes the notion that Verdi was affiliated with either Freemasonry or with Giuseppe Mazzini in the secret society of the *Carbonari*.

297. Martin, George. "Verdi and the Risorgimento." In *Aspects of Verdi* (item 244), 3–28.
An earlier version of this article appeared in *The Verdi Companion* (item 5), 13–41.

Examines the political milieu of Europe during the time of Verdi, focusing on the unification of Italy and the Risorgimento movement. The author also discusses the composer's treatment of political topics in his music and the influence of Verdi's political milieu on the general tone of his works. Martin proposes that even in many of his later works, Verdi continued to use Risorgimento themes, translated into "abstractions."

298. Parakilas, James. "Political Representation and the Chorus in Nineteenth-Century Opera." *19th Century Music* 16 (1992–93): 181–202.

Argues that partisan political disputes were a distinctive feature of nineteenth-century opera, carried out largely through the medium of the chorus. The author traces the historical roots of this phenomenon to the period of pre-revolutionary France and examines the subsequent use of the chorus to represent "the people," divided choruses to represent opposing factions, and staging to reinforce the representation of individuals as proxies for the people. The discussion includes examples from the Verdi repertory, including *Don Carlos*, *Simon Boccanegra*, and *Aida*.

299. Parker, Roger. *"Sull'ali dorate": The Verdian Patriotic Chorus in the 1840s*. Parma: Istituto Nazionale di Studi Verdiani, forthcoming.

This forthcoming volume will, among other things, reassess the extent to which Verdi's early choruses represented a political agenda.

300. Pauls, Birgit. *Giuseppe Verdi und das Risorgimento: Ein politischer Mythos im Prozeß der Nationenbildung.* Ph.D. dissertation, U. Frankfurt am Main, 1996. Berlin: Akademie Verlag, 1996. 353 p. ISBN 3–05–003013–5. ML 410 .V4 P18 1996.

This important new study challenges long-held notions about the extent to which Verdi and his music played a decisive role in the unification of Italy in the mid-nineteenth century. Pauls argues that historians have selectively manipulated evidence to suggest that Verdi's music promoted a strong political agenda. She analyzes Verdi's elevation to the stature of a national hero at the end of the nineteenth century and his posthumous reputation based on the model of mythical systems developed by cultural anthropologists Hans Blumenberg and Claude Lévi-Strauss. The volume contains an extensive discussion of the Risorgimento movement in Italy. Compositions examined in special detail include: Verdi's hymns, occasional pieces, and "patriotic" choruses; *La battaglia di Legnano; Les vêpres siciliennes; Simon Boccanegra;* and *Un ballo in maschera.* For the latter opera, the author compares Somma's libretto with a heavily censored version (proposed by the Neapolitan authorities but rejected by Verdi) that placed the conflict between the Guelfs and the Ghibellines in fourteenth-century Florence. Pointing to details in *La traviata, Luisa Miller,* and *Falstaff,* Pauls proposes that Verdi's operas are more important as reflections and commentary on contemporary social conflicts than for their reputed political messages. Other topics discussed include Verdi's service as a Senator, his representation in nineteenth-century school books, reassessments of his reception by Mussolini and the fascists and by Franz Werfel, and the composer's relationship to Wagner. The volume features a substantial bibliography and a name index.

301. Petrobelli, Pierluigi. "Verdi, la Francia, e l'Italia unita: Una lettera a Léon Escudier." In *Omaggio a Gianfranco Folena,* 2:1749–57. Padua: Editoriale Programma, 1993. 2 vols. ISBN 88–71231–05–8. PC 1026 .F65 O63 1993.

Examines Verdi's attitudes toward the unification of Italy and the political aspirations of Napoleon III in France. A previously unpublished letter written to Léon Escudier on 11 November 1860 serves as focal point for the discussion, although the author provides a wealth of background information touching on the composer's relationship to both his French and Italian publishers, his future compositional plans, and the historical-political milieu of the period.

302. Rindo, John Patrick. "A Structural Analysis of Giuseppe Verdi's Early Operas and Their Influence on the Italian Risorgimento." Ph.D. dissertation, University of Oregon, 1984. xi, 322 p.

Examines the influences of the Italian Risorgimento movement on *Nabucco, I lombardi, Ernani, Giovanna d'Arco, Attila, Macbeth,* and *La battaglia di Legnano* and ways in which these operas may have influenced the movement. The author focuses on the areas of dramatic structure, characterization, themes, and theatrical imagery. The dissertation also provides useful information about the Risorgimento movement as a political and social force.

CHAPTER 9

Performance History; Reception; Locative Studies

Studies cited in this chapter concern the reception of Verdi's music in general as well as more specialized examinations about the performance and reception of his music in specific locations. The locative studies are listed by country except for the Italian peninsula, which is categorized by city. Readers wishing to pursue an investigation of Verdi's music in particular cities or opera houses should also consult the numerous published theater chronicles and general musical histories of cities and regions, which are not listed in this bibliography.

PERFORMANCE HISTORY & GENERAL STUDIES OF RECEPTION

303. Kaufman, Thomas G. *Verdi and His Major Contemporaries: A Selected Chronology of Performances with Casts.* With the Research Assistance of Marion Kaufman. Garland Reference Library of the Humanities, 1016. New York: Garland, 1990. xxiv, 590 p. ISBN 0–8240–4106–2. ML 128 .O4 K4.

About half of the main chronology is devoted to Verdi; the remainder covers nearly 200 operas by seventeen of his contemporaries (including figures such as Emanuele Muzio, Arrigo Boito, Giovanni Bottesini, Saverio Mercadante, and Franco Faccio). An appendix lists the most successful works of about another dozen composers (including some works written jointly by several composers). Nineteenth-century performances are generally covered more thoroughly than those from the twentieth century. The geographical coverage is very broad, although the author notes that there are gaps, especially in Spain, southern Italy, the Balkans, and Eastern Europe. This volume will be especially useful for those interested in the reception of Verdi's operas outside the largest centers in Italy, which often have their own published chronologies. The author has included a bibliography and list of newpapers and periodicals consulted. The index contains only titles of operas. Linda B. Fairtile has published separate indexes for composers and librettists listed in the volume (see item 304).

304. Fairtile, Linda B. "Two Appendices for Thomas G. Kaufman's *Verdi and His Major Contemporaries.*" *Verdi Newsletter* 20 (1992): 16–21.

Provides an index of composers and an index of librettists for Kaufman's volume (item 303).

305. Mila, Massimo. "Fétis e Verdi, ovvero gli infortuni della critica." *Atti 3* (item 226), 312–21.

Examines the negative treatment of Verdi's music in the writings of the music critic François-Joseph Fétis, with special attention given to an article published in the *Revue et gazette musicale* on 13 September 1850.

306. ———. "Verdi e Hanslick." *La rassegna musicale* 21 (1951): 212–24. Reprinted in *L'arte di Verdi* (item 375), 316–30.

After surveying Eduard Hanslick's position among nineteenth-century music critics who were familiar with Verdi's works, the author offers an important examination of Hanslick's reaction to Verdi's music in his *Die moderne Oper* and other writings. With the exception of *Ernani*, the Viennese music critic did not regard Verdi's early operas favorably. He saw a new, more elevated style developing with the grand trilogy of *Rigoletto*, *Il trovatore*, and *La traviata*, which he attributed to the influence of French elements from the music of Meyerbeer. For Verdi's later operas, Hanslick carefully argues against any direct influence from the music of Wagner. He sees *Aida* as the peak of Verdi's production, criticizing *Otello* for a lack of youthful fire and spirit. Mila argues that Hanslick was one of the first important critics to subscribe to the idea, still accepted by some today, that Verdi's best creations were those written in a "popular" idiom, and that *Otello* and *Falstaff* show a deterioration of style.

* Parker, Roger. "On Reading Nineteenth-Century Opera: Verdi through the Looking Glass." See item 429.

* Pestelli, Giorgio. "Verdi come compositore nazionale ed europeo." See item 278.

307. Petrobelli, Pierluigi. "Un caso di trasmissione e recezione delle forme di cultura musicale: La musica di Verdi." In *Atti del XIV Congresso della Società Internazionale di Musicologia: Trasmissione e recezione delle forme di cultura musicale*, 1: 693–98. Ed. by Angelo Pompilio, Donatella Restani, Lorenzo Bianconi, and F. Alberto Gallo. 3 vols. Turin: Edizioni di Torino, 1990. ISBN 88–7063–084–6.

Reprinted in English translation as "The Music of Verdi: An Example of the Transmission and Reception of Musical Culture." *Verdi Newsletter* 15 (1987): 3–6.

Some of Verdi's operas achieved immediate and lasting popularity, primarily due to catchy tunes that could be performed and enjoyed outside the context of the entire opera. This type of reception contrasts sharply with the composer's own aesthetics, which focused on the dramatic unity of the entire work, achieved primarily through subtle musical means. The author proposes that the recognition of this dramatic unity has been the most important factor leading to the recent interest in live performances of the entire corpus of Verdi's works.

308. Tintori, Giampiero. "Da *Oberto* a *Falstaff*: Le prime." *Musica e dossier* 2 (December 1986), special insert, 33–42.

This profusely illustrated article surveys the reception of each of Verdi's operas at their premiere.

LOCATIVE STUDIES

Belgium

309. Van Der Linden, Albert. "Les "premières' d'*Aida* et d'*Othello* en Belgique." In *Giuseppe Verdi: Scritti raccolti in occasione delle "Celebrazioni Verdiane" dell'VIII Settimana Musicale* (item 243), 87–92.

After reviewing the early history of Verdi performances in Belgium, the author examines the reception of performances of *Aida* and *Otello* at the Théâtre de la Monnaie in 1877 and 1902 respectively. Van Der Linden also briefly discusses the negative views of Belgian music critic François-Joseph Fétis toward Verdi.

Chile

310. Hamlet-Metz, Mario. "Verdi nell'ultimo confine del nuovo mondo: La diffusione della sua musica in Cile durante l'ottocento." *Quadrivium: Studi di filologia e musicologia* 27 (1986): 177–88. This volume of *Quadrivium* is listed in some indexes as a monograph: *Universalità della musica, prestigio dell'Italia, attualità di Verdi: Studi in onore di Mario Medici*, Vol. 2. Ed. by Giuseppe Vecchi. Bologna: Antiquae Musicae Italicae Studiosi, 1986.

Surveys the performance and reception of Verdi's operas in nineteenth-century Chile. Almost all performances of Verdi's music were well received due, in part, to the excellent singers who travelled from Europe. The article includes a short bibliography of general materials dealing with musical life in Chile.

England

311. Chusid, Martin. "Casts for the Verdi Premieres in London (1845–1977)." *AIVS Newsletter* 5 (June 1978): 13–17; 6 (March 1979): 15–19.

     A chronological list of London premieres of Verdi's works, with information about place, date, casts, and conductors. The author provides biographical and explanatory notes about many of the cast members. One additional item is included as an addendum in *Verdi Newsletter* 11 (March 1983): 31.

312. Hussey, Dyneley. "Verdi in England." In *Giuseppe Verdi: Scritti raccolti in occasione delle "Celebrazioni Verdiane" dell'VIII Settimana Musicale* (item 243), 27–36.

     A brief study of the reception of Verdi's works in England divided into two periods: 1839–1901 and 1901–1950. The author includes a discussion of Verdi's two trips to England (1847 and 1862). The second portion of the article focuses on the effect of Wagner's popularity on the reception of Verdi's works during the early decades of the twentieth century and the renewal of interest in his music during the period following the end of World War I.

313. Schlitzer, Franco. "Verdi a Londra nel 1847." In *Giuseppe Verdi: Scritti raccolti in occasione delle "Celebrazioni Verdiane" dell'VIII Settimana Musicale* (item 243), 61–79.

     A detailed study of Verdi's trip to London to supervise the premiere performance of *I masnadieri*, relying largely on the letters of Emanuele Muzio (item 72). The author includes citations from contemporary reviews of the performances.

France

314. Bloom, Peter. "A Note on Verdi in Paris." *Verdi Newsletter* 16 (1988): 18–21.

     Examines Verdi's mixed feelings about France. While the composer admired many traits of French culture and musicians, he disliked the insolence he felt they displayed. The author discusses in detail Verdi's confrontation with Pierre-Louis Dietsch, conductor at the Paris Opéra, just before the premiere of *Les vêpres siciliennes* in 1863.

315. Goury, Jean. "Verdi et la France." *Atti 2* (item 225), 565–72.

     An overview of the reception of Verdi's music in France.

316. Mancini, Roland. "Y a t-il une renaissance-Verdi en France?" *Atti 3* (item 226), 258–73.

Discusses the increasingly favorable reception of Verdi's works in France since World War II and analyzes issues that have either hindered or helped the popularity of Verdi's operas among the French public. The article concludes with a list of operas broadcast over radio in Paris from 1948 through 1972 with major cast members and directors.

317. Meloncelli, Raoul. "Giuseppe Verdi e la critica francese." *Studi verdiani* 9 (1993): 97–122.

Surveys the reception of Verdi's music in France, focusing particularly on reviews published in the *Revue des deux mondes*. Paul Scudo's reviews of early and middle works tended to be critical, although he wrote more positively about *Les vêpres siciliennes* and *Un ballo in maschera*. Later critics, including Henry Blaze de Bury, Camille Bellaigue, and Arthur Pougin were generally both enthusiastic and laudatory. The article contains extensive quotations from French periodicals and other sources, primarily between 1850 and 1910.

318. Petit, Pierre. "Verdi et la France." In *Giuseppe Verdi: Scritti raccolti in occasione delle "Celebrazioni Verdiane" dell'VIII Settimana Musicale* (item 243), 37–47.

A concise study on Verdi's activities in France and the initial reception of his French operas in that country.

319. Pistone, Danièle. "Verdi et la critique musicale française: Aspects et évolution de 1860 à 1993." In *Le parole della musica, II: Studi sul lessico della letteratura critica del teatro musicale in onore di Gianfranco Folena*, 295–305. Ed. by Maria Teresa Muraro. Studi di musica veneta, 22. Florence: Olschki, 1995. ISBN 88-222-4340-4. ML 63 .P26 1994.

A survey of the reception of Verdi's music in France based on a linguistic analysis of 500 articles drawn from five periodicals (*L'art musicale* [1860–94], *Diapason* [1992–93], *Le ménestrel* [1860–1940], *Le monde de la musique [1978–93]*, and *Musica* [1902–14]) and three archives (the Bibliothèque de l'Opéra, the fonds *Montpensier* of the Départment de la Musique at the Bibliothèque Nationale, and the fonds *Paul-Marie Masson* at the Bibliothèque de Musicologie at the Université de Paris-Sorbonne). Across the entire spectrum of time, the terms *"force," "passion"* and *"dramatique"* remain exceptionally important. The author also considers how descriptive terms have changed over time, tending to become more visual, more precise, and less tactile in their orientation.

Genoa

320. Resasco, Ferdinando. *Verdi a Genova: Ricordi, aneddoti, e episodi.* Genoa: Fratelli Pagano, 1901. 111 p. ML 410 .V48 R42.

Presents a series of anecdotes, primarily concerned with events that took place in Genoa and the reception of Verdi's works there. The volume also reproduces some correspondence, contains a series of short reminiscences by Giuseppe De Amicis, and reproduces what is billed as the last photograph of Verdi, taken by Enrico Alberto d'Albertis on a visit to Sant'Agata in September 1900.

Germany/Austria

321. Conati, Marcello. "Saggio di critiche e cronache verdiane dalla *Allgemeine musikalische Zeitung* di Lipsia." In *Il melodramma italiano dell'ottocento: Studi e ricerche per Massimo Mila*, 13–43. Ed. by Giorgio Pestelli. Saggi, 575. Turin: Einaudi, 1977. ML 1733.4 .M5.

A survey of writings about Verdi's works in the *Allgemeine musikalische Zeitung* through 1848. These reviews of Verdi's early works were, for the most part, somewhat negative, paralleling the sentiment of reviews about the composer's music in other Germanic periodicals of the era.

322. Hermet, August. "Verdi e la civiltà germanica." In *Giuseppe Verdi: Scritti raccolti in occasione delle "Celebrazioni Verdiane" dell'VIII Settimana Musicale* (item 243), 9–26.

Discusses a variety of topics, including: Verdi's relationship to the aesthetics of German romanticism, the historical positions of Verdi and Wagner, and the Verdi Renaissance in Germany beginning in the 1920s with the efforts of Franz Werfel.

323. Hortschansky, Klaus. "Die Herausbildung eines deutsch-sprachigen Verdi-Repertoires im 19. Jahrhundert und die zeitgenössische Kritik. In *Colloquium "Verdi-Wagner" Rom 1969: Bericht* (item 227), 140–84.

An important study of the reception of Verdi's works performed in translation in Germanic lands during the nineteenth century. An appendix lists performances discussed in the article by opera and city, allowing ready access for readers interested in specific locales or/and operas. After a list of general sources, the bibliography also contains a section categorized by individual city. A summary table lists the dates for first performances of *Nabucco, Ernani, Rigoletto, Trovatore, Traviata, Ballo, Aida, Otello,* and *Falstaff* on 23 German-speaking stages (both German and Italian performances are listed for Vienna).

324. Martin, George. "Franz Werfel and the 'Verdi Renaissance.'" In *Aspects of Verdi* (item 244), 61–77.

Outlines the decline in popularity in Verdi's works, which reached a low point in the first two decades of the twentieth century, the reasons for the decline, and the role of Franz Werfel in starting a "Verdi Renaissance" in German-speaking countries. Although his semi-historical *Verdi: Ein Roman der Oper*, published in 1924, became enormously popular in Europe, Werfel's subsequent activities presenting speeches, publishing articles as well as the first collection of the composer's letters in a language other than Italian, translating librettos, and freely arranging *La forza del destino* were also important in reviving Verdi's popularity. The author includes a detailed description of *Verdi: Ein Roman der Oper*.

325. Walker, Frank. "Verdi and Vienna: With Some Unpublished Letters." *Musical Times* 92 (1951): 403–05, 451–53.
Reprinted in Italian translation. "Verdi a Vienna (con alcune lettere inedite)." In *Giuseppe Verdi: Scritti raccolti in occasione delle "Celebrazioni Verdiane" dell'VIII Settimana Musicale* (item 243), 49–60.

Describes Verdi's trips to Vienna in 1843 for performances of *Nabucco* and in 1875 for performances of the *Requiem*. Perhaps the most valuable part of this article are the citations of Verdi's letters that refer to Vienna in some way. Walker also cites contemporary reviews of the performances supervised by the composer.

Holland

326. Bottenheim, S.A.M. "La musica di Verdi in Olanda." In *Giuseppe Verdi: Scritti raccolti in occasione delle "Celebrazioni Verdiane" dell'VIII Settimana Musicale* (item 243), 103–4.

A cursory summary of early performances of Verdi's operas in the Netherlands. The most successful works were *Ballo in maschera* and *Il trovatore*.

Hungary

327. Várnai, Péter Pál. "Verdi magyarországon." *Verdi: Bollettino dell'Istituto di Studi Verdiani* 2 [No. 5] (1966): 949–87; 3 [No. 7] (1969–82): 246–86, and 3 [No. 8] (1973): 1038–82. An Italian translation appears in vol. 2, 988–1030 and vol. 3, 287–332, 1083–1129; English and German translations may be found in vol. 2, 1429–1503 and vol. 3, 718–89, 1409–1484.
Later reissued in monograph form (Budapest: Zeneműkiadó, 1975, 219 p.). This version contains a table showing first performances of Verdi's works in Hungary and a discography.

The first portion of the article dealing with the reception of Verdi's works in Hungary covers the years 1846–84 and concentrates on performances held in Pest. The earliest complete operas to be performed in Hungary were *Ernani* and *Nabucco*; they were more successful in Hungarian-language performances than the very first ones in Italian. Verdi's works were championed by Ferenc Erkel, manager of the National Theater. Although Erkel brought most of

Verdi's later works to the stages of Hungary, their success never quite equalled that of the *Ernani* and *Nabucco*. Part two of the article (published in vol. 3) examines the period from the closing of the National Theater (1885) through the post-World War II era. *Otello* was particularly successful in early Hungarian performances. The early years of the twentieth century saw a revival of interest in Verdi's operas, which were frequently revived with modern stage settings. After World War II, Verdi performances continued to flourish in Hungary, including some works performed for the first time in the country.

Japan

328. Fukuhara, Nobuo. "Verdi in Giappone." *Atti* 2 (item 225), 560–64.

A cursory overview of the reception of Verdi's music in Japan from 1913 through the 1960s.

Milan

*   Morazzoni, G., ed. *Verdi: Lettere inedite*; G.M. Ciampelli. *Le opere verdiane al Teatro alla Scala (1839–1929)*. See item 33.

329. Tintori, Giampiero. "Verdi in Milan." *The Verdi Companion* (item 5), 43–66.

A short essay followed by a set of illustrations that include paintings and photographs of people associated with the composer, facsimile reproductions from Verdi's autograph scores, librettos, production books, musical scores, and costume designs associated with productions at La Scala.

Montecatini

330. Lubrani, Mauro, with Vasco Ferretti. *Giuseppe Verdi a Montecatini: L'ultima grande stagione creative del Maestro (1880–1901)*. Edizioni Montecatini, 7. Montecatini Termi: Edizioni Montecatini, 1981. 137 p.

Documents in essays and pictures Verdi's many trips to this well-known resort during the last decades of his life. The volume contains a wealth of iconographic material; it also includes a chronology of Verdi's life, a list of works with information about premieres, and a short bibliography.

Naples

331. Conati, Marcello. "Verdi per Napoli." In *Il Teatro di San Carlo 1737–1987. Vol. 2: L'opera, Il ballo*, 225–66. Ed. by Bruno Cagli and Agostino Ziino. Naples: Electa Napoli, 1987. ISBN 88–435–2414–3 (set). ML 290.8 N2 M3 1987.

A detailed examination of the performance and reception of Verdi's operas in Naples between 1841 and 1873, focusing on his personal involvement in productions of *Alzira* (1845), *Luisa Miller* (1849), *Un ballo in maschera* (scheduled for 1858, but not performed there), *Don Carlo* (1872) and *Aida* (1873).

Poland

332. Chodkowski, Andrzej. "Verdi sulle scene di Varsavia." *Quadrivium: Studi di filologia e musicologia* 27 (1986): 189–98. This volume of *Quadrivium* is listed in some indexes as a monograph: *Universalità della musica, prestigio dell'Italia, attualità di Verdi: Studi in onore di Mario Medici*, Vol. 2. Ed. by Giuseppe Vecchi. Bologna: Antiquae Musicae Italicae Studiosi, 1986.

A brief survey of the performance and reception of Verdi's music in nineteenth-century Warsaw. Verdi's music reached a new level of popularity in the late 1850s and early 1860s when *Rigoletto, Il trovatore,* and *La traviata* became his first work to be performed in Polish.

333. Glinski, Matteo. "Verdi e la Polonia." In *Giuseppe Verdi: Scritti raccolti in occasione delle "Celebrazioni Verdiane" dell'VIII Settimana Musicale* (item 243), 93–101.

A short description of the reception of Verdi's works in Poland is followed by an assessment of the influence of his style on several Polish composers of opera, including: Jozef Brzowski, Stanislaw Moniuszko, Wladyslaw Zelenski, and Ignac Jan Paderewski.

Rome

334. Belli, Adriano, and Ceccarius. *Verdi e Roma: Celebrazione verdiana 27 gennaio 1951.* Preface by Salvatore Rebecchini. Rome: Teatro dell'Opera di Roma, 1951. 60 p. ML 410 .V4 E5.

This elegantly illustrated, limited edition commemorative volume contains essays about Verdi's operas written for Rome and the first Roman performances of his other works.

Russia

335. Martinov, Ivan. "Verdi in Russia." *Quadrivium: Studi di filologia e musicologia* 27 (1986): 167–76. This volume of *Quadrivium* is listed in some indexes as a monograph: *Universalità della musica, prestigio dell'Italia, attualità di Verdi: Studi in onore di Mario Medici*, Vol. 2. Ed. by Giuseppe Vecchi. Bologna: Antiquae Musicae Italicae Studiosi, 1986.

Surveys the reception of Verdi's music in Russia, beginning with the St. Petersburg performance of *I lombardi* in 1845. Much of the article focuses on Verdi's trips to Russia for the premiere of *Forza*. The author also examines Tchaikovsky's reaction to Verdi's music.

Trieste

336. Manganaro, Ciro. *Verdi cantore del Risorgimento nella passione degli Irredenti.* Trieste: Unione degli Istriani, [1993]. 45 p.

    A short study of Verdi as a political and social hero among the people of Trieste and the surrounding regions of Istria and Dalmatia.

337. *La passione verdiana di Trieste: Giuseppe Verdi e Trieste.* Trieste: Comune di Trieste, 1951. 87 p. + 11 plates. ML 410 .V4 P17.

    A commemorative volume containing a number of short essays dealing with the reception of Verdi's works (with a special emphasis on *Stiffelio*, which was premiered there, and on the first performances of other Verdi operas in Trieste) and the history of the Teatro Comunale G. Verdi.

338. Stefani, Giuseppe. *Verdi e Trieste.* Trieste: Comune di Trieste, 1951. 291 p. ML 410 .V48 S816.

    Presents a detailed study of the reception of Verdi's music in Trieste, focusing on performances during the composer's lifetime, with particular emphasis on the two operas composed especially for the city: *Il corsaro* and *Stiffelio*. The volume includes a useful index of names and titles of works, a large number of illustrations, and a bibliography that emphasizes other specialized studies about Verdi and Trieste or works about Verdi published in Trieste.

United States

339. Bello, John. "Verdi a New York." *Atti 2* (item 225), 509–15.

    A brief overview of the history of Verdi performances in New York, focusing on the American premiere of *Don Carlo* in 1877.

340. Chusid, Martin. "Casts for the Verdi Premieres in the U.S. (1847–1876)." *AIVS Newsletter* 2 (December 1976): 16–18; 3 (June 1977): 11–12.

    Lists U.S. premieres of Verdi's works chronologically, with information about place, date, casts, and conductors. The author provides biographical and explanatory notes about many of the cast members. One additional item is included as an addendum in the *Verdi Newsletter* 11 (March 1983): 31.

341. Hixon, Don L. *Verdi in San Francisco, 1851–1869: A Preliminary Bibliography.* [Irvine, Calif.: the author], 1980. vi, 89 p. ML 410 .V4 H591.

A listing, by opera, of performances in San Francisco, including dates, theaters, cast information, and references to reviews in five area newspapers.

342. Martin, George. *Verdi at the Golden Gate: Opera and San Francisco in the Gold Rush Years.* Berkeley: University of California Press, 1993. xxii, 321p. ISBN 0–520–08123–4. ML 1711.8 .S2 M37.

This volume offers an unusually detailed analysis of the reception of Verdi's operas in San Francisco from 1851–1860, framed within a larger-scale study of the way in which opera reached the far Western frontier of America. Operas performed during this period included *Ernani, Il trovatore, La traviata, I due Foscari, Nabucco, I lombardi, Rigoletto,* and *Attila.* There were also a number of performances of a pastiche entitled *Judith,* with music taken from several of Verdi's early operas. Martin suggests that audiences reacted favorably to Verdi's works to a large extent because they identified with issues raised by the plots. A series of useful appendices list opera premieres with theater, cast, and number of performances; information about the principal theaters in the city; maps of San Francisco's theater district; a short essay on tuning and transposition practices; a comparative table showing world, Western hemisphere, and San Francisco premieres of Verdi's operas, with cast information for productions in San Francisco; and performances of Verdi's operas in San Francisco by decade from 1851 through 1899.

Venice

343. Antolini, Bianca Maria. "Cronache teatrali veneziane: 1842–1849." In *Musica senza aggettivi: Studi per Fedele d'Amico,* 1:297–322. Ed. by Agostino Ziino. Quaderni della Rivista italiana di musicologia, 25. Florence: Olschki, 1991. 2 vols. ISBN 88–222–3903–2. ML 55 .D22 1991. ML 55 .D22 1991.

Describes musical life in Venice during the 1840s as seen in the letters of Faustina Capranica to her father, Bartolomeo, an important impresario, and to other family members. Some of the letters include significant information about the preparations for the 1844 premiere of *Ernani* and its subsequent reception. Other letters discuss the early reception of *I lombardi, I due Foscari,* and *Giovanna d'Arco.* This previously unpublished material comes from a collection at the Archivio Storico Capitolino in Rome.

344. Conati, Marcello. *La bottega della musica: Verdi e La Fenice.* Opere e libri. Milan: Il Saggiatore, 1983. 452 p. + 32 p. plates. ML 410 .V4 C67 1983.

The most detailed and authoritative discussion of Verdi's dealings with La Fenice in Venice, drawing largely on the rich trove of primary source material in the archives of the opera house. In addition to several general sections, individual chapters provide documentary histories of five operas that premiered at La Fenice: *Ernani, Attila, Rigoletto, La traviata* and *Simon Boccanegra* (first version). Extant documentary material is particularly rich in the case of *Ernani* and *Simon Boccanegra,* but the volume reveals previously unknown facts or circumstances about all five. The complete or partial reproduction of over 350 letters and other documents (indexed by date at the end of the volume) are a particularly valuable resource for the researcher. Conati's transcriptions of letters from Verdi to La Fenice correct many errors in earlier publications by Morazzoni (item 33) and Nordio (item 35), although the latter sometimes contains passages omitted in the present volume.

345. Tintori, Giampiero, ed. *Verdi e la Fenice.* Venice: Teatro La Fenice, 1980. 47 p. ML 141 .V3 V47 1980.

An exhibition catalogue with rich illustrative material relating to the five operas that premiered there. Illustrations include playbills, photographs, scene and costume designs, and illustrated title pages.

346. Valeri, Diego, ed. *Verdi e la Fenice.* Venice: Ente Autonomo del Teatro la Fenice, 1951. 83 p. + 19 p. plates. ML 410 .V4 V3.

This commemorative volume, issued for the fiftieth anniversary of the composer's death, is divided into two main sections. The largest study, "Verdi e la Fenice" by Mario Nordio (item 35), presents a series of letters from Verdi to members of the theater's presidency with commentary. The remainder of the volume presents six short essays by different authors each focusing on one of the operas that Verdi wrote for the theater: *Ernani, Attila, Rigoletto, La traviata,* and *Simon Boccanegra.* The book contains nineteen illustrations, including facsimile reproductions of several playbills and a letter to Guglielmo Brenna dated 19 October 1850.

CHAPTER 10

Verdi's Influence & Historical Position

This chapter contains citations for studies that discuss Verdi's influence on his contemporaries and subsequent generations and general assessments of Verdi's place in history.

347. Abert, Anna Amalie. "Verdi und Wagner." In *Colloquium "Verdi-Wagner" Rom 1969: Bericht* (item 227), 1–13.
   Republished in *Wagner in Italia*, 305–14. Ed. by Giancarlo Rostirolla. Turin: EDT, 1982. ML 410 .W12 W24.

   A concise comparative essay on the two composers' aesthetic views and their contributions to nineteenth-century opera.

348. Bacchelli, Riccardo. "Esperienze e conclusioni di un'annata verdiana." In *Giuseppe Verdi nel cinquantenario della morte* (item 230), 28–37.

   Reviews some of the activities commemorating the 50th anniversary of the composer's death and the stature of Verdi as a historical figure.

349. Berlin, Isaiah. "The Naiveté of Verdi." *The Verdi Companion* (item 248), 1–12.
   Also published in *The Hudson Review* 21 (Spring 1968): 138–47; *Atti 1* (item 224), 27–35; and in *Against the Current: Essays in the History of Ideas*, 287–96. Ed. by Henry Hardy. London: Hogarth Press; New York: Viking Press, 1980. ISBN 0701204397; 0–670–10944–4. Reprint. Oxford: Clarendon, 1989. ISBN 0–19–283028–7. B29 .B445 1991.

   Discusses Verdi as a "naive" artist in the sense used by Friedrich Schiller in his essay *Über naive und sentimentalische Dichtung* (1796): artists not conscious of any break between themselves and their milieu and who did not intend their art for any "spiritual end" beyond itself. The author argues that for the most part, Verdi's contemporaries fit Schiller's category of "sentimental" artists, who feel alienated from society and consequently fill their artistic production with a strong sense of satire.

350. Bonavia, Ferruccio. "Verdi and His Contemporaries." *Music and Letters* 4 (1923): 178–83.

This short essay offers a strong defense of Verdi and his music. The main portion of the article examines the influence of Rossini on Verdi and ways in which Verdi rose above the accomplishments of his predecessors. Bonavia attacks several "myths" about the composer, including his "lack" of religious belief and the dependence of his later style on Wagner. The essay provides an interesting assessment of attitudes toward Verdi and his music in England during the early decades of the twentieth century. The author calls for the writing of an "authoritative and completely trustworthy" biography of the composer, a task which he himself would later undertake (see item 135).

351. Cantoni, Angelo. "Verdi e Stravinskij." *Studi verdiani* 10 (1994–95): 127–54.

Although in the early 1940s Stravinsky considered *Otello* and *Falstaff* tainted by Wagnerian influence, he later completely reversed himself with regard to *Falstaff*, which he held up as a highly original work that "resisted" Wagnerism. The main part of the article considers the influence of Verdi's compositions (particularly *Falstaff*) on Stravinsky's musical style in works like *The Rake's Progress, Oedipus Rex, Jeux de cartes* and *The Dumbarton Oaks Concerto* and, in special detail, the influence of Verdi's *Requiem* on Stravinsky's *Requiem Canticles*.

352. Della Seta, Fabrizio. "Verdi: La tradizione italiana e l'esperienza europea." *Musica/realtà* No. 32 (August 1990): 135–58.

Examines Verdi's parallel roots in the tradition of Italian music and European Romanticism and ways in these contrasting sources have influenced the assessments of historians from the time of Verdi's death to the present. The author argues that the composer's cultural background was broader and richer than many historians have supposed. He draws particular attention to key Romantic texts and manifestos with which Verdi was familiar and suggests that August Wilhelm Schlegel's *Über dramatische Kunst und Literatur* may have exercised a pivotal influence on his aesthetics, particularly the idea of "dramatic unity." Della Seta also contends that Verdi's operas differ fundamentally in concept from those of his predecessors (such as Bellini and Donizetti) because they offer a true musical realization of Romantic theater without being filtered by "Classical" notions of the Enlightenment. In conclusion, the author asserts that the genre of French *grand opéra*—particularly the works of Meyerbeer—provided Verdi with an important dramaturgical model linking progressive Romantic literary aesthetics to opera. He discusses an illustrative example comparing the quartet for solo voices in Act II of *Luisa Miller* with an analogous trio for solo voices in Act III of Meyerbeer's *Robert le diable.*

353. Eösze, László. "Aspetti comuni dell'arte poetica di Verdi, Bartók, e Kodály." *Atti 1* (item 224), 97–105.

Compares and contrasts Verdi's feelings about nationalism in music to that of Bartók and Kodály.

354. Escudier, Léon. "Giuseppe Verdi." In *Mes souvenirs*, 69–96. Littérature musicale. Paris: E. Dentu, 1863. ML 395 .E73.

This short essay by Verdi's French publisher offers a description of the composer's character and a contemporary assessment of the unique features and significance of his work.

355. Gresch, Donald. "The Fact of Fiction: Franz Werfel's *Verdi: Roman der Oper.*" *Current Musicology* 28 (1979): 30–40.

Analyzes the position of Werfel's historical novel, which contributed to the growing popularity of Verdi's music during the 1920s. Although there are many elements of fiction in the volume, the author concludes that Werfel's characterization of Verdi as a spiritually regenerated man who renounces egoistic selfishness for humility and love of fellow man closely matches portraits drawn by later biographers, notably Francis Toye (see item 144).

356. Kühner, Hans. "Franz Werfel und Giuseppe Verdi." *Verdi: Bollettino dell'Istituto di Studi Verdiani* 1 [No. 3] (1960): 1391–1400. Italian and English translations are printed on pp.1790–1804.

Assesses the role of Franz Werfel in promoting the music of Verdi in the early twentieth century. The author provides a summary of Werfel's views about the composer, as seen in *Verdi: Roman der Oper* and examines its significance for later studies.

* Mila, Massimo. *L'arte di Verdi.* See item 375.

357. Moravia, Alberto. "La volgarità di Verdi." In *Opere, 1948–1968*, 1345–51. Milan: Bompiani, 1989. ISBN 88–452–1451–6. PQ 4829 .O62 A6 1989. Reprinted in many other collections of Moravia's essays.
English translation by Bernard Wall. "The 'Vulgarity' of Giuseppe Verdi." In *Man as End: A Defense of Humanism. Literary, Social, and Political Essays*, 248–54. New York: Farrar, Straus & Giroux, 1966. PQ 4829 .O62 U613 1966.

French translation by Madame Claude Poncet. "La 'vulgarité' di Verdi." In *L'avant scène opera 126* (item 716): 110–13.

Adopting the premise that Verdi sprang from peasant stock and peasant culture [a premise promoted by the composer but discredited by recent biographers], Moravia argues that Verdi's operas promulgate Renaissance humanist ideals, filtered through a vulgarized folkloric tradition. An interesting part of this essay is the author's comparison of Verdi to other intellectual figures such as Alessandro Manzoni, Giacomo Leopardi, Victor Hugo, and William Shakespeare.

* Parker, Roger. "On Reading Nineteenth-Century Opera: Verdi Through the Looking Glass." See item 429.

358. Moser, Hans Joachim. "Giuseppe Verdi." *Rassegna musicale* 12 (1939): 149–58.

A thought-provoking essay by a leading German musicologist of his day on Verdi's historical position. Moser considers Verdi to have initated a new surge of Romanticism in Italy, drawing on the past tradition of composers such as Astorga, Durante, and Tartini in combination with a strong interest in non-Italian writers such as Victor Hugo, Alexandre Dumas, Friedrich Schiller, and William Shakespeare. The main portion of the article compares Verdi's historical position to that of Wagner against the broader background of general tendencies in Italian and German music.

359. Petrobelli, Pierluigi. "Einige Thesen zu Verdi." In *Komponisten auf Werk und Leben befragt: Ein Kolloquium*, 138–56. Ed. by Harry Goldschmidt, Georg Knepler, and Konrad Niemann. Leipzig: VEB Deutscher Verlag für Musik, 1985. ML 390 .K756 1985.

Discusses several issues surrounding the composer and his music, including: 1) the myth, partly created and fostered by the composer himself, of Verdi as an untutored, largely self-taught peasant who rose to greatness against overwhelming odds and its subsequent influence on the history of Verdi biography; 2) the issue of Verdi's stylistic and artistic development, which is complicated by the fact that he was productive over such a long period in which musical style generally went through tremendous changes; and 3) the tradition of Verdi as a "political" composer, particularly with respect to the Risorgimento movement—a tradition that the author feels has been exaggerated. The latter part of the article contains the text of the ensuing discussion among conference participants.

* Pizzi, Italo. *Per il I° centenario della nascita di Giuseppe Verdi: Memorie—aneddoti—considerazioni.* See item 247.

360. Pizzetti, Ildebrando. "Giuseppe Verdi: Maestro di teatro." In *Giuseppe Verdi nel cinquantenario della morte* (item 230), 14–27.
Republished in *Verdi: Bollettino dell'Istituto di Studi Verdiani* 1 [No. 2] (1960): 751–66; English and German translations are provided on pp. 1013–38.

Proposes that the composer's greatness lay first and foremost in his ability to express human nature. The article also provides a useful summation of the reception of Verdi's music and the state of Verdi studies at mid-century, when the 50th anniversary of the composer's death was being commemorated.

361. ———. "La grandezza di Verdi." In *La musica italiana dell'ottocento*, 248–78. Turin: Edizioni Palatine di R. Pezzani & C., 1947. Reprint, with introductory essays by Marzio Pieri, Gian Paolo Minardi, and Evelina Schatz. Parma: Battei, 1988. ML 290.4 P69.

After surveying various aspects of Verdi's life, career, and music, the author concludes that his most notable contribution was the development of a new, rich, and powerfully expressive musical language coupled with an equally powerful and distinctive dramatic art.

362. Spada, Marco. "La scoperta di Verdi: Le tappe di una rinascita." *Musica e dossier* No. 35 (1989): 18–22.

Traces the increasing interest in Verdi in both performance and musicological realms starting in the 1950s and 60s. Includes a survey of activities by the Istituto di Studi Verdiani.

363. Tomlinson, Gary. "Verdi After Budden." *19th Century Music* 5 (1981–82): 170–82.

This important essay-review offers a significant evaluation of Julian Budden's magisterial three-volume study of Verdi's operas (item 365) and of the state of Verdi research ca. 1980. In his own assessment of Verdi's historical position, Tomlinson asserts that the simple melodic forms found in the composer's early works do not simply represent a continuation of the traditions of Bellini and Donizetti but rather a purposeful reaffirmation of them in contrast to the more circumspect approach of contemporaries such as Mercadante and Pacini.

364. Vecchi, Giuseppe. "Giuseppe Verdi e la missione nazionale e sociale della musica nel pensiero di Giuseppe Mazzini." In *Studi e ricerche sui libretti delle opere di Giuseppe Verdi* (item 444), 201–4.

This brief essay examines the nationalistic reverence for the music of Verdi in Italy as the fulfillment of the aesthetic ideas of Giuseppe Mazzini, which emphasize both nationalism and the mysterious, divine nature of music.

CHAPTER 11
General Studies About Verdi's Music

This chapter contains citations of studies that are concerned with the broad range of Verdi's music or encompass more than a single work. Subcategories include: Verdi's aesthetics and dramaturgy, compositional process, stylistic and analytical studies, vocal and orchestral performance practice, and staging and scenography. Cross-references will direct the reader to some significant writings listed in other parts of this volume; the index provides a comprehensive listing of all materials dealing with a particular area.

365. Budden, Julian. *The Operas of Verdi.* Rev. ed. Vol. 1, *From "Oberto" to "Rigoletto"*; Vol. 2, *From "Il trovatore" to "La forza del destino"*; Vol. 3, *From "Don Carlos" to "Falstaff."* Oxford: Clarendon, 1992. xiii, 524; ix, 532; 546 p. ISBN 0–19–816261–8; 0–19–816262–6; 0–19–816263–4. ML 410 .V4 B88 1991.

Italian translation. *Le opere di Verdi.* Ed. by Giorgio Pestelli. Biblioteca di cultura musicale. Turin: Edizioni di Torino, 1986. xii, 600; x, 601; vi, 629 p. ISBN 88–7063–038–2; 88–7063–042–0; 88–7063–058–7. ML 410 .V4 B88 1986.

This set, first published from 1973–81, has become the standard survey of Verdi's operas for musically knowledgeable connoisseurs. It has also become important as a standard point of departure by Verdi specialists for more technical discussions of topics relating to musical style. Chapters devoted to individual operas detail the historical background and genesis of the works and then provide a descriptive analysis of the plot and music. Additional chapters interspersed throughout the set provide useful information about the cultural and artistic milieu of Italy at the outset of Verdi's career, at mid-century, and in the years from 1870–90, and consider general characteristics of Verdi's early operas and the formation of his mature style at mid-century. Budden's level of discussion, especially in his description of the individual operas, never becomes extremely technical or difficult for the uninitiated reader to follow. For a detailed critique of the first edition (1973–81) and an assessment of this study's place in the history of Verdi studies, see Gary Tomlinson's penetrating essay-review "Verdi after Budden" (item 363).

366. Cabourg, Jean, ed. *Guide des opéras de Verdi.* Les indispensables de la musique. Paris: Fayard, 1990. 1283 p. ISBN 2–213–02409–X.

For each opera, this guide provides a summary of the plot, a brief compositional history and survey of the work's reception, and an annotated discography. Complete librettos (in French translation) are included for fifteen of the more popular operas. Appendices include a brief chronology of Verdi's life, a tabular summary of main events in the Risorgimento movement and unification of Italy, brief biographies of Verdi's main librettists, and a glossary of technical terms often found in the Verdi literature. The discographies, among the most comprehensive available and which contain substantial discussions of each recording, are among the most useful features of this reference work.

367. Chusid, Martin. "Toward an Understanding of Verdi's Middle Period." In *Verdi's Middle Period, 1849–1859: Source Studies, Analysis, and Performance Practice* (item 235), 1–15.

This introductory essay to the volume surveys musical characteristics of Verdi's middle-period style, including a new orientation toward drama, greater continuity, more sophisticated musical organization, replacement of choruses with more dramatic ensemble numbers, the employment of the stage band to represent specific social occasions, and a change in aria style reflecting, in part, influences from French opera. The author proposes several factors that led to these stylistic changes, such as personal artistic growth, increasing financial security, longer contemplation of possible subjects for new operas, failure of the revolutions of 1848–49, and the increasing creative influence of Giuseppina Strepponi on Verdi's thought.

368. Dallapiccola, Luigi. *Appunti, incontri, meditazioni.* Milan: Suivini Zervoni, 1970. 193 p. ML 60 .D18.
   Republished as *Parole e musica.* Rev. and enl. ed. Ed. by Fiamma Nicolodi. La cultura: Saggi di arte e letteratura, 53. Milan: Il Saggiatore, 1980. 603 p. ML 60 .D18 1980.
   English translation by Rudy Shakelford. *Selected Writings of Luigi Dallapiccola.* Vol. 1. *Dallapiccola on Opera.* Musicians on Music, 4. [London]: Toccata Press, 1987. 291 p. ISBN 0–90768–909–4 (cloth); 0–90768–910–8 (paper). ML 1700 .D18 A25 1987.
   French translation. *Paroles et musique.* Collection musique ouverte. Paris: Minerve, 1992. 239 p. ISBN 2–869310–59–5.

This edition of Dallapiccola's critical writings includes four chapters pertaining to Verdi: "Parole e musica nel melodramma" (see item 262), "Pagine di diario sul *Rigoletto*," "Considerazioni sul *Simon Boccanegra*," and "Su un passo del *Falstaff.*"

369. Degrada, Francesco. *Il palazzo incantato: Studi sulla tradizione del melodramma dal Barocco al Romanticismo.* Fiesole: Discanto Edizioni, 1979. 2 vols. vii, 215; 170 p. ML 1700 .D43.

The second volume of this anthology contains articles on *Macbeth, Don Carlos,* and *Otello.* See items 622, 758, and 812.

370. Della Corte, Andrea. *Le sei più belle opere di Giuseppe Verdi.* [Milan]: Istituto d'Alta Cultura, [1946]. 209 p. The publisher reissued the work in an elegantly bound limited edition in 1957. ML 1733.3 C656.

A collection of previously published essays on six operas: *Rigoletto, Il trovatore, La traviata, Aida, Otello,* and *Falstaff.* For each work, the author devotes the first part of his discussion to the history of the work, followed by an extensive descriptive analysis. The volume also contains facsimile reproductions of a letter dated 28 March 1845 written to Felice Romani and a small album leaf in which Verdi wrote the first bars of "Di quel amor" from *La traviata.*

371. Engelhardt, Markus. *Verdi und Andere: "Un giorno di regno," "Ernani," "Attila," "Il corsaro" in Mehrfachvertonungen.* Premio Internazionale Rotary Club di Parma "Giuseppe Verdi," 1. Parma: Istituto di Studi Verdiani, 1992. xv, 389 p. ISBN 88–85065–09–0. ML 410 .V4 E494 1992.

An invaluable source for background on the literary and musical milieu for Verdi's early operas. Engelhardt investigates significant features of Verdi's early style through a comparison with operas based on the same stories written by his contemporaries. Individual chapters are devoted to *Un giorno di regno* (with settings by Giuseppe Mosca, Adalbert Gyrowetz, and Verdi), *Ernani* (settings by Vincenzo Bellini, Vincenzo Gabussi, Constantino Quaranta, Alberto Mazzucato, Verdi, Henri Louis Hirchmann, and Antonio Laudamo), *Attila* (Francesco Malipiero and Verdi), and *Il corsaro* (Giovanni Pacini, Alessandro Nini, Verdi, and Francesco Cortesi). The study demonstrates how Verdi's librettos, in contrast to many of his contemporaries, avoid placing most of the dramatic and musical interest on one or two leading characters and instead adopt a more complex approach to the drama that often runs closer to the original literary model. Engelhardt also argues that Verdi's operas contain deeper, more arresting, and more dynamic dramatic and musical development than many operas by his contemporaries. The volume contains a summary essay in Italian; separate indexes for names, musical works, and places/institutions facilitates use of the material. An earlier, more concise treatment of the *Ernani* chapter entitled "Versioni operistiche dell'*Hernani*" may be found in *"Ernani" ieri e oggi* (item 228), 104–22.

372. Godefroy, Vincent. *The Dramatic Genius of Verdi: Studies of Selected Operas.* 2 vols. London: Victor Gollancz, 1975; New York: St. Martin's Press, 1977. 287; 348 p. ISBN 0–575–01979–4; 0–312–21946–6. ML 410 .V4 G6 1976.

This set is intended for the general reader rather than the Verdi specialist. Each chapter provides a descriptive analysis of an opera, focusing on dramaturgy and early reception of the works. While the treatment is not as comprehensive, imaginative, or up to date as Julian Budden's set (item 365), many readers will find valuable some of Godefroy's thoughts and points of view. Operas discussed in the first volume include: *Nabucco, I due Foscari, Giovanna d'Arco, Attila, Macbeth, I masnadieri, Luisa Miller, Rigoletto, Il trovatore,* and *La traviata.* The second volume includes essays on *Les vêpres siciliennes, Un ballo in maschera, La forza del destino, Don Carlos, Aida, Simon Boccanegra, Otello, Falstaff,* and a thought-provoking chapter on the aborted *Re Lear* project. Neither volume contains an index.

373. Hughes, Spike. *Famous Verdi Operas: An Analytical Guide for the Opera-Goer and Armchair Listener.* Philadelphia: Clinton Book Co., 1968. MT 100 .V47 H8.

An act-by-act description of twelve Verdi operas intended for the uninitiated listener or reader. There is no attempt to incorporate scholarly research available at the time of the book's publication; most serious readers will prefer to use Budden (item 365) as a point of departure.

374. Levi, Primo. *Verdi.* Rome: Stabilimento Tipografico della "Tribuna," 1901. 42 p. ML 410 .V4 L47.

This short monograph, originally published in the *Rivista politica e letteratura,* focuses on a discussion of stylistic innovation in the composer's later works, including the *Requiem, Otello, Falstaff,* and the *Pezzi sacri.* The volume includes facsimiles and transcriptions of four letters from Verdi to Levi.

375. Mila, Massimo. *L'arte di Verdi.* Saggi, 627. Turin: Giulio Einaudi, 1980. xiv, 384 p. ML 410 .V4 M57.
       Spanish translation by Carlos Guillermo Perez de Aranda and Cristina Smeyers Tamargo. *El arte de Verdi.* Madrid: Alianza, 1992. 355 p. + 16 p. plates. ISBN 84–206–8559–3.

This important volume contains a significant series of essays dealing with various facets of Verdi's music and aesthetics. It represents, in part, a complementary publication to the author's earlier work *La giovinezza di Verdi* (item 171), although this collection is organized quite differently and has a much broader focus. The four sections of the book deal with Verdi's concept of drama; the composer's musical style; individual compositions beginning with *Vêpres*, including a chapter on religious music; and Verdi's place in history and art, including his role as a political figure and the reception of his works by Eduard Hanslick (see item 306). Some chapters were originally published as articles or presented as papers. This volume, together with *La giovinezza di Verdi*, is an amplification and revision of the author's earlier works entitled *Il melodramma di Verdi* (Bari: Laterza, 1933; 2nd ed., Milan: Feltrinelli, 1960) and *Giuseppe Verdi* (Bari: Laterza, 1958). A useful feature of the present study is a large bibliography (p. 357–78), organized by type of publication and current through ca. 1980. This bibliography includes specialized sections that list the contents of special and commemorative issues of periodicals, the *Quaderni dell'Istituto di Studi Verdiani*, the *Bollettino dell'Istituto di Studi Verdiani*, and the Acts of the first three *Congressi Internazionali di Studi Verdiani*. See item 401 for an analysis and critique of some of the author's ideas.

376. Osborne, Charles. *The Complete Operas of Verdi*. London: Victor Gollancz, 1969. 485 p. New York: Alfred A. Knopf, 1970. 472, xiii p. ISBN 0–575–00273–5. MT 100 .V47 O8. Reprinted several times by various publishers.

   Italian translation by Giampiero Tintori. *Tutte le opere di Verdi: Guida critica*. Milan: Mursia, 1975. 477 p. MT 100 .V47 O8 1975b.

A guide to the composer's operas written in a popular style and intended for a general audience. A final chapter briefly discusses the non-operatic works. The volume contains a short bibliography and an index.

377. Parker, Roger. *Studies in Early Verdi, 1832–1844: New Information and Perspectives on the Milanese Musical Milieu and the Operas from Oberto to Ernani*. Outstanding Dissertations in Music from British Universities. New York and London: Garland, 1989. 219 p. ISBN 0–8240–2020–0. ML 410 .V4 P157.

A photographic reprint of the author's doctoral dissertation (Ph.D., University of London, 1981). Individual chapters include: Verdi and the *Gazzetta privilegiata di Milano* (see item 176), "Classical" music in Milan during Verdi's formative years (item 277), the autograph score of *Oberto* (item 803), the genesis of *Un giorno di regno* (item 743), the early performance history of *Nabucco* (item 799), the influence of the singer in Verdi's early operas (item 490), levels of motivic definition in *Ernani* (item 689), and the structure of Act I, Scene 2 of *Il trovatore* (item 958).

378. Petrobelli, Pierluigi. *Music in the Theater: Essays on Verdi and Other Composers.* Translations by Roger Parker and William Drabkin. Princeton Studies in Opera. Princeton: Princeton University Press, 1994. ix, 192p. ISBN 0–691–09134–X. ML 410 .V2 P28.

This anthology contains English translations of eight articles dealing with Verdi, most of which had been previously published in various journals and conference reports. Their compilation here is especially valuable for readers who wish to study in English some significant writings of one of the world's foremost Verdi scholars. The introduction also contains a useful summary of nomenclature relating to Italian prosody. Individual articles from this collection are abstracted separately as items 452, 576, 587, 733, 782, 798, 868, and 959.

379. Rinaldi, Mario. *Le opere meno note di Giuseppe Verdi.* Historiae musicae cultores biblioteca, 29. Florence: Olschki, 1975. 302 p. + 12 plates. ML 410 .V4 R545.

A study of *Oberto, Un giorno di regno, I lombardi, I due Foscari, Giovanna d'Arco, Alzira, Attila, I masnadieri, Il corsaro, La battaglia di Legnano,* and *Stiffelio.* For each opera, the author discusses the work's genesis and reception, provides a short plot summary, and a descriptive analysis of the music. Although this volume presents a substantial discussion of operas that have not attracted much scholarly attention, readers should use it in tandem with more recent research. The volume contains a short bibliography.

380. ———. *Le opere più note di Giuseppe Verdi.* Historiae musicae cultores biblioteca, 41. Florence: Olschki, 1986. 513 p. + 16 plates. ISBN 88–222–3411–1. ML 410 .V4 R547 1986.

A study of the operas not included in item 379 above, organized in a similar format, plus a short essay on the *Requiem.* Unfortunately, the author does not always incorporate recent research about the operas and therefore it should be used with some caution. This volume lacks a bibliography, and all but the first three chapters lack footnotes.

381. Roncaglia, Gino. *L'ascensione creatrice di Giuseppe Verdi.* Rev. ed. Florence: Sansoni, 1940. 457 p. ML 410 .V4 R65.

Provides an overview of Verdi's compositions, emphasizing changing trends in the composer's style. Much of the volume is a reworking of the author's earlier and less judicious *Giuseppe Verdi: L'ascensione dell'arte sua* (Naples: Francesco Perrella, 1914). Although this study is somewhat out of date, it still makes lively and useful reading. Appendices provide a work list and a list of librettos in tabular form as well as a selective bibliography.

382.   ———. *Galleria verdiana.* Milan: Curci, 1959. 197 p. ML 410 .V4 R66.

A collection of essays previously published in periodicals. Individual topics include: the "tema-cardine" (see item 498), the aborted opera *Re Lear*, Verdi and La Scala, the sketch for *Rigoletto*, and evil operatic characters that reflect the composer's sense of pessimism.

383.   Soffredini, A. *Le opere di Verdi: Studio critico analitico.* Milan: Carlo Aliprandi, 1901. 299 p. MT 100 .V48 S6 1901.

An expansion of the author's critiques and reviews that were earlier serialized in the *Gazzetta musicale di Milano.* An individual chapter is devoted to each of the operas and the *Requiem*; a final chapter considers the remaining "minor" works. Although many of Soffredini's critiques are extensive, some of the lesser-known works receive only cursory comments. This volume is particularly useful as a reflection of contemporary reception.

384.   Tintori, Giampiero. *Invito all'ascolto di Giuseppe Verdi.* Milan: Mursia, 1983. 289 p. ML 410 .V4 T56 1983.

Tintori divides his volume into two main parts: a short biography of the composer, followed by a more discursive examination of the compositions, examining both their historical context and outlining the stories of each of the operas. A final concluding essay evaluates a few of the most important publications in the Verdi bibliography. The volume also contains a longer bibliography in conventional format, a work list, discography, and separate indexes for names and compositions.

385.   Torchi, L[uigi]. "L'opera di Giuseppe Verdi e i suoi caratteri principali." *Rivista musicale italiana* 8 (1901): 279–325.

This extensive survey, issued in commemoration of the composer's death, provides an assessment of his works, emphasizing comparisons and contrasts among different operas and trends in stylistic development throughout his career.

386.   Unterholzner, Ludwig. *Giuseppe Verdis Opern-Typus.* Ph.D. dissertation, Friedrich-Alexanders-Universität, Erlangen, 1927. Hannover: Hannoverscher Anzeiger, A. Madsack & Co., 1927. 59 p. ML 410 .V48 U61.

An early attempt to describe systematically Verdi's musical style and dramaturgical principles. The study focuses on the role of the libretto in determining musical treatment and Verdi's use of recurring musical ideas to underscore parallel situations or "affects."

387. Zecchi, Adone, ed. *Collana di saggi verdiani.* Bologna: F. Bongiovanni, 1951.
      94 p. ML 410 .V4 Z4.

      A commemorative collection of essays by a dozen different authors, each
      discussing some aspect of one of Verdi's compositions. The volume features
      writings about *Ernani, Giovanna d'Arco* and *I vespri siciliani,* in addition to
      many of his better known works.

388. Zeppegno, Luciano. *Il manuale di Verdi.* With the collaboration of Maurizio
      Rinaldi. Roma: Lato Side, 1980. 397 p. MT 100 .V47 Z46.

      A guide to Verdi's operas written in popular style for a general audience. For
      each opera, the author presents a concise summary of the plot and a descriptive
      analysis of the music.

DRAMATURGY & AESTHETICS

389. Abert, Anna Amalie. "Über Textentwürfe Verdis." In *Beiträge zur Geschichte
      der Oper,* 131–38. Ed. by Heinz Becker. Studien zur Musikgeschichte des
      19. Jahrhunderts, 15. Regensburg: Gustav Bosse, 1969. ML 1700.1 .B43.

      Verdi's preparation of preliminary scenarios illustrates how thoroughly he
      involved himself in the earliest stages of shaping the librettos for his operas.
      While the composer generally wanted to preserve the spirit of the original
      model as much as possible, his earlier works take some liberties in the
      presentation of the material. Verdi struggled with the dramatic shape more
      intensively than usual in *Macbeth* and *Re Lear,* his first two attempts at
      working with Shakespeare. In the case of *Re Lear,* the composer appears to
      have reached a point where he could not reconcile his desire to remain utterly
      faithful to the text and yet present the work in a manner suitable to the operatic
      stage.

390. Alper, Clifford. "Comprimario 'in excelsis'." *The Opera Journal* 5 (Winter
      1972): 18–20.

      Examines several comprimario roles in Verdi's operas in which the composer
      wrote unusual or distinguished music for a "minor" character. Examples
      include, among others, Monterone in *Rigoletto,* Paolo in *Simon Boccanegra,*
      Cassio in *Otello,* and the friar in *Don Carlos.*

391. Baldacci, Luigi. "La figura del padre nel rapporto Schiller-Verdi." *Quadrivium:
      Studi di filologia e musicologia* 27 (1986): 105–13. This volume of *Quadrivium*
      is listed in some indexes as a monograph: *Universalità della musica, prestigio
      dell'Italia, attualità di Verdi: Studi in onore di Mario Medici,* Vol. 2. Ed. by
      Giuseppe Vecchi. Bologna: Antiquae Musicae Italicae Studiosi, 1986.

Compared to his predecessors or successors, Verdi placed more emphasis on the role of fathers in the dramaturgy of his operas. The three first plays by Schiller that Verdi chose to adopt—*Giovanna d'Arco, I masnadieri,* and *Luisa Miller*—share the common element of children who turn against their fathers. Schiller's other plays, some of which were considered by Verdi, do not emphasize conflict between father and child. *Don Carlos,* written when Schiller had left behind his *Sturm und Drang* period, departs from the playwright's—and Verdi's—earlier dramaturgical focus by not emphasizing tension between family members. The author argues that this change fits better with the temperament of French culture, an important consideration for the composer since *Don Carlo* would premiere in that country.

392. ———. "I libretti di Verdi." In *Il melodramma italiano dell'ottocento: Studi e ricerche per Massimo Mila,* 113–23. Ed. by Giorgio Pestelli. Saggi, 575. Turin: Einaudi, 1977. ML 1733.4 .M5.

A concise overview of Verdi's approach to selecting and refining a libretto and his interaction with librettists. The author argues that the composer took such a significant role in the shaping and refining of the librettos for his operas that they are as much his creation as the music itself (see item 442 for a recent examination and refinement of this idea). Baldacci further asserts that the entire corpus of Verdi's librettos may be regarded as a coherent, cohesive dramaturgical entity.

393. Barblan, Guglielmo. "L'opera di Giuseppe Verdi e il dramma romantico." *Rivista musicale italiana* 45 (1941): 93–107.

Outlines Verdi's aesthetic principles and their relationship to European literary Romanticism. The author proposes that the most fundamental element that Verdi drew from his literary counterparts was a strong sense of contrast. The conclusion of the article argues that Verdi reflects the Romantic ideal of drama every bit as much as Wagner, although they approached it in different ways.

394. ———. "Il sentimento dell'onore nella drammaturgia verdiana." *Atti 3* (item 226), 2–13.

Honor in its various forms—heroic honor, nationalistic honor, and familial honor—is a central impetus to the dramatic action in many of Verdi's operas. The study focuses particularly on *Oberto, rnani, La battaglia di Legnano, Jérusalem, Luisa Miller, Un ballo in maschera, La forza del destino, Don Carlos,* and *Falstaff.*

395. Baroni, Mario. *Il declino del patriarca: Verdi e le contraddizioni della famiglia borghese.* Musica dramatica in aemiliae romandiolae civitatibus archivium;

Studi e testi verdiani, 3. Bologna: Antiquae Musicae Italicae Studiosi, 1979. 159 p. ML 410 .V48 B37.

A detailed examination, using semiotic theory, of Verdi's treatment of the family and family themes—particularly the role of the father—compared with that of his immediate predecessors.

396. Beghelli, Marco. "Per un nuovo approccio al teatro musicale: L'atto performativo come luogo dell'imitazione gestuale nella drammaturgia verdiana." *Italica* 64 (1987): 632–53.

A semiotic study of stereotypical musical gestures found throughout Verdi's operas that carry to completion particular actions witnessed on the stage. Specific categories examined in this article include crying (or lamenting), laughing, reading, narrating, singing, conjuring, fainting, and dying. A distinction between performative act and its subsequent realization in musical gesture helps to explain, for example, the apparent paradox of a person dying on stage who can sing at full strength throughout his or her final agony. This article presents some of the ideas in the author's doctoral dissertation (Università di Bologna, 1986), entitled "Atti performativi nella drammaturgia verdiana."

397. Bradshaw, Graham. "A Shakespearean Perspective: Verdi and Boito as Translators." In James A. Hepokoski, *Giuseppe Verdi: "Falstaff"* (item 695), 152–71.

Discusses Verdi and Boito as interpreters of Shakespeare. Bradshaw asserts that in many ways, Boito's libretto for *Otello* parallels the story in Cinthio Giraldi's *Gli hecatommithi* more closely than Shakespeare's recasting of it for his play. In contrast, the many linguistic and formal subtleties in Boito's libretto for *Falstaff* give the work a genuinely "Shakespearean" aura. Verdi's musical treatment in both cases shows remarkable insight into the great playwright's creative milieu. The article also includes a critical assessment of Daniel Sabbeth's dissertation on *Falstaff* (item 711).

398. Carrara Verdi, Gabriella. "La parola scenica in Verdi." *Archivio storico per le province parmensi*. 4th series. 34 (1982): 529–38.

Discusses Verdi's concept of the "parola scenica" with illustrations from the finale of Il *trovatore*, the first scenes of *Aida*, and the beginning of *Otello*. In each case, the author shows how the composer altered a portion of the libretto to increase its dramatic impact.

399. Cisotti, Virginia. *Schiller e il melodramma di Verdi*. Florence: La Nuova Italia Editrice, 1975. xii, 172 p. ML 423 .S35 C6.

A detailed study of Verdi's operas based on plays by Schiller and their literary and social background. After a preliminary discussion of the reception of Schiller's works in nineteenth-century Italy, with particular focus on Andrea Maffei's translations, the author considers, in turn, Verdi's operas *Giovanna d'Arco, I masnadieri, Luisa Miller*, the third act of *La forza del destino*, and *Don Carlos*. In each case, Cisotti provides a detailed comparison of the opera with their respective prototypes in Schiller's dramas and presents information relating to the works' relationship to the cultural milieu of the ottocento. The volume contains a useful index of names.

400. Conati, Marcello. "Verdi et la culture parisienne des années 1830." In *Music in Paris in the Eighteen-Thirties/La musique à Paris dans les années mil huit cent trente*, 209–27. Ed. by Peter Bloom. Musical Life in 19th-Century France/La vie musicale en France au XIXe siècle, 4. Stuyvesant, N.Y.: Pendragon, 1987. ISBN 0–918728–71–1. ML 270.8 .P2 M76.

While Verdi's trips to the French capital beginning in 1847 significantly influenced his musical style and aesthetic preferences, French culture undoubtedly also affected his early development as a composer. The works of Eugène Scribe and other French playwrights and librettists were often performed in Milan, and French operas by composers such as Auber, Halévy, Rossini, and Meyerbeer were widely performed in important opera houses throughout Italy. While it is not known whether Verdi was familiar with Victor Hugo's Preface to *Cromwell*, many of his own aesthetic views parallel those announced by the famous French author including: the superiority of artistic creation over simple reflections of nature, the enhancement of drama by contrasting heroic figures with ridiculous or grotesque counterparts, and the need to abolish fine distinctions between traditional genres.

401. D'Amico, Fedele. "Note sulla drammaturgia verdiana." In *Colloquium "Verdi-Wagner" Rom 1969: Bericht* (item 227), 272–87.
Reprinted in *Fedele d'Amico: Un ragazzino all'Augusteo. Scritti musicali*, 41–58. Ed. by Franco Serpa. Turin: Giulio Einaudi, 1991. ISBN 88–06–12385–8. ML 160 .D195 1991.

D'Amico asserts that authors' own ideas about drama strongly influence their estimation of Verdi's aesthetic principles. After discussing contrasting points of view in writings by Ildebrando Pizzetti (items 360 and 494), Massimo Mila (item 375), and Leo Karl Gerhartz (item 408), the present author suggests that a fundamental operative principle of Verdi's aesthetics parallels that proposed by literary critic György Lukás: the essence of dramatic effect consists in its *immediate*, collective effect on a group of spectators. For additional commentary on D'Amico's ideas, see Fabrizio Della Seta's essay (item 352).

402. ———. "Shakespeare pietra di paragone di Verdi." In *Fedele d'Amico: Un ragazzino all'Augusteo. Scritti musicali*, 75–84. Ed. by Franco Serpa. Turin: Giulio Einaudi, 1991. ISBN 88–06–12385–8. ML 160 .D195 1991.

Examines ways in the composer's aesthetic sense of "realism" interacted with the Shakespearean models in *Macbeth* and *Otello*.

403. Della Seta, Fabrizio. "'Parola scenica' in Verdi e nella critica verdiana." In *Le parole della musica, I: Studi sulla lingua della letteratura musicale in onore di Gianfranco Folena*, 259–86. Ed. by Fiamma Nicolodi and Paolo Trovato. Studi di musica veneta, 21. Florence: Olschki, 1994. ISBN 88–222–4284–X. ML 63 .P26 1994.

This important study surveys the differing ways in which Verdi scholars have treated the idea of "parola scenica." The author proposes that Verdi may have arrived at the term as a felicitous expression to convey a specific idea at a particular moment to his librettist, Antonio Ghislanzoni, and that it should perhaps not be elevated to a general dramaturgical principle. Della Seta cites a number of passages in which Verdi uses the term "scenico" or "teatrale" to describe a word, a phrase, a verse, a situation, an effect, or a movement, all to designate a certain theatrical effect that directly draws the attention of the public to something of significance. He argues that the "scenic aspect" ["*scenicità*"] of the word is something that Verdi required continually from his librettist in a general way, and that it was not limited to occasional phrases that launch a new formal section or piece. The author also suggests that the "scenic aspect" applied in Verdi's mind to the music itself every bit as much as it does the words of the libretto and that a concept of "musica scenica" might be more useful to analysts than the more limited "parola scenica." An appendix reproduces the two instances in Verdi's correspondence that use the term "parola scenica" (both to Ghislanzoni) as well as a passage to Antonio Somma and one to Boito that refer to the same concept without using the term. The appendix also reproduces citations from 23 secondary sources in which Verdi scholars discuss the concept of "parola scenica." See item 102 for another recent study dealing with the term, albeit from a more traditional standpoint.

 *   ———. "Verdi: La tradizione italiana e l'esperienza europea." See item 352.

404. Donà, Mariangela. "Verdi e il romanticismo tedesco." *Atti 2* (item 225), 180–85.

An overview of the reception of German Romantic ideas in nineteenth-century Italy and specifically by Verdi.

405. Drenger, Tino. *Liebe und Tod in Verdis Musikdramatik: Semiotische Studien zu ausgewählten Opern*. Hamburger Beiträge zur Musikwissenschaft, 45.

Eisenach: Verlag der Musikalienhandlung Karl Dieter Wagner, 1996. ISBN 3–88979–070–4. 382 p. MT 100 .V47 D7 1996.

The first section of the study examines the Romantic conception of love and death, the idea of death as redemption, symbols and metaphors of love and death in nineteenth-century literature and music, and Verdi's own feelings and experiences with love and death. The latter portion of the volume discusses the themes of love and death in five specific operas: *I lombardi, La battaglia di Legnano, La traviata, Don Carlos,* and *Otello*. In each case, the author includes a relatively detailed musical-dramatic analysis of selected scenes from the work. The author provides a substantial bibliography, but the book lacks an index.

406. Edwards, Geoffrey and Ryan Edwards. *The Verdi Baritone: Studies in the Development of Dramatic Character.* Bloomington and Indianapolis: Indiana University Press, 1994. x, 193 p. ISBN 0–253–31949–8. ML 410 .V4 E3.

Surveys Verdi's characterization of leading baritone roles in *Nabucco, Ernani, Macbeth, Rigoletto, La traviata, Simon Boccanegra* and *Otello*. An appendix provides a plot summary for each of the operas discussed.

* Folena, Daniela Goldin. "Lessico melodrammatico verdiano." See item 102.

407. Fricke, Harald. "Schiller und Verdi: Das Libretto als Textgattung." In *Oper und Operntext*, 95–115. Ed. by Jens Malte Fischer. Reihe Siegen: Beiträge zur Literatur- und Sprachwissenschaft, 60. Heidelberg: Carl Winter Universitätsverlag, 1985. ISBN 3–533–03665–0 (cloth); 3–533–03664–2 (paper). ML 2110 .O645 1985.

After briefly reviewing Verdi's involvement with the works of Schiller, the author carefully compares *Luisa Miller* and *Don Carlos* with their literary prototypes. Fricke proposes that *Luisa Miller* served as a trial "sketchbook" for ideas and procedures in his later works, while *Don Carlos* transcended many of the limitations of Schiller's idealistic historical drama.

408. Gerhartz, Leo Karl. *Die Auseinandersetzungen des jungen Giuseppe Verdi mit dem literarischen Drama: Ein Beitrag zur szenischen Strukturbestimmung der Oper.* Berliner Studien zur Musikwissenschaft, 15. Berlin: Merseburger, 1968. 523 p. ML 410 .V4 G39.

Examines Verdi's attitudes and ideas regarding the adaptation of theatrical dramas as opera librettos. The study focuses on the period from *Ernani* to *Rigoletto* and includes a discussion of the composer's unrealized plans for *Re Lear*. A series of tables at the end of the volume provide outlines of the original plays, showing material that was added or omitted in the librettos. See item 401 for further discussion and critique of some of the author's ideas.

409. Gräwe, Karl Dietrich. "Shakespeares dramatische Charaktere und Verdis Operngestalten: Über das Verhältnis von Dramentext und Opernlibretto." *Atti 1* (item 224), 120–25.

Examines reasons why Boito's adaptation of Shakespeare's texts for *Otello* and *Falstaff* work so effectively as operatic librettos.

410. ――――. "L'uno e gli altri: Osservazioni sulla drammaturgia verdiana di conflitto interumano e della sua soluzione." *Atti 3* (item 226), 27–33.

Shows how Verdi effectively used dance or party music, typically played by a stage band, to underscore conflicts among individuals and between individuals and society. The author's discussion focuses on examples from *Rigoletto*, *La traviata*, *Otello*, and *Falstaff*.

411. Guccini, Gerardo. "La drammaturgia dell'attore nella sintesi di Giuseppe Verdi." *Teatro e storia* 4 (October 1989): 245–82.

This wide-ranging and important essay examines the development of Verdi's aesthetic ideals in the 1840s and early 1850s, focusing on parallels between the techniques of contemporary stage actors in Italy, particularly Gustavo Modena, and Verdi's creative process. Guccini investigates the composer's association during the mid-1840s with a group of Milanese intellectual figures that included Francesco Hayez, Alessandro Sanquirico, Tommaso Grossi, Carlo Cattaneo, Andrea Maffei, Giulio Carcano, and Gustavo Modena. All these shared an interest in aesthetics of the theater and theatrical reform, and their discussions no doubt fueled the composer's passion for Shakespeare and Schiller that soon manifested itself in *Macbeth*, *I masnadieri*, and the never completed *Re Lear*. The author argues that while Verdi's attraction to literature that displayed strongly contrasting characters and situations and that focused on deviations from societal norms was at odds with general trends in Italian theater, his ideas were in sympathy with broader pan-European developments. A large part of the essay explores Verdi's dramaturgical ideals in the famed trilogy of the early 1850s: Rigoletto, La *traviata,* and *Il trovatore*, as well as in Verdi's unrealized plans for an opera based on Alexandre Dumas père's play *Kean, ou désordre et génie* (1834), based on the life of then recently deceased British actor Edmund Kean.

412. Herrmann, William A., Jr. "Religion in the Operas of Giuseppe Verdi." Ph.D dissertation, Columbia University, 1963. v, 291 p.

While the *Requiem* represents Verdi's only explicitly religious work during the main part of his career, the author points out that he began and ended his career writing religious music and argues that religious scenes in his operas represent a cohesive and coherent part of that tradition. Topics examined include Verdi's attitude toward religion, religious elements in his librettos, religious choruses and liturgical scenes, depiction of the clery, prayers sung by sopranos, and death scenes. The author concludes that the *Requiem* and the *Pezzi sacri* are a direct outgrowth of religious scenes in his operas and therefore should not be expected to display a distinctive style of their own.

413. Hudson, G. Elizabeth. "Narrative in Verdi: Perspectives on His Musical Dramaturgy." Ph.D. dissertation, Cornell University, 1993. x, 294 p.

An important study that considers narrative in the aesthetics of Italian opera and the relationship of Verdi's treatment of narrative texts to nineteenth-century conventions. The second portion of the dissertation examines in detail narrative aspects of three operas: *Rigoletto* (later published separately; see item 863), *Il trovatore* and *Otello*. The chapter dealing with *Il trovatore* focuses on how three *racconti* (one sung by Ferrando and two by Azucena) give dramatic shape to events concerning Azucena and her mother that occurred in the distant past. The discussion of *Otello* centers on the way in which expectations about narrative conventions affect the dramaturgy of the entire opera.

414. Jeuland-Meynard, Maryse. "L'Europe, pour quoi faire? Dans les opéras de Verdi." In *Les innovations théâtrales et musicales italiennes en Europe aux XVIIIᵉ et XIXᵉ siècles*, 191–206. Ed. by Irène Mamczarz. Paris: Presses Universitaires de France, 1991. ISBN 2–13–044030–4. PN 2570 .I55 1991.

Examines the tendency of Verdi's librettos to focus on locations outside of his native land and their portrayal of foreigners.

415. ———. "Images et discours sur le corps dans le livret de Verdi." In *La représentation du corps dans la culture italienne: Actes du Colloque de 1981, Centre d'Études Italiennes d'Aix-en-Provence*, 217–39. Aix-en Provence: Université de Provence, 1983. ISBN 2–85399–079–6. NX 552.1 A1 R46 1983.

Surveys imagery relating to the human body found in both the lyrical text and the stage directions of Verdi's librettos. The author devotes particular attention to images of blood and death that frequently dominate the operas' final scenes.

416. Kunze, Stefan. "Fest und Ball in Verdis Opern." In *Die 'Couleur locale' in der Oper des 19. Jahrhunderts*, 269–78. Ed. by Heinz Becker. Studien zur Musikgeschichte des 19. Jahrhunderts, 42. Regensburg: Gustav Bosse Verlag, 1976. ISBN 3–7649–2101–3. ML 1704 .C68.

Explores the function of party and dance scenes—including the use of stage band music—in Verdi's dramaturgy. While dance and party scenes in operas by earlier composers centered largely on the practical consideration of bringing everyone onto stage in one place, Verdi begins to use these scenes as a dramatic harbinger of an ensuing catastrophe. The author surveys Verdi's use of these scenes, with special emphasis on *Rigoletto, Un ballo in maschera, La traviata, Ernani,* and *Otello.* Kunze suggests that Mozart's ballroom scene in *Don Giovanni* provided a prototype for the composer's new way of handling these scenes.

417. Lavagetto, Mario. *Quei più modesti romanzi. Il libretto nel melodramma di Verdi: Tecniche costruttive, funzioni, poetica di un genere letterario minore.* Argomenti. Milan: Garzanti, 1979. 205 p. ML 410 .V4 L33.

A comprehensive study of Verdi's librettos (excluding *Un giorno di regno* and *Falstaff*), including topics such as general approach to dramaturgy; characterization; organization of plots; use of the chorus; and elements of language, meter, and poetic structure. The author details the special contributions of Solera, Piave, and Cammarano to the corpus of Verdi's librettos and provides a detailed assessment of the final act from *Un ballo in maschera.* Although the volume lacks an index, it contains a sizeable bibliography of items dealing with Verdi's librettos and the literary aspects of his operas.

418. ———. "Tredici proposte intorno ai libretti." *Per un "progetto Verdi" anni '80* (item 232), 45–54.

Asserts that the study of librettos is yet in an infant state, and their usefulness for shedding light on a wide range of matters has not yet been totally realized. The author suggests several avenues that need to be explored, including a critical edition of Verdi's librettos, an exploration of the precise sources and literary archetypes on which individual librettos are based, a comprehensive study of censorship in Verdi's operas, and examination of the sociological, historical, and linguistic components of librettos.

419. López-Calo, José. "La Spagna in Verdi." *Atti 3* (item 226), 244–49.

Verdi's operas set in Spain—*Il trovatore, La forza del destino,* and *Don Carlos*—show an interest in exoticism that emphasizes the Romantic and mystical atmosphere of bygone eras.

420. Loschelder, Josef. *Das Todesproblem in Verdis Opernschaffen.* Italienische Studien. Stuttgart: Deutsche Verlags-Anstalt, 1938. 101 p. ML 410 .V4 L6.

Surveys the treatment of death in both the librettos and music of Verdi's operas. The discussion includes the way in which death is handled for various character types, the portrayal of death scenes themselves, the relationship of death to love and religion, and the use of tonal structure and recurring motives in connection with the idea of death.

421. Manlove, John. "The Dramaturgy of Shakespeare and Verdi: A Study of Form." Ph.D. dissertation, University of Minnesota, 1964. vii, 281 p.

Compares the dramaturgical elements (action, dialogue, character, and theme) in Verdi's three operas based on Shakespearean plays to the original dramas, concluding that faithfulness to the original model is not a prerequisite for successful dramaturgy in opera but at times may impede it.

422. Marcozzi, Rudy T. "The Interaction of Large-Scale Harmonic and Dramatic Structure in the Verdi Operas Adapted from Shakespeare." Ph.D. dissertation, Indiana University, 1992. viii, 308 p.

Using Schenkerian analytical methodology and plot analysis based on Bernard Beckerman's *Dynamics of Drama*, the author concludes that there is a strong correlation between dramatic design and tonal design in Verdi's three Shakespeare operas at both local and more fundamental structural levels. Appendices include reductive graphs showing the middleground tonal structure of each of the three operas under consideration.

423. Metzger, Heinz-Klaus, and Rainer Riehn, eds. *Giuseppe Verdi*. Musik-Konzepte, 10. Munich: edition text + kritik, 1979. ISBN 3–88377–016–7. ML 410 .V4 G57.

A collection of five articles that focus on aesthetic issues in Verdi's music. Includes a list of works and a selective discography. See items 262, 438, 557, 886, and 928.

424. Minardi, Gian Paolo. "Temporali e battaglie nell'opera verdiana." *Atti 3* (item 226), 232–37.

Verdi uses storm scenes in his operas not merely for pictorial effect but for dramatic reasons: a ferocious release of primal energy that evokes a sense of impending doom beyond human control. The presence of a battle scene creates a similar effect, symbolically representing the violent release of tension between opposing groups of people. The author argues that Verdi's musical depictions of storms and battles represent some of his most imaginative writing.

425. Nicastro, Aldo. "Il teatro francese nell'evoluzione del melodramma verdiano." *Atti 3* (item 226), 338–48.

Verdi's involvement with the Paris Opéra became a major influence on the development of his style. The author argues that the composer's first opera written expressly for the Opéra, *Les vêpres siciliennes*, shows a new orientation and sophisticated refinement in his psychological approach to human passion and love that permeates *La forza del destino, Don Carlos, Aida,* and especially *Un ballo in maschera.*

426. ———. "Verdi e la parola scenica." *Musica e dossier* No. 36 (January 1990): 47–55.

This nicely illustrated article surveys Verdi's aesthetic ideals with respect to opera librettos and examines how changes in his musical style paralleled changes in the style of the librettos. One particularly interesting table illustrates similarities in construction between roughly parallel scenes in two librettos by Salvatore Cammarano: the entrance scene of Leonora in *Il trovatore* and that of Lucia in Donizetti's *Lucia di Lammermoor*. This article is part of a larger group of essays in this issue entitled "Musica e libretti nell'opera italiana dell'ottocento."

427. Paduano, Guido. *Noi facemmo ambedue un sogno strano: Il disagio amoroso sulla scena dell'opera europea*. Palermo: Sellerio, 1982. 203 p. ML 3858 .P3 1982

The volume includes substantial chapters devoted to an investigation of dramaturgy in *Ernani* and *Don Carlos*, focusing particularly on the conflict between love and political ambition.

428. ———. "Shakespeare e la parola scenica." In *Il giro della vita: Percorsi dell'opera lirica*, p. 115–66. Discanto/contrappunti, 30. Scandicci: La Nuova Italia, 1992. ISBN 88–221–1090–0.

Argues that while Verdi's operas based on Shakespeare contain substantial changes from the original plays, both artists, in their own way, have an uncanny ability to use language to conjure up the essence of a situation which, in Verdi's case, is reinforced by the music. This article offers significant insights into the genesis of the librettos to *Macbeth, Otello,* and *Falstaff.*

429. Parker, Roger. "On Reading Nineteenth-Century Opera: Verdi Through the Looking Glass." In *Reading Opera*, 288–305. Ed. by Arthur Groos and Roger Parker. Princeton: Princeton University Press, 1988. ISBN 0–691–09132–3. ML 2110 .R4 1988.

Proposes that for Verdi the gradual move away from the traditional libretto with its distinction between rhymed metrical verse (intended for arias) and unrhymed, irregular *versi sciolti* (intended for recitative), and the conventional musical structures engendered by these librettos created an "abyss of freedom," resulting in a gradual loss of creative energy in the latter part of his career. No longer could he easily dash off an *opera di getto* in a single burst of creative activity. The extraordinary linguistic ability and musical talents of Boito allowed him to cross into new territory with *Otello*, particularly because of its unity of conception and lack of subplots, and *Falstaff*, in which the comic mode unleashed unprecedented musical diversity. The author draws parallels to Wagner's aesthetic development, in which the changing literary style fueled, rather than hampered, his creative energy. Parker also argues that an implicit acceptance of Wagner's aesthetic premises has colored the critical reception of Verdi's operas up to the present, resulting in more favorable acceptance of "progressive" operas such as *Rigoletto* and *La traviata*, than more conservatively grounded works such as *Il trovatore*.

430. Pinagli, Palmiro. *Romanticismo di Verdi.* Florence: Vallecchi, 1967. 172 p. ML 410 .V4 P48.

A study of Verdi's aesthetic principles, based primarily on ideas expressed in his correspondence. The volume is organized around general topics presented in a relatively chronological framework, including the composer's relationship to his immediate predecessors and contemporaries, the issue of nationalism in Verdi's music, his conception of opera, and his changing musical style. While much territory has been explored more thoroughly since this book's publication, it remains an excellent concise introduction to Verdi's aesthetic thought.

431. Pinzauti, Leonardo. "Le due 'stupende lettere' del Petrarca e il romanticismo di Giuseppe Verdi." *Quadrivium: Studi di filologia e musicologia* 27 (1986): 115–21. This volume of *Quadrivium* is listed in some indexes as a monograph: *Universalità della musica, prestigio dell'Italia, attualità di Verdi: Studi in onore di Mario Medici*, Vol. 2. Ed. by Giuseppe Vecchi. Bologna: Antiquae Musicae Italicae Studiosi, 1986.

Verdi's reference to "two stupendous letters by Petrarch" in a letter to Giulio Ricordi (20 November 1880) has often been associated with his revision of *Simon Boccanegra*. The author argues that sentiments from the Petrarch letters have a much more global association with the composer's aesthetics, particularly as seen in Giuseppe Fracassetti's 1865 translation, which imbues the letters with a highly romantic, melodramatic, and nationalistic spirit. Pinzauti also points to other aspects of Fracassetti's translation that may have influenced the tone and color of the revised *Simon Boccanegra*. See Daniela Goldin's study (item 887) for additional exploration of the influence of Petrarch on Verdi.

432. Pizzagalli, Franco. "La religiosità nei melodrammi di G. Verdi." *Rivista internazionale di musica sacra/International Church Music Review* 5 (1984): 23–34.

Argues that Verdi, contrary to some assertions in the secondary literature, was neither opposed nor indifferent to the philosophical tenets of Christianity. The composer's portrayal of religion and religious sentiments in his operas suggests a powerful faith in God, albeit a mysterious God who neither intervenes directly in the course of human lives—even in response to direct prayer—nor mediates the suffering of innocent people. The article includes a brief survey of religious scenes in Verdi's operas.

433.   Porter, Andrew. "Verdi and Schiller." In *Opera Annual No. 3*, p. 52–63. Ed. by Harold Rosenthal. London: John Calder; New York: Lantern Press, 1956. ML 21 .O6 no. 3.

A concise examination of the way in which Verdi and his librettists adapted Schiller's plays in *Giovanna d'Arco, I masnadieri*, and *Luisa Miller*. The author proposes that the two artists' styles have much in common, emphasizing passion, powerful effects, and directness.

434.   Rinaldi, Mario. *Verdi critico: I suoi giudizi, la sua estetica*. Roma: Edizioni Ergo, 1951. 449 p. + 7 p.

A study of Verdi as an intellectual figure, focusing on his aesthetic conceptions and his opinions about music and culture in general. Individual chapters cover a wide variety of topics, including: the influence of the composer's personality on the works he produced, the role of inspiration in his creative process, his choice and rejection of various topics for operas, his adaptation of conventional formal procedures, his ideas about the direction of music in Italy and in Europe north of the Alps, and his reaction to reviews and critiques of his works. This volume is well worth study, although it should be used in tandem with more recent scholarship, especially in the area of the composer's creative process. The volume contains a selective bibliography and a short name dictionary of people associated with Verdi.

435.   ———. *Verdi e Shakespeare: "Macbeth" — "Otello" — "Falstaff."* Collezione Dorica 1039. Rome: Fratelli De Santis, n.d. 53 p. ML 410 .V4 R5.

Offers a short essay on each of Verdi's operas based on Shakespeare. The essays focus on the issue of dramaturgy, pointing out aspects of Verdi's treatment of the material that make the operas convincing and spell-binding.

436.   Roccatagliati, Alessandro. "Drammaturgia romantica verdiana: *Luisa Miller* e *Rigoletto*." Quaderni de Il Coretto, 3. Bari: Associazione Musicale Il Coretto, 1989. 79 p. ML 410 .V4 R63 1989.

Examines Verdi's aesthetic ideas relating to dramaturgy— focusing on *Luisa Miller* and *Rigoletto*, works composed at the end of the *primo ottocento*—against the background of general debates and discussions about dramaturgy during the Romantic period in Italy and throughout Europe in general. The author focuses special attention on the significance of Alessandro Manzoni's essay

Lettre à M. C[hauvet] sur l'unité de temps et de lieu dans la tragédie (1823) and the role of musical conventions in establishing the shape and tone of opera librettos.

437. Santi, Piero. "Etica verdiana ed etica schilleriana." *Atti 2* (item 225), 209–33.

An important, detailed study that explores Verdi's approach to realism throughout his works and its relationship to his sense of ethics. The author uses Schiller's dramas as a major points of comparison and contrast; however, he also includes considerable discussion of operas not based on stories by Schiller, particularly *Rigoletto, La traviata*, and *Falstaff.*

438. Schnebel, Dieter. "Die schwierige Wahrheit des Lebens—Zu Verdis musikalischem Realismus." In *Giuseppe Verdi: Musik-Konzepte* 10 (item 423): 51–111.

The first portion of the article compares the aesthetic approaches of Verdi and Wagner by examining several sets of roughly parallel scenes in their operas. In the second part, the author provides a detailed study of Verdi's aesthetic development from *Nabucco* through *Falstaff.*

439. Tomlinson, Gary. "Opera and *Drame*: Hugo, Donizetti, and Verdi." In *Studies in the History of Music*. Vol. 2: *Music and Drama*, 171–192. New York: Broude Brothers, 1988. ISBN 0–8450–7402–4. ML 1700 .M88.

Victor Hugo set a new tone in dramas such as *Cromwell, Hernani, Le roi s'amuse, Lucrèce Borgia,* and *Angelo.* His search to represent "truth" and "reality" led to a new, more natural poetic style, fidelity to details of time and locale, a mixing of the sublime and the grotesque, and an emphasis on political, moral, and social reform. Donizetti's *Lucrezia Borgia* initiated a new tradition that applied Hugo's aesthetic principles to Italian opera. *Ernani* imbued Verdi with a new sense of purpose, reflected in his sophisticated use of a more "popular" musical style; he later realized Hugo's more artistic goals in *Rigoletto.*

440. Van, Gilles De. "L'eroe verdiano." In *Opera & Libretto I*, 265–80. Studi di musica veneta. Florence: Olschki, 1990. ISBN 88–222–3825–7. ML 1700 .O655 1990.

A study of Verdi's dramaturgical approach to the hero, i.e., a man (usually a tenor) who wants to be united with the heroine but is frustrated by the actions of one or more antagonists. The author discusses the fundamental difference between the hero and other protagonists and the inherent double paradox typically found in Verdi's operas: 1) the hero is both extraneous to society yet fully belongs to it and 2) the hero is morally superior to his fellow characters but also capable of making terrible mistakes. The concluding portion of the article considers the mechanics of how Verdi and his librettists resolve the fate of the hero throughout his operas.

441.   ————. "Notes sur Verdi humoriste." In *Omaggio a Gianfranco Folena*, 2:1739–48. 2 vols. Padua: Editoriale Programma, 1993. ISBN 88-71231-05-8. PC 1026 .F65 O63 1993.

Proposes that the use of comic—or lighter—moments to bring out more sharply the overall tragic or melodramatic mood remains a constant part of Verdi's dramaturgy from the early 1850s, and that the composer's knowledge of Mozart's *Don Giovanni* strongly influenced this aesthetic approach. The bulk of the article, in which the author draws many direct parallels to *Don Giovanni*, focuses on *La forza del destino*. Van also examines the interplay of tragedy and comedy in *Un ballo in maschera* and in the second act finale of *Il trovatore*. The author criticizes the commonly held viewpoint that Verdi—at least in the first part of his career—"zig-zagged" between innovative "pioneering" operas and conservative "throwback" works, proposing instead that the composer drew from a wide range of aesthetic procedures to support a consistent dramaturgical ideal.

442.   ————. "Parole, musique, drame: Les rapports de Verdi avec ses librettistes." In *Le livret malgré lui: Actes du Colloque du Groupe de Recherche sur les Rapports Musique-Texte (G.R.M.T.), Paris-Sorbonne, le 23 novembre 1991*, 69–78. Paris: Éditions Publimuses, 1992. ISBN 2-909861-00-7.

Argues that the extent of Verdi's influence on the librettos for his operas has long been overemphasized by writers who wish (consciously or not) to portray him favorably with respect to his contemporary, Richard Wagner. While Verdi actively collaborated with his librettists, his primary concern involved issues of dramaturgy, not a precise, polished version of the language to be used.

443.   ————. *Verdi: Un théâtre en musique*. Paris: Fayard, 1992. 473 p. ISBN 2-213-02895-8. ML 410 .V4 V26 1992.
        Italian translation by Rita De Letteriis. *Verdi: Un teatro in musica*. Discanto/contrappunti, 31. Florence: La nuova Italia, 1994. ISBN 88-221-1446-9.
        English translation by Gilda Roberts. *Verdi, Man of the Theater: Creating Drama Through Music*. Chicago: University of Chicago Press, forthcoming.

An important detailed study of the evolution and development of Verdi's ideas about dramaturgy. The volume begins by surveying Verdi's work set in the context of works by his contemporaries, presenting a concise examination of the way in which librettos typically took shape and establishing a general typology of Verdian characters. The author suggests that Verdi's work was influenced both by the format of simple conflict found in the contemporary *mélodrame* and by the more sophisticated examination of people's emotions and moral dilemmas associated with the musical drama. The volume contains a substantial bibliography, a glossary of technical terms, an index of names, and a separate index of Verdi's compositions.

444. Vecchi, Giuseppe. *Studi e ricerche sui libretti delle opere di Giuseppe Verdi.* Dulce melos, 6. Miscellanee saggi convegni, 30. Bologna: Antiquae Musicae Italicae Studiosi, 1990. 204 p.

Four of the essays were previously published as a group entitled "Annotazioni su alcuni libretti delle opere di Verdi." *Quadrivium: Studi di filologia e musicologia* 20 (1979): 77–192.

A collection of eight new and previously published essays dealing with specific works. See items 364, 616, 646, 771, 857, 891, 968, and 978.

445. Weaver, William. "Aspects of Verdi's Dramaturgy." *The Verdi Companion* (item 5), 131–43.

An overview of Verdi's ideas about effective drama based on selected correspondence with his librettists.

446. ———. "Verdi and the Drama of Love." *Atti 3* (item 226), 523–28.

Although a love duet between hero and heroine was a standard feature of nineteenth-century opera, Verdi almost never employs it in a conventional manner. He typically adds a dramatic dimension to his duets between lovers by starting with one or the other accused of unfaithfulness or cruelty. This charge is refuted in a middle section and, in conclusion, the lovers reconcile themselves to each other and to their fate. In general, love is not often a chief motivating force in Verdi's works. The operas that place the most attention on love duets are *Don Carlos* and *Les vêpres siciliennes*, both written for French audiences.

447. Weiss, Piero. "Verdi and the Fusion of Genres." *Journal of the American Musicological Society* 35 (1982): 138–56.

Italian translation by Alessandro Roccatagliati: "Verdi e la fusione dei generi." In *La drammaturgia musicale*, 75–92. Ed. by Lorenzo Bianconi. Bologna: Società Editrice il Mulino, 1986. ISBN 88–15–01127–7. ML 1700 .D72 1986.

Explores Verdi's use of comic elements in several middle-period works to heighten dramatic intensity and suggests that this aesthetic notion was strongly influenced by the composer's knowledge of Shakespeare and Victor Hugo. The author makes particularly insightful comments about the intellectual relationship between Verdi and Cammarano as it developed during the genesis of *Luisa Miller* and the never-completed *Re Lear* and offers an analysis of

comic elements in *Rigoletto*. See item 411 for a further development of some of
Weiss's ideas.

448. Wiesmann, Sigrid. "'Disposizioni sceniche' oder 'Gesamtkunstwerk': Wagner,
Verdi und die Große Oper." In *Atti del XIV Congresso della Società
Internazionale di Musicologia: Trasmissione e recezione delle forme di cultura
musicale*, 1: 714–20. Ed. by Angelo Pompilio, Donatella Restani, Lorenzo
Bianconi, and F. Alberto Gallo. Turin: Edizioni di Torino, 1990. 3 vols.
ISBN 88–7063–084–6.

Using *Otello* and *Götterdämmerung* as points of reference, the author asserts
that Verdi, like Wagner, conceived the visual aspects of his later works as
having a fundamental, integral status, analogous in importance to both text and
music. The two composers also share a common interest in using musical
dialogue to carry out the essence of the drama. Finally the author considers the
relationship of both composers to the earlier tradition of French *grand opéra*,
as embodied in the works of Giacomo Meyerbeer.

449. Zoppelli, Luigi. "Verdi 'narratore': Onniscienza, timbro puro, e oggetto
psichico." *Studi verdiani* 7 (1991): 57–78.

A study of narrative strategies in Verdi's operas. In particular, the author
examines the function of passages featuring instrumental solos ("pure timbres"),
often associated with the entry of a character deep in thought, to represent a
precise psychic object that cannot be shown or acted out literally on stage. The
author devotes particular attention to Philip's monologue that opens Act IV of
Don Carlos.

COMPOSITIONAL PROCESS

450. Hepokoski, James A. "Compositional Emendations in Verdi's Autograph
Scores: *Il trovatore*, *Un ballo in maschera*, and *Aida*." *Studi verdiani* 4
(1986–87): 87–109.

Analyzes selected revisions made during the skeleton-score stage of the
compositional process in the following pieces: Leonora's Act I cavatina "Tacea
la notte placida" and the first appearance of Count Luna in Act I, Scene 2 of
Il trovatore; Amelia's Act III preghiera "Morrò, ma prima in grazia" from *Un
ballo in maschera*; and "Celeste Aida" and the opening of Act IV, Scene 2 from
Aida.

451. Lawton, David, and David Rosen. "Verdi's Non-Definitive Revisions: The
Early Operas." *Atti 3* (item 226), 189–237.

This significant study examines substitute pieces, transpositions, and revisions made by Verdi for individual singers (*puntature*) in specific productions of operas through *Attila*. With one exception from *Les vêpres siciliennes*, Verdi stopped writing substitute arias when he reached *Macbeth* and began to demand tight control over all important productions of his subsequent works. He continued, however, to write *puntature* on occasion even late in his career. An extensive section of the article, based upon several chapters in Lawton's doctoral dissertation (see item 480), analyzes three versions of Fenena's preghiera in *Nabucco* and assesses their differing effects on the tonal structure of the final act of the opera. The authors include a concise checklist of Verdi's non-definitive revisions through *Attila*, a prose description detailing the history of each of the revisions, and a catalogue listing documentation, texts, and musical sources for each of the revisions.

* Marvin, Roberta Montemorra. "Aspects of Tempo in Verdi's Early and Middle-Period Italian Operas." See item 531.

452. Petrobelli, Pierluigi. "Osservazioni sul processo compositivo in Verdi." *Acta musicologica* 43 (1971): 125–42.
    English translation by Roger Parker. "Remarks on Verdi's Composing Process." In *Music in the Theater: Essays on Verdi and Other Composers* (item 378), 48–74.

The opening portion of this article considers general issues involved in studying Verdi's composing process. Problems faced by researchers include the unavailability of most compositional drafts and sketches, the complexity of Verdi's composing process, which often continued even after the early performances of a work, and lack of previous research on which to build (the situation in all three of these areas has improved substantially since the article was first published). The author then offers specific thoughts related to two compositional documents: 1) a bifolio containing a fragmentary draft for the conclusion of *I due Foscari* and 2) the previously published continuity draft for *Rigoletto*. The sketch for *I due Foscari* shows that while the composer remained close to his early ideas about rhythmic scansion, he altered the melodic shape considerably while expanding and broadening his original conception of the passage to achieve greater dramatic impact (the author provides additional thoughts about this sketch in item 671). The *Rigoletto* draft shows, among other things, how Verdi achieved a "negative" characterization of Rigoletto, and how he worked out the sophisticated interaction of vocal and orchestral lines in the Rigoletto-Sparafucile duet.

453. Powers, Harold S. "One Halfstep at a Time: Tonal Transposition and 'Split Association' in Italian Opera." *Cambridge Opera Journal* 7 (1995): 135–64.

The concluding portion of this article discusses sections from three operas in which Verdi originally wrote a passage in a key one-half step distant from its final version: the final scene of *Il trovatore* (originally written in Eb major and later transposed to E); two of Gilda's arias in *Rigoletto* ("Caro Nome," transposed from F to E Major and the *tempo d'attacco* and slow movement of Gilda's duet-finale with her father in Act II, tranposed from Db to C major); and the second stanza of Gabriele's aria in Act II of *Simon Boccanegra* (originally written in Eb, but transposed up to E major). Powers demonstrates reasons for each of the changes, concluding—in support of an idea stated earlier by James Hepokoski (item 827)—that the transpositions are neither random nor merely practical for the convenience of the singers but affect the expressive significance created by the "web of tonalities" present in each opera.

STYLISTIC & ANALYTICAL STUDIES

454. Abbate, Carolyn, and Roger Parker, eds. *Analyzing Opera: Verdi and Wagner.* Berkeley: University of California Press, 1989. viii, 304 p. ISBN 0–520–06157–8. MT 95 .A59 1989.

Contains papers presented at the Cornell Verdi-Wagner Conference held in October 1984. The editors' introduction (pp. 1–24) contains a useful historical summary of trends in analytical studies dealing with Verdi's operas. Individual articles from this volume are abstracted separately as numbers 477, 573, 575, 683, 827, and 861. James Webster later offered an informal response to the conference (see item 511 below).

455. Abert, Anna Amalie. "Leidenschaftsausbrüche zwischen Rezitativ und Arie." *Atti 3* (item 226), 56–70.

Discusses examples of highly dramatic or emotional outbursts in Verdi's operas in which the composer momentarily shifts to a declamatory texture that is neither pure recitative nor aria. While these passages are found throughout Verdi's works, they are particularly notable in operas written during the late 1850s and early 1860s as the composer sought to transform conventions from the first part of the century into a distinctive new style.

456. Alper, Clifford D. "Thematic Similarities in Early and Middle Verdi." *Verdi Newsletter* 11 (1983): 16–21.

Illustrates Verdi's process of self-borrowing with two sets of melodic patterns that recur in more than one opera. The author first compares a melody that appears at the beginning of *La battaglia di Legano,* at a parallel structural point in *Rigoletto,* and again in Act III of *Rigoletto.* A second set of similar melodies may be found in Act I of *Attila* and *Il corsaro,* Act III of *La battaglia di*

Legnano, Acts I and III of *Rigoletto* and Act II, Scene I of *La traviata*. The author argues that this second melody type, which Verdi may have modelled after a passage in Donizetti's *Pia de'Tolomei*, undergoes a process of thematic development throughout these operas, reaching a peak in *La traviata*.

457. Balthazar, Scott L. "Analytic Contexts and Mediated Influences: The Rossinian *Convenienze* and Verdi's Middle and Late Duets." *Journal of Musicological Research* 10 (1990): 19–45.

Focusing on Verdi's handling of the duet in operas from *Luisa Miller* through *Aida*, the author argues that the significance of formal features should be assessed not against an archetypal structure that coalesced at the time of Rossini but rather against the way in which that standard formal procedure had evolved at various points in time. Balthazar proposes that Verdi's handling of form in his middle and later operas not only drew on conventions of the past for purposes of continuity but also for their inherent flexibility and ambiguity. Specific examples illustrate tendencies toward an increasingly dramatic content and structure in the duet, breaking down its traditional balance between active and contemplative sections in favor of a less regimented, additive approach in which a chain of sections produce a cumulative effect. The author concludes with a discussion of the Amonasro-Aida duet from Act III of *Aida*, offering a counter-interpretation to that proposed by Harold Powers in item 496 below.

458. ———. "Music, Poetry, and Action in *Ottocento* Opera: The Principle of Concurrent Articulations." *Opera Journal* 22 (June 1989): 13–34.

Discusses the practice of synchronizing musical, dramatic, and poetic articulations as a means of formal organization in nineteenth-century opera, particularly in duets. The author examines representative passages from *Ernani* (Act II duet for Ernani and Silvia) and *La forza del destino* (Act II, "Scena Osteria"), illustrating how the composer and his librettists gradually began to place less emphasis on the structural implications of poetic form, substituting fast-moving articulations based on personality, mood, situation, and expressive nuances of the text.

459. Baroni, Mario. "Le formule d'accompagnamento nel teatro del primo Verdi." *Studi verdiani* 4 (1986–87): 18–64.

Argues that accompanimental figuration in Verdi's early operas is rooted in the tradition of popular band music rather than a native symphonic tradition. The author finds in five early operas (*Oberto*, *Ernani*, *I due Foscari*, *Attila*, and *Luisa Miller*) nearly 300 different accompanimental formulas that can be grouped in nine categories. Verdi typically delineated or underscored specific types of dramatic situations by drawing accompanimental formulas from particular categories.

460. Basevi, Abramo. *Studio sulle opere di G. Verdi.* Florence: Tofani, 1859.
     Reprint. Bologna: Antiquae Musicae Italicae Studiosi, 1978. xi, 324 p. ML
     410 .V5 B3.

     An English translation by Edward Schneider, *Study of the Operas of Giuseppe
     Verdi,* with annotations and an Introduction by Stefano Castelvecchi, has
     been announced by the University of Chicago Press. See item 892 for a
     recently published English translation of Chapter 19 on *Simon Boccanegra.*

     Basevi, a contemporary of Verdi, was a music critic in Florence, where each
     chapter of this book originally appeared as an independent article in the
     Florentine music journal *L'armonia.* After the introduction, each chapter
     explores a single opera, beginning with *Nabucco* and ending with *Aroldo*; an
     important concluding chapter summarizes stylistic qualities of Verdi's music and
     assesses his historical position at mid-century. Of particular interest is Basevi's
     division of the composer's works into two periods, a *prima* and *seconda maniera.*
     He discusses this in the chapter devoted to *Luisa Miller,* the opera that Basevi
     regards as Verdi's first work in the new style. While the first period emphasizes
     a feeling of grandeur in the manner of the last operas of Rossini, the second
     period resembles more the style of Donizetti with less grandeur, fewer effects
     predicated on sonority, lighter *cantilene,* more flexible rhythms, more tuneful
     melodic ideas, and greater use of *parlante* passages. The volume contains a
     detailed index. In recent years many Verdi scholars have frequently drawn on
     Basevi's writings, which have acquired a quasi-canonical status. Roger Parker
     (item 491) has recently offered a critique of this trend as well as a detailed
     consideration of Basevi's historical significance and an assessment of the
     Studio's strengths and weaknesses.

461. Budden, Julian. "Problems of Analysis in Verdi's Works." *Nuove prospettive
     nella ricerca verdiana* (item 231), 125–29.

     Argues that Basevi's concept of *tinta* is limited as an analytical tool because of
     its vagueness. Unifying features such as tonality and recurring motives are more
     specific but also pose difficulties. Only two of Verdi's operas begin and end in
     the same key; therefore, tonal structure must be viewed differently from
     traditional "closed" instrumental cycles. Likewise, Verdi wrote his early operas
     in a way that did not allow for the possibility of thematic development. Motivic
     unity is perhaps heard more easily in Verdi's *Requiem* than in any of his operas.

462. Celletti, Rodolfo. "Caratteri della vocalità di Verdi." *Atti* 3 (item 226), 81–88.
     English translation by Harold Barnes. "On Verdi's Vocal Writing." In *The
     Verdi Companion* (item 5), 216–38.

     Examines Verdi's characteristic writing for various voice types, focusing on the
     ways in which he departed from the style of earlier nineteenth-century
     composers.

463. Chusid, Martin. "The Organization of Scenes with Arias: Verdi's Cavatinas and Romanzas." *Atti 1* (item 224), 59–66.

Examines the characteristics of pieces that Verdi himself labelled cavatina or romanza. Cavatinas, most frequently written for the heroine, always occur at the first appearance of a character on stage. They use an "Andante" tempo, compound meter, shown either by the meter signature or by the consistent use of triplet subdivisions and, with one exception, feature the major mode. Verdi wrote romanzas most frequently for the leading tenor, and they occur anywhere in the opera. Most are in simple meters, and a substantial number utilize minor mode. Many use a bipartite formal structure.

464. Cone, Edward T. "The Old Man's Toys: Verdi's Last Operas." *Perspectives USA* 6 (1954): 114–33.

Reprinted in *Music: A View from Delft*, 159–75. Chicago: University of Chicago, 1989. ISBN 0–276–11469–4 (cloth); 0–276–11470–8 (paper). ML 60 .C773 M9 1989.

German translation. "Verdis letzte Opern: Die Spielzeuge eines alten Mannes. Die Spätwerk Verdis im Lichte der moderne Kritik." *Perspektiven* 3 (1953): 127–46.

French translation. "Les derniers ouvrages de Verdi ou les passe-temps d'un vieillard." *Profils* 6 (1954): 115–35.

Rebuts criticism that *Otello* and *Falstaff* demonstrate waning inspiration and were written as mere pastimes in the composer's late years. The author sees sophisticated advances in these operas in the use of elaborate melodic development, rich orchestral treatment, utmost concentration of ideas, and sophisticated shaping of the drama.

465. Dalmonte, Rossana. "Da *Oberto* a *Rigoletto*: Precisione di una formula." *Ricerche musicali* 3 (1979): 53–69.

In every opera from *Oberto* to *Rigoletto*, Verdi includes at least one passage of recitative on a single note to reflect heightened emotion, premonition, or remembrance of past events. The author examines the structure of some of these passages, including cadential formulas, treatment of rhythm, harmony, and timbre. The article concludes with a comprehensive survey of this type of passage in *Oberto*.

466. Dean, Winton. "Some Echoes of Donizetti in Verdi's Operas." *Atti 3* (item 226), 122–47.

Examines a series of passages in which Verdi subconsciously responded to a dramatic situation in a similar way to Donizetti. The author suggests that these passages became more frequent as Verdi's dramatic imagination and powers of characterization matured.

467. Engelhardt, Markus. *Die Chöre in den frühen Opern Giuseppe Verdis.* Würzburger musikhistorische Beiträge, 11. Tutzing: Hans Schneider, 1988. 374 p. ISBN 3–7952–0551–4. ML 410 .V4 E49 1988.

This important study, originally the author's doctoral dissertation, is the most extensive examination to date of the chorus in Verdi's operas from *Oberto* to *Luisa Miller*. The main body of the study analyzes Verdi's use of the chorus according to its function within the operas: introductory numbers or tableaus, solo or duet scenes, independent choral numbers during an act, or as preparation for part of a finale. Other sections of the book examine Verdi's choruses with respect to their literary models, the relationship between literary and musical form, and general stylistic characteristics of the music. A brief, but important, introductory section of the book deals with issues of performance practice relating to the chorus in early nineteenth-century opera in general and Verdi's operas in particular. Separate indexes for names and for compositions by Verdi (further broken down by act, scene, and number) facilitate the use of this volume for researchers. See item 754 for an updated version of the author's discussion of the choruses in *Luisa Miller*.

468. Finscher, Ludwig. "Wort und Ton in den Opern Verdis." *Colloquium "Verdi-Wagner" Rom 1969: Bericht* (item 227), 255–71.

Traces the stylistic evolution of Verdi's approach to declamation through his early operas. Changes can be seen as early as *Nabucco* and reach a new plateau with *Macbeth* and *Luisa Miller*.

469. Gallico, Claudio. "Struttura e funzione di pezzi sacri nell'opera e radici del linguaggio verdiano." In *Tornando a "Stiffelio"* (item 234), 265–71.

Verdi's evocation of religious music in his operas is an area that requires further study. The author suggests several areas for further exploration, including the degree of stylistic consistency among passages in various operas, their precise function, and the influence of music by earlier composers.

470. Girardi, Michele. "Per un inventario della musica in scena nel teatro verdiano." *Studi verdiani* 6 (1990): 99–145.

Verdi included stage music, performed either on or off stage, in each of his operas except *Un giorno di regno*. The author provides an overview of this stage music, which includes offstage vocal interjections, serenades, and choruses, as well as music for solo instruments and stage bands. Girardi then discusses Verdi's use of stage music to heighten the sense of drama in various ways: to signal an event that is about to take place or has just taken place or to impart special color to party or religious scenes.

471. Goold, William C. "The Verdi Baritone: A Study of Six Representative Operas." D.M.A. dissertation, University of Kentucky, 1981. iv, 242 p.

Explores Verdi's creation of significant baritone roles in *Nabucco, Ernani, Macbeth, Rigoletto, Otello,* and *Falstaff.* The author argues that the increased prominence given to baritones in these and other contemporary operas resulted from a change in style from *bel canto* to a more powerful type of singing. Verdi established a clear baritone type in his early career: a philosopher given to introspection and, with the exception of Falstaff, possessed of a serious nature. The author also concludes that while the composer established a clear baritone range in his earliest operas, his later operas more frequently exploit the extremes of that range.

472. Gossett, Philip. "The Chorus in *Risorgimento* Opera." *Cambridge Opera Journal* 2 (1990): 41–64.

Assesses the role of Verdi's choruses as conveyors of political ideas in light of the tradition established by earlier Italian composers, notably Rossini. The chorus in Rossini's later operas, particularly those premiered in Naples, becomes a dramatic force in its own right. Verdi develops this tendency further. Contemporary audiences interpreted some of his monumental choruses as political hymns partly on the basis of their musical style, despite being dramatically neutralized by the censors. The author examines political meaning in "Immenso Jeovha" from *Nabucco,* "Morte colga" from *Ernani,* "Viva Italia!" the opening chorus of knights in *I lombardi* (which is closely related to the second act finale of Rossini's *Guillaume Tell*), and the council chamber scene in the revised version of *Simon Boccanegra.* This last example suggests that Verdi continued to endow his choral scenes with political messages even after the unification of Italy—in this case, to promote reconciliation and unity among the various regions of the new country.

473. Hale, Virgil Edward. "The Tenor Arias in the Operas of Giuseppe Verdi." D.M.A. dissertation, University of Kentucky, 1973. v, 375 p.

A study of selected examples of Verdi's writing for tenors across the course of his career. The extensive vocal ranges and the style of writing in his first two operas suggests that the composer had the relatively light "tenorino" voice in mind. By *La forza del destino,* however, Verdi had created a new style for a *tenore di forza,* requiring much more forceful singing using chest voice.

*   Hepokoski, James. "*Ottocento* Opera as Cultural Drama: Generic Mixtures in *Il trovatore.*" See item 956.

474. Huebner, Steven. "Lyric Form in Ottocento Opera." *Journal of the Royal Music Association* 117 (1992): 123–47.

Proposes a new system for analyzing melodic structure (particularly for pieces that move away from symmetrical sixteen-bar patterns) based on the function of individual phrases: opening, middle (development), and closure. Illustrative examples include: prologues from *Attila, Giovanna d'Arco*, and *Simon Boccanegra*; "Tacea la notte" from *Il trovatore*; and "Alla vita che t'arride" from *Un ballo in maschera*.

475. Jablonsky, Stephen. "The Development of Tonal Coherence in the Revised Operas of Giuseppe Verdi." Ph.D. dissertation, New York University, 1973. 2 vols. 465 p.

A comparative analysis of twelve pairs of musical numbers from six operas that Verdi revised during the course of his career (*I lombardi* and *Jérusalem, Stiffelio* and *Aroldo*, and early and late versions of *Macbeth, Forza, Simon Boccanegra*, and *Don Carlos*). The revisions show a larger number or greater variety of tonal centers, which are more clearly established than in the original versions.

476. Kerman, Joseph. "Verdi's Use of Recurring Themes." In *Studies in Music History: Essays for Oliver Strunk*, 495–510. Ed. by Harold S. Powers. Princeton: Princeton University Press, 1968. Reprint. Westport, Conn.: Greenwood, 1980. ISBN 0–313–22501–X. ML 3797.1 .S88 1980.
        Reprinted in Joseph Kerman. *Write All These Down: Essays on Music*, 274–87. Berkeley: University of California Press, 1994. ISBN 0–250–08355–5. ML 60 .K37.

Distinguishes two types of recurring themes in Verdi's music: "identifying themes," which are sung or played when a group, person, or idea is strongly in evidence, and "recalling themes," which recall a dramatic situation. About two-thirds of Verdi's early operas use recurring themes—most of them "identifying themes"— although an example of a "recalling theme" can be found as early as *Oberto*. Beginning with *Rigoletto*, Verdi's works show sophisticated and imaginative use of "recalling themes," culminating in his powerful, but economical use of two themes in *Otello*. *Falstaff* opens a new path by using recurring themes for musical organization as well as identification and recall.

477. Kerman, Joseph, and Thomas S. Grey. "Verdi's Groundswells: Surveying an Operatic Convention." In *Analyzing Opera: Verdi and Wagner* (item 454), 153–79.

Examines Verdi's use of a stereotypical climatic gesture, which Julian Budden has called a "groundswell" effect. Although this convention had traditionally been associated with concerted finales, Verdi began to use the device in other contexts, at times reducing it to very small proportions while at other times transforming it into sophisticated designs that only hint at past tradition.

478. Kovács, János. "Zum Spätstil Verdis." *Atti 1* (item 224), 132–44.

Singles out as the most important hallmark of Verdi's late style his replacement of traditional operatic forms with a more continuous, through-composed structure that often utilizes forms associated with instrumental music. The author also discusses, with examples, characteristic melodic shapes and harmonic vocabulary from Verdi's later works.

479. Langford, Jeffrey. "Text Setting in Verdi's *Jérusalem* and *Don Carlos*." *Verdi Newsletter* 12 (1984): 19–31.

The text of *Jérusalem* shows that Verdi, even in his first French opera, was very conscientious about matters of stress. A comparison to the composer's treatment of prosody in *Don Carlos* shows that Verdi's general procedure for setting French text remained the same and indeed followed the procedure he used in Italian operas: 1) primary accents fall on downbeats; 2) secondary accents normally fall on some sort of stressed beat; 3) exceptions are made when rhythmic-melodic symmetry is critical for musical-dramatic reasons. The author criticizes Julian Budden's assertion (item 651) that Verdi attempted to create a new kind of liberated French melody in *Don Carlos* based on the "suppleness" of the French language, asserting that in French poetry, stress patterns (especially of secondary accents) are not totally fluid but are fixed by syntactical relationships. Langford concludes that changes of melodic style in *Don Carlos* cannot be attributed to any unique characteristics of the French language. This article contains an excellent summary of principles of French and Italian prosody. For related examinations of Verdi's approach to French prosody, see items 645 and 971.

480. Lawton, David. "Tonality and Drama in Verdi's Early Operas." Ph.D. dissertation, University of California, Berkeley, 1973. 2 vols. xii, 638 p.

Explores Verdi's use of tonal structure to underscore dramatic action in his operas through *Rigoletto*, using techniques such as referential use of keys, double cycles (a distinctive tonal plan used in two different numbers), expanded introductions and tonally unified acts, and recurring themes. Analysis of Verdi's use of tonality in his early operas shows that *Macbeth* is a crucial turning point, in which he attempts to structure an entire act from a single set piece as a focal point. The author provides detailed discussions of the duet from Act III of *Nabucco*, the final trio of *Ernani*, the duet from Act I of *Macbeth*, and the final duet in *Luisa Miller*, in addition to examining tonal structure in *Rigoletto* as a whole. See item 485 below for a creative criticism of some aspects of Lawton's analytical methodology.

481. Leibowitz, René. "Tempo and Character in the Music of Verdi." *Atti 3* (item 226), 238–43.

   Analyzes Verdi's use of different tempos and meters. Although the composer's metronome markings for certain tempo categories are fairly consistent (as in the ⅜ andantino, typically marked ♪=72–96), others (such as the ¢ allegro, ¢ presto, and ⁴⁄₄ allegro agitato) vary considerably, both within a particular opera and from opera to opera.

482. Lendvai, Ernő. *Verdi and Wagner.* Trans. by Monika Palos and Judit Pokoly. Budapest: International House, 1988. 504 p. ISBN 963–521–1627. MT 95 .L5213 1988.

   This study, based on the analytical premises of the Kodály system, advances the thesis that the harmonic and tonal structure in much of the music of Verdi (and Wagner) presages the more explicit development of modal harmony in the music of Bartók. A major section of the volume is devoted to the "tonal dramaturgy" of *Falstaff*, which the author analyzes scene by scene.

483. Mila, Massimo. "La dialogizzazione dell'aria delle opere giovanili di Verdi." *Atti 1* (item 224), 222–31.
   Also published in *L'arte di Verdi* (item 375), 85–94.

   Verdi's early works show a concern for replacing the idea of the aria as a static reflection (typified by the da capo form of the preceding era) with a more dramatically intense role characterized by an open two-part form (slow—fast) and a tendency to include dramatic interaction with other characters or/and the chorus.

484. ———. "L'unità stilistica nell'opera di Verdi." *Nuova rivista musicale italiana* 2 (1968): 62–75.
   Also published in *L'arte di Verdi* (item 375), 336–49.

   This interesting essay points out difficulties in two extreme positions: one, that throughout his career Verdi's musical style is so strongly rooted in a homogeneous dramatic conception that it makes little sense to talk about different style periods; the other, that there is a huge gulf between the early works, which draw on conventions of early nineteenth-century Italian opera, and the last works, which absorb the musical style and language of Wagner. Mila suggests that a useful compromise might be to isolate central features of Verdi's style that serve as means of recognizing the transformation of style from his early career through his last works and proposes that the composer's treatment of melody and the relationship between vocal and orchestral parts would well serve in this role.

485. Moreen, Robert Anthony. "Integration of Text Forms and Musical Forms in Verdi's Early Operas." Ph.D. dissertation, Princeton University, 1975. vi, 332 p.

This study, one of the first to examine in detail the relationships among Italian prosody, the structure of Verdi's early opera librettos (through *La traviata*), and the composer's treatment of musical-dramatic designs in those operas, is an important point of departure for anyone interested in analyzing Verdi's music. The introductory section offers a particularly valuable starting point for any analytical discussion of Verdi's work. It presents a clear but concise discussion of Italian prosody and its terminology with examples drawn from Verdi's librettos. The ensuing section discusses mid-nineteenth century Italian musical-dramatic terminology as outlined in Abramo Basevi's *Studio sulle opere di G. Verdi* (item 460). The main body of the work first examines the basic way in which Verdi set music to verse, both with lines of regular syllable count and with more irregular patterns. Correspondence among Verdi and his librettists shows that the composer usually requested poetic lines with a particular structure to provide variety, although occasionally he wanted to create a strong metric effect through the use of decasyllabic lines. The second major portion of the text considers Verdi's construction of solo and ensemble numbers, starting from Basevi's description of a standard four-part sequence (*tempo d'attacco*, adagio, *tempo di mezzo*, and cabaletta/stretta) and then examines exceptions and variations to this pattern. Moreen argues that any formal analysis of Verdi's early works should begin with the structure of the text and its adherence to or departure from expected norms. He discusses at length the duet between Macbeth and Lady Macbeth in Act I of *Macbeth* and criticizes David Lawton's analysis (see item 480) for relying on musical texture and dramatic weight rather than the structure of the text as the primary point of departure. See item 502 for a closely related study; item 457 offers a recent assessment of the strengths and weaknesses of Moreen's analytical approach.

486. Noske, Frits R. "The Notorious Cabaletta." In *The Signifier and the Signified* (item 488), 271–93.

After briefly outlining the history and development of the cabaletta in the early nineteenth century, the author examines Verdi's use of the cabaletta in operas from *Oberto* to *Aida*. Although Verdi never abandoned the cabaletta, the author proposes that he was largely responsible for its gradual demise. At times he omitted it or treated it as a separate, independent piece; at other times he adopted irregular formal structures or used it to express subtle feelings, such as tenderness, concern, and sadness, that were not normally associated with the cabaletta. Above all, Verdi generally insisted on a change of mood or situation in the libretto to justify dramatically the presence of a cabaletta.

487.   ———. "Ritual Scenes." In *The Signifier and the Signified* (item 488), 241–70.

Defines a ritual scene in Verdi as one that: 1) deals with a solemn act relating in some way to a supernatural element, 2) sets up conflict between an individual and a group associated with the supernatural element, and 3) is structured in a symmetrical fashion. Beyond investigating the musical and dramatic structure of ritual scenes in *Giovanna d'Arco, Macbeth, I masnadieri, Jérusalem, La forza del destino, Don Carlos,* and *Aida,* the author examines scenes from *Simon Boccanegra, Un ballo in maschera,* and *Falstaff* that contain some elements associated with his definition of ritual. Verdi often makes his ritual scenes part of a large ensemble, with a formal division into three sections: the first sung by the person conducting the ritual, the second by the protagonist, and the third by the chorus.

488.   ———. *The Signifier and the Signified: Studies in the Operas of Mozart and Verdi.* The Hague: Martin Nijhoff, 1977. Reprint. Oxford: Clarendon Press, 1990. x, 418 p. ISBN 0–19–816201–4. ML 1700.1 .N67.

This important volume collects a number of essays on Verdi's operas, some previously published in other sources. See items 486, 487, 489, 656, 831, and 884.

489.   ———. "Verdi and the Musical Figure of Death." In *The Signifier and the Signified* (item 488), 171–214.
An earlier version appears in *Atti 3* (item 226), 349–86.

Verdi frequently associates three interrelated versions of an anapestic rhythmic figure with the idea of death. The article begins by surveying the use of this rhythmic idea in opera and related genres starting with Lully and ending with Mayr and Berlioz. The author then examines Verdi's use of this formula, concluding that *Macbeth* marks a turning point after which the composer uses the device with increasing subtlety and dramatic effectiveness.

490.   Parker, Roger. "The Influence of the Singer in Early Verdi Opera." In *Studies in Early Verdi* (item 377), 143–70.

Examines the influence that particular singers had on Verdi's vocal writing in his early operas. A comparison of the parts for Leonora in *Oberto* and the Marchesa in *Un giorno di regno,* both of which were created for Antonietta Rainier-Marini, shows similar exploitation of specific vocal effects. Moreover, the close parallels between individual numbers in the two operas suggest that Verdi modelled not only musical style and form but also dramatic development of the Marchesa's character on Leonora in the earlier opera. The author proposes that Verdi's operas after *Nabucco* show a new creative relationship between the composer and the performers in which the strengths of particular performers inspired the composer to develop his own original vocal style. Parker discusses the career of Erminia Frezzolini, who created the role of Giselda in *I lombardi* and the title role in *Giovanna d'Arco* and analyzes her first solo number in *I lombardi*: the *preghiera* "Salve Maria!" Verdi explores different vocal styles in the two stanzas of the hymn, but both are marked by a total absence of traditional ornamentation. The author suggests that this approach capitalized on Frezzolini's ability to convince dramatically, both with singing and acting.

491. ———. "Insolite forme,' or Basevi's Garden Path." In *Verdi's Middle Period, 1849–1859: Source Studies, Analysis, and Performance Practice* (item 235), 129–46.

Assesses the modern reception of Abramo Basevi's *Studio sulle opere di G. Verdi* (item 460), particularly as seen in recent writings that invoke normative expectations of form and genre by Verdi's contemporaries as an analytical tool. Parker suggests that Harold S. Powers' article "'La solita forma' and 'The Uses of Convention'" (item 496) was largely responsible for elevating Basevi's work to canonical status. He examines Basevi's own background as a failed opera composer and suggests that the *Studio* was atypical of most contemporary writing about opera, addressed primarily to composers rather than the general public and perhaps imbued with an element of self-justification. He suggests that Basevi's formal descriptions, constructed into a model by Powers and others, may not have been as normative for nineteenth-century listeners as these scholars have argued. In particular, Parker suggests that Basevi did not think of a *tempo d'attacco* as a standard formal section as some modern analysts have done. In the closing portion of his article, the author examines other influences on Basevi's writings. For example, his religious beliefs, strongly affected by the philosophy of Vincenzo Gioberti, no doubt led to a critical view of *La traviata*. Parker notes that he did not intend this article as a vituperation of a currently popular analytical approach but hopes that it might stimulate new dialogue about analytical ideas and methodologies.

492. ———. *Leonora's Last Act: Essays in Verdian Discourse*. Princeton: Princeton University Press, 1997. ISBN 0–691–01557–0. ML 410 .V4 P155 1997.

493. Pizzetti, Ildebrando. "Contrappunto e armonia nell'opera di Verdi." *La rassegna musicale* 21 (1951): 189–200.

A broad survey of Verdi's harmonic style, with particular emphasis on his ability to create unusual modulations and his use of counterpoint. While Verdi's music contains relatively few full-blown passages, many places demonstrate a sophisticated contrapuntal balance between vocal and/or orchestral parts. The closing section of the article examines stages in Verdi's harmonization of "Quel vecchio maledivami" as shown in the sketches for *Rigoletto*.

494. ———. "Giuseppe Verdi." In *Musicisti contemporanei: Saggi critici*, 1–36. Milan: Fratelli Treves, 1914.

Briefly surveys main characteristics of Verdi's musical style, such as strongly contrasting situations with powerful dramatic interest, subtle use of counterpoint, and a distinctive melodic style that features forceful recitative passages that never become extraneous but bring the audience into the drama. See item 401 for a critique of some of the author's ideas.

495. Powers, Harold S. "Il 'do del baritono' nel 'gioco delle parti' verdiano." In *Opera & Libretto II*, 267–81. Studi di musica veneta. Florence: Olschki, 1993. ISBN 88–222–4064–2. ML 1700 .O655 1993.

Discusses Verdi's dramatic and structural use of the high c' (sometimes coupled with its upper neighbor note, db') for baritone voice. Powers proposes that Verdi probably discovered the potential effects of this sonority in the voice of Giorgio Ronconi, who created the role of Nabucco. His most stunning use of it, however, occurs in the roles created by Felice Varesi: *Macbeth* and *Rigoletto*. In the case of the latter opera, it is even possible to see how Verdi places increasingly greater emphasis on the sonority in his sketches for the work. The conclusion of the article considers *Otello*, where the $c'-db'/c\sharp'$ sonority is fundamental for Iago and c'' is a significant sonority for Desdemona. The author also responds to earlier writings about tonality in *Otello* by David Lawton (item 830) and by Roger Parker and Matthew Brown (item 832).

496. ———. "'La solita forma' and 'The Uses of Convention.'" *Acta musicologica* 59 (1987): 65–90.

A slightly earlier version appears in *Nuove prospettive nella ricerca verdiana* (item 231), 74–105.

This classic article laid the foundation for much later analytical research about Verdi, both by Powers himself and by other authors. Powers argues that many analyses of Verdi's operas have been unduly biased by an approach that is preoccupied with "forward-looking" traits and seeking unity in *topoi* and tonality. He proposes instead scrutinizing writings by the composer and his contemporaries, as well as the music itself, in order to focus on musical and dramatic presuppositions of Verdi and the audience for whom he was writing. The author proceeds to examine normative scene types for the grand duet, the aria/cavatina, and the central finale, based in large part on writings by Abramo Basevi and Emanuele Muzio. Rebutting the position taken by Julian Budden (item 365), Powers argues that the duet scene, not the aria scene, should be regarded as the fundamental structural shape in nineteenth-century Italian opera. The article also critically responds to Philip Gossett's on Verdi's "Uses of Convention" (item 572), David R.B. Kimbell's analysis of the Violetta-Germont duet from Act II of *La traviata* (item 162), Pierluigi Petrobelli's analysis of the Amonasro-Aida duet in Act III of *Aida* (item 576) and Budden's analysis of the Act I finale in *Luisa Miller* (item 365). Special attention is also given to the structure of the Coronation Scene in *Giovanna d'Arco*. Powers concludes that even in his later works, Verdi frequently manipulated conventional expectations about form and structure in a very sophisticated manner to achieve maximum dramatic effect. See items 457 and 491 for discussions and critiques of Powers' methodology; item 457 provides another assessment, with a specific critique of Powers' analysis of the Amonasro-Aida duet.

497. ———. "*Tempo di mezzo*: Three Ongoing Episodes in *Verdian Musical Dramaturgy.*" *Verdi Newsletter* 19 (1991): 6–36.

The title refers to three *tempo di mezzo* passages that underwent substantial alteration when Verdi revised their respective operas. This article only touches on Amelia's *racconto* in the central finale of the 1857 *Simon Boccanegra*, which was later integrated into the Council Chamber scene in the 1881 version; the author refers readers to his published discussion of this scene (item 896 below). More space here is devoted to the cavatina of the lost ring from Act I of *Stiffelio* and *Aroldo*, focusing on the unconventional aspects of the *Stiffelio* version (this portion of the article is essentially an abridged version of item 917 below). The third passage examined in this article is the conclusion of *Macbeth*, from the announcement of Lady Macbeth's death to the end of the battle. Verdi's nomenclature in the autograph of the 1847 version of the opera and in a letter to Felice Varesi, who first sang the role of Macbeth, suggests that the composer conceived everything following the sleepwalking scene to the final curtain as a colossal single number based on the aria-scene convention. The composer eliminated the generic expectations of this portion of the opera when he revised the work for Paris.

498. Roncaglia, Gino. "Il 'tema-cardine' nell'opera di Giuseppe Verdi." *Rivista musicale italiana* 47 (1943): 218–29.

Suggests that Verdi often uses throughout an opera a central "pivot theme" that contains the central musical-dramatic essence of the work. As primary examples of this idea, Roncaglia cites the theme associated with the pact in *Ernani* and the curse theme in *Rigoletto*. He proposes that operas following *Rigoletto* (notably *La traviata*, *Un ballo in maschera*, *Don Carlo*, and *Aida*) set up a contrast between two or three of these "pivot themes," while *Otello* and *Falstaff* abandon this device for more sophisticated ways of unifying the opera. See item 476 above for Joseph Kerman's discussion of the *tema-cardine* in context of other types of recurring themes in Verdi's operas and his constructive criticism of the concept in operas other than *Rigoletto* and *La traviata*. The author also points out differences between this technique and that of Wagner's Leitmotiv.

499.   Rosen, David. "How Verdi Operas Begin: An Introduction to the *Introduzioni*." In *Tornando a "Stiffelio"* (item 234), 203–21.
Republished with minor revisions. *Verdi Newsletter* 16 (1988): 3–18.

Analyzes Verdi's use of the term *Introduzione* in his autograph scores (often later excised or altered by his publishers). The designation always indicates the presence of a chorus, which may be a simple opening chorus, a chorus followed by an aria or cavatina, or a chorus integrated in a longer and more complex structure. Verdi's treatment of the *Introduzione* differs markedly from a contemporary theoretical description by Carlo Ritorni in his *Ammaestramenti alla composizione d'ogni poema e d'ogni opera appartenente alle musica* (Milan: Pirola, 1841). Rosen offers several possible reasons why Verdi suppressed in *Aroldo* the elaborate *Introduzione* that begins *Stiffelio*, including lack of dramatic motivation for the *largo concertato*, insufficient development of the characters, and too great a weight in relationship to the finale. An appendix to the article reproduces extensive citations from Ritorni's treatise.

500.   ———. "How Verdi's Serious Operas End." In *Atti del XIV Congresso della Società Internazionale di Musicologia: Trasmissione e recezione delle forme di cultura musicale*, 3: 443–50. Ed. by Angelo Pompilio, Donatella Restani, Lorenzo Bianconi, and F. Alberto Gallo. 3 vols. Turin: Edizioni di Torino, 1990. ISBN 88–7063–070–6.
Republished in *Verdi Newsletter* 20 (1992): 9–15.

Establishes a typology for Verdi's operas that end with the death of a principal character. While the composer adopted a variety of approaches during the 1840s, most of the later works contain a death scene with mourners, and the end of the set piece usually coincides with the principal victim's death. Exceptions to this pattern result from dramatic reasons: typically, the commission of a serious crime for which an extended aria or consolatory ensemble is inappropriate. Verdi wrote most of his death scenes in keys with at least three flats; finales without death scenes utilize fewer flats or the sharp side of the circle of fifths.

501.   ———. "Meter, Character, and *Tinta* in Verdi's Operas." In *Verdi's Middle Period, 1849–1859: Source Studies, Analysis, and Performance Practice* (item 235), 339–92.

Examines the influence of meter on character and *tinta*, concentrating on Verdi's use of $\frac{3}{8}$. The author argues that Verdi makes a clear distinction between his use of $\frac{3}{8}$ and related meters, such as $\frac{3}{4}$ and $\frac{6}{8}$, and that this difference is not merely a notational convention but a stylistic feature that is audible to listeners and should be carefully distinguished by performers. At the beginning of his career, Verdi typically used ³⁄₈ within a restricted tempo range (centering around Andantino), gradually expanding its use to serve as kinetic music in *parlante* passages. The composer used ³⁄₈ with the greatest frequency during his middle period (between *Luisa Miller* and *Un ballo in maschera*), with the greatest concentration in *Il trovatore* and *La traviata*, which the author examines in particular detail. In the case of *Il trovatore*, Rosen argues that the frequent use of ³⁄₈ contributes to the work's distinctive *tinta*, with connections between the pieces in ³⁄₈ reinforced by melodic and dramatic similarities.

502. Ross, Peter. "Studien zum Verhältnis von Libretto und Komposition in den Opern Verdis." Ph.D. dissertation, Universität Bern, 1979. 307 p.

A detailed study of the influence of versification and formal structure in the librettos on Verdi's musical settings. Much of the material touches on ideas presented in Robert Moreen's dissertation (item 485) and Harold Power's "La solita forma" (item 496), published about the same time and with which the author was apparently unfamiliar. In the case of the former, however, Ross discusses the entire corpus of Verdi's operas, while Moreen restricts his discussion to the early works.

503. Serafin, Tullio, and Alceo Toni. *Stile, tradizioni, e convenzioni del melodramma italiano del settecento e dell'ottocento.* Milan: Ricordi, 1958. 2 vols. xii, 167; 323 p. ML 1733 .S45.

The entire second volume of this set is devoted to Verdi. A preliminary chapter assesses the relationship of Verdi's operas to those by his Italian predecessors. Successive chapters provide lengthy descriptive analyses of *Nabucco, Ernani, Macbeth, Rigoletto, Il trovatore,* and *La traviata.*

504. Siegmund-Schultze, Walther. "Gedanken zum Verdischen Melodie-Typus." *Verdi: Bollettino dell'Istituto di Studi Verdiani* 2 [No. 4] (1961): 255–84. English and Italian translations are published on pp. 671–710.

Suggests that Verdi's mastery of characterization is largely based on his use of melody and proposes general categories into which his melodies may be grouped. The author surveys Verdi's use of melody throughout his career; the greatest attention, however, is given to *Aida.*

505. Travis, Francis Irving. *Verdi's Orchestration.* Ph.D. dissertation, Universität Zürich, 1956. Zurich: Juris-Verlag, 1956. 105 p. ML 410 .V4 T74.

This study surveys the evolution of Verdi's orchestral technique, technical aspects relating to his treatment of individual instrumental families, and his use of orchestration to support dramatic development. The dissertation contains numerous musical examples, a chart indicating orchestral forces required for each of Verdi's compositions, and a useful, if outdated, bibliography.

506. Tyler, Linda L. "Striking up the *Banda*: Verdi's Use of the Stage Band in His Middle-Period Operas." *The Opera Journal* 23 (March 1990): 2–22.

Suggests that Verdi began to use the stage band in new and more creative ways starting with *Macbeth* in 1847. In particular, the composer exploited stage band music to increase dramatic effect and to deemphasize the sense of formal disjunction between sections. The author examines a number of specific scenes from operas through *Un ballo in maschera*.

507. Van, Gilles De. "Musique et narration dans les operas de Verdi." *Studi verdiani* 6 (1990): 18–54.

A survey of stylistic and formal techniques used by Verdi in narrative passages. For secondary characters, Verdi frequently uses strophic form and rhythmic regularity, lending a "popular" tone to the music. For narration of important events by primary characters, the composer adopts a more dramatic tone with a sectional form that changes mood as the narration progresses.

508. ———. "La notion de 'tinta': Mémoire confuse et affinités thématiques dans les opéras de Verdi." *Revue de musicologie* 76 (1990): 187–98.

Verdi's concept of *tinta* involves the use of many different aspects of the music—including, among other things, melodic resemblances, orchestral timbres, and choice of keys—to create a sense of unity in the minds of the audience. *Tinta* is meant to be felt subconsciously and intuitively. The composer does not expect individual listeners to be able to recognize or articulate precise connections during the course of hearing a performance; the connections can only be clarified through careful analysis. After a general discussion of the concept of *tinta*, the author illustrates the concept through a detailed analysis of thematic resemblances in Act II, Scene 2 of *La forza del destino*.

509. Vlad, Roman. "Alcune osservazioni sulla struttura delle opere di Verdi." *Atti 2* (item 226), 495–522.

Argues against the assertion that Verdi's harmonic treatment is fundamentally conservative and has little relation to "progressive" harmonic tendencies of the nineteenth century. Examples, drawn primarily from the period of *Rigoletto* and after, demonstrate the composer's use of chromatic harmony, modality, and his striking treatment of dissonance.

510. ———. "Anticipazioni nel linguaggio armonico verdiano." *La rassegna musicale* 21 (1951): 237–45.

Surveys harmonic idioms in Verdi's music that look forward to twentieth-century styles including polytonality, use of modal scales, unusual pivot-tone modulations, harmonic ellipses and substitutions in cadential progressions, and treatment of dissonance. The author points out that these forward-looking ideas are found throughout Verdi's works, not just in his final operas, and argues against the proposition that they are strongly influenced by the music of Wagner.

511. Webster, James. "To Understand Verdi and Wagner We Must Understand Mozart." *19th Century Music* 11 (1978–88): 175–93.

Suggests that the need for developing new analytical and explanatory models for nineteenth-century opera should begin with a closer examination of Mozart's operatic music and proposes that analyzing *coherence* in opera (and other musical works) will be more productive than engaging in debates over "unity" or "organicism." The author includes a useful summary of recent developments in the analysis of Verdi's operas.

512. Wedell, Friedrich. *Annäherung an Verdi: Zur Melodik des jungen Verdi und ihren musiktheoretischen und ästhetischen Voraussetzungen.* Ph.D. dissertation, Kiel Universität, 1995. Kieler Schriften zur Musikwissenschaft, 44. Kassel: Bärenreiter, 1995. xix, 344 p. ISBN 3–7618–1259–0. ML 290.4 W43 1995.

This significant volume offers the most detailed exploration to date of the young Verdi's approach to melody and its conceptual background in both the music and the theoretical writings of his immediate predecessors. The largest portion of the study examines in detail theoretical works such as Francesco Galeazzi's *Elementi teorico-pratici di musica* (1791, 1796), Carlo Gervasoni's *La scuola della musica* (1800), Antoine Reicha's *Traité de mélodie* (1814, translated into Italian as *Trattato della melodia* in 1830), Bonifazio Asioli's *Il maestro di composizione* (1832), and Raimondo Boucheron's *Filosofia della musica o estetica applicata a quest'arte* (1842). Wedell summarizes what these authors—and others—say about melodic form and style, vocal forms and genres, and principles of text setting and their relationship to Italian prosody. A short central section considers the melodic style of Bellini and Donizetti, and a final portion of the volume examines Verdi's approach to melody in *Oberto* and *Nabucco*, focusing on styles and formal principles discussed in the theoretical writings. An appendix reproduces passages from the treatises in the original language. A substantial bibliography is divided into four sections: musical editions, publications dating prior to ca. 1900 (a fairly comprehensive listing of ottocento treatises and monographs), more recent studies dating after ca. 1900, and a short group of books dealing with analytical and philosophical methodology. The lack of an index hampers the use of this interesting study.

513. Werner, Klaus G. "Verdi auf dem Weg zum Spätwerk: Zwei Ouvertüren im Spannungsfeld zwischen Instrumentalmusik und Oper." *Musikforschung* 44 (1991): 130–55.

A detailed comparison of Verdi's revised overture to *La forza del destino* (1869) with the overture for *Aida* (1871), which the composer withdrew before it was ever performed. The revised *Forza* overture exhibits a dramatic development, using the principle of sonata form, that runs parallel to the opera itself, while the *Aida* overture utilizes the traditional "potpourri" approach with sophisticated contrapuntal treatment and some affinities to sonata procedure.

514. Witzenmann, Wolfgang. "Grundzüge der Instrumentation in den Opern Verdis und Wagners." In *Colloquium "Verdi-Wagner" Rom 1969: Bericht* (item 227), 304–27.

Compares and contrasts Verdi's and Wagner's styles of orchestration and their conceptions of the role of the orchestra in opera.

VOCAL & ORCHESTRAL PERFORMANCE PRACTICE

515. *Les introuvables du chant verdien.* Special issue of *L'avant scène opéra.* Paris: L'Avant-Scène, 1986. 173 p. ISSN 0764–2873. ML 410 .V4 I4 1986.

This volume was prepared as the companion to an eight-disk set of recordings with the same title released by Pathé-Marconi. While much of the special issue is devoted to presenting the text of the recorded selections, the volume contains a great many short biographies and several longer articles dealing with historically renowned or important Verdi interpreters, together with a wealth of iconographic material.

516. Battaglia, Elio. "Problemi esecutivi della vocalità verdiana." *Per un "progetto Verdi" anni '80* (item 232), 119–28.

Examines ways in which modern performers typically depart from an "authentic Verdi voice" and argues for a return to historically accurate vocal performance styles.

517. ———. "Voci verdiane: Equivoco di scuola?" *Nuova rivista musicale italiana* 6 (1972): 526–44.

Traces the roots of Verdi's vocal style to the works of Rossini, drawing on examples from the roles of Violetta (*La traviata*), Leonora (*La forza del destino*), and Gilda (*Rigoletto*), and assesses the composer's own thoughts on singing style, drawing primarily on comments about some of the roles in *Otello*. The author concludes that current singing styles are not historically accurate.

518.   Bragaglia, Leonardo. *Verdi e i suoi interpreti (1839–1978): Vita scenica delle opera del cigno di Busseto attraverso una antologia critica e uno studio delle ventotto opere di Giuseppe Verdi.* Rome: Bulzoni, 1979. 375 p. ML 410 .V4 B76.

This guide to the performance history of Verdi's operas considers both live and recorded performances, focusing on productions mounted by larger Italian theaters. For each opera, the author presents a short account of its origins and a summary of the plot, followed by a discussion of a few of the most significant productions of the work. Lists at the end of each opera provide cast information for a larger, but selective, group of performances. A name index is useful in locating discussions about particular performers.

519.   Cavicchi, Adriano. "Problemi di prassi esecutiva storica: Dall'architettura teatrale alla vocalità." *Per un "progetto Verdi" anni '80* (item 232), 87–93.

A concise, but useful overview of issues involved in arriving at an understanding of historical performance practices in Verdi's music.

*   Chusid, Martin. "A Letter by the Composer about *Giovanna d'Arco* and Some Remarks on the Division of Musical Direction in Verdi's Day." See item 745 below.

520.   Celletti, Rodolfo. "'Nessuno può impormi un cantante.' Prima riflessione sulla vocalità in Verdi: Intransigente sulle voci, proponeva personalmente i cast, enunciava i tipi vocali, faceva nomi, poneva veti." *Musica viva* 8 (May 1984): 68–71.

Based on the composer's correspondence, examines Verdi's attitudes toward singers who would be performing his works. At the beginning of his career, Verdi considered the quality of his singers of importance paramount to none else; later, he placed the abilities of the orchestra, chorus, conductor, the costumes, scenery, and acting on an equally high level, without diminishing his interest in the singers.

521.   ———. "Oltre alla voce ci vuole 'talento grande, anima e sentimento di scena.' Terzo e ultima riflessione sulla vocalità di Verdi: Cantanti e interpreti non sono sempre la stessa cosa." *Musica viva* 8 (July/August 1984): 66–69.

Presents evidence from Verdi's correspondence about his desire for performers with superior interpretative ability but who would also follow his instructions and indications precisely.

522.   ———. "'Pel cantante vorrei: profonda conoscenza della musica, emissione del
        suono, esercizi vocali lunghissimi, pronuncia perfetta.' Seconda riflessione
        sulla vocalità di Verdi: Lo studio di canto." *Musica viva* 8 (June 1984):
        58–61.

        Presents a compendium of Verdi's comments about the training of singers and
        his expectations of their musical ability and background. The composer's
        comments clearly show that he preferred singers who adopted—in terms of his
        time—the declamatory style, excelling in forcefulness of delivery and careful
        phrasing. Verdi also showed a strong aversion to "metronomical" performance
        of rhythm.

523.   ———. "Voci romantiche piene di pathos." *Musica e dossier* No. 2 (December
        1986) special insert, 43–53.

        Discusses performance style in singing at the time of Verdi. Examines the
        composer's aesthetic ideals in areas such as virtuosity, ornamentation, execution
        of dynamics, and the distribution of parts among vocal types. The article is
        richly illustrated with contemporary illustrations of scenes from Verdi's later
        operas.

524.   Chusid, Martin. "Verdi's Own Words: His Thoughts on Performance, with
        Special Reference to *Don Carlos, Otello,* and *Falstaff.*" *The Verdi Companion*
        (item 5), 144–92.

        A perusal of Verdi's ideas about the performance of his later operas as seen in
        selected correspondence. Topics include choice of singers, staging, the chorus,
        solo vocal performance and characterization of leading roles, and orchestral
        playing.

   *   Conati, Marcello, and Marcello Pavarani, eds. *Orchestre in Emilia-Romagna
        nell'ottocento e novecento.* Cited above as item 261.

   *   Cordell, Albert O. "The Orchestration of Verdi: A Study of the Growth of
        Verdi's Orchestral Technique as Reflected in the Two Versions of *Simon
        Boccanegra.*" Cited below as item 900.

525.   Crutchfield, Will. "Authenticity in Verdi: The Recorded Legacy." *Opera* 36
        (1985): 858–66.

        The article opens with a general discussion of nineteenth-century vocal
        performance practices based on phonographic evidence including: the literalness
        of Verdi's *pianissimo* markings, use of legato, and rhythmic freedom. The
        closing section on ornamentation is a condensed version of item 526 below.

526.   ———. "Vocal Ornamentation in Verdi: The Phonographic Evidence." *19th Century Music* 7 (1983–84): 3–54.

This important article examines Verdi's use of vocal ornamentation and his attitude toward the insertion of new cadenzas or the alteration of his own ornamentation by performers. A discussion of improvised vocal ornamentation by singers whose careers began before or around 1900, based on a group of over 1200 early Verdi recordings, forms the central core of the study. Appendices present transcriptions of 207 examples from 142 recordings by 74 singers, some of whom had worked with Verdi, biographical data on the singers, and data about the recordings.

527.   Fairtile, Linda B. "The Violin Director and Verdi's Middle-Period Operas." In *Verdi's Middle Period, 1849–1859: Source Studies, Analysis, and Performance Practice* (item 235), 413–426.

Examines the tradition of the violin director in early and mid-nineteenth-century opera, based largely on a study of microfilmed parts at the American Institute for Verdi Studies and focusing on performances of Verdi's operas during the 1840s and 50s. The *primo violino* parts typically emphasize rhythmic activity more than any other feature of the music, suggesting that the main jobs of the violin director were to indicate the tempo and character of a passage and to ensure that all important musical lines were present, even if he had to supply it himself. The article reproduces pages from manuscript parts to *Rigoletto* and *Il trovatore* and a more elaborate printed part of *Un ballo in maschera*, which is laid out as a short score that could be used either by a violin director or a baton conductor. An appendix lists violin director parts in the AIVS microfilm collection grouped first by period (prior to 1849, 1849–59, and after 1859), and secondarily by type (complete operas [10 sets across the 3 categories], individual numbers in original orchestrations [20 sets], and arrangements of individual numbers [29 sets]). See item 960 below for another article by the author on this topic dealing specifically with *Il trovatore* and *Le trouvère*.

528.   Hajtas, Franz. *Studien zur frühen Verdi-Interpretation: Schalldokumente bis 1926.* Europäische Hochschulschriften, series 36, vol. 47. Frankfurt am Main: Peter Lang, 1990. 210, xxxiii p. ISBN 3–631–42950–9. ML 457 .H23 1990.

After discussing some of Verdi's comments about performance practice, the author examines 205 early recordings involving a total of 108 singers and fifteen Verdi operas to determine the frequency and degree of taking "liberties" in performance. An especially useful feature is extensive biographical information about the singers, which is presented in short paragraphs in the body of the study and summarized in a table in an appendix. Other appendices list the performers by their teachers, and lists of the analyzed recordings organized by chronology, performer, and opera.

529. Harwood, Gregory W. "Verdi's Reform of the Italian Opera Orchestra." *19th Century Music* 10 (1986–87): 108–34.

Traces the development of Verdi's ideas about orchestral size, balance among instruments, and seating arrangements and the composer's efforts to compel the most important theaters in Italy to conform to set minimum standards, particularly during the late 1860s and early 1870s. Verdi's experience at the Paris Opéra strongly influenced his ideas about the overall size and balance of the orchestra. He preferred to have the double basses split on both sides of the orchestra or in a line across the entire back and to group the second violins, violas, and cellos together. Verdi also supported the Italian tradition of positioning the conductor in front of the orchestra, near the audience, rather than the French tradition of placing him next to the stage with the orchestra to his back.

* Jensen, Luke. "The Emergence of the Modern Conductor in 19th-Century Italian Opera." See item 266.

530. Leibowitz, René. "Vérisme, véracité, et vérité de l'interprétation de Verdi." *Atti 1* (item 224), 145–56.

Allowing some latitude for stylistic interpretation, the author argues that Verdi's operas achieve their greatest effect when a sincere effort is made to represent the composer's intentions faithfully.

531. Marvin, Roberta Montemorra. "Aspects of Tempo in Verdi's Early and Middle-Period Italian Operas." In *Verdi's Middle Period, 1849–1859: Source Studies, Analysis, and Performance Practice* (item 235), 393–411.

After surveying nineteenth-century theoretical writings about tempo, the author investigates the composer's thoughts about tempo and about the use of the metronome, his procedure for assigning tempo, and the use and meaning of his tempo adjectives. Verdi began noting metronome markings as early as *Attila*, and he continued using them in most of his subsequent operas. A careful examination of Verdi's compositional process demonstrates that he normally inserted basic tempo adjectives at main structural divisions when he prepared the skeleton score; he added and refined designations constantly during the later stages of scoring and orchestral rehearsals. The composer's autograph scores show increasingly specific and detailed tempo adjectives to convey the sense of both speed and character. An appendix lists all of Verdi's tempo designations in Italian operas from *Oberto* to *Un ballo in maschera* (excluding

Simon Boccanegra) based on the autograph scores, noting the opera in which they first appeared.

532. ———. "Verdi and the Metronome." *Verdi Newsletter* 20 (1992): 4–8.

The use of metronome markings to indicate precise tempos initially encountered substantial resistance in Italy. A series of articles by Luigi Casamorata in the *Gazzetta musicale di Milano* may have been influential in Verdi's decision to designate metronomic equivalents in *Attila*. Verdi continued to use metronome markings or their equivalent in most of his operas after *Attila*.

533. Meucci, Renato. "Il cimbasso e gli strumenti affini nell'ottocento italiano." *Studi verdiani* 5 (1989–90): 109–62.

An important discussion of low brass instruments used in Italy during the nineteenth century, focusing on the term "cimbasso," which Verdi specified in his scores from *Oberto* through *Aida*. The author proposes that "cimbasso" evolved from the term "c. basso" or "c. in basso," abbreviations for the corno basso (also called "corno di basso"). This low brass instrument was basically a "serpentone" with six to nine finger holes but shaped in the form of a bassoon. Instruments were made of brass, ebony, or mahogany. It seems to have been first used in Italy at La Scala about 1825 and soon became popular in other orchestras and bands. In the mid-1830s, the all-metal ophecleide, with either keys or valves, enjoyed a brief popularity, followed by the bombardone. Considerable evidence suggests that the name "cimbasso" was also frequently applied to these other low brass instruments as a generic term. In *Otello*, Verdi called for a "trombone basso" in B♭ that would blend better with the timbre of the tenor trombones. For modern performances of Verdi's operas, the author recommends tubas with proportional dimensions of 1/2 or, at most 3/4. Appendices lists manuscript sources for nineteenth-century Italian operas and other works that call for cimbasso or related instruments. The article contains many helpful illustrations and diagrams as well as a bibliography for further study.

534. Petrobelli, Pierluigi. "La fedeltà al testo: Una lettera verdiana." In *Festschrift Wolfgang Rehm zum 60. Geburtstag am 3. September 1989*, 234–47. Ed. by Dietrich Berke and Harald Heckmann. Kassel: Bärenreiter, 1989. ISBN 3–7618–0971–9. ML 55 .R424 1989.

Presents the text of a previously unpublished draft for a letter (the letter itself is not known to exist) in which Verdi unequivocally states that his operas are sold to his publishers with the strict condition that the works be performed integrally, exactly as they were composed, without cuts, alterations, transpositions or changes of any kind. The draft has some additions and corrections in the hand of Giuseppina; from the salutation and contents of the letter, the author concludes that the intended recipient was most likely Luigi Mancinelli, an orchestral director and composer whose wife, Luisa Cora Mancinelli, had a long friendship with the Verdis. Petrobelli cites several other letters in which the composer expresses the same ideas about the performance of his works.

STAGING & SCENOGRAPHY

535.   Bordowitz, Harvey. "Verdi's *Disposizioni sceniche*: The Stage Manuals for Some Verdi Operas." M.A. thesis, Brooklyn College, 1976. 143 p.

Examines the role of Verdi as stage director as seen in a broad study of six *disposizioni sceniche*: *Giovanna de Guzman (Les vêpres siciliennes), Un ballo in maschera, La forza del destino, Don Carlo, Aida* and *Otello*. The author reproduces diagrams from the staging manuals as well as quotations of extensive sections in English translation.

536.   Cohen, H. Robert. *The Original Staging Manuals for Twelve Parisian Operatic Premières/Douze livrets de mise en scène lyrique datant des créations parisiennes.* Musical Life in 19th-Century France/La vie musicale en France au XIXe siècle. Stuyvesant, NY: Pendragon, 1991. xxxiv, 282 p. ISBN 0–918728–70–3. ML 1727.8 .P207.

Reprints in facsimile the staging books for performances at the Paris Opéra of *Le trouvère* (12 January 1857) and *Les vêpres siciliennes* (13 June 1855).

 *   ———. "A Survey of French Sources for the Staging of Verdi's Operas: *Livrets de mise en scène*, Annotated Scores, and Annotated Libretti in Two Parisian Collections." Cited above as item 24.

 *   Cohen, H. Robert, with the collaboration of Sylvia L'Écuyer Lacroix and Jacques Léveillé. *Les gravures musicales dans* L'Illustration *1843–1899*. See item 109.

537.   Cohen, Robert and Marcello Conati. "Un element inexploré de la mise en scène du XIX siècle: Les *figurini* italiens des operas de Verdi (état de la question)." In *Opera & Libretto I*, 281–97. Studi di musica veneta. Florence: Olschki, 1990. ISBN 88–222–3825–7. ML 1700 .O655 1990.

Figurini (costume designs) are found in the archives of many opera houses and were sometimes reproduced as lithographs in contemporary periodicals. The authors survey the available resources for Verdi's operas and propose ways in which they contribute valuable information to our understanding of contemporary scenography and performance practices. The article includes 30 illustrations, primarily from Verdi's middle-period operas.

538. Covre, Jolanda Nigro. "Artisti contemporani in scena: Come rivivere l'opera verdiana." In *"Sorgete! Ombre serene!" L'aspetto visivo dello spettacolo verdiano* (item 545), 27–29.

Discusses issues faced by modern stage directors relating to the use of historical visual ideas and materials from productions mounted during Verdi's lifetime.

*   Ferrari, Luigi. *La collezione Gallini: Gusto, usanze, odi del teatro musicale italiano nel secondo ottocento.* See item 110.

539. Guccini, Gerardo. "Giuseppe Verdi: Autore di mises en scène." In *Giuseppe Verdi: Vicende, problemi e mito di un artista e del suo tempo* (item 237), 81–92.

Examines Verdi's involvement with the staging of his operas in the context of nineteenth-century practice. Proposes that the first version of *Macbeth* marks a critical juncture in Verdi's career, in which he began to involve himself more thoroughly and systematically in all aspects of the production of his works.

540. Jürgensen, Knud Arne. *The Verdi Ballets.* Foreword by Julian Budden. Premio Internazionale Rotary Club di Parma "Giuseppe Verdi" 4. Parma: Istituto Nazionale di Studi Verdiani, 1995. xiii, 398 p. + 97 p. plates. ISBN 88–85065–12–0. ML 410 .V4 J87 1995.

The first full-scale study of Verdi's ballet music in a beautifully produced volume. A short introduction (taken from article below) precedes a series of eight chapters, each devoted to a specific opera: *Jérusalem* (the 1847 premiere at the Paris Opéra), *Nabuchodonosor* (an 1848 performance at the Théâtre de la Monnaie in Brussels), *Les vêpres siciliennes* (the 1855 premiere at the Paris Opéra), *Le trouvère* (a new French version of the opera premiered at the Paris Opéra in 1857), *Macbeth* (the 1865 Parisian premiere at the Théâtre Lyrique), *Don Carlos* (the 1867 premiere at the Paris Opéra), *Aida* (the world premiere in Cairo, 1871, but with important new choreography by Joseph Hanssen for a staging at the Paris Opéra in 1880), and *Othello* (the French version performed at the Opéra in 1894). For each opera, the author provides historical background, as known, for the genesis of the ballet music, a description of the staging and costuming, and its reception. Appended to each chapter is a more detailed survey of the ballet music and variants among the musical and choreographic sources with incipits, indications concerning *décor* and *régie*, and contemporary diagrams from the *disposizioni sceniche* and other sources. A wealth of illustrations include contemporary stage designs, *figurini*, facsimile reproductions of pages from the manuscript scores, *disposizioni sceniche*, and annotated libretto pages. The volume contains five appendices. The first provides details concerning a female variation from *Troubadouren* Act III, as it was performed in Copenhagen in 1865 choreographed by August Bournonville. The second appendix contains a complete transcription of Joseph Hanssen's notation of the original choreography for *Aida* as performed at the Théâtre de la Monnaie in Brussels (1877) and the Paris Opéra (1880). Appendix III reproduces portions of articles and reviews of the premieres of Verdi's ballets. Appendix IV provides a biographical dictionary of choreographers and principal dancers in Verdi's ballets. Appendix V offers an annotated chronological survey of the non-ballet dances and "dance arias" in Verdi's operas. The author has included exemplary reference material at the back of the volume: a list of the 100 illustrations and their sources, a bibliography, a name index, an index of ballets and divertissements, an index of operas and plays, and an index of periodicals.

541.   ————. "The Verdi Ballets: An Unmasked Ball." *Dancing Times* 83 (1992–93): 250–51, 346–47.
        Italian version. "I balletti verdiani: Un ballo smascherato." *Chorégraphie* 1 (Spring 1993): 56–68.

        Surveys ballet music Verdi wrote for eight of his operas (*Les vêpres siciliennes, Don Carlos, Jérusalem, Nabucodonosor, Le trouvère, Macbeth, Aida*, and *Otello*). Provides general background about the "Second Empire Ballet," including some of the individual dancers, such as Caterina Beretta and Claudina Cucchi, for whom Verdi wrote. Argues that Verdi's ballet scenes deserve closer study based on knowledge about the choreographers and dancers, the original set designs and costumes, and contemporary reviews of the early performances. The article provides a brief overview of material in the author's full-length study of Verdi's ballet music (item 540).

542.   Kahane, Martine. "La danza nelle versioni parigiane delle opere di Verdi parigiano." *Danza italiana* 1 (autumn 1984): 43–60.

        Provides background information relating to the place of ballet in nineteenth-century French opera, and aspects of choreography, staging, and reception for Verdi's ballet music, focusing on *Les vêpres siciliennes* and *Don Carlos*. Also examines some evidence regarding details of costuming for *Don Carlos*.

543.   Mariani, Valerio. "Scenografia verdiana." In *Giuseppe Verdi nel cinquantenario della morte* (item 230), 3–13.

        One of the earliest specialized studies focusing on Verdi's scenic conception of his operas, developments in Italian scenography during the nineteenth century, and the design work of some of the composer's contemporaries, including Domenico Morelli and Carlo Ferrario. The article contains a half-dozen illustrations of early scene designs.

    *   Monaldi, Gino. *Saggio di iconografia verdiana.* See item 114.

544.   Petrobelli, Pierluigi. "'Infine io non me ne intendo, ma mi pare che. . .' Passato e presente della visione scenica verdiana." In *"Sorgete! Ombre serene!" L'aspetto visivo dello spettacolo verdiano* (item 545), 17–26.

    This important essay provides an overview of the composer's involvement with scenic and visual aspects of his operas and the influence of French theater on the development of his ideas regarding elements of staging. Petrobelli argues that visual imagery often kindled the composer's imagination, and that the visual element, in synthesis with the dramatic and musical elements, formed a crucial aspect of Verdi's fundamental aesthetic principles.

545.   Petrobelli, Pierluigi, Marisa Di Gregorio Casati, and Olga Jesurum, eds. *"Sorgete! Ombre serene!" L'aspetto visivo dello spettacolo verdiano.* 2nd ed. Parma: Istituto Nazionale di Studi Verdiani, 1996. 200 p. ISBN 88–85065–13–9. ML 141 .P2 V476 1996.

    An exhibition catalogue dealing with scenography and other visual aspects of Verdi's operas. The first portion of the catalogue reproduces scenery and costume designs in which the composer is known to have collaborated with the artists or designers in some way; operas represented include *Attila*, *Macbeth*, *Don Carlo*, and *La forza del destino*. Illustrations in the following section present an overview of scenography from Verdi's day to the present for *Rigoletto*, *Simon Boccanegra*, *Otello*, *Falstaff*, and *Aida*; a separate section is devoted to *Il trovatore*. The concluding portion of the volume provides descriptions, documentation, and bibliography relating to the more than one hundred illustrations in the catalogue. Two particularly useful features of this volume are a biographical dictionary of 29 scenographers associated with productions of Verdi's operas and a substantial bibliography of 100 items dealing with scenographic aspects of Verdi's works. The volume includes an important introductory article by Petrobelli (item 544) and a short essay by Jolanda Nigro Covre (item 538).

546.   Quattrocchi, Arrigo. "I balletti di Verdi." *Musica e dossier* No. 51 (September–October 1991): 66–70.

    A survey of Verdi's ballet music and a discussion of the circumstances in France that led to their composition. The author briefly describes differences between Joseph Hanssen's elaborate choreography for *Aida* at the Paris Opéra and the simpler style used at the work's Italian premiere at La Scala.

    *   *La realizzazione scenica dello spettacolo verdiano: Atti del Congresso Internazionale di Studi, Parma, 28–30 settembre 1994.* See item 233.

547. Ronconi, Luca and Gianfranco Capitta. "Verdi che abbraccia l'Europa." *Musica e dossier* 2 (December 1986), special insert, 44–48.

   A modern stage director discusses special challenges posed by Verdi's operas using examples from recent productions throughout Europe.

548. Rosen, David. "The Staging of Verdi's Operas: An Introduction to the Ricordi *Disposizioni sceniche*." In *International Musicological Society, Report of the Twelfth Congress, Berkeley, 1977,* 444–53. Ed. by Daniel Heartz and Bonnie Wade. Kassel: Bärenreiter, 1981. ISBN 3–7618–0649–3.
   Italian translation by Alessandro Roccatagliati. "La mess'in scena delle opere di Verdi: Introduzione alle 'disposizioni sceniche' Ricordi." In *La drammaturgia musicale,* 209–22. Ed. by Lorenzo Bianconi. Bologna: Società Editrice il Mulino, 1986. ISBN 88–15–01127–7. ML 1700 .D72 1986.

   Provides a general overview of the *disposizioni sceniche* published by Ricordi for each opera of Verdi from *Les vêpres siciliennes* to *Falstaff.* Verdi considered them binding instructions for the performances of his works; therefore, they provide authoritative evidence of how he wanted his operas to be staged. Taken as a whole, the production books provide valuable evidence regarding performance practice in the nineteenth century. Of special interest was the typical practice of changing scenes within an act (as opposed to those between acts) rapidly and in full view of the audience. Rosen suggests that Verdi does not seem to have been interested in visual symbolism as much as issues of realism and visual magnificence. The production books also offer solutions to specific problems in individual works, such as the manner in which to portray the ending of *Les vêpres* and the way in which Iago should act upon finishing his "Credo" in *Otello.* Appendices list bibliographical information and locations for the *disposizioni sceniche,* an inventory of French *livrets de mise en scène* based on productions supervised by Verdi, and a selective list of *disposizioni sceniche* issued by Ricordi for works by other composers.

549. Tomasi, Gioacchino Lanza. "Tradizione e rinnovamento nella pratica esecutiva verdiana." *Per un "progetto Verdi" anni '80* (item 232), 55–62.

   Discusses the difficulties in recreating the original ambience of Verdi's operas caused by today's cultural and artistic milieu, which is vastly different from that in which Verdi's operas were first performed.

550. Viale Ferrero, Mercedes. "Da *Norma* a *Attila*: Scene del Teatro Regio di Torino durante il regno di Carlo Alberto." In *Opera & Libretto I,* 235–51. Studi di musica veneta. Florence: Olschki, 1990. ISBN 88–222–3825–7. ML 1700 .O655 1990.

A study of scenography at the theater, including designs by Giuseppe Bertoja for *Oberto* (1840) and *I lombardi* (1844) and designs by Luigi Vacca for *Attila* (1848–49). Includes excerpts from reviews published in contemporary newspapers and periodicals and reproductions of some of the stage designs.

*   Wiesmann, Sigrid. "'Disposizioni sceniche' oder 'Gesamtkunstwerk': Wagner, Verdi und die Große Oper." See item 448.

CHAPTER 12
Studies About Individual Operas

This chapter contains citations of studies that are concerned with one particular opera arranged first by work, then by categories paralleling those in the preceding chapter. Cross-references will direct the reader to some significant writings listed in other parts of this volume. To find additional materials dealing with a particular work, readers should also consult the subject index.

AIDA

Aida, always one of Verdi's most popular operas, has inspired many scholarly studies, many of which focus on either its relatively long and complicated genesis or its unusual, exotic scenario.

Guides to the Work

551. *Aïda. L'avant-scène opéra* 4 (July/August 1976). Paris: L'Avant-Scène, 1976. 130 p. ISSN 0395–0670. MT 95 .A94 no. 4.
2nd ed. Paris: Société Premières Loges, 1993. 151 p. ISSN 0764–2873. ML 410 .V4 A54 1993.

Over a half dozen articles consider topics such as the influence of nineteenth-century archeological and anthropological studies on Verdi's conception of the opera, its compositional history, and the significance of the work. The libretto is presented in the original Italian with a modern French translation by Georges Farret. The volume also includes a discography of complete recordings and individual arias or sections accompanied by a prose essay, tables listing the earliest performances of the opera in major centers, as well as more detailed information about performances in major houses up to the present, all of which are updated in the second edition. The original bibliography contains about 150 items, including complete editions and arrangements of individual numbers from the opera, librettos, and secondary literature dealing with Verdi in general and *Aïda* in particular; the second edition presents a shortened list emphasizing the most recent publications; it also contains a videography with a prose discussion of five complete recordings through 1989.

552. *Aida*. English National Opera Guides, 2. London: John Calder; New York: Riverrun, 1980. 96 p. ISBN 0–7145–3770–5. ML 50 .V484 A2 1980.

In addition to reproducing the libretto in both Italian and English translation, this guide contains essays describing the work's genesis and evaluating the opera's place in Verdi's career. The volume contains a descriptive analysis of the opera, a discography, and a very brief selective bibliography.

553. Csampai, Attila, and Dietmar Holland, eds. *Giuseppe Verdi, "Aida": Texte, Materialien, Kommentare*. Rororo Opernbücher. Reinbek bei Hamburg: Rowohlt Taschenbuch Verlag, 1985. 282 p. ISBN 3–499–17974–1. ML 50 .V484 A45 1985.

Histories and General Studies

554. Abdoun, Saleh, ed. *Genesi dell'"Aida" con documentazione inedita*. Quaderni dell'Istituto di Studi Verdiani, 4. [Parma: Istituto di Studi Verdiani], 1971. xxiv, 189 p. + 39 plates. ML 410 .V4 A48 vol. 4.

A commemorative volume issued for the centenary of the opera's premiere. The major portion of the book reproduces 203 letters and documents dealing with the genesis of the work, its earliest performances (particularly the premiere in Cairo), and its early reception. A substantial number of documents, especially those from the archives of the Cairo Opera, had not been previously published (see item 559 below for additional documents that supplement this collection). Footnotes to the letters provide helpful background information. The volume also contains essays by Saleh Abdoun on the history of the Cairo Opera and by Claudia Dolzani on the authenticity of Egyptian motifs in the opera. A chronological list of early performances (1871–1881), prepared by Marcello Conati, provides information about lead singers and, in many cases, other personnel. Illustrations include exterior and interior views of the Cairo Opera, jewelry worn by Amneris, and costume designs for the premiere performance. A series of indexes allows easy access to the documentary portion of the volume. One lists letters and documents by date, another inventories names cited in the letters and documents, a third tabulates cities cited in the chronology.

*   Busch, Hans, ed. and trans. *Verdi's "Aida": The History of an Opera in Letters and Documents*. See item 93 above.

555. Codignola, Mario, and Riccardo De Sanctis, eds. *"Aida" in Cairo: The Birth of an Opera by a Famous Italian Composer*. N.p.: Banca Nazionale di Lavoro, n.d. 204 p. ML 410 .V4 A57 1982.

A number of short essays by various authors discuss the genesis of the libretto and the music (items 561 and 569), the singers in the original production (item 583), scenery and costumes used at the work's premiere in Cairo and in the first Italian performance at La Scala (item 582), issues in performance practice (item 579), and assessments of work's significance and place in history (item 568). Copious illustrations, mainly in color, are perhaps the most valuable feature of this volume. They include, among other things, reproductions of set designs, costumes, facsimiles of early scores, posters, and other publicity for performances of the work.

* Conati, Marcello. "Verdi, il *grand opéra* e il *Don Carlos*." Cited above as item 260.

556. Colombati, Claudia. "Esotismo e archeologia nell'*Aida* di G. Verdi." *Quadrivium: Studi di filologia e musicologia* 27 (1986): 127–47. This volume of *Quadrivium* is listed in some indexes as a monograph: *Universalità della musica, prestigio dell'Italia, attualità di Verdi: Studi in onore di Mario Medici*, Vol. 2. Ed. by Giuseppe Vecchi. Bologna: Antiquae Musicae Italicae Studiosi, 1986.

Discusses the late nineteenth-century fascination with archeology and antiquity as an important influence on the conception of *Aida*. The latter part of the article contains a descriptive analysis of exotic effects throughout the opera. The author also cites some of the writings of music critic Filippo Filippi describing his trip to Cairo for the work's premiere.

557. Csampai, Attila. "*Aida*—Ende aller Utopie." In *Giuseppe Verdi: Musik-Konzepte* 10 (item 423): 46–50.

Evaluates *Aida* as a final glorification of the Romantic "bourgeois" opera and proposes that its enduring popularity stems from a combination of grand spectacle with themes that are timeless.

558. Erasmi, Gabriele. "*Norma* ed *Aida*: Momenti estremi della concezione romantica." *Studi verdiani* 5 (1988–89): 85–108.

Proposes that *Aida* may be viewed, to some extent, as a parody of *Norma*. While Bellini's opera celebrates the rise of Romantic ideals, Verdi's provides a commentary on their decline. The author criticizes Hussey's interpretation of Aida (item 149) as a grand celebration of the success of the Italian Risorgimento movement.

559. Günther, Ursula. "Zur Entstehung von Verdis *Aida*." *Studi musicali* 2 (1973): 15–71.

Publishes 48 letters, primarily from the Bibliothèque de l'Opéra and Sant'Agata, concerning the early history of *Aida*. These documents show that Camille Du Locle was the key figure in persuading Verdi to undertake the new opera and that he approached the composer on behalf of Egyptian authorities as early as December 1869 in Genoa. The author also concludes that Du Locle spent about a week at Sant'Agata during the second half of June 1870, which would have allowed time for an extensive discussion of the drama and terms of the contract for the new opera. Günther's important documentary study supplements the historical examination of the opera's genesis in item 554 above—especially by extending it backwards in time—and offers corrections and additions to the documents published in items 29 and 52.

560. Luzio, Alessandro. "Come fu composta l'*Aida*." In *Carteggi verdiani* (item 29), 4:5–27.

The author cites portions of correspondence by Verdi, Camille Du Locle, and Antonio Ghislanzoni to illustrate the genesis of the *Aida* libretto. To a large extent, this material has been superseded by more complete studies of the documents, such as items 554, 559, and 572.

561. Nello Vetro, Gaspare. "The Genesis of *Aida*: Verdi's Letters." In Aida *in Cairo* (item 555), 117–124.

An overview of the work's compositional history, based on Verdi's correspondence. The article lacks notes and critical references; for a more comprehensive overview in English, see item 93.

562. Pirrotta, Nino. "Semiramis e Amneris, un anagramma o quasi." In *Il melodramma italiano dell'ottocento: Studi e ricerche per Massimo Mila*, 5–12. Ed. by Giorgio Pestelli. Saggi, 575. Turin: Einaudi, 1977. ML 1733.4 .M5.

Discusses parallels between *Aida* and Rossini's *Semiramide* including the plots of the two operas, the characterization of Semiramide and Amneris, and the opening scene of Act II of *Aida* with the second part of Act I in *Semiramide*, which both feature a *boudoir* scene. The author argues that the similarities, especially in this last case, stem primarily from Verdi's own initiative.

563. Righini, Pietro. "Dalle trombe egizie per l'*Aida* alle trombe di Tut-ank-amon." *Nuova rivista musicale italiana* 11 (1977): 591–605.

Compares the size, shape, timbre, and possible pitches on the ceremonial trumpets Verdi had fabricated for *Aida* with that of actual Egyptian trumpets excavated from the tomb of King Tutankhamen in 1922. While the physical shape of Verdi's trumpets matched the ancient instruments, they differed substantially in size and acoustical properties.

564. Robinson, Paul. "Is *Aida* an Orientalist Opera?" *Cambridge Opera Journal* 5 (1994): 133–40.

Criticizes Edward W. Said's interpretation of *Aida* as a product of European imperialist philosophy (see item 565). Robinson argues that since the opera portrays Egypt as the imperialist aggressor and evokes strong sympathy for the Ethiopian "victims," the opera is more convincingly viewed as anti-imperialist in tone, closely related to the underlying sentiments of Verdi's Risorgimento operas of the 1840s. Robinson also examines Verdi's use of "exotic" music in the opera, noting that these short episodes always lead to   more powerful passages, sung in a purely Western idiom by characters who are Egyptian.

565. Said, Edward W. "The Empire at Work: Verdi's *Aida*." In *Culture and Imperialism*, 111–32. New York: Alfred A. Knopf, 1993. ISBN 0–394–58738–3. PN 761 .S28.
An earlier version of this chapter appeared as "The Imperial Spectacle." *Grand Street* 6 (Winter 1987): 82–104.

Summarizes the unusual (for Verdi) events surrounding the opera's commission and initial conceptualization, arguing that despite some effort to gather and incorporate accurate historical and cultural details about Egypt, the opera presents a strongly biased and Orientalized view of Egypt based on prevailing European attitudes about the Near East. The author draws parallels between the national rivalries portrayed in the opera and the nineteenth-century imperial aspirations of both Britain and France in northeast Africa. The essay provides some interesting insights into the career of Auguste Mariette, who provided the original scenario for the opera; the political milieu surrounding the reign of Khedive Ismail, who commissioned the opera; and the place of the new Opera House in the cultural milieu of mid- to late nineteenth-century Cairo. See item 564 for a response by Paul Robinson to some of the author's main assertions about the tone of the opera.

Dramaturgy; Studies of the Libretto

566. Humbert, Jean-Marcel. "À propos de l'égyptomanie dans l'oeuvre de Verdi: Attribution à Auguste Mariette d'un scénario anonyme de l'opéra *Aïda*." *Revue de musicologie* 62 (1976): 229–56.

Reviews the role of Auguste Mariette as preparer of the original scenario for Verdi's *Aida* and reviews some of the major differences between this scenario and the final version of the opera. The 23-page scenario was originally published in a very limited edition in Cairo in 1871, but all copies had long been presumed lost until the recent discovery of one at the Bibliothèque de l'Opéra. The Verdi heirs at Sant'Agata have confirmed that their archives contain a manuscript Italian translation of the scenario, Acts I and II in the

hand of Verdi himself, Acts III and IV in the hand of Giuseppina (the article
reproduces in facsimile the first and final pages of this manuscript). A
significant contribution of this study is a complete reproduction of the original
French scenario, side by side with the Italian translation from the manuscript
at Sant'Agata.

567. Kitson, John Richard. "Verdi and the Evolution of the *Aida* Libretto." Ph.D.
      dissertation, University of British Columbia, 1985. 2 vols. viii, 996 p.

      The most complete study to date of the genesis of the libretto for *Aida*. Kitson
      bases almost all of his discussion on primary source documents, including the
      composer's correspondence with Ghislanzoni and several "working" manuscripts
      (some previously unpublished) that he transcribes in a series of appendices.
      These include: a manuscript showing modifications made by Verdi and Camille
      Du Locle to Mariette's original scenario, Verdi's own scenario or "groundplan"
      for the opera, the composer's prose libretto, Ghislanzoni's draft manuscript of
      the versified libretto (including later revisions), and Verdi's selections and
      alterations of Ghislanzoni's versified draft for parts of Acts 2 and 3 and all of
      Act 4. A final appendix provides an overview of Italian operatic prosody. The
      author argues that Verdi's involvement in the preparation of this and other
      librettos was so extensive that he should essentially be considered their author.
      For a recent re-examination and refinement of this idea, see item 442.

568. Marchesi, Gustavo. "*Aida* come fiaba." *Quadrivium: Studi di filologia e
      musicologia* 14 (1973): 283–94.
      English translation. "*Aida*, A Fairy Tale." In "*Aida*" *in Cairo* (item 555),
      91–99.

      Suggests that the libretto of *Aida* has many characteristics in common with the
      genre of fable, albeit without a happy ending. Radames and Aida are cast as
      "hero-victims," and both must pass through a test to determine their
      steadfastness while Amneris, as antagonist, may be regarded as a type of witch.
      The author suggests that Verdi drew on characteristics of the fable to evoke an
      aura of superstition, intolerance, and fatality that permeates the opera. Marchesi
      also proposes that Verdi turned to the outdated gesture of the cabaletta several
      times in the opera as a static, "empty" form that expresses the futile effort of the
      main characters to rise above their fateful circumstances.

569. Rescigno, Eduardo. "The Birth of the Libretto." In "*Aida*" *in Cairo* (item 555),
      199–204.

      An overview of the way in which Verdi and Ghislanzoni shaped the libretto for
      Aida based, in part, on recently discovered documentary evidence.

Studies of Compositional Process

570. Conati, Marcello. "Aspetti di melodrammaturgia verdiana: A proposito di una sconosciuta versione del finale del duetto Aida-Amneris." *Studi verdiani* 3 (1985): 45–78.

 Begins with a thorough review of Verdi's approach to formal structure in arias and typical differences in duets and finales, emphasizing in particular the distinction between cabalettas and strettas. The author then reviews the compositional history of the Aida-Amneris duet in Act II which, in its original version, avoided using a cabaletta form for its conclusion but did maintain the character of a stretta finale. Verdi created a more subtle, yet stunning effect in the revised version by reaching a deceptive conclusion, then ending *pianissimo* with a reminiscence of Aida's Act I *romanza*. The article reproduces, in facsimile, the score pages showing the original version of the duet.

* Lawton, David. "The Autograph of *Aida* and the New Verdi Edition." See item 1033.

* Osthoff, Wolfgang. "Oper und Opernvers: Zur Funktion des Verses in der italienischen Oper." See item 276.

Stylistic and Analytical Studies

571. Della Seta, Fabrizio. "'O cieli azzurri': Exoticism and Dramatic Discourse in *Aida*." *Cambridge Opera Journal* 3 (1991): 49–62.

 An evaluation of exotic style in *Aida* based on semiotic methods and concepts suggests that Verdi's approach differs substantially from *fin de siècle* decadent exoticism. Aida's love of country, which is especially important in generating the turning point of the drama, can be viewed not only as in its most obvious sense but also as the vision of an imaginary otherworld, free of the restrictions created by collective relationships. Verdi's distinctive *tinta* for this aspect of exoticism in "Celeste Aida," the scenes with Aida in Act III, and the Act IV finale differs markedly from the *tinta* of the choruses and dances associated with religious or political scenes. The author argues that the composer added Aida's romanza "O cieli azzurri" after the opera was completed not solely to expand the soprano role for Teresa Stolz, but also to clarify the idealized vision of the otherworld in the subsequent duets for Aida/Amonasro and Aida/Radames.

572. Gossett, Philip. "Verdi, Ghislanzoni, and *Aida*: The Uses of Convention." *Critical Inquiry* 1 (1974): 291–334.

 The author points out that Ghislanzoni's letters to Verdi are reproduced in the wrong order, sometimes with fabricated dates and errors of transcription, in the *Copialettere* (item 28) and other later publications, such as Abbiati (item 145) and Osborne (item 37). He postulates a revised chronology for the 35 letters and summarizes their content in tabular form. In the remainder of the article, Gossett examines the compositional history of the five duets in *Aida*, demonstrating how formal conventions established at the time of Rossini influenced Verdi's approach to both text and music in the opera, even in a piece such as the Act III Amonasro-Aida duet, which gives the impression of being relatively unorthodox. See item 457 above for a recent assessment of the strengths and weaknesses of Gossett's analytical approach in this article.

573. Lawton, David. "Tonal Systems in *Aida*, Act III." *Analyzing Opera: Verdi and Wagner* (item 454), 262–75.

Examines Verdi's use of motivic and tonal relationships to unify Act III of *Aida*. Analyzes the tonal plan of the act as a double cycle, each one moving from G major or minor through F major to Db major/minor; each cycle, however, preserving its own characteristic *tinta*. The article builds upon and responds to earlier studies by Gossett (item 572), Petrobelli (item 576), and Powers (item 496).

574. Lendvai, Ernő. "Verdi's Formgeheimnisse." *Atti 1* (item 224), 156–71.

Using examples from *Aida*, the author suggests that symphonic structures, particularly the sonata principle and the idea of continuing variation, play a significant role in Verdi's music.

575. Parker, Roger. "Motives and Recurring Themes in *Aida*." *Analyzing Opera: Verdi and Wagner* (item 454), 222–38.

The core of the article concentrates on the recurring theme associated with Aida and its complex interaction with the musical and dramatic structure of the opera. Verdi underscores the development of Aida's character through subtle variation of the theme and the way in which it interacts with differing tonal schemes and musical environments throughout the opera. The article also discusses ways in which the composer unifies the prelude and opening scene through the use of small "developmental motives."

576. Petrobelli, Pierluigi. "Music in the Theater (à propos of *Aida*, Act III)." In *Themes in Drama 3: Drama, Dance, and Music*. Ed. by James Redmond. Cambridge: Cambridge University Press, 1981), 129–42.
The essay is reprinted in Petrobelli's *Music in the Theater: Essays on Verdi and Other Composers* (item 378), 113–26 and in *"Aida" in Cairo* (item 555), 63–70.
Italian version. "La musica nel teatro: A proposito dell'atto III di *Aida*." In *La drammaturgia musicale*, 143–56. Ed. by Lorenzo Bianconi. Bologna: Società Editrice il Mulino, 1986. ISBN 88–15–01127–7. ML 1700 .D72 1986.

An examination of the interaction of dramatic action, verbal organization, and music in the opening portion of *Aida*, Act III. Petrobelli proposes that while dramatic structure and verbal organization contain the essence of the episode, music serves to provide an additional descriptive layer and also determines the temporal dimension of the work. Based on his discussion of this scene, the author proposes five general principles that "govern the unfolding of the dramatic 'language' of opera." Petrobelli's analytical methodology is heavily indebted to Frits Noske's application of semiotics to opera and can be best understood after gaining familiarity with this earlier study (see item 488).

* Werner, Klaus G. "Verdi auf dem Weg zum Spätwerk: Zwei Ouvertüren im Spannungsfeld zwischen Instrumentalmusik und Oper." See item 513.

Performance Practice, Staging, Scenography

577. Alberti, Luciano. "'I progressi attuali [1872] del dramma musicale': Note sulla *Disposizione scenica per l'opera "Aida"* compilata e regolata secondo la messa in scena del Teatro alla Scala da Giulio Ricordi." In *Il melodramma italiano dell'ottocento: Studi e ricerche per Massimo Mila*, 125–55. Ed. by Giorgio Pestelli. Saggi, 575. Turin: Einaudi, 1977. ML 1733.4 .M5.

Examines Verdi's changing aesthetic ideas and their application in *Aida*, using numerous illustrations from the production book and the composer's personal correspondence, comparing them to Wagner's reform of opera in Germany.

578. De Sanctis, Riccardo, and Pierluigi Petrobelli, eds. *Immagini per "Aida"*. Parma: Istituto di Studi Verdiani, 1983. 94 p. ISBN 88–8506–501–5. ML 141 .P2 V475 1983.

An exhibition catalogue featuring reproductions of costumes and set designs for the opera's premiere in Cairo and its first performance at the Paris Opéra in 1880, accompanied by short interpretive essays in Italian, French, English, and German. Some costume designs for other early productions are also included. Much of the iconographic material, reproduced here for the first time, was later republished in item 555 above.

579. Gavazzeni, Gianandrea. "Conducting Aida." In *"Aida" in Cairo* (item 555), 41–47.

Gavazzeni, a contemporary opera director, discusses special performance difficulties related to this opera.

580. Jürgensen, Knud Arne. "Le coreografie originali di *Aida*." *Studi verdiani* 6 (1990):146–58.

Examines Verdi's attitude toward the inclusion of ballet music for operas performed in Paris, surveys the composer's ballet music written for French productions, and discusses in detail his expansion of the ballet music in *Aida* for the 1880 production at the Opéra. The author compares the choreography for this production, preserved by Joseph Hanssen in a manuscript at the Bibliothèque de l'Opéra, with that of the Milanese premiere, described in the printed *disposizione scenica*. Jürgensen notes that Hanssen probably created the choreography for the "Danse des petits esclaves Maures" for an 1877 performance of *Aida* at the Théâtre Royal de la Monnaie in Brussels.

581. Olivero, Gabriella. "*Aida* tra egittologia ed egittomania." *Studi verdiani* 10 (1994–95): 118–26.

Discusses several sets of visual material at the Archivio Storico Ricordi associated with the staging of the opera at its Milanese premiere and soon after in Parma. These include: two sets of scenery designs by Girolamo Magnani, two scene designs by Carlo Ferrario, various stage props, and extensive costume designs. The author also examines the main literary and artistic sources that designers used to create the staging and scenography for early Italian performances of the opera. The article includes ten plates (most in color) showing reproductions of some of the iconographic material.

582. Viale Ferrero, Mercedes. "Scenery and Costumes for *Aida*: Cairo (1871) Milan (1972)." In *"Aida" in Cairo* (item 555), 139–44.

Examines the genesis of the scenography for the work's premiere in Cairo, focusing on the influence of Auguste Mariette. Discusses changes in the scenography for the opera's European premiere at La Scala, suggesting that these increased the work's expressive force and dramatic coherence. The volume includes color reproductions of many of the designs and costumes for these two productions.

Performance History; Reception

583. Gualerzi, Giorgio. "The Singers." In *"Aida" in Cairo* (item 555), 175–82.

Examines the history surrounding the choice of singers for the lead roles at the opera's Cairo premiere. The volume contains photographs of many of these performers.

584. Nello Vetro, Gaspare. "Cieli azzurri sì, cieli azzurri no." *Quadrivium: Studi di filologia e musicologia* 27 (1986): 123–25. This volume of *Quadrivium* is listed in some indexes as a monograph: *Universalità della musica, prestigio dell'Italia, attualità di Verdi: Studi in onore di Mario Medici*, Vol. 2. Ed. by Giuseppe Vecchi. Bologna: Antiquae Musicae Italicae Studiosi, 1986.

Reproduces a review of performances in Cairo, published in the Roman musical journal *Il liuto* in January 1872. The review clarifies that, contrary to some reports in the secondary literature, Aida's *romanza* "Cieli azzurri" was not a later addition for the Italian premiere.

585. Pinzauti, Leonardo. "*Aida* e *Lohengrin* a confronto nella Firenze di cent'anni fa." *Atti 3* (item 226), 401–7.

Suggests reasons for the lukewarm reception of *Aida* by Florentine music critic Girolamo Alessandro Biaggi. Biaggi generally disliked the music of both Verdi and Wagner. After having heard both *Lohengrin* and *Aida*, however, he reserved his sharpest criticism for Verdi, who to him had not only renounced the principles of Italian *bel canto* but had gone beyond Wagner's use of melodic declamation in *Lohengrin*.

ALZIRA

Alzira marked Verdi's first collaboration with Salvatore Cammarano and was his first opera written for Naples. The work received only a lukewarm reception during its initial performances, and it remains one of Verdi's least performed operas and one about which relatively little has been written.

Histories and General Studies

586. Mila, Massimo. "Verdi minore: Lettura dell'*Alzira*." *Rivista italiana di musicologia* 1 (1966): 246–63.

A brief summary of the opera's history and reception, followed by a descriptive analysis of the work. The author repeatedly points to characteristic passages that foreshadow ideas from later operas.

Studies of Compositional Process

587. Petrobelli, Pierluigi. "Pensieri per *Alzira*." *Nuove prospettive nella ricerca verdiana* (item 231), 110–24.
    English translation by Roger Parker. "Thoughts for *Alzira*." In *Music in the Theater: Essays on Verdi and Other Composers* (item 378), 75–99.

Discusses a manuscript in the collection of the Gesellschaft der Musikfreunde in Vienna that contains sketches for two sections of *Alzira*. The first sketch demonstrates how the composer refined his ideas for the chorus that concludes the Prologue to Act I. Cammarano had originally planned a hymn of rejoicing to be sung by the entire chorus of Incas; Verdi expanded this idea by adding solo passages for the young hero Zamoro. A second sketch in this manuscript contains a passage from the Act I finale, where the composer also modified some of Cammarano's ideas to make the passage more effective musically and dramatically.

ATTILA

Although *Attila* received a lukewarm premiere, the opera enjoyed tremendous popularity during the politically turbulent decade of the 1850s. The genesis of the work presents some particularly interesting problems. Solera, who formulated the libretto, abandoned work on the project after moving to Spain; Piave completed it under close supervision by the composer.

Histories and General Studies

*   Engelhardt, Markus. *Verdi und Andere: "Un giorno di regno," "Ernani," "Attila, "Il corsaro" in Mehrfachvertonungen*. See item 371.

588.   Mila, Massimo. "Lettura dell'*Attila* di Verdi." *Nuova rivista musicale italiana* 17 (1983): 247–76.

A short history of the work's genesis and reception, followed by a detailed descriptive analysis.

Studies of Compositional Process

589.   Gossett, Philip. "A New Romanza for *Attila*." *Studi verdiani* 9 (1993): 13–53.

Recounts the history of two substitute arias Verdi wrote for Russian tenor Nicolai Ivanov under encouragement from Rossini. The aria with chorus "Odi il voto, o grande Iddio" for *Ernani* has long been known. The Romanza "Sventurato! alla mia vita," written for *Attila*, disappeared until the 1960s. Its recent purchase by the Library of Congress has made it available to scholars for the first time. The author briefly discusses the music, which he presents in a full transcription. The article also reproduces the first page of the manuscript in facsimile.

Stylistic and Analytical Studies

*   Balthazar, Scott Leslie. "The *Primo Ottocento* Duet and the Transformation of Rossinian Code." See item 251.

590.   Noiray, Michel, and Roger Parker. "La composition d'*Attila*: Étude de quelques variantes." *Revue de musicologie* 62 (1976): 104–23.

Presents a comparative reading of passages from an early draft preserved at the Bibliothèque Nationale containing a portion of the prologue and the corresponding passage in the autograph full score, now located at the British Museum. Passages examined in particular detail include the introduction

Odabella's cavatina "Allor che i forti corrono," and her cabaletta "Da te questo or m'è concesso." The authors suggest that heightened dramatic effect stimulated most of the revisions and that Verdi's concern for drama and musical unity points toward an even stronger realization in the soon-to-be-composed *Macbeth*.

591. Edwards, Geoffrey, and Ryan Edwards. "A Reconsideration of Verdi's Early Musical Characterization: Ezio in *Attila*." *The Opera Journal* 23 (June 1990): 2–12.

Verdi's musical characterization of Ezio, the Roman general, does not suggest a flat, "cardboard" character but rather a complex individual with strengths, weaknesses, and conflicting emotions.

592. Rhodes, Terry Ellen. "Love vs. Duty: A Study of Odabella in Verdi's *Attila*." *The Opera Journal* 25 (June 1992): 12–29.

Argues that Odabella's duality of character allowed Verdi to write strongly dramatic and contrasting music for her, although her characterization in the libretto has sometimes been criticized as inconsistent. The author briefly examines the genesis of Odabella's character in the libretto, then surveys her pieces in the opera, focusing on her prologue aria, the *Scena e Romanza* from Act I, and her duet with Foresto from Act I.

* Smart, Mary Ann. "'Proud, Indomitable, Irascible': Allegories of Nation in *Attila* and *Les vêpres siciliennes*." See item 973.

Performance Practice, Staging, Scenography

593. Giovagnoli, Attilio. "Due bozzetti di Romolo Liverani per l'opera *Attila* di Verdi al Teatro Comunale Provvisorio di Fano." *Nuovi studi fanesi* 3 (1988): 165–72.

Discusses two sketches by Romolo Liverani (reproduced in the article) for the Teatro Comunale's production of *Attila* in January 1850. One sketch pertains to the Prologue, Scene 2; the other represents the final scene of Act I. The author discusses the work of Liverani in general and compares his approach in *Attila* to that of Giuseppe Bertoja, who designed the staging for the work's Venetian premiere in 1846.

* Viale Ferrero, Mercedes. "Da *Norma* a *Attila*: Scene del Teatro Regio di Torino durante il regno di Carlo Alberto." See item 550.

Performance History; Reception

594. Pestelli, Giorgio. "L'opera al Teatro Regio di Torino durante il Regno d
    Carlo Alberto." In *Opera & Libretto I*, 253–64. Studi di musica veneta
    Florence: Olschki, 1990. ISBN 88–222–3825–7. ML 1700 .O655 1990.

    Much of the article concerns the reception of *Attila* in Turin during 1848–49
    including interventions by the censors.

UN BALLO IN MASCHERA

The troubled genesis of this opera, as well as its unusual style, have led to many
interesting studies. Although the work was intended for the Teatro San Carlo in
Naples, the censors rejected the essentially completed opera and proposed a radically
altered version, *Adelia degli Adimari*. The composer, in turn, renounced the
bowdlerized libretto, noting scathing comments in its margins (see item 601)
Eventually he moved the work's premiere to the Teatro Apollo in Rome, but censor
there still demanded modifications, including a change of locale from Sweden to
America. The style of *Ballo* is unique among Verdi's works, a blend of tragedy and
comedy and of Italian and French traditions; this feature has also led to a number of
fascinating analytical and historical studies.

Guides to the Work

595. *Un bal masqué. L'avant-scène opéra* 32 (March/April 1981). Paris: L'Avant-
    Scène, 1981. 178 p. ISSN 0395–0670. MT 100 .V48 B32.
    2nd ed. Paris: Société Premières Loges, 1992. 146 p. ISSN 0764–2873. ML
    410 .V4 B134 1992.

    This bulk of this issue is devoted to *Ballo*. Essays focus on the genesis of the
    work and the trouble Verdi encountered with the censors, the historical
    background of the story behind the libretto, and the characterization of the
    leading roles in the opera. The libretto is presented in Italian with a parallel
    French translation by Gilles De Van, with a running commentary by Sylvaine
    Falcinelli. The volume also includes a discography of complete recordings and
    individual arias or sections (accompanied by a prose essay dealing with the
    complete recordings), tables listing the earliest performances of the opera in
    major centers, as well as more detailed information about performances in
    major houses up to the present (updated in the second edition). The
    bibliography in the first edition contains about 150 items, including general
    studies about Verdi as well as items pertaining directly to *Ballo*; the second
    edition has a much smaller list of about two dozen items.

596. *A Masked Ball/Un ballo in maschera*. English National Opera Guides, 40.
    London: John Calder; New York: Riverrun, 1989. 96 p. ISBN
    0–7145–4167–2. ML 50 .V484 B22 1989.

This guide features an outstanding essay by Pierluigi Petrobelli on Verdi's fusion of styles in the opera (see item 598) and a detailed study of the "Laughing Chorus" by Harold Powers (item 608). The volume also presents a descriptive analysis of the work, a discography and selective bibliography. An English translation of the libretto by Edmund Tracey, presented side by side with the Italian original, restores the action to the court of Gustavus III, King of Sweden, as well as the original names of the characters before censors forced Verdi to change the locale to Boston.

Histories and General Studies

597. D'Amico, Fedele. "Il *Ballo in maschera* prima di Verdi." *Verdi: Bollettino dell'Istituto di Studi Verdiani* 1 [No. 3] (1960): 1251–1328. English and German translations are printed on pp. 1663–1714.

Compares Verdi's opera with several earlier settings of the same story: 1) *Gustave III ou Le bal masqué* (libretto by Eugène Scribe, music by Daniel-François-Esprit Auber, first performed in 1833), 2) *Clemenza di Valois* (libretto by Gaetano Rossi, music by Vincenzo Gabussi, first performed in 1841), and 3) *Il reggente* (libretto by Salvatore Cammarano and music by Saverio Mercadante, first performed in 1843).

*   Gerhard, Anselm. *Die Verstädterung der Oper.* See item 265.

598. Petrobelli, Pierluigi. "The Fusion of Styles." In *A Masked Ball/Un ballo in maschera.* English National Opera Guides 40 (item 596), 9–14.

Ballo represents a unique work among Verdi's compositions in his use of music to underscore the contrast between the "light/comic" and "dark/tragic" areas of the plot. This creates a strong sense of contrast in musical and dramatic style that draws on both Italian and French theatrical conventions. The author also argues that Verdi ultimately adopted Scribe's original subtitle—*Le bal masqué*—as a "neutral" title capable of reflecting the ambiguities in the drama rather than settling on the interim title, *Una vendetta in domino*, which would have underscored the tragic element alone.

599. *Verdi: Bollettino dell'Istituto di Studi Verdiani*, 1. Parma: Istituto di Studi Verdiani, 1960. cxliv, 1804 p. + 97 p. ML 410 .V4 A5.

Most articles in the three numbers comprising this volume of the *Bollettino* concern *Un ballo in maschera.* They cover a wide range of topics, including the history and genesis of the work, and its reception, and a descriptive analysis of the opera. Most articles are printed in Italian, English, and German; some of the most significant items are listed separately as numbers 94, 597, 610–13, and 1017. A separately issued and paginated index fascicle contains, in addition to the actual index, a bibliography of materials dealing with *Ballo in maschera*, a discography (including recordings of selections from the opera), and a listing of 39 printed librettos with full information from their respective title pages.

* Walker, Frank. "Unpublished Letters: A Contribution to the History of *Un ballo in maschera*." See item 94.

Dramaturgy; Studies of the Libretto

600. Flora, Francesco. "Il libretto." *Verdi: Bollettino dell'Istituto di Studi Verdiani* [No. 1 and 2] (1960): 44–72, 662–78. English and German versions of the text may be found on pp. 305–53, 863–93.

Examines the genesis of the libretto to *Ballo*, including difficulties with the censors, followed by a descriptive analysis of the plot.

601. Luzio, Alessandro. "Il libretto del *Ballo in maschera* massacrato dalla censura borbonica." In *Carteggi verdiani* (item 29), 1:241–75.

A detailed description of the censors' proposed revision of the *Ballo* libretto into a substantially new work to be called *Adelia degli Adimari*. The commentary is based on the manuscript prepared by the censors, onto which Verdi made extensive and largely acerbic annotations. The author reproduces three pages of the manuscript in facsimile.

Stylistic and Analytical Studies

602. Bollert, Werner. "Auber, Verdi, und der *Maskenball*-Stoff." In *Bericht über den Internationalen Musikwissenschaftlichen Kongress, Bonn 1970*, 349–52. Ed. by Carl Dahlhaus et al. Kassel: Bärenreiter, 1971. ISBN 3–6718–0146–7. ML 36 .I6277.

Compares Verdi's *Ballo* with Auber's *Gustave III ou Le bal masqué*, written a quarter-century earlier. Bollert illustrates how Verdi's conception of several scenes parallels closely that of the earlier composer yet reaches beyond them in dramatic and musical sophistication.

* Della Seta, Fabrizio. "Il tempo della festa: Su due scene della *Traviata* e su altri luoghi verdiani." See item 934.

603. Espinosa, Alma. "The Tonality of B♭ in Verdi's *Ballo in maschera*: Fate, Foreshadowing, and Dramatic Unity." *Verdi Newsletter* 23 (1996): 4–7.

Asserts that Verdi associated the key of B♭ with the conspiracy to kill Riccardo and the misunderstanding that brings Renato into the assassination plot. The author points out how the key serves both as a foreshadowing device and a means of dramatic irony.

604. Hudson, Elizabeth. "Making Music: A Reconsideration of Light and Shade in *Un ballo in maschera.*" In *Verdi's Middle Period, 1849–1859: Source Studies, Analysis, and Performance Practice* (item 235), 257–72.

Critiquing the frequently cited metaphor of "light" and "dark" to represent the powerful sense of contrast in *Ballo*, the author suggests that the notion of "masking" and "unmasking" better represents the constantly shifting play of many types of opposition (including the tension between major and minor) in this work.

605. Levarie, Siegmund. "Key Relations in Verdi's *Un ballo in maschera.*" *19th Century Music* 2 (1978–79): 143–47.

After outlining the tonal structure of the work, the author proposes that the three pieces from the opera in C Major (Ulrica's invocation in Act I, the love duet in Act II, and Riccardo's *romanza* in Act III) serve as musical and dramatic "piers" that balance and mediate between the sharp keys that dominate the first half of the opera and the flat keys that dominate its second half. Responses to this article by Joseph Kerman and Guy Marco are published in the same journal on pages 186–91 and in vol. 3 (1979–80): 83–88; Levarie offers a rejoinder to Kerman's critique on pages 88–89.

606. Parker, Roger, and Matthew Brown. "Motivic and Tonal Interaction in Verdi's *Un ballo in maschera.*" *Journal of the American Musicological Society* 36 (1983): 243–65.

A close analysis of Act I, Scene 1 from several points of view shows that words, music, and drama together form a symmetrical structure emphasizing "classical balance." The apparently anomalous excursions to Db major in this scene launch an entire series of parallel tonal movements that become increasingly complex and more closely related to the central dramatic event of Riccardo's assassination. The authors conclude, however, that the network of motivic and tonal associations throughout this opera are so complex that any single explanatory model by itself will be insufficient.

607. Powers, Harold S. "'La dama velata': Act II of *Un ballo in maschera.*" In *Verdi's Middle Period, 1849–1859: Source Studies, Analysis, and Performance Practice* (item 235), 273–336.

A detailed study of Act II, with particular emphasis on the material leading up to the inadvertent unveiling of Amelia, which Powers argues is the dramatic and musical high point of the act (see item 608 below for another article by the author concentrating on the concluding portion of this act). The article emphasizes the interaction between drama, music, and staging in the act's evolution from initial conception through an intermediate version (*Una vendetta in domino*) to its final state. The closing section of the essay focuses on the use of moonlight in the stage setting. The dramatic use of moonlight during the scene was an important feature of Somma's revisions of the libretto for the abortive *Una vendetta in domino*, possibly influenced by Salvatore Cammarano's 1843 adaptation of the story for Mercadante's *Il reggente*; it also played a significant part in Giuseppe Cencetti's published *disposizione scenica* for *Ballo*'s Roman premiere in February 1859. The author contends that the gradual unveiling of the moon from behind the clouds, which provides constantly greater illumination to the scene, parallels the rise in dramatic tension and reaches a peak at the same point that Amelia's veil falls.

608.   ———. "The 'Laughing Chorus' in Contexts." In *A Masked Ball/Un ballo in maschera*. English National Opera Guides, 40 (item 596), 23–40.

A detailed analysis of the Act II finale, focusing on how the composer emphasized the sharp contrast between tragic and comic elements. The author compares Somma's and Verdi's treatment of this scene with that of earlier versions of the story—Scribe's original libretto written for Auber (*Gustave III, ou Le bal masqué*); Gaetano Rossi's libretto written for Vincenzo Gabussi (*Clemenza di Valois*); and Cammarano's libretto written for Mercadante (*Il reggente*)—emphasizing the way in which the Italians modified aspects of the French libretto to suit their own national traditions. Somma's revisions of the finale indicate that he borrowed some ideas from Cammarano's libretto. For his part, Verdi planned an unusual structure, substituting in place of the final stretta a mixture of text and music from the preceding section, further developing a scheme he had already tried in *Luisa Miller* and *Il trovatore*. The concluding portion of the article considers Verdi's emphasis on sharply contrasting major and minor tonalities (especially Bb major and Bb minor) in the quintets at the end of Acts I and III.

609.   Ross, Peter. "Amelias Auftrittsarie im *Maskenball*: Verdis Vertonung in dramaturgisch-textlichem Zusammenhang." *Archiv für Musikwissenschaft* 40 (1983): 126–46.

A close textual and musical examination of Amelia's aria "Ma dall'arido stelo divulsa," focusing on revisions in the text and their influence on the rhythmic shape of the music. In addition, Ross compares the rhythmic character of certain passages to sections of other operas by Verdi.

610. Zecchi, Adone. "Il coro nel *Ballo in maschera*." *Verdi: Bollettino dell'Istituto di Studi Verdiani* 1 [No. 3] (1960): 1137–54. English and German translations of the article appear on pp. 1470–96.

A descriptive analysis of choral sections in *Ballo*, focusing on the Introduction.

* Casale, Stephen. "A Newly-Discovered Letter from Verdi to Léon Escudier." See item 54 above.

Performance History; Reception

611. Della Corte, Andrea. "Saggio di bibliografia delle critiche al *Ballo in maschera*." *Verdi: Bollettino dell'Istituto di Studi Verdiani* 1 [No. 3] (1960): 1165–97. English and German translations of the article are found on pp. 1516–71.

A selection of citations from periodicals and books, ranging from Verdi's times to the present, assessing *Ballo in maschera*. Most entries contain short quotations from the original source; a few contain only short summaries.

612. Gara, Eugenio. "Il cammino dell'opera in un secolo d'interpretazioni." *Verdi: Bollettino dell'Istituto di Studi Verdiani* 1 [No. 1, 2, and 3] (1960): 112–33, 704–19, 1155–64. English and German translations of the article are printed on pp. 418–57, 928–57, and 1497–1515.

Surveys the reception of *Un ballo in maschera* through letters, documents, and published reviews, concentrating primarily on nineteenth- and early twentieth-century performances in Italy.

Miscellaneous

613. Mila, Massimo. "Problemi di filologia e d'interpretazione intorno alla partitura del *Ballo in maschera*." *Verdi: Bollettino dell'Istituto di Studi Verdiani* 1 [No. 1 and 2] (1960): 134–56, 720–31. English and German versions of the article may be found on pp. 458–93, 720–31.

A detailed discussion of differences between the original published orchestral score (1914) and a new "revised and corrected" edition issued by Ricordi in 1959.

LA BATTAGLIA DI LEGNANO

La battaglia di Legnano is Verdi's most openly political opera, inspired by the revolutions of 1848 in which the Milanese temporarily forced their Austrian overlords from the city. Noske provides an excellent analysis of the political features of the opera, although recent studies have begun to question the extent of Verdi's political activism in this and other operas (see, for example, item 300). Very little scholarly work has appeared dealing with the music itself.

Histories and General Studies

614. Noske, Frits. "Verdi und die Belagerung von Haarlem." In *Convivium musicorum: Festschrift Wolfgang Boetticher zum sechzigsten Geburtstag am 19. August 1974*, 236–45. Ed. by Heinrich Hüschen and Dietz-Rüdiger Moser. Berlin: Merseburger, 1974. ISBN 3–87537–085–6. ML 55 .B6 1974.

Argues that *La battaglia di Legnano*, more than any other opera by Verdi, reflects the composer's assertive patriotism, with a clear parallel between the plot and recent events during the revolutions of 1848. The author examines patriotic elements in both the opera's libretto and music and subsequent difficulties with the censors, which eventually led to an alternative version called *L'assedio di Arlem*, with the locale changed from northern Italy to Holland. Noske discusses the major changes made in this alternative version, including some of the resulting inconsistencies or weaknesses in the story. Although the opera was never performed in nineteenth-century Holland, the author compares it to several operas by other composers dealing with the parallel topic of the siege of Leiden. An appendix reproduces a letter from Salvatore Cammarano to Giovanni Ricordi discussing the altered libretto, as well as a contract signed by Verdi, Cammarano, and Ricordi establishing rights of ownership for *La battaglia* and specifying conditions under which the alternative *Assedio* libretto could be used.

Stylistic and Analytical Studies

615. Budden, Julian. "*La battaglia di Legnano*: Its Unique Character with Special Reference to the Finale of Act I." *Atti 3* (item 226), 71–80.

Analyzes the Act I duet between Arrigo and Lida as a modified sonata form in which the return to home key, following a development section, presents new thematic material. The author draws parallels between Verdi's procedure and that used by Beethoven in the terzetto "Gut, Söhnchen, gut" (No. 5) from *Fidelio*.

IL CORSARO

Although the composer was initially enthusiastic about the story of *Il corsaro*, he eventually wrote the work under a certain amount of duress in order to fulfill an unhappy contract with the publisher Lucca. Verdi neither took into consideration the premiere cast when writing the work, nor did he supervise the opera's premiere. Today, *Il corsaro* remains one of Verdi's most neglected operas, both in terms of research and performance.

Histories and General Studies

* Engelhardt, Markus. *Verdi und Andere: "Un giorno di regno," "Ernani," "Attila," "Il corsaro" in Mehrfachvertonungen*. See item 371.

616. Medici, Mario, ed. *Il corsaro*. Quaderni dell'Istituto di Studi Verdiani, 1. [Parma: Istituto di Studi Verdiani], 1963. 75 p. + 11 plates. ML 410 .V58 A48 no. 1.

   A commemorative booklet containing two major essays and illustrative material, issued in connection with a performance of the opera at the Palazzo Ducale in Venice during 1963. Giuseppe Vecchi traces the history of the libretto and analyzes its plot (also reprinted in item 444), while Mario Medici contributes an analytical-descriptive essay on the music.

617. Mila, Massimo. "Lettura del *Corsaro* di Verdi." *Nuova rivista musicale italiana* 5 (1971): 40–73.

   After a brief discussion of the work's genesis and reception, the main portion of the article provides a substantial descriptive analysis of the opera.

618. Zambon, Rita. "Quando il ballo anticipa l'opera: *Il corsaro* di Giovanni Galzerani." In *Creature di Prometeo: Il ballo teatrale dal divertimento al drama. Studi offerti a Aurel M. Milloss*, 305–13. Ed. by Giovanni Morelli. Studi di musica veneta, 23. Florence: Olschki, 1996. ISBN 88–22–4415–X. GV 1655 .C64 1996.

   Presents evidence that Galzerani's ballet influenced Piave's conception of the libretto for Verdi's opera, particularly in terms of its dramatic structure. The ballet was presented many times in Italian theaters beginning with its premiere at La Scala in 1826. An appendix traces these performances, publications of Byron's *Corsair* in Italian translation, and operas based on the story through 1848, the year of Verdi's setting.

DON CARLOS

The complex history of this work, the longest and perhaps the grandest of Verdi's operas, has led to a large number of studies in the areas of genesis and compositional process. The length and demands of the work forced the composer to make revisions even before the curtain went up on the first production, and the ensuing years saw many more revisions, with the most substantial alterations in 1882–83. The massive amount of primary source material, particularly at the Paris Opéra, have allowed thorough documentation of this process. A basic starting point for any thorough study of the opera should be the *Atti del II° Congresso Internazionale di Studi Verdiani* (item 225), devoted entirely to this opera.

Guides to the Work

619. *Don Carlos. L'avant-scène opéra* 90/91 (September/October 1986). Paris
      L'Avant-Scène, 1986. 226 p. ISSN 0764-2873. ML 5 .A9 v. 90–91.
      2nd ed. Paris: Société Premières Loges, 1990. 191 p. ISSN 0764-2873. ML
      410 .V4 V353 1990.

Nearly 200 pages of this special issue (and all of the 2nd edition) are devoted to
Don Carlos. Approximately a dozen articles focus on topics such as the genesis
of the work, the relationship of the libretto to Schiller's drama, musical
characterization of individual roles in the opera, Verdi's major reworking and
abridgment of the work in 1883, and the opera's reception history. The volume
also includes a French translation of item 643 below, originally published in
Italian. One of the most significant contributions of this volume is the first
publication of Joseph Méry's and Camille Du Locle's original scenario (1865)
for the opera. The guide also presents the original French libretto, restoring
several passages that were cut before the first performance, together with a
parallel Italian translation based on the work of Achille De Lauzières and
Angelo Zanardini, with new passages translated by Piero Faggioni. The
descriptive analysis accompanying the libretto includes an assessment of
modifications made by the composer for the four-act Italian version of the
opera. The volume contains much other useful material, including a
discography of complete and partial recordings accompanied by a prose essay,
tables listing the earliest performances of the opera in major centers, as well as
more detailed information about performances in major houses up to the
present. A substantial specialized bibliography lists nearly 350 items, including
principal editions, musical studies, studies and documents relating to the
historical Don Carlos, Philippe II, and Schiller's play. The second edition
contains only a few unsubstantial changes.

620. *Don Carlos/Don Carlo.* English National Opera Guides, 46. Ed. by Jennifer
      Batchelor. London: John Calder; New York: Riverrun, 1992. 160 p. ISBN
      0-7145-4208-3. ML 50 .V484 D613 1992.

Essays in this guide deal with the genesis of the opera and its place among
Verdi's works; the transformation of Schiller's play into the libretto for the
opera; Saint-Réal's novel, *Don Carlos*, the primary source for Schiller's play;
Verdi's characterization of the main figures; and aspects of the work's post-
premiere revisions. The guide reproduces the libretto based on the original
Paris score rather than the original printed libretto but restores the cuts Verdi
made before the first performance; it also includes parallel translations in Italian
(based on the version by Achille De Lauzières and Angelo Zanardini) and
English (a new translation by Andrew Porter). An appendix provides passages
that were added for the four-act version in Italian that premiered at La Scala
in 1884. The editors have noted significant variants from the printed libretto

and have also included diagrams and information from the third edition (1884) of the *disposizione scenica* that provide interesting details about the composer's conception of the opera's staging. The volume contains a selective discography accompanied by a brief comparison of different productions and a highly selective bibliography.

521. Mioli, Piero. *Invito all'opera "Don Carlos" di Giuseppe Verdi.* Milan: Mursia, 1990. 195 p. ISBN 88–425–0134–4. ML 50 .V484 D6 1990.

This substantial guide offers a survey of the work's genesis, performance, and reception; the transformation of Schiller's play into the libretto; an overview of the plot and musical form; and a brief bibliography with selected excerpts from the secondary literature. The libretto reproduced here is the Italian translation by Achille De Lauzières and Angelo Zanardini. The author's extensive annotations detail changes made from the original French version and point to significant features of the music.

Histories and General Studies

* *Atti del II° Congresso Internazionale di Studi Verdiani.* See item 225.

* Conati, Marcello. "Verdi, il *grand opéra* e il *Don Carlos*." Cited above as item 260.

522. Degrada, Francesco. "*Don Carlos*: Il teatro musicale e la sua funzione critica." In *Il palazzo incantato* (item 369), 2:143–53.

Examines the element of social commentary in *Don Carlos* and the way in which the French *grand opéra* tradition helped to shape Verdi's ideological approach.

523. Günther, Ursula. "La genèse du *Don Carlos* de Verdi: Nouveaux documents." *Revue de musicologie* 72 (1986): 104–17.

Describes newly found sheets at the Bibliothèque-Musée de l'Opéra that were excised from a copy of the autograph manuscript during the final rehearsals and after the first performance. The author also reproduces and discusses iconographic material, including a title page design; a caricature published in the *Journal d'images: Journal comique, critique, satirique*; and costume designs for several of the characters.

524. ———. "La genèse de *Don Carlos*, opéra en cinq actes de Giuseppe Verdi, représenté pour la première fois a Paris le 11 mars 1867." *Revue de musicologie* 58 (1972): 16–64; 60 (1974): 87–158.

This formidable and important study is one of the earliest to document th
history of the original version of the opera and establish its compositiona
chronology. The author's main sources are letters and documents (includin,
some previously unpublished items originally housed at the Archives de l'Opér
and later transferred to the Archives Nationales) and excised musical materia
(preserved at the Bibliothèque de l'Opéra). The article presents in transcriptio
some of the music that was later deleted or modified. In addition, sixteen plate
provide facsimile reproductions of pages from manuscript and publishe
librettos and from manuscript scores and parts. See item 95 for related materia

625. ———. "Wagnerismen in Verdis *Don Carlos* von 1867?" In *Wagnerliteratur–
       Wagnerforschung: Bericht über das Wagner-Symposium München 1983*
       101–08. Ed. by Carl Dahlhaus and Egon Voss. Mainz: Schott, 1985. ISBN
       3–7957–2202–0. ML 410 .W131 W22 1983.

A number of nineteenth-century composers and critics, including George
Bizet, found features in the original version of *Don Carlos* that suggested th
influence of Wagner. The author argues that these features are in realit
further developments of techniques and ambitions already attempted by Verd
in many of his earlier works. Since Verdi knew little of Wagner's music at thi
point in his career, the most significant foreign influence on his style in *Do
Carlos* undoubtedly came from Meyerbeer, especially in the areas of scoring
melodic shape, and stage effects. The author suggests that some critics hav
deceptively tried to argue for Wagnerian influence in order to underplay an
possible role by Meyerbeer.

626. ———. "Zur Entstehung der zweiten französischen Fassung von Verdis *Do
       Carlos.*" In *Report of the Eleventh Congress [of the International Musicologica
       Society], Copenhagen 1972*, 1:396–402. Ed. by Henrik Glahn, Søre
       Sørensen, and Peter Ryom. Copenhagen: Wilhelm Hansen, 1974. 2 vols
       ISBN 87–7455–026–8. ML 36 .I67 1972.

Describes documents from the Archives Nationales in Paris that contai
information relating to Verdi's revision of the opera into a second Frenc
version in the years 1882–83. See item 96 for a reproduction and more detaile
assessment of these documents.

  *   Günther, Ursula, and Gabriella Carrara Verdi. "Der Briefwechsel Verdi
       Nuitter-Du Locle zur Revision des *Don Carlos.*" See item 96.

627. Osborne, Charles. "*Don Carlo*: The Extra Dimension—Music?" *Atti 2* (item
       225), 348–54.

Argues that the compassionate tone of Verdi's music in the *auto-da-fé* scene, a scene not found in Schiller's drama, sets a completely different tone for the entire opera from that of the original play.

28. Pugliese, Giuseppe. "Gli studi verdiani e il *Don Carlos* oggi." *Atti 2* (item 225), 2–14.

This introductory essay to the *Don Carlos* conference begins by surveying the state of Verdi research at the start of the 1970s and the contributions of the Istituto di Studi Verdiani. Later, the author considers some of the particular problems associated with the study of *Don Carlos* and suggests that the moral-psychological tone of the opera is one important area that needs much further research and discussion.

29. Robinson, Paul. "Realpolitik: Giuseppe Verdi's *Don Carlo*." In *Opera & Ideas from Mozart to Strauss*, 155–209. New York: Harper & Row, 1985. ISBN 0–06–015450–0. ML 1720 .R6 1985.

Proposes that Verdi's middle-period operas, especially *Don Carlos*, contain elements of *Realpolitik* philosophy: politics guided by considerations of power and opportunism rather than ideology. In general, these political elements are conveyed through such things as Verdi's direct (rather than symbolic) approach to opera, his use of musical patterns fashioned after rhetorical devices, and his emphasis on "power voices": the high baritone and the dramatic mezzo-soprano. The concluding section of the article considers how Verdi's treatment of each of the principal characters in *Don Carlos* conveys political ideology. In particular, King Philip emerges as a true political leader, who is willing to sacrifice his own peace and contentment for the greater good of the people.

30. Sutcliffe, James Helme. "Die sechs 'Fassungen' des *Don Carlos*: Versuch einer Bilanz." *Oper heute* 7 (1984): 69–89.

Examines the history of the opera, focusing on the various versions in which it was performed during Verdi's lifetime and their relationship to Schiller's original play. Includes a comparative table that outlines in parallel columns the main structure of the five-act Parisian *Don Carlos* (1866–67), the revised four-act version performed in Milan in 1882–83, and Schiller's original drama.

Dramaturgy; Studies of the Libretto

31. Alonso, María Rosa. "El tema de Don Carlos en la literatura: Sus orígenes y desarrollo." *Atti 2* (item 225), 16–58.

A thorough overview of the historical figure of Don Carlos as seen through the eye of both historians and literary figures since the period of the Renaissance. The article provides indispensable background for understanding Schiller's

treatment of historical characters and events and its influence on Verdi and h
librettists.

632. Chusid, Martin. "Schiller Revisited: Some Observations on the Revision
     Don Carlos." *Atti 2* (item 225), 156–69.

     Notes that Verdi's revision of *Don Carlos* into four acts during the early 188(
     created a closer parallel to Schiller's original play. In addition to excising man
     passages, most of which had no parallel in Schiller, revisions in the meetin
     between Philip and Posa and the scene between Elizabeth and Eboli convey th
     tone of Schiller's play more faithfully. In particular, an added reference i
     Eboli's aria to her previous seduction by Philip greatly improves the coherenc
     of the opera's plot.

633. Cusatelli, Giorgio. *"Don Carlos* di Schiller tradotto da Andrea Maffei." *Atti*
     (item 225), 170–79.

     Examines Andrea Maffei's cultural background, the relationship of h
     translation of *Don Carlos* to other contemporary Italian translations of Schille
     and the way in which Maffei's linguistic choices frequently alter the historic
     and ideological content of Schiller's drama.

634. Döhring, Sieghart. *"Grand opéra* als historisches Drama und als privat
     Tragödie: Meyerbeers *Le prophète* und Verdis *Don Carlos.*" In *Atti del XI
     Congresso della Società Internazionale di Musicologia: Trasmissione e recezior
     delle forme di cultura musicale*, 1: 727–33. Ed. by Angelo Pompilio, Donatell
     Restani, Lorenzo Bianconi, and F. Alberto Gallo. 3 vols. Turin: Edizioni
     Torino, 1990. ISBN 88–7063–084–6.

     Examines similarities and differences in the dramaturgy of the two opera:
     focusing on the cathedral scene in *Le prophète* and the *auto-da-fè* scene fror
     Don Carlos and on the ways in which the two composers integrated epi
     conflict between large groups of people and personal conflict among individu:
     characters.

635. Edelman, Susanne Popper. *"Don Carlo*: Schiller, Verdi, and the Marquis
     Posa." *The Opera Journal* 17/3 (1984): 16–22.

     Examines the complex characterization of the Marquis di Posa in Schiller
     original play, based largely on the playwright's own commentary. Posa
     motivations and goals are sometimes unclear in Verdi's opera because
     simplifies his political and philosophical side.

636. Freeman, John W. "The Ambivalence of Personal Relationships in Dc
     Carlo." *Atti 2* (item 225), 331–35.

Argues that the characters in *Don Carlos* show a depth in subtle psychological development that is unsurpassed in the rest of Verdi's operas. Individual characters harbor ambivalent feelings; interaction between characters also tends to be ambivalent due to inner conflicts. The author suggests that Verdi's command of musical language had matured to the extent that his music could at times underscore or even suggest the interplay of these ambivalent ideas.

* Fricke, Harald. "Schiller und Verdi: Das Libretto als Textgattung." See item 407.

637. Gerhartz, Leo Karl. "Il sogno di Fontainebleau: Alcune riflessioni sulla tecnica dell'introduzione nel dramma schilleriano e nell'opera verdiana." *Atti 2* (item 225), 186–192.

Demonstrates that while Schiller conveys some essential "background" information as a subtle part of long narrative passages, Verdi presents the same ideas in a more direct and dramatic fashion, utilizing theatrical and musical gestures that forcefully convey the emotional intensity behind significant situations. The author argues that the visual aspect of the opera is of paramount importance to its dramaturgical development.

638. Ghisi, Federico. "Sogno e realtà nell'introduzione al terzo atto del *Don Carlo*." *Atti 2* (item 225), 343–47.

A detailed comparison of the king's monologue in Schiller's original drama with the same scene in Méry and Du Locle's libretto for *Don Carlos*. The opera expands Philip's introspective meditation considerably, rendering explicit some ideas to which Schiller only alludes in his play.

639. Günther, Ursula. "Le livret français de *Don Carlos*: Le premier acte et sa révision par Verdi." *Atti 2* (item 225), 90–140.

This substantial and important article examines Verdi's collaboration with Joseph Méry and Camille Du Locle in fashioning the libretto for *Don Carlos*. In particular, the author analyzes Verdi's revisions in the first act, based on the autograph score and on other manuscript and early printed materials.

640. Hamlet-Metz, Mario. "The Full Circle: Don Carlos of Spain in History, Schiller, and Verdi." In *Friedrich von Schiller and the Drama of Human Existence*, 29–35. Ed. by Alexej Ugrinsky. Contributions to the Study of World Literature, 25. New York: Greenwood, 1988. ISBN 0–313–26262–4. PT 2492 .F75 1988.

A detailed comparison of the historical Don Carlos and the treatment of his life by Schiller and Verdi. The author proposes that while Schiller enervates the character of Don Carlos at the expense of the Marquis of Posa, Verdi endows him with larger-than-life stature as a hero, visionary, and redeemer.

641. López-Calo, José. "Il conflitto tra chiesa e stato nel *Don Carlos/Don Carlo.*" *Atti 2* (item 225), 80–89.

Examines the views of the historical King Philip II toward the relationship between religion and politics. Although Schiller does not emphasize the question of religion in his play, he does expound his views in his *Geschichte des Abfalls der vereinigten Niederlande von der spanischen Regierung*. In the opera, Verdi's anticlerical attitude led him to criticize the church's institutional invasion into state affairs.

642. Martin, George. "Posa in *Don Carlos*: The Flawed Hero." *Opera Quarterly* 5 (Summer/Autumn 1987): 59–80.
Also published in *Aspects of Verdi* (item 244), 93–116.

Reevaluates dramaturgy in *Don Carlos* in light of the new perception of Schiller's plays in recent years. These new studies view the dramatist's primary theme as the moral ambiguity of political action and how it affects character rather than focusing on the opposition of political and/or religious ideas. The author reviews the story of *Don Carlos* in Verdi's adaptation, arguing that the composer understood its relevance to contemporary political and social events, but was also attracted to the ambiguity surrounding the actions of several characters, particularly Posa. Illustrated jackets to the published scores, in fact, suggest that the late nineteenth-century viewed Posa as the hero of the opera, while critics from our century have been unsympathetic toward Verdi's characterization of him.

643. ———. "Verdi, la chiesa, e il *Don Carlo.*" *Atti 2* (item 225), 14–47.
Republished in a French translation by Michel Orcel in item 619, 153–55.

Discusses Verdi's treatment of religion and the church in *Don Carlos* in light of the contemporary political and religious milieu in Italy and throughout Europe, with particular attention given to Pope Pius IX's Syllabus of Errors (1864). The author concludes that the *Don Carlos* libretto is so powerful because it confronts the conflict between the ideas of liberty and intolerance, one of the greatest issues that the world has faced and continues to face.

644. Stringham, Scott. "Schiller and Verdi: Some Notes on Verdi's Dramaturgy." *Atti 2* (item 225), 234–40.

A study of the issues faced by Méry and Du Locle in transforming Schiller's extraordinarily long play into an opera libretto, underscored by many points of comparison between Schiller's play and Verdi's libretto.

645. Van, Gilles De. "La musique de la langue: Le français de *Don Carlos.*" In *D'un opéra à l'autre: Hommage à Jean Mongrédien*, 125–32. Ed. by Jean Gribenski, Marie-Claire Mussat and Herbert Schneider. Paris: Presses de l'Université de Paris-Sorbonne, 1996. ISBN 2-840500–63–9. ML 1700 .D89 1996.

After reviewing the major differences between French and Italian prosody, the author notes show how Verdi adopted the rhythm of the French text to his own melodic-rhythmic style, frequently utilizing anapestic rhythmic patterns. Beyond the matter of simple prosody, the author argues that the implicit musical qualities of the French language fundamentally affected the composer's approach in setting *Don Carlos* and that this experience, in turn, influenced the increased suppleness and flexibility of his melodic-rhythmic style in his two last operas, *Otello* and *Falstaff.* See items 479 and 971 for a related examination of Verdi's approach to French prosody.

646. Vecchi, Giuseppe. "Per il libretto di *Don Carlos.*" In *Studi e ricerche sui libretti delle opere di Giuseppe Verdi* (item 444), 193–200.

A brief overview of the genesis of the libretto for *Don Carlos* and its subsequent revisions which, in the author's view, render the work more elegant and comprehensive.

Studies of Compositional Process

647. Günther, Ursula. "Die Pariser Skizzen zu Verdis *Don Carlos.*" In *Bericht über den Internationalen Musikwissenschaftlichen Kongress, Bonn 1970*, 412–14. Ed. by Carl Dahlhaus et al. Kassel: Bärenreiter, 1971. ISBN 3-6718-0146-7.

Describes 28 pages of sketches for the first version of *Don Carlos* preserved in the Bibliothèque de l'Opéra. The sketches contain music for the Act III ballet and for a rejected scene for Don Carlos that was to open Act V. The sketches show that Du Locle and Verdi fashioned the replacement aria for Elisabeth so that it closely resembled the original aria for Don Carlos, particularly in the third and fourth strophes. In contrast, Verdi composed an entirely new orchestral introduction, based on choral music from the Act II cloister scene.

648. Porter, Andrew. "The Making of *Don Carlos.*" *Proceedings of the Royal Music Association* 98 (1971–72): 73–88.

A concise overview of the compositional history of *Don Carlos*, based on recently discovered manuscript material. Proposes that Verdi intended to imbue the French tradition of *grand opéra* with new nobility, adding his own stylistic strengths of characterization, dramatic impact and "warmth." The author views Verdi's 1883 condensation into four acts as closer to Schiller's drama, strengthening places where the dramatic motivation in the original was unclear or passages where musical shape had been unbalanced by early cuts.

649. Pestelli, Giorgio. "Le riduzioni del tardo stile verdiano: Osservazioni su alcune varianti del *Don Carlos*." *Nuova rivista musicale italiana* 6 (1972): 372–90.

    Expands the line of inquiry begun in item 650 below, with a detailed comparison of one portion of the duet in three different versions (the author does not consider the original version suppressed before the opera's premiere). The successive variants show a progressive condensation of musical material, using fewer bars and more direct musical means to accomplish the same dramatic purpose.

650. Rosen, David. "Le quattro stesure del duetto Filippo—Posa." *Atti 2* (item 225), 368–88.

    Compares and contrasts four extant drafts for the duet between Philip and Posa. The successive versions show a gradual move away from a conventional design with closed sections and the adoption of a more declamatory style for the vocal part, reserving lyrical moments for points of emphasis. The article includes musical examples, a facsimile reproduction of several pages from the manuscript score at the Bibliothèque de l'Opéra, and a helpful chart summarizing the structure of the different versions.

Stylistic and Analytical Studies

651. Budden, Julian. "L'influenza della tradizione del grand opéra francese sulla struttura ritmica di *Don Carlo*." *Atti 2* (item 225), 311–18.

    Proposes that fundamental characteristics of French prosody led to greater flexibility in the rhythmic shaping of phrases in *Don Carlos* that was unprecedented in Verdi's earlier works. For a critique of some of the ideas in this article, see item 479.

652. Chusid, Martin. "The Inquisitor's Scene in Verdi's *Don Carlos*: Thoughts on the Drama, Libretto, and Music." In *Studies in Musical Sources and Analysis: Essays in Honor of Jan LaRue*, 505–34. Ed. by Eugene K. Wolf and Edward H. Roesner. Madison, WI: A-R Editions, 1990. ISBN 0–89579–253–2. ML 55 .L217.

    A detailed analysis of this scene, focusing on unusual musical syntax or procedure to underscore abnormal events or atypical emotions in the drama. Verdi's setting of the prosody, for example, emphasizes Philip's weak position in relation to the Inquisitor. Similarly, the Inquisitor's music, full of chromatically inflected third-related harmonic progressions, reflects his supreme power over both church and state. The conclusion of the article discusses a little-known album leaf in Verdi's hand that provides some interesting variants for the opening of the Inquisitor's scene.

653. Eösze, László. "Mondo ideale ed espressione musicale nel *Don Carlos.*" *Atti 2* (item 225), 323–30.

Proposes that *Don Carlos* may be interpreted on two levels: 1) the collapse of the concepts of freedom and liberty and 2) a tragedy involving the fate of particular individuals. The main part of the article focuses on the ways in which Verdi's music underscores the characterization of specific individuals and their interrelationships. The author argues that in certain key scenes throughout the opera, the more serious the philosophical thrust of the scene, the less tightly the music adheres to conventional formal procedures.

654. Gallico, Claudio. "Scena ed aria." *Atti 2* (item 225), 336–42.

Analyzes Elisabetta's monologue "Tu che le vanità conoscesti del mondo," the only section of *Don Carlo* specifically labelled by the composer "scena ed aria." The author proposes that here Verdi fused musical gestures typically associated with "scenes" and "arias" into an organic whole. The resulting unit, unique among all of the composer's writings, brilliantly supports the unusually complex dramaturgy in this portion of the opera.

655. Gräwe, Karl Dietrich. "Dialogo e duetto come attività intermediarie di personaggi drammatici: Struttura e modi della funzione del dialogo in *Don Carlo*—Dramma di Schiller e opera di Verdi." *Atti 2* (item 225), 193–203.

A study of Verdi's *gran scena e duetto* from Act II in which Don Carlo and Elisabetta first meet after her marriage to Filippo. The author focuses on the way in which Verdi transfers the climactic point of crisis from the beginning of the episode in Schiller's play to its end in the operatic setting.

* Langford, Jeffrey. "Text Setting in Verdi's *Jérusalem* and *Don Carlos.*" See item 479.

656. Noske, Frits. "*Don Carlos*: The Signifier and the Signified." In *The Signifier and the Signified* (item 488), 294–308.

Asserts that distinctive musical ideas constituting the *tinta* of *Don Carlos* are: 1) a motive ascending from the tonic to the sixth, then descending to the fifth, 2) a non-ornamental chromatic rotation around the fifth, and 3) a rhythmic motive consisting of a half or quarter note tied to a number of triplets. The author proposes that these ideas are associated with the characters Don Carlos, Elisabeth, and King Philippe (and to a lesser extent in Eboli and Posa) in their mutual frustration about the reigning system—the Spanish court—impeding their own individual goals.

657. ———. "From Idea to Sound: Philip's Monologue in Verdi's *Don Carlos*." In
      *From Idea to Sound: Proceedings of the International Musicological Symposium
      held at Castle Nieborów in Poland, September 4–5, 1985*, 77–93. Ed. by Anna
      Czekanowska, Miloš Velimirović, and Zbigniew Skowron. Cracow: Wydano
      Nakladem Fundacij Zjednoczoney Europy, 1993. ISBN 83–900574–0–9.
      ML 3800 .I58 1985.
      Also published in *Studi verdiani* 10 (1994–95): 76–92.

      A semiotic analysis of Philip's monologue at the beginning of Act IV,
      demonstrating how Verdi creates musical and dramatic intensity by "shaping"
      the sound around three interrelated "signs." The author argues that these signs
      express the idea that Philip, although an absolute monarch, remains a human
      being, frustrated by the rigid political-social system in which he is operating
      and vacillating in his decisions about his present political and domestic
      difficulties.

658. Shawe-Taylor, Desmond. "The Extended Formal Arias in *Don Carlo*." *Atti
      2* (item 225), 389–93.

      Analyzes Philip's large-scale aria at the beginning of Act IV as the counterpart
      to a symphonic sonata form and the Queen's aria at the beginning of Act V as
      an expansive ternary structure.

659. Várnai, Péter Pál. "Unità musicale e drammaturgica nel *Don Carlo*." *Atti 2*
      (item 225), 402–11.

      Examines Verdi's use of recurring melodic and harmonic gestures in *Don
      Carlos* to provide a sense of musical and dramatic unity. The article focuses on
      a pattern that consists of an alternation between tonic and submediant chords.

Performance Practice, Staging, Scenography

660. Celletti, Rodolfo. "La vocalità nel *Don Carlo*." *Atti 2* (item 225), 475–83.

      Much of Verdi's vocal writing in *Don Carlo* is reminiscent of a style he had
      largely abandoned in his immediately preceding works. After speculating about
      possible reasons for this, the author examines the vocal demands Verdi requires
      of each of the main roles in the opera.

   * De Bellis, Frank V., and Federico Ghisi. "Alcune lettere inedite sul *Don Carlos*
      dal carteggio Verdi-Mazzucato." Cited above as item 70.

661. Cavicchi, Adriano. "Le prime scenografie del *Don Carlo*, con alcune
      considerazioni fra spettacolarità e musica." *Atti 2* (item 225), 516–24.

A study of the staging for the Parisian premiere of *Don Carlos* based on extant scene designs, a series of illustrations by G. Gonin based on the original staging, and Verdi's detailed instructions in the published *disposizione scenica*. The author also presents iconographic evidence regarding early performances at La Scala in Milan and La Fenice in Venice. The article includes 20 plates, among them a series of 8 lithographs included in the piano-vocal score issued by Ricordi in 1867 and a series of stage designs by Giuseppe and Pietro Bertoja for La Fenice and by Carlo Ferrario for La Scala.

662. Porter, Andrew. "Verdi's Ballet Music, and *La pérégrina*." *Atti 2* (item 225), 255–67.

After briefly reviewing the place of ballet music in Verdi's operas, the article examines the history, background, and aesthetic role of the ballet scene entitled *La pérégrina* that Verdi wrote for the third act of *Don Carlos*. Includes a description of the ballet scenario for the original production based on the 1867 libretto, comments in the autograph and conducting score, and the *disposizione scenica*.

Performance History; Reception

* Bello, John. "Verdi a New York." Cited below as item 339.

663. Cvetko, Dragotin. "*Don Carlos* nella luce della critica contemporanea slovena." *Atti 2* (item 225), 525–30.

After an overview of the reception of Verdi's works in Slovenia during the nineteenth and early twentieth centuries, the author examines the 1962 premiere performance of *Don Carlos* in Slovenia.

664. Gualerzi, Giorgio. "Un secolo di *Don Carlos*." *Atti 2* (item 225), 494–504.

An overview of the performance history of *Don Carlos/Don Carlo* from its premiere through 1969.

665. Martinov, Ivan. "*Don Carlos* de Verdi et le théâtre russe." *Atti 2* (item 225), 546–49.

A brief description of the Russian premiere of *Don Carlos* mounted by Fedor Chaliapine at the Bolshoi Theater in 1917.

666. Rosenthal, Harold. "The Rediscovery of *Don Carlos* in Our Day." *Atti 2* (item 225), 550–58.

An overview of the reception of Verdi's opera, focusing particularly on England.

Miscellaneous

667. Günther, Ursula. "*Don Carlos*: Edizione integrale—Critical Edition." *Nuove prospettive nella ricerca verdiana* (item 231), 29–48.

Clarifies the differences between the piano-vocal score of the *Edizione integrale delle varie versioni in cinque e quattro atti* (Milan: Ricordi, 1980) with the version that will be published as part of the new Verdi Edition. The former is a practical edition, presenting comprehensive material relating to all versions of the opera, including material that the composer eliminated during the rehearsals before the premiere. The new critical edition will use as its point of departure the version presented at the first public performance in 1867.

I DUE FOSCARI

While few studies have been written specifically about this opera, they have raised some important points about Verdi's compositional process in his early works.

Histories and General Studies

* Tomlinson, Gary. "Italian Romanticism and Italian Opera: An Essay in Their Affinities." See item 290.

Dramaturgy; Studies of the Libretto

668. Stringham, Scott. "*I due Foscari*: From Byron's Play to Verdi's Opera." *Philological Papers [West Virginia University]* 17 (June 1970): 31–40.

Outlines the plot of Byron's *The Two Foscari*, discusses the genesis of Verdi's opera libretto, and describes the major changes in the original play made by Verdi and Piave. The author suggests that the libretto suffers from loose ends, unclear motivations, and a less impressive use of language than Byron's original play; nevertheless, he argues that it functions acceptably as a libretto.

Studies of Compositional Process

669. Biddlecombe, George. "The Revision of 'No, non morrai, chè i perfidi': Verdi's Compositional Process in *I due Foscari*." *Studi verdiani* 2 (1983): 59–77.

Piano-vocal scores published by Cramer, Beale & Co. (London) and Blanchet (Paris) transmit an early version of this duet, which Verdi replaced before the premiere performance of the opera. The composer's revisions to the opening Andantino show his concern for a more powerful dramatic effect through more concise treatment and increased musical momentum. An appendix contains a facsimile reproduction of the original version as published by Cramer, Beale & Co.

70. Lawton, David. "A New Sketch for Verdi's *I due Foscari*." *Verdi Newsletter* 22 (1995): 4–16.

    Describes a page from Verdi's continuity draft for *I due Foscari*, recently purchased by a private collection, that contains the music for the first 68 bars of Act II, no. 8 ("Introduzione, Scena ed Aria Jacopo"). The sketch, which is reproduced here both in facsimile and in transcription, is particularly significant because it is the earliest known sketch or draft for any of Verdi's operas, with the exception of several short sketches from *Alzira* (see item 587 above). Verdi's revisions to the prelude strengthen formal symmetry and heighten the impact of a striking diminished-seventh chord in bar 33 of the recitative by eliminating a similar sonority at the end of the prelude. Revisions in the *scena* produce greater motivic coherence and reinforce the tonal structure of the piece.

71. Petrobelli, Pierluigi. "L'abbozzo di Busseto e la creazione musicale in Verdi." *Biblioteca '70* 3 (1973): 17–22.

    Poses a list of questions that need to be better understood about the composer and suggests that one of the principal avenues for that understanding will come from a study of Verdi's compositional process. The main part of the article discusses a sketch fragment belonging to *I due Foscari*, supplementing observations made in item 452. In particular, the author draws attention to Verdi's specific notation of dynamics at this early stage of the compositional process as well as an isolated B♭, representing the tolling of a bell, that forebodes the coming disaster.

RNANI

rnani has provoked the most scholarly study of any of Verdi's earliest operas. It arked the composer's first collaboration with Francesco Maria Piave, and it was erdi's first opera to be premiered in a theater other than La Scala. The composer's rrespondence with Piave and with the Presidency of La Fenice about the shaping of e libretto and matters of censorship is particularly fascinating. *Ernani's* stylistic aturation in the areas of dramatic effect and in treatment of traditional solo and duet rms has inspired several notable analytical articles.

uides to the Work

72. Lanza Tomasi, Gioacchino. *"Ernani" di Giuseppe Verdi: Guida all'opera.* Oscar musica. Milan: Mondadori, 1982. 132 p. ML 50 .V484 E7 1982.

    Provides a short history of the opera's compositional genesis, a discussion of Verdi's attraction to the works of Victor Hugo, a descriptive analysis of the music, a reproduction of the libretto, and a discography.

Histories and General Studies

* Cagli, Bruno. "'. . . Questo povero poeta esordiente': Piave a Roma, un carteggio con Ferretti, la genesi di *Ernani*." See item 206.

* Della Corte, Andrea. "La composizione dell'*Ernani* nelle lettere di Verdi." See item 97.

* Engelhardt, Markus. *Verdi und Andere: "Un giorno di regno," "Ernani," "Attila," "Il corsaro" in Mehrfachvertonungen.* See item 371.

* "*Ernani*" ieri e oggi: Atti del Convegno Internazionale di Studi, Modena, Teatro San Carlo, 9–10 dicembre 1984/"Ernani" Yesterday and Today: Proceedings of the International Congress, Modena, Teatro San Carlo, 9/10 December 1984. See item 228.

673. Marchesi, Gustavo. "Gli anni di *Ernani*." In "*Ernani*" *ieri e oggi* (item 228), 19–42.

    A close examination of the genesis of *Ernani*, focusing on its relationship to Verdi's other compositions from this period and on preparations for its premiere at La Fenice.

674. Spada, Marco. "*Ernani* e la censura napoletana." *Studi verdiani* 5 (1988–89): 11–23.

    Chronicles difficulties with the censors that prevented *Ernani* from being performed in Naples for more than three years after its premiere in Venice. Police documents show the theater's unsuccessful attempts to mount the opera as *Elvira d'Aragona*, a version that had recently been performed in Palermo, or as *Demetrio Alvexi*, with the locale changed to Greece. A third version, *Il proscritto*, was finally performed in March 1848, alternating between the Teatro del Fondo and San Carlo. Ironically, it was only a short time later that the Revolutions of 1848 opened the way for the original version to be performed at San Carlo. Appendices reproduce the scenario for *Demetrio Alvexi* and several contemporary reviews of *Il proscritto*.

Dramaturgy; Studies of the Libretto

675. Jeuland-Meynard, Maryse. "De l'*Hernani* de Victor Hugo a l'*Ernani* di Giuseppe Verdi." *Cahiers d'études romanes* 3 (1977): 117–51.

    Examines ways in which that the highly charged social, philosophical, and political atmosphere of early nineteenth-century society strongly influenced Hugo's conception of *Hernani*. The author proposes that this miliet contributed both to the initial success of Hugo's play as well as Verdi's operatic setting; later, its absence led to a relative lack of interest in the opera. Much of the article compares dramaturgy in the opera's libretto to Hugo's original play.

676. Ross, Peter. "Zur Dramaturgie des Finalaktes von Verdis *Ernani.*" *Jahrbuch für Opernforschung* 2 (1986): 27–50.
Italian translation. "Per un'analisi drammaturgica dell'atto finale di *Ernani.*" In *"Ernani" ieri e oggi* (item 228), 176–94.

Investigates the genesis of the final act of *Ernani* by comparing various drafts for the libretto with Hugo's play. The author concludes that this act of *Ernani* represents a high point among all of Verdi's operas in its dramatic concision.

677. Schulz-Buschhaus, Ulrich. "*Ernani* and *Hernani*: Zum 'Familialismus' der Verdischen Oper." In *Opern und Opernfiguren: Festschrift für Joachim Herz,* 161–73. Wort und Musik: Salzburger Akademische Beiträge, 2. Ed. by Ursula Müller and Ulrich Müller, with the assistance of Gerhard Heldt and Georg F. Mielke. Anif/Salzburg: Verlag Ursula Müller, 1989. ISBN 3-85145-002-7. ML 1720 .O64 1989.

Examines the way in which Piave and Verdi adapted Hugo's play *Hernani* for their opera libretto, focusing on differences in dramaturgical conception. The author suggests that among the most fundamental changes made by Verdi and Piave was a greater emphasis on popular, middle-class elements and familial relationships.

678. Stocker, Leonard. "The Treatment of the Romantic Literary Hero in Verdi's *Ernani* and in Massenet's *Werther.*" Ph.D. dissertation, Florida State University, 1969. vi, 182 p.

Although much research has been done on *Ernani* since the completion of this dissertation, it remains a valuable source for information on the literary background of the libretto, including its relationship to Hugo's play and to the Romantic literary movement in general.

679. Stringham, Scott. "Giuseppe Verdi and Victor Hugo: Some Notes on the Transformation of *Hernani* into *Ernani.*" *Philological Papers [West Virginia University]* 18 (September 1971): 42–50.

A detailed comparison of Verdi and Piave's libretto with the original play by Victor Hugo. Although the operatic version drastically simplified the original plot (including the removal of all vestiges of comedy or humor), the author proposes that several minor changes, particularly in the final act, are an improvement over the original play. Verdi's alteration of the ending likely resulted from difficulties in dealing with the censors.

680. Zanichelli, Silvana. "Alcuni appunti sulla trasformazione dell'*Hernani* di Hugo."
    In *"Ernani" ieri e oggi* (item 228), 43–59.

    This study focuses on how Verdi's demands for conciseness and the
    requirements of the censors helped shaped the libretto for *Ernani*. Count Alvise
    Mocenigo, Presidente agli spettacoli at La Fenice, played a particularly
    important role in guiding and advising Piave about dealing with the censors.
    The article concludes with a useful comparison of Piave's libretto with the
    original drama by Hugo.

681. ———. "Genesi di un libretto d'opera: l'*Ernani* di F.M. Piave." Ph.D.
    dissertation, Università degli Studi di Bologna, 1980. 431 p.

    The most detailed study of the libretto for *Ernani*, including its genesis, Verdi's
    negotiations with the theater and the censors, his collaboration with Piave, and
    the relationship among the different drafts of the libretto and the original
    drama by Hugo. The volume contains a substantial bibliography.

Studies of Compositional Process

682. Gallico, Claudio. "Verso l'edizione critica di *Ernani* di Verdi." *Nuove prospettive
    nella ricerca verdiana* (item 231), 20–28.

    The author published a later version of this article entitled "Il restauro del testo
    di *Ernani*" in *"Ernani" ieri e oggi* (item 228), 92–103.

    The process of preparing a new critical edition for *Ernani* has provided many
    insights into Verdi's compositional process. The autograph manuscript was
    prepared in three distinct stages: 1) a skeleton score (all the vocal parts, the
    instrumental bass part, and the instrumental parts that carry the melody);
    2) the full score, with complete orchestration; and 3) revisions, probably made
    during orchestral rehearsals before the premiere performance. The author
    discusses examples of late revisions made in Act III, No. 10 and the Act I
    finale. One of the most interesting problems that emerged in studying the
    musical sources involves dynamic markings. When Luigi Truzzi prepared a
    reduction of the orchestral parts for the piano-vocal score, he sometimes
    changed an accent mark in the original into a specific dynamic level in the piano
    reduction. The author demonstrates how many of these alterations became part
    of tradition and eventually even found their way into Ricordi's published full
    score.

683. Gossett, Philip. "The Composition of *Ernani*." In *Analyzing Opera: Verdi and
    Wagner* (item 454), 27–55.

    Italian translation by Stefano Castelvecchi. "La composizione di *Ernani*." In
    "Ernani" ieri e oggi (item 228), 60–91.

Describes a number of revisions, both simple and elaborate, as well as structural alterations found in the autograph score. Some revisions probably resulted from trying to show off the voices of the singers to best advantage or, in one case, from the availability of a bass clarinet player in the orchestra at La Fenice. Although the original version of the opera's closing trio is not extant, some of its features may be adduced through clues in the musical manuscript and Verdi's autograph copy of the libretto.

Stylistic and Analytical Studies

684. Beltrami, Cesare. *Musica e libretto d'opera nell'analisi metrica dell'"Ernani."* Turin: Il Piccolo Editore, 1986. 85 p.

    The final section of this brief monograph discusses the metrical structure of the main lyrical portions of the libretto. The author's commentary tends to be more descriptive than analytical. The bulk of the volume provides general background regarding opera during the *primo ottocento* and on the genesis of *Ernani*.

685. Budden, Julian. "Il linguaggio musicale di *Ernani.*" In *"Ernani" ieri e oggi* (item 228), 123–32.

    Discusses several significant stylistic characteristics in *Ernani*, including: obtaining maximum effect from limited musical means, avoidance of symmetry in melodic phrases, subtle use of harmony to bolster dramatic effects, and occasional mixture of declamatory and cantabile textures as a substitution for traditional recitative.

686. Della Seta, Fabrizio. "L'atto di Carlo Quinto." In *"Ernani" ieri e oggi* (item 228), 161–75.

    A close examination of the formal structure of Act III, focusing on Verdi's use of tonality.

687. Kerman, Joseph. "Notes on an Early Verdi Opera." *Soundings* 3 (1973): 56–65. Republished, in tandem with item 748, as "Two Early Verdi Operas; Two Famous Terzetti." In *Write All These Down: Essays on Music*, 288–306. Berkeley: University of California Press, 1994. ISBN 0–520–08355–5. ML 60 .K37.

    The author analyzes the terzetto finale of Act IV and argues that its relationship to the preceding music in the act shows the young Verdi's masterful command of large-scale tonal and thematic architecture.

688. Parker, Roger. "'Infin che un brando vindice' e le cavatine del primo atto di *Ernani.*" In *"Ernani" ieri e oggi* (item 228), 142–60.

An earlier version of the article was published as "'Infin che un brando vindice': From *Ernani* to *Oberto.*" *Verdi Newsletter* 12 (1984): 5–7.

Cites newly discovered evidence that Silva's Act I cabaletta, "Infin che un brando vindice" is a revision by Verdi of a *puntatura* originally written for Ignazio Marini for a performance of *Oberto* in Barcelona. The second part of the article considers the three cavatinas in Act I of *Ernani* and illustrates their crucial dramatic and musical function within the context of the entire act.

689.   ———. "Levels of Motivic Definition in Verdi's *Ernani.*" *19th Century Music* 6 (1982–83): 141–50.

A revised version of a chapter from the author's doctoral thesis (see item 377). Verdi's use of several recurring melodic motives throughout the opera to underscore the ideas of love and the dictates of honor is not entirely successful, since the motives themselves are not distinctive enough or used often enough to establish a strong dramatic thread. In a smaller dimension, however, Verdi repeatedly employed several motivic ideas during Elvira's Act I *scena* "Surta è la notte" that create a strong sense of unity and dramatic force.

Performance Practice, Staging, Scenography

690.   Viale Ferrero, Mercedes. "Le prime scene per *Ernani*: Appunti di scenografia verdiana." In *"Ernani" ieri e oggi* (item 228), 195–206.

Investigates the scenography for early performances of *Ernani*, focusing on the premiere at La Fenice (1844), a performance the same year at Faenza with scenery designed by Romolo Liverani, and a 1846 revival at La Fenice with scenery by Giuseppe Bertoja.

Performance History; Reception

*   Antolini, Bianca Maria. "Cronache teatrali veneziane: 1842–1849." See item 343.

691.   Conati, Marcello. "*Ernani* di Verdi: Le critiche del tempo—Alcune considerazioni." In *"Ernani" ieri e oggi* (item 228), 207–72.

A brief essay reviewing the overwhelmingly positive reception of *Ernani* in its early years is followed by two useful appendices. The first reproduces 31 published reviews of *Ernani* from its premiere through July 1847. The second appendix lists nearly 200 early performances of *Ernani* with dates, location, and principal members of the cast.

FALSTAFF

Verdi's final opera, with its unprecedented exploration of the comic vein, explores new stylistic approaches in all areas of the drama and the music. To date, a large number of studies have examined the composer's advances in style, his close collaboration with Boito, and his compositional process, which extends as late as refinements made during the preparation of printed parts.

Guides to the Work

692. Csampai, Attila, and Dietmar Holland, eds. *Giuseppe Verdi, "Falstaff": Texte, Materialien, Kommentare.* Rororo Opernbücher. Reinbek bei Hamburg: Rowohlt Taschenbuch Verlag, 1986. 300 p. ISBN 3–499–18095–2. ML 410 .V4 F2 1986.

This guide contains a number of fine essays on the genesis of the opera and its place among Verdi's works and Italian comic opera; Boito's libretto; Boito's and Verdi's relationship to Shakespeare; and the opera's reception history, including reviews of early performances by Charles Villiers Stanford, George Bernard Shaw, and Eduard Hanslick. The editors have also included a selection of nearly three dozen letters to and from Verdi concerning the opera. The libretto is reproduced in side by side format in Italian and a German translation by Ragni Maria Gschwend. The volume concludes with a selective bibliography and a discography of complete recordings, with an accompanying essay.

693. *Falstaff. L'avant-scène opéra* 87/88 (May/June 1986). Paris: L'Avant-Scène, 1986. 194 p. ISSN 0764–2873. ML 5 .A9 v. 87–88.

This entire issue is devoted to *Falstaff.* Nearly a dozen articles focus on topics such as the genesis of the work, Verdi's relationship to Shakespeare and his treatment of the Falstaff figure, and Victor Maurel, who created the first Sir John Falstaff. The libretto is presented in the original Italian with a parallel French translation by Pierre Malbos. The volume also includes a discography of complete recordings and individual arias or sections accompanied by a prose essay and tables listing the earliest performances of the opera in major centers as well as more detailed information about performances in major houses up to the present. A substantial specialized bibliography contains over 200 items, including principal editions, musical studies, and studies and documents relating to Shakespeare and his play.

694. *Falstaff.* English National Opera Guides, 10. London: John Calder; New York: Riverrun, 1982. 128 p. ISBN 0–7145–3921–X. ML 50 .V484 F32 1982.

The guide contains an assessment of the place of *Falstaff* among Verdi's works and the history of Italian opera in general; a descriptive analysis of the work, prefaced by a discussion of Boito's sources for the libretto; and a brief essay by

Andrew Porter discussing his translation of the libretto. The concluding portion of the volume contains the libretto in Italian and an English translation by Andrew Porter and a brief, selective discography and bibliography.

695. Hepokoski, James A. *Giuseppe Verdi: "Falstaff."* Cambridge Opera Handbooks. Cambridge: Cambridge University Press, 1983. x, 181 p. ISBN 0–521–23534–0; 0–521–28016–8. ML 410 .V4 H46 1983.

A most valuable general study of the opera. After a detailed synopsis of the plot, subsequent chapters outline the genesis of the work, the preparation of the libretto, and the compositional history of the opera, including a substantial discussion of the revisions Verdi made for productions after its premiere. In addition to describing innovative formal and harmonic features, Hepokoski's discussion of musical technique and structure traces the work's roots in traditional ottocento opera. The analytical section of the volume gives special attention to the complex structure of the scene at the Garter Inn (Act II, scene i), arguing that the composer frequently disrupts symmetrical formal structures in the small and middle dimensions in order to underscore the many unexpected dramatic twists of the plot. A brief overview of major productions of the work since its premiere is coupled with a study of its reception history, focusing on long-standing controversies surrounding its relationship to Wagnerian style. An important chapter of the volume discusses the composer's guidelines for performing the work, based primarily on his supervision of the premiere, and reproduces costume and set designs for the original production. This, coupled with Hepokoski's discussion of how various modern editions deal with Verdi's post-premiere revisions, provides particularly useful information for modern conductors and stage directors. An epilogue to the volume contains an article by Graham Bradshaw on Verdi and Boito as interpreters of Shakespeare (see item 397). See the author's dissertation (item 705 below) for a more detailed and technical discussion of the composer's process of revision in the work.

Histories and General Studies

* Busch, Hans, ed. and trans. *Verdi's "Falstaff" in Letters and Contemporary Reviews.* See item 98.

696. *"Falstaff": Numero speciale della "Illustrazione italiana."* Milan: Fratelli Treves, 1891. 28 p. ML 410 .V484 V4.

A beautifully illustrated commemorative edition issued just before the premiere of Verdi's last work. The issue includes essays on Shakespeare's *Falstaff* and its reception in Italy, the plot, the performers, staging, and costuming for the first production, and general articles on Verdi and Shakespeare. See item 712 below for an assessment of Giulio Ricordi's article, published in this collection, on how Verdi composed and rehearsed.

697. Gerhartz, Leo Karl. "Versuch über *Falstaff*: Zu autobiographischen Aspekten von Verdis letzter Oper." In *Musik, Deutung, Bedeutung: Festschrift für Harry Goldschmidt zum 75. Geburtstag*, 21–29. Ed. by Hanns-Werner Heister and Hartmut Lück. Dortmund: Pläne-Verlag, 1986. ISBN 3–88569–018–7. ML 55 .G64 1986.

An essay written to accompany a new production of the opera in Frankfurt am Main in 1985. Argues that *Falstaff* stands out among all of Verdi's operas for its autobiographical suggestions. The author sees Falstaff's speech near the end of the final scene as a key passage, alluding to the role of the artist in society. In this passage, Falstaff points out that while everyone enjoys making fun of him, they have nothing without him, for their wit is engendered by his. This becomes more poignant with the unexpected combination of the serious form of the fugue with the gesture of the "last laugh" at the end of the play. At the same time, the opera serves as a recapitulation of Verdi's career in which many of the tiny "mosaics" from which it is built recall scenes or passages from earlier works.

Dramaturgy; Studies of the Libretto

698. Dürr, Karl-Friedrich. *Opern nach literarischen Vorlagen: Shakespeares "The Merry Wives of Windsor" in der Vertonungen von Mosenthal-Nicolai, "Die lustigen Weiber von Windsor" und Boito-Verdi, "Falstaff." Ein Beitrag zum Thema Gattungstransformation*. Stuttgarter Arbeiten zur Germanistik, 62. Stuttgart: Akademischer Verlag Hans-Dieter Heinz, 1979. ii, 282 p. ISBN 3–88099–063–8. ML 2100 .D83.

A detailed comparison of Verdi's opera with an earlier setting of the Falstaff story by Otto Nicolai and with Shakespeare's play. The author places particular emphasis on aspects of contrasting dramaturgy in the three works and examines issues relating to questions of genre and convention.

699. Girardi, Michele. "Fonti francesi del *Falstaff*: Alcuni aspetti di drammaturgia musicale." In *Arrigo Boito: Atti del Convegno Internazionale di Studi* (item 199), 395–430.
English translation. "French Sources of *Falstaff* and Some Aspects of Its Musical Dramaturgy." *Opera Quarterly* 11 (Autumn 1995): 45–63.

Boito's autograph notes, written in his copy of the *Oeuvres complètes de W. Shakespeare*, translated by François-Victor Hugo (Paris: Alfonse Lemerre, [1871+]), demonstrate that this French translation was his primary source for the libretto to *Falstaff*. Boito carefully underlined passages in *The Merry Wives*

of Windsor that would be used in the libretto. In the two parts of *Henry IV*, he
made annotations showing how material might be related to the main plot line
derived from *The Merry Wives*, primarily in order to heighten the comic tone
and better delineate the character of Falstaff. These sources for the libretto
show that at times Boito creatively mixed words and images from different
passages and exchanged lines among different characters. Girardi also points out
how significantly the actual text influenced Verdi's fertile imagination by
examining several passages from the opera. An appendix presents selected
passages from the Hugo translations side by side with parallel lines from Boito's
libretto.

700. Melchiori, Giorgio. "Di Falstaff in *Falstaff*." In *Semeia: Itinerari per Marcello
      Pagnini*, 427–32. Ed. by Loretta Innocenti, Franco Marucci, and Paola
      Pugliatti. Bologna: Società Editrice il Mulino, 1994. ISBN 88–15–04712–3.
      PR 14 .S396 1994.

      Proposes that the genius of *Falstaff* lies in Boito's adroit synthesis of Falstaff's
      character from multiple Shakespearean sources.

701. Osthoff, Wolfgang. "Il sonetto nel *Falstaff* di Verdi." Trans. by Lorenzo
      Bianconi. In *Il melodramma italiano dell'ottocento: Studi e ricerche per
      Massimo Mila*, 157–83. Ed. by Giorgio Pestelli. Saggi, 575. Turin: Einaudi,
      1977. ML 1733.4 .M5.

      A detailed examination of Fenton's sonnet at the start of the second part of Act
      III and Verdi's musical realization of it. The author suggests possible sources
      for the idea of the sonnet, including Shakespeare's *Romeo and Juliet* and Sonnet
      No. 8, Manzoni's *I promessi sposi*, and plays by Calderón and Goldoni.

Studies of Compositional Process

702. Barblan, Guglielmo. *Un prezioso spartito del* Falstaff. [Milan]: Edizioni della
      Scala, [1957]. 34 p. ML 410 .V48 B237.

      Describes ideas for revisions that Verdi jotted down in a printed piano-vocal
      score during the premiere performances of the opera. These changes involve all
      aspects of the work: the text, melody, rhythm, harmony, and staging. The
      monograph contains numerous facsimile reproductions from the annotated
      score, which is now housed in the library at the Conservatorio "G. Verdi" in
      Milan.

703. ———. "Spunti rivelatori nella genesi del *Falstaff*." *Atti 1* (item 224), 16–21.

      Examines Verdi's revisions in the aria "Dal labbro il canto estasiato vola."

704. Gál, Hans. "A Deleted Episode in Verdi's *Falstaff.*" *Music Review* 2 (1941): 266–72.

Describes a passage of 16 bars from the Act II finale, present in the first piano-vocal edition but later deleted and replaced by a substitute passage of six bars. The excised passage featured a lyrical duet for Nanetta and Fenton, who are hiding behind a screen as Ford and his men search the house for Falstaff. Gál concludes that Verdi must have felt that the episode impeded the pace of the drama at this crucial juncture in the score. The article reproduces the original passage and its replacement in their entirety.

705. Hepokoski, James A. "The Compositional History of Verdi's *Falstaff*: A Study of the Autograph Score and the Early Editions." Ph.D. dissertation, Harvard University, 1979. 2 vols. xiv, 526 p.

The most extensive study to date of compositional process in Verdi's last opera and the work's early performance and publication history. The composer made corrections and revisions at every stage of the work's genesis to eliminate unnecessary repetition, to make the vocal parts fit better with the abilities of individual performers, and to intensify important dramatic passages. The author includes transcriptions of sections from the skeleton score that differ most significantly from the final version and diagrams that show the gathering structure of the autograph full score. Because Hepokoski physically studied the autograph score, this study should be used in tandem with any serious examination of the facsimile reproduction of the score (item 715). A more succinct and less technical discussion of the most significant revisions can be found in the author's Cambridge Opera Handbook (item 695 above).

706. ———. "Verdi, Giuseppina Pasqua, and the Composition of *Falstaff.*" *19th Century Music* 3 (1979–80): 239–250.

Despite the composer's protests that he wrote *Falstaff* only for his own gratification and without considering theatrical and vocal resources, the author demonstrates that the choice of Giuseppina Pasqua to sing Mistress Quickly strongly influenced his conception of her part. In particular, Hepokoski examines the compositional genesis of her monologue, "Giunta all'Albergo della Giarrettiera," which the composer interpolated into the previously composed opening of Act II, scene 2.

Stylistic and Analytical Studies

707. Baumann, Thomas. "The Young Lovers in *Falstaff.*" *19th Century Music* 9 (1985–86): 62–69.

Criticizes Cone's and Noske's interpretation (items 464 and 487) that Fenton and Nanetta represent a static idealization of young love. Baumann argues that

Verdi and Boito took pains to dramatize a gradual process of maturation in these two characters. The author also proposes that Verdi used an intricate system of tonal areas throughout the opera centered around the pitches *a*, *c*, and *e*, the "musical letters" in the name Alice.

708. Beghelli, Marco. "Lingua dell'autocaricatura nel *Falstaff*." In *Opera & Libretto II*, 351–80. Studi di musica veneta. Florence: Olschki, 1993. ISBN 88–222–4064–2. ML 1700 .O655 1993.

     Examines ways in which Verdi parodies characteristic or stereotypical musical gestures from his earlier operas to create a comic effect in *Falstaff*. Includes many musical examples showing these "parallel" effects.

   * Cantoni, Angelo. "Verdi e Stravinskij." See item 351.

   * Lendvai, Ernö. *Verdi and Wagner*. See item 482.

709. Linthicum, David. "Verdi's *Falstaff* and Classical Sonata Form." *Music Review* 39 (1978): 39–60.

     Analyzes the opening scene at the Garter Inn as a traditional sonata form. Rather than using a traditional tonic-dominant relationship, Verdi establishes a polarity between third-related keys: C major and E major. The author suggests that the structural emphasis on mediant relationships and Verdi's use of motivic development in this scene may have come from his study of Beethoven's music.

710. Sabbeth, Daniel. "Dramatic and Musical Organization in *Falstaff*." *Atti 3* (item 226), 415–42.

     An overview of the dramatic and musical shape of the opera. The musical analysis concentrates on the use of the final fugue's subject as a unifying motive throughout the work, the tonal structure of the opera, and the importance of the pitch class *Ab/G#*. The author argues that Verdi and Boito present an idealized vision of the world in which individual members go through a growth process to arrive at a point at which they mutually accept and take joy in other members of society.

711. ———. "Principles of Tonal and Dramatic Organization in Verdi's *Falstaff*." Ph.D. dissertation, City University of New York, 1976. ix, 225 p.

     Uses a bass graph technique to analyze foreground, middleground, and background levels of the opera's tonal organization. The author proposes that *Falstaff* is built on large-scale motions that are diatonic and that this traditional approach creates organic unity in the work in place of the traditional framework of the number opera. The author also suggests that certain tonalities and pitch classes have significant associative properties in the opera. See item 397 for a critical assessment of some of Sabbeth's ideas.

Performance Practice, Staging, Scenography

712. Hepokoski, James A. "Under the Eye of the Verdian Bear: Notes on the Rehearsals and Première of *Falstaff*." *Musical Quarterly* 71 (1985): 135–56.

Discusses documents and other materials relating to the early rehearsals and premiere production of *Falstaff*, which were closely supervised by the composer. In sessions with the singers, Verdi rigorously oversaw various matters such as pronunciation and gestures. He was also strict about allowing encores only in pre-planned places. The article provides an overview of reactions from contemporary reviewers. The author also discusses Victor Maurel's 1907 recording of "Quand'ero paggio," concluding that the composer would have disagreed with its slow tempo, rhythmic liberties, and careless pronunciation. An appendix reproduces in translation Giulio Ricordi's article, "Come scrive e come prova Giuseppe Verdi" ("How Giuseppe Verdi Writes and Rehearses"), published just before the premiere of *Falstaff* in *L'illustrazione italiana* (see item 696 above). While Ricordi (no doubt spurred by the composer) focused on elements of spontaneous inspiration and little or no subsequent revision in his characterization of Verdi's composing process, his description of the rehearsals appears to be more accurate. A second appendix reproduces in translation some of Verdi's written instructions made during rehearsals.

713. Viale Ferrero, Mercedes. "Boito inventore di immagini sceniche: Rapporti significativi tra immagine poetica e immagine scenica." In *Arrigo Boito: Atti del Convegno Internazionale di Studi* (item 199), 275–96.

The article examines, among other things, the influence of Boito on the costumes and staging of *Otello* and *Falstaff*. Includes reproductions of a dozen designs relating to *Falstaff*, including engravings of scenery and costume designs.

Performance History; Reception

714. *"Falstaff," dramma lirico in quattro atti, versi di Arrigo Boito, musica di Giuseppe Verdi: Giudizi della stampa italiana e straniera.* Milan: Ricordi, n.d. 296 p.

A conveniently anthologized set of reviews and articles issued after the premiere performance of the work. The volume unfortunately lacks an index or table of contents, so individual reviews must be found by browsing.

Miscellaneous

715. *Falstaff.* Facsimile reproduction of the autograph score. Milan: Ente Autonomo del Teatro alla Scala, 1951. 790 p.

   This publication of the *Falstaff* score was issued in a limited, numbered edition in commemoration of the 50th anniversary of the composer's death. It is a highly significant document for anyone interested in studying Verdi's compositional process in the opera. Because many significant physical details are not apparent in the reproduction, however, users should ideally examine it in tandem with James Hepokoski's dissertation (item 705), which provides critical information about the manuscript's gathering structure, ink colors, and cancelled or revised passages.

* Hepokoski, James A. "Overriding the Autograph Score: The Problem of Textual Authority in Verdi's *Falstaff.*" See item 1032.

LA FORZA DEL DESTINO

La forza del destino appeared after the first minor hiatus in Verdi's production of new works and marks an important turning point in his career in which he took on new projects strictly at his own pace and only when he was fully satisfied with all aspects of the proposed production. Verdi constantly revised *Forza* from the time of its premiere in 1862 through a thoroughly revised version that premiered seven years later at La Scala. These revisions have led to many interesting studies about compositional process in this opera. The opera's position at a crucial juncture in Verdi's career has also led to significant studies dealing with issues of style and reception.

Guides to the Work

716. *La force du destin. L'avant-scène opéra* 126 (December 1989). Paris: L'Avant-Scène, 1989. 162 p. ISSN 0764–2873.

   This bulk of this issue is devoted to *Forza*. Three major articles focus on the genesis of the work, political and social conditions in Italy at the time of its composition, and influences on the libretto. The original 1862 libretto is presented in Italian with a parallel French translation by Michel Orcel, together with a running descriptive analysis by Gilles De Van. The volume also includes a discography of complete recordings and individual arias or sections, accompanied by an essay describing the complete recordings, tables listing the earliest performances of the opera in major centers, as well as more detailed information about performances in major houses up to the present. A short bibliography contains nearly two dozen items, including principal editions, musical studies, and studies and documents relating to the libretto and its sources. Finally, there is a short discussion of the principal roles and a brief synopsis of the entire opera.

717. *The Force of Destiny/La forza del destino.* English National Opera Guides, 23. London: John Calder; New York: Riverrun, 1983. 112 p. ISBN 0–7145–4007–2. ML 50 .V484 F62 1983.

This guide contains essays tracing the history of the work and Verdi's later large-scale revision of it, a detailed descriptive analysis of the opera, and a highly selective discography and bibliography. The volume presents the libretto in an English translation by Andrew Porter printed side by side with the original Italian. Passages from the earlier version of the opera are included in footnotes or in appendices.

718. Rescigno, Eduardo. *"La forza del destino" di Verdi.* Il formichiere. Milan: Emme Edizioni, 1981. 288 p.

A sophisticated opera guide that examines the opera's origins, presents a copy of the libretto with copious and detailed annotations, an extensive descriptive analysis of the music, and an annotated discography of significant recordings from 1943 through 1978.

History and General Studies

* Gerhard, Anselm. *Die Verstädterung der Oper: Paris und das Musiktheater des 19. Jahrhunderts.* See item 265.

719. Marchesi, Gustavo. "Gli anni della *Forza del destino.*" *Verdi: Bollettino dell'Istituto di Studi Verdiani* 2 [No. 4, 5, and 6] (1961–66): 17–42, 713–44, 1505–42. English and German translations of the article are found on pp. 313–58, 1033–87, 1995–2059.

A detailed narrative of the genesis and first performances of *Forza*, organized around a collation of letters (primarily already published) from Verdi to various correspondents.

720. Parmentola, Carlo. "*Rataplan*: Confessioni sulla *Forza del destino.*" In *Il melodramma italiano dell'ottocento: Studi e ricerche per Massimo Mila*, 91–111. Ed. by Giorgio Pestelli. Saggi, 575. Torino: Einaudi, 1977. ML 1733.4 .M5.

Discusses the role of crowd scenes in Acts II, III, and IV that evoke a "popular" style and their relationship to Verdi's characterization of Trabuco, Preziosilla, and Melitone. The author argues that these scenes express an autonomous, collective meaning that becomes far more powerful than a simple evocation of local color.

721. *Verdi: Bollettino dell'Istituto di Studi Verdiani*, 2. Parma: Istituto di Studi Verdiani, 1961–66. cviii, 2617 p. + 128 p. index. ML 410 .V4 A5.

Most articles in the three numbers comprising this volume of the *Bollettino* concern *La forza del destino*. They cover a wide range of topics, including the history and genesis of the libretto and the music, the opera's reception, a descriptive analysis by Guido Pannain, and a transcription of the first German translation of the opera. Most articles are printed in Italian, English, and German; some of the most significant items concerning *Forza* are listed separately as numbers 719, 722, 725, 730, 732, 734–36, and 738–40. A separately issued and paginated index contains, in addition to the actual index, a bibliography of materials dealing with *La forza del destino*, a discography (including recordings of selections from the opera), and a listing of 42 printed librettos with full information from the title pages.

722. Walker, Frank. "Introduction to a Biographical Study (Parliamentary Deputy at Turin, Opera Composer at St. Petersburg)." *Verdi: Bollettino dell'Istituto di Studi Verdiani* 2 [No. 4] (1961): 1–16. Italian and German translations may be found on pp. 278–312.

A short biographical essay, based largely on letters and other documents, dealing with Verdi's activities during the first half of 1861. The author suggests artistic, patriotic, and financial reasons that may have led Verdi to decide to write *La forza del destino*.

Studies of the Libretto; Dramaturgy

723. Blommers, Thomas J. "Rivas and Verdi: *The Force of Destiny*." Ph.D. dissertation, University of Iowa, 1978. vii, 186 p.

An extensive exploration of differences between the play by Rivas and the libretto for Verdi's opera. Although the opera eliminates some of the minor characters, it expands the role of several supporting characters, in particular Preziosilla, Melitone, and Trabuco. Verdi's opera joins the original characters of Don Carlo and Don Alvaro into one person, necessitating several substantial changes in plot from the original play. The volume contains a selected bibliography that is useful for tracing materials relating to Rivas and his play.

724. Busquets, Loreto. *Rivas y Verdi: Del "Don Alvaro" a "La forza del destino."* Università degli Studi di Milano, Facoltà di Lettere. Quaderni della Ricerca, 6. Rome: Bulzoni, 1988. 91 p. ML 410 .V4 F328 1988x.

Offers a detailed examination of the genesis of the libretto for *Forza* and its subsequent revision for the 1869 production at La Scala. The major portion of this monograph provides a detailed comparison of Verdi's libretto with the original play by Ángel de Saavedra, Duke of Rivas. The author suggests that Verdi was particularly attracted to the play because of its philosophical explication of human liberty and its interaction with forces of good and evil.

725. Gerhartz, Leo Karl. "Verdi und Schiller: Gedanken zu Schillers *Wallensteins Lager* und den Schlußszenen des dritten Aktes der *Forza del destino*." *Verdi: Bollettino dell'Istituto di Studi Verdiani* 2 [No. 6] (1966): 1589–1610. English and Italian translations are found on pp. 2063–95.

Proposes that the choral and other vocal pieces between the opening chorus of the final part of Act III and Fra Melitone's sermon function in the same way as the pictorial descriptions in Schiller's *Wallensteins Lager*.

* Van, Gilles De. "Notes sur Verdi humoriste." See item 441.

726. Martin, George. "Verdi's Imitation of Shakespeare: *La forza del destino*." In *Aspects of Verdi* (item 244), 79–91.
First published in *Opera Quarterly* 3 (Spring 1985): 19–29.

Argues that in *Forza* Verdi attempted to create a Romantic drama in Shakespearean style filtered through the critical reception of Schlegel, which emphasized the mixing of tragic and comic elements and the abandonment of unities of time and action. The 1882 revision for French houses, either made by Verdi or with his approval, backs away from Schlegel's ideals, as do the composer's later operas based on Shakespeare.

Studies of Compositional Process

727. Conati, Marcello. "'Ei mi raggiunse . . . m'insultò . . . l'uccisi': Una lettera di Verdi sul finale della *Forza del destino*." *Musica viva* 8 (October 1984): 68–71.

Examines Verdi's conception of the final scene of the opera based on his correspondence with Ghislanzoni via Giulio Ricordi. In a previously unpublished letter from a private collection, written on 8 [January 1869], Verdi makes specific suggestions about how a portion of the text needed to be altered to better fit the music he had composed. The letter, reproduced here in both transcription and facsimile, fits into a sequence of correspondence already published in Abbiati's biography (item 145) and clears up a comment by the composer in a letter dated 11 January.

728. Holmes, William C. "The Earliest Revisions of *La forza del destino*." *Studi verdiani* 6 (1990): 55–98.

A study of revisions made by Verdi during preliminary rehearsals prior to the premiere performance in St. Petersburg. The earlier readings can be largely reconstructed from performance material now located in the Kirov Library in St. Petersburg and a score prepared by the composer for performances of the work in Madrid, now located at the Bibliothèque Nationale in Paris. The composer made minor changes in several numbers from Acts I, II and IV. In

Act III, Verdi inserted a newly composed cabaletta for Don Alvaro and chorus at the end of the finale, which showed off Enrico Tamberlick's famous high *c′*, and he completely rewrote Don Carlo's cabaletta, "Egli è salvo" from his aria "Urna fatale." This new information suggests that despite the composer's later revisions in the finale to Act IV, it was Act III that posed the most extensive problems for him.

729.   ————. "Verdi's Changing Attitudes Towards Dramatic Situations as Seen in Some of His Revisions in *La forza del destino*." *La musique et le rite sacré et profane: Actes du XIII ‘ Congrès de la Sociéte Internationale de Musicologie, Strasbourg, 29 août—3 septembre 1982.* Vol. 2: Communications libres, 657–73. Ed. by Marc Honegger and Paul Prevost. Strasbourg: Association des Publications près les Universités de Strasbourg, 1986. ISBN 86–820–107–5. ML 3797.1 .I59 1982.

Analyzes revisions made between the St. Petersburg premiere and the 1869 production at La Scala in two numbers: the duet between Leonora and the Padre Guardiano that precedes the Act II finale and the opening scene (the "soup-kitchen" scene) of Act IV. In revising both scenes, Verdi left intact the opening portion, which set the dramatic mood, while intensifying dramatic and theatrical elements in the latter portion of the scenes.

730.   Mompellio, Federico. "Musica provvisoria nella prima *Forza del destino*." *Verdi: Bollettino dell'Istituto di Studi Verdiani* 2 [No. 6] (1966): 1610–80. English and German translations of the article are printed on pp. 2096–114.

Catalogues and discusses significant revisions made by the composer based on differences among a piano-vocal score by Luigi Truzzi of the original version of *Forza* and two piano-vocal scores of the revised version of the opera. The author concludes that Verdi's revisions, without exception, improve the corresponding passages in the original version.

731.   Nádas, John. "New Light on Pre-1869 Revisions of *La Forza del destino*." *Verdi Newsletter* 15 (1987): 7–29.

Evidence from correspondence and other documents at Sant'Agata show that Verdi began revising *Forza* as early as mid-August 1863, when he first returned home after a series of trips initiated by the premiere of *Forza* in St. Petersburg two years earlier. Pressure to revise the work came both from the prospects of a performance in Paris and from Ricordi, who had not been able to realize a profit from it. Verdi turned first to Piave for help, but the librettist was unable to come up with a satisfactory solution. Léon Escudier, who visited Verdi in Genoa during June 1864 specifically to discuss *Forza*, put him in contact with Achille De Lauzières, who would later translate *Don Carlos* into Italian. De Lauzières drafted revisions for the final three scenes of Act IV (reproduced in an appendix to the article), but Verdi also found these unsatisfactory. Changes proposed by Camille Du Locle and Charles Nuitter, who translated the work into French during the summer of 1865, were similarly rejected. Yet another formal set of revisions was proposed in 1868 by Antonio Ghislanzoni, based in part on the work by Du Locle and Nuttier, but these also failed to satisfy the composer fully. Appendices to the article reproduce a tableaeu for Act I, as sent to Verdi by Emile Perrin, and a chronology of events during the *Forza* years.

Stylistic and Analytical Studies

732. Lawton, David. "Verdi, Cavallini, and the Clarinet Solo in *La Forza del destino*." *Verdi: Bollettino dell'Istituto di Studi Verdiani* 2 [No. 6] (1966): 1723–48. Italian and German translations are found on pp. 2149–85.

Much circumstantial information supports the tradition that Verdi wrote the clarinet solo at the beginning of Act III for Ernesto Cavallini. An analysis of the solo itself suggests that Verdi attempted to mitigate the weaknesses of the older six-key clarinet, which Cavallini preferred. Appendices provide an extensive biographical essay about Cavallini and reproduce previously unpublished letters written to Cavallini by Mercadante, Liszt, and Berlioz.

733. Petrobelli, Pierluigi. "More on the Three 'Systems': The First Act of *La forza del destino*." In *Music in the Theater: Essays on Verdi and Other Composers* (item 378), 127–40.

Petrobelli's analytical overview evaluates the dramatic power generated by the interaction of dramatic action, verbal organization, and music. The "introduzione-scena" does not utilize the recitative style normally associated with *versi sciolti*; instead, Verdi adds musical interest and dramatic relevance by creating a short musical number articulated primarily by the orchestral part. Likewise, the "Scena-Finale I°," built around only fourteen lines of *settenari doppi*, utilizes sonata form with key words occurring at principal junctures in the form. Petrobelli demonstrates that the text for Leonora's romanza was not adopted literally from the libretto to *Re Lear*, as is sometimes asserted, but instead utilizes a different poetic meter that better suits the character and function of this section. Finally, Verdi breaks conventional structure from the inside in the concluding portion of the Leonora-Alvaro duet by fusing the end of the cabaletta onto the ensuing recitative.

734. Ugolini, Giovanni. "Fra Melitone." *Verdi: Bollettino dell'Istituto di Studi Verdiani* 2 [No. 6] (1966): 1711–22. English and German translations are provided on pp. 2135–48.

Investigates Verdi's musical characterization of Fra Melitone, focusing on his "sermon" in Act III. The jeering, sarcastic quality of Fra Melitone's music, created by disjunct intervals and rapid changes in surface rhythm and texture creates a strong dramatic impression. The author shows how Verdi later developed this particular characterization even further in *Otello* and *Falstaff.*

735. Várnai, Péter Pál. "Leonóra és Don Alvaro: Dallamdramaturgiai jegyzetek." *Verdi: Bollettino dell'Istituto di Studi Verdiani* 2 [No. 6] (1966): 1681–94. An Italian translation is printed on pp. 1695–1710; English and German translations appear on pp. 2115–34.

Analysis of the music of Leonora and Don Alvaro reveals a consistent melodic formula containing the characteristic interval of a sixth. A version in minor refers to the psychological aspects of the tragedy shared by these characters; a variant in the major occurs in a few places when the protagonists enjoy a temporary respite from the blows of fate.

* Werner, Klaus G. "Verdi auf dem Weg zum Spätwerk: Zwei Ouvertüren im Spannungsfeld zwischen Instrumentalmusik und Oper." See item 513.

736. Zecchi, Adone. "Il coro nella *Forza del destino.*" *Verdi: Bollettino dell'Istituto di Studi Verdiani* 2 [No. 5] (1962): 793–814. English and German translations of the article appear on pp. 1155–88.

A descriptive analysis of choral sections in *Forza*, found almost exclusively in the second and third acts.

Performance Practice, Staging, Scenography

737. Benois, Nicola. "Nota sulla scenografia della *Forza del destino.*" *Verdi: Bollettino dell'Istituto di Studi Verdiani* 2 [No. 6] (1966): 1749–68. English and German translations are supplied on pp. 2186–216.

Surveys the history of the work's staging. The most lavish early staging took place at La Scala in 1869 under the artistic direction of Carlo Ferrario. It served as a point of departure for many ensuing productions. Later artists whose work is discussed include, among others: Edoardo Marchioro (La Scala, 1927), Alberto Scaioli (Teatro Reale dell'Opera, Rome, 1929), Camillo Parravicini (Terme di Caracalla, 1951; Teatro dell'Opera, Rome, 1954), Cipriano Efisio Oppo (Maggio Musicale Fiorentino, 1942), Giovanni Grandi (Palazzo dello Sport, Milan, 1945), Orlando di Collalto (Maggio Musicale Fiorentino, 1956), and Cesare Maria Cristini (Teatro San Carlo, Naples, 1957). Illustrations following p. 2216 show 45 set designs for various scenes of the opera in different stagings.

erformance History; Reception

'38. Barblan, Guglielmo. "Un po' di luce sulla prima rappresentazione della *Forza del destino* a Pietroburgo." *Verdi: Bollettino dell'Istituto di Studi Verdiani* 2 [No. 5] (1962): 833–79. English and German translations of the article are located on pp. 1217–1302.

The most detailed and thorough analysis published to date on the reception of *Forza* at its St. Petersburg premiere. Articles from the Russian press (reproduced in their entirety), and reports of eyewitnesses indicate, contrary to information found in some biographical sources, that there were apparently no organized protests, only isolated hecklers. The author suggests that the highly charged atmosphere, created by tension between the pro-German musicians and the Russian nationalists, was a major factor that led to the opera's mixed reception. An appendix to the article examines a few significant revisions and information about performance forces derived from a copyist's manuscript and parts in the Russian theater archives.

'39. Della Corte, Andrea. "Saggio di bibliografia delle critiche alla *Forza del destino*." *Verdi: Bollettino dell'Istituto di Studi Verdiani* 2 [No. 6] (1966): 1863–1906. English and German translations of the article are found on pp. 2391–2470.

A selection of citations from periodicals and books, ranging from Verdi's times to the present, assessing *La forza del destino*. Most entries contain short quotations from the original source; a few contain only short summaries.

'40. Gualerzi, Giorgio. "Il cammino dell'opera: Ricerche per una storia dell'interpretazione." *Verdi: Bollettino dell'Istituto di Studi Verdiani* 2 [No. 4, 5, and 6] (1961–66): 147–76, 880–903, 1769–1862. English and German translations of the article are printed on pp. 487–540, 1303–46, 2217–2390.

A comprehensive study of the work's reception from its first performances through the early twentieth century. The author focuses most attention on nineteenth-century performances, drawing on letters and reviews published in contemporary periodicals.

N GIORNO DI REGNO

erdi's second opera—and only comedy until *Falstaff*—has probably experienced the oorest reception of all of his works from the time of its premiere until the present. Ithough few independent studies have been devoted to this work, the ones cited elow offer useful insights into the beginning of Verdi's career.

Histories and General Studies

741. Engelhardt, Markus. "Nuovi dati sulla nascita dell'opera giovanile di Verdi *U* *giorno di regno.*" Trans. by Raoul Precht. *Studi verdiani* 4 (1986–87): 11–1?

Materials in the Archivio Storico Civico di Milano confirm long-held doub? about the accuracy of this work's genesis as presented in two early source? Lessona's *Volere è potere* (item 128), based largely on interviews with th? composer, and Verdi's own recollections published in Pougin's *Vita aneddotic* (item 131). Communications from Merelli to the administration of the theate? show that in mid-May 1840, the impresario was planning to revive *Oberto* a? part of the following season. Sometime between mid-May and 20 June, Ver? agreed to undertake the comic opera, making the gestation time for this wor? much shorter than had previously been thought. After the failure of *Giorno*, ? remains unclear why Merelli decided to mount a revival of *Oberto* rather tha? demand Verdi write another opera.

* Engelhardt, Markus. *Verdi und Andere: "Un giorno di regno," "Ernani," "Attila,* *"Il corsaro" in Mehrfachvertonungen.* See item 371.

742. Mioli, Piero. "Il povero Stanislao." *Musica e dossier* No. 51 (September-Octobe? 1991): 60–65.

A brief description of the work and its genesis, an assessment of the music, an? an evaluation of reasons for its poor reception.

Dramaturgy; Studies of the Libretto

743. Parker, Roger. "*Un giorno di regno*: From Romani's Libretto to Verdi's Opera? In *Studies in Early Verdi* (item 377), 83–109.
Republished in *Studi verdiani* 2 (1983): 38–58.

A slightly revised version of a chapter from the author's doctoral dissertatio? (see item 377). The libretto for Verdi's *Un giorno di regno* differs considerabl? from Romani's original libretto, *Il finto Stanislao*, and unless evidence to th? contrary surfaces, it must be assumed that the composer had a hand in recastin? the libretto for his opera. The author discusses each of the major textu? changes and analyzes the corresponding musical passages for features that ma? have prompted the change. On the basis of the literary style of the replacemen? texts, Parker proposes that Solera was the likely collaborator of Verdi i? revising the libretto.

Stylistic and Analytical Studies

* Parker, Roger. "The Influence of the Singer in Early Verdi Opera." See iter? 490.

GIOVANNA D'ARCO

Although *Giovanna d'Arco* was well received at its premiere, Verdi became disenchanted with the production, and the opera marks a period of time in which the composer withdrew all association with La Scala. While *Giovanna* has received little scholarly attention, the following two studies provide an outstanding examination of its literary roots and performance practice.

Dramaturgy; Studies of the Libretto

744. Engelhardt, Markus. "Shakespeare-Anleihen in Verdis 'Schiller'-Oper *Giovanna d'Arco*." In *Über Musiktheater: Eine Festschrift für Arthur Scherle anläßlich seines 65. Geburtstages*, 71–83. Ed. by Stefan G. Harpner and Birgit Gotzes. Munich: Ricordi, 1992. ISBN 3-980-3090-0-2. ML 1700 .U24 1992.

    After reviewing the history of the Joan of Arc story in European literature and on the operatic stage, the author examines the literary sources of Verdi's opera. Although it is clear that Solera used Schiller's play as a major source, the author argues that several ideas in his libretto for Verdi's opera come from Shakespeare's *Henry VI, Part One*. These include the way in which the relationship between Giovanna and Lionello is presented, the chorus of good and bad spirits, and the treatment of Giacomo, the father of Giovanna. To conclude the article, Engelhardt examines the way in which Solera compiled the libretto for *Giovanna* and compares Solera's treatment of the story to that by Gaetano Rossi, set to music by Nicola Vaccai in 1827.

Performance Practice, Staging, Scenography

745. Chusid, Martin. "A Letter by the Composer about *Giovanna d'Arco* and Some Remarks on the Division of Musical Direction in Verdi's Day." *Performance Practice Review* 3 (1990): 7–57.
    Republished in *Studi verdiani* 7 (1991): 12–56.

    Presents, for the first time in transcription and English translation, a letter from Verdi to Pietro Romani, *maestro direttore* at the Teatro La Pergola in Florence, dated 28 March 1845. The letter is particularly significant because Verdi discusses his feelings about tempo for most of the individual numbers in the opera. The second portion of the article examines the way in which the first violinist and the maestro al cembalo, or vocal director, shared responsibility for directing operas in Italy during this period. Evidence suggests that the vocal director was typically considered a higher rank than the violin director. Information from librettos in which Verdi himself directed the premiere of his works suggests that in these cases he temporarily took over the role of vocal director. An extensive appendix to this article, organized by theater, provides useful documentation regarding vocal and orchestral directors and the titles

describing their function in selected performances of Verdi's operas betwee
1839–93. Appendices list 1) performances directed by Verdi in which th
libretto, by omitting the name of the vocal director, suggests that the compose
himself served this function and 2) operas not directed by Verdi for which n
separate vocal director is listed in the libretto. Two complementary articles a
item 960, which focuses on the *violino principale* as conductor in *Il trovatore* an
item 266, which focuses on the shift to baton conductors in nineteenth-centur
Italian opera.

I LOMBARDI / JÉRUSALEM

I lombardi was the earliest opera that Verdi revised substantially at a later period in h
life. It became *Jérusalem*, his first work written expressly for the Paris Opéra. Th
composer later reissued *Jérusalem* in an Italian translation, *Gerusalemme*; it neve
caught the attention of the Italian public, however, who continued to prefer th
original version.

Histories and General Studies

746. Günther, Ursula. "Giuseppe Verdis erster Erfolg in Paris." *Lendemains* 31/3
     (1983): 53–62.

     Verdi, like Rossini, achieved his first Parisian success with a reworking of a
     earlier Italian opera. The author details the history of *Jérusalem*'s genesi
     discusses its main differences from *I lombardi*, arguing that it is musically an
     dramatically superior to the earlier opera, describes the *mise-en-scène*, for whic
     no expense was spared, summarizes the early reviews of the work in the Parisia
     press, and recounts Verdi's reactions to working with the French system c
     opera production. One of the author's most interesting discoveries about th
     autograph manuscript is that the transposition of certain passages for sopran
     Mme. Julian Van Gelder in the love duet is partly in the hand of Giuseppin
     Strepponi. Her hand alternates with Verdi's twice during the text of the passag
     in which Gaston and Hélène pledge love to each other suggesting, on
     different level, a sort of secret message to each other. This evidence suggest
     that the liaison between Giuseppe and Giuseppina began earlier than previous
     thought, since these manuscript pages were written at the end of Septembe
     or at the latest, early October 1847.

747. Medici, Mario, ed. *Gerusalemme*. Quaderni dell'Istituto di Studi Verdiani, 2
     [Parma: Istituto di Studi Verdiani], 1963. 109 p. + 20 p. plates. ML 410 .V
     A48 vol. 2.

     A commemorative booklet, issued in connection with a performance of th
     opera at the Teatro La Fenice in Venice on 24 September 1963, containin
     three major essays by Giuseppe Pugliese, reprinted reviews of earl

performances, and a wealth of illustrative material. The essays consider the place of the libretto to *I lombardi* among the librettos to Verdi's other operas, a descriptive analysis of *I lombardi*, and a discussion of the most substantial changes made in transforming the work into *Jérusalem* and *Gerusalemme*. Illustrations and early reviews published in the volume concern all three versions.

Stylistic and Analytical Studies

748. Kerman, Joseph. "*I lombardi* in San Diego." *19th Century Music* 3 (1979–80): 259–64.

Republished, in tandem with item 687, as "Two Early Verdi Operas; Two Famous Terzetti." In *Write All These Down: Essays on Music*, p. 288–306. Berkeley: University of California Press, 1994. ISBN 0–520–08355–5. ML 60 .K37.

This article, partly a review of the first American performance of *I lombardi* since the nineteenth century, also offers an analytical discussion of the Act III terzetto. The author responds to Budden's criticism (item 365) that the return to tonic at the end of the terzetto seems unmotivated after the strong tonal movement in the middle of the piece, and he proposes several possible explanations for the distinctive tonal shape of the number.

749. Kimbell, David R.B. "Verdi's First Rifacimento: *I lombardi* and *Jérusalem*." *Music and Letters* 60 (1979): 1–36.

Discusses the changes Verdi made, after a distance of only four and a half years, to convert *I lombardi* into the French opera *Jérusalem*. The author considers first the significant changes made by Alphonse Royer and Gustave Vaez in Solera's libretto for *I lombardi*. He then discusses changes in the music in two categories: 1) borrowings from the earlier opera and 2) more substantial reworkings. The author concludes that while some changes were made to fit the expectations of the French public, others reflect the rapid maturation of Verdi's own musical style during the preceding years.

* Langford, Jeffrey. "Text Setting in Verdi's *Jérusalem* and *Don Carlos*." See item 479.

* Parker, Roger. "The Influence of the Singer in Early Verdi Opera." See item 490.

750. Quattrocchi, Arrigo. "Da Milano a Parigi: *Jérusalem*, la prima revisione di Verdi." *Studi verdiani* 10 (1994–95): 13–60.

The most thorough study to date of the genesis of *Jérusalem*. After examining the history of Verdi's revisions to *I lombardi* to create the new French opera the author provides a detailed discussion of the most significant musical and dramaturgical changes and proposes reasons for the alterations. Quattrocch furnishes several sets of comparative musical examples. Tables at the end of the article provide detailed formal schemes for both operas, showing areas o correspondence, newly composed sections, and passages with substantia revision.

Staging; Scenography

* Viale Ferrero, Mercedes. "Da *Norma* a *Attila*: Scene del Teatro Regio d Torino durante il regno di Carlo Alberto." See item 550.

LUISA MILLER

This opera, which since the time of Abramo Basevi has frequently been hailed as th beginning of a new stylistic period in Verdi's compositional career, has been the subjec of surprisingly few individual studies.

Guides to the Work

751. *Luisa Miller. L'avant-scène opéra* 151 (January/February 1993). Paris: Sociét Premières Loges, 1993. 110 p. ISSN 0764–2873. ML 410 .V4 L85 1993.

The bulk of this special issue is devoted to *Luisa Miller*, including articles o the genesis of the libretto, Verdi and Schiller, and the singers who created th principal roles in the premiere production. The libretto is presented in th original Italian with a modern French translation by Michel Orcel, togethe with a parallel descriptive analysis by Gilles de Van. The volume also include a discography of complete recordings and individual arias or sections accompanied by a prose essay. Tables list the earliest performances of the oper in major centers as well as more detailed information about performances ir major houses up to the present. The short bibliography of 24 items (includin editions of the work, general studies of Verdi, and studies focusing on *Luis Miller* or Schiller) emphasizes only the most recent publications.

Dramaturgy; Studies of the Libretto

* Fricke, Harald. "Schiller und Verdi: Das Libretto als Textgattung." See item 407.

* Roccatagliati, Alessandro. "Drammaturgia romantica verdiana: *Luisa Miller* e *Rigoletto*." See item 436.

752. Ross, Peter. "*Luisa Miller*—Ein kantiger Schiller-Verschnitt? Sozialkontext und ästhetische Autonomie der Opernkomposition im Ottocento." In *Zwischen Opera buffa und Melodramma: Italienische Oper im 18. und 19. Jahrhundert*, 159–78. Ed. by Jürgen Maehder and Jürg Stenzel. Perspektiven der Opernforschung, 1. Frankfurt am Main: Peter Lang, 1994. ISBN 3–631–41917–1. ML 1733 .Z95 1994.

A detailed and incisive comparison of Cammarano's and Verdi's libretto with Schiller's *Kabale und Liebe*. The author examines various factors that influenced the play's adaptation as a libretto, including exigencies of the operatic medium, availability of vocal soloists, and demands of the Neapolitan censors.

Analytical and Stylistic Studies

753. Alper, Clifford D. "Verdi's *Luisa Miller*: Her Ancestors and Descendants." *The Opera Journal* 13 (Summer 1980): 3–11.

Offers a short descriptive analysis of the opera, focusing on passages that seem to presage stylistic features in later works, particularly *La traviata*, *Il trovatore*, *Don Carlos*, and the *Requiem*.

754. Engelhardt, Markus. "'Something's Been Done to Make Room for Choruses': Choral Conception and Choral Construction in *Luisa Miller*." In *Verdi's Middle Period, 1849–1859: Source Studies, Analysis, and Performance Practice* (item 235), 197–205.

While the operatic chorus has a primarily decorative function in Verdi's early operas, it becomes an integral part of the dramaturgy in *Luisa Miller*. The village chorus and hunting chorus in Act I and the peasant chorus in Act II clarify the characterization of Luisa and interact dramatically with her, while the *Scena e coro* in Act III (the first time Verdi used that designation) fuses the drama of Luisa with external events and the comments of the group around her. The article updates and expands a portion of the author's doctoral dissertation, item 467.

MACBETH

Macbeth marks the first time that Verdi undertook to work with a story based on Shakespeare, and documentary evidence shows that he took particular interest in working through details concerning the libretto, singing, and staging. The composer himself called attention to the new musical style of *Macbeth*, and Verdi scholars consider it a major turning point in his career. The composer later made considerable revisions in the work for its 1865 Parisian premiere at the Théâtre-Lyrique. The most important single reference tool for research on this opera is the *"Macbeth" Sourcebook*, based on presentations made at an International Verdi Conference held in 1977 at Danville, Kentucky.

Guides to the Work

755. *Macbeth. L'avant-scène opéra* 40 (March/April 1982). Paris: L'Avant-Scène, 1982. 143 p. ISSN 0395–0670. ML 410 .V4 V356 1982.

The bulk of this issue is devoted to *Macbeth*. A dozen articles focus on topics such as the genesis of the libretto and the music, Verdi's major revision of the work in 1865, his characterization of Lady Macbeth and some important interpreters of that role, and issues involving staging and scenography. The guide reproduces the 1847 libretto, with a modern French translation by Michel Orcel. The volume also includes a discography of complete recordings and individual arias or sections, accompanied by a prose essay. Tables list the earliest performances of the opera in major centers as well as more detailed information about performances in major houses up to the present. The bibliography in this issue, containing both general sources about Verdi and publications regarding *Macbeth*, is highly selective and substantially slimmer than in some other volumes of the series.

756. *Macbeth*. English National Opera Guides, 41. London: John Calder; New York: Riverrun, 1990. 96 p. ISBN 0–7145–4148–6. ML 50 .V484 M22 1990.

This guide contains an introductory essay by Giorgio Melchiori discussing the general history of the opera and the major changes Verdi made in the revised version; an article by Harold Powers dealing with Verdi's compositional process (see item 776); a discussion by Michael R. Booth about *Macbeth* and the Nineteenth-Century Theater (see item 786); a translation by Andrew Porter of August Wilhelm Schlegel's "Nota al *Macbeth*," published in Carlo Rusconi's translation of the play which was used as a main source of the libretto; and Porter's translations of the standard preface published in the Ricordi libretto and of Piave's intended preface for the 1847 libretto. The volume reproduces the 1865 version of the libretto in Italian with a performing English translation by Jeremy Sams; in addition, deleted passages from the 1847 version are presented in an appendix. The volume contains a discography and a very brief selective bibliography.

757. Rescigno, Eduardo. *"Macbeth" di Giuseppe Verdi: Guida all'opera*. Oscar musica 8. Milan: Mondadori, 1983. 284 p. ML 410 .V4 R431 1983.

Provides a short history of the opera and its libretto, a descriptive analysis of the music (based on the revised version, but with references to the first version), a reproduction of the libretto for the revised version (changes from the first version are noted in footnotes), a bibliography, discography, and a partial index, in which the reader may look up references to particular numbers in the opera.

Histories and General Studies

758. Degrada, Francesco. "Lettura del *Macbeth*." *Studi musicali* 6 (1977): 207–67. Reprinted in *Il palazzo incantato* (item 369), 2:79–137.

A concise history and analysis of the work, including discussions of the respective contributions of Piave and Maffei, Verdi's emphasis on the "fantastic" and his new approach to dramaturgy, and the revisions for the production in Paris. An appendix reproduces a section from August Wilhelm Schlegel's *Über dramatische Kunst und Literatur*, published by Carlo Rusconi in his Italian translation of *Macbeth*, that strongly influenced Verdi's dramatic conception of the opera.

759. Guandalini, Gina. "I due *Macbeth* e i molti *Lear* di Verdi." In *Il teatro del personaggio: Shakespeare sulla scena italiana dell'800*, 115–46. Ed. by Laura Caretti. Biblioteca teatrale, 27. Rome: Bulzoni, 1979. PR 3019 .I8 T4.

Surveys the genesis of Verdi's *Macbeth*, with an emphasis on the libretto (including changes made for the 1865 version) and Verdi's conception of the dramaturgy. The concluding portion of the article traces the composer's repeated intentions to compose an opera based on *King Lear* and the gradual evolution of his ideas about the work's libretto and dramaturgy.

760. Moscatelli, Cledes. *Il "Macbeth" di Giuseppe Verdi: L'uomo, il potere, il destino.* Ravenna: A. Longo, 1978. 133 p.

A short history of the genesis and reception of *Macbeth* with a concise analysis of the opera, written primarily for the non-Verdi specialist. Appendices present some of Verdi's letters and reproduce the libretto. For a more detailed and scholarly approach to the history and analysis of the opera, see item 762 below.

761. Noske, Frits. "Verdi's *Macbeth*: Romanticism or Realism?" In *Ars musica, musica scientia: Festschrift Heinrich Hüschen zum fünfundsechzigsten Geburtstag am 2. März 1980*, 359–63. Ed. by Detlef Altenburg. Cologne: Gitarre und Laute Verlagsgesellschaft, 1980. ISBN 3–88583–0002–7. ML 55 .H87 1980.

Macbeth breaks with the tradition of Italian Romantic opera in several significant ways: romantic love plays no part in the opera, there is no role for a *primo tenore*, Duncan has a silent role, and the introductory chorus is sung by a group of witches. Noske proposes that Duncan serves as a representation of goodness as a secular agent of God on earth and therefore stands in opposition to the witches, who represent the idea of evil. Musical references to the witches occur at many key dramatic points in the opera, underscoring the infiltration of evil into the acts of individuals. The author suggests that the opera is best understood as a Realistic rather than a Romantic opera.

762. Rosen, David and Andrew Porter, eds. *Verdi's "Macbeth": A Sourcebook.* New York: Norton; London: Cambridge, 1984. xvi, 527 p. ISBN 0–393–95073–8 (Norton); 0–521–26520–7 (Cambridge). ML 410 .V4 V35 1984.

Contains the most significant recent scholarship dealing with this opera. Includes selected reports from the Fifth International Verdi Conference, held on 10–12 November 1977 at Danville, Kentucky, together with valuable source materials. Among the most important of these are a chronological reproduction in both the original language and English translation of surviving letters and documents relating to the opera. A number of documents are published here for the first time; others contain significant corrections from previously published versions. The letters and documents are lightly annotated. Other documentary materials include English translations of reviews and other published commentary relating to the premiere of both versions and some other early productions; reproductions of five costume designs for the original production with historical commentary; a list of autographs, manuscript copies, and selected editions of both versions and their locations; and a discussion by David Rosen of scores, arrangements, and performance materials published by Ricordi. The volume also contains transcriptions of the "Scala" libretto in Verdi's hand with revisions by Andrea Maffei, and of draft fragments for the 1865 libretto in Verdi's hand. Appendices show productions of *Macbeth* from 1847–1947 in major cities or performed with major artists, list music for *Macbeth* written by other composers, and present a table of revisions and a concordance of four piano-vocal scores (the list of early performances is updated in item 790 below). The volume also includes a piano-vocal transcription by David Lawton of the principal passages of the original production that Verdi later revised or recomposed for the 1865 Paris production. The *Sourcebook* concludes with a useful bibliography, index, discography, glossary, and name dictionary. The libretto for the original 1847 libretto is reproduced in facsimile. Articles on individual topics are listed separately as items 215, 763, 764, 769, 772–74, 779–81, 783–85, 787, 788, and 791.

Dramaturgy; Studies of the Libretto

763. Barish, Jonas. "Madness, Hallucination, and Sleepwalking." In *"Macbeth" Sourcebook* (item 762), 149–55.

Discusses the way in which Verdi adapted Shakespeare's *Macbeth* for his opera. Focuses particularly on the sleepwalking scene, comparing Verdi's treatment to the portrayal of sleepwalking scenes in operas by other composers.

764. Degrada, Francesco. "Observations on the Genesis of Verdi's *Macbeth*." In *"Macbeth" Sourcebook* (item 762), 156–73.

A detailed examination of the various stages in the genesis of the libretto for *Macbeth*, including the composer's prose drafts, Piave's construction of the libretto, and refinements and corrections in the versification by Andrea Maffei.

765. Goldin, Daniela. "Il *Macbeth* verdiano: Genesi e linguaggio di un libretto." *Analecta musicologica* 19 (1979): 336–372.
Reprinted in *La vera fenice*, 230–82. Turin: Einaudi, 1985. ISBN 88–06–57398–5. ML 2110 .G64 1985.

The most detailed examination available of the formulation of the libretto for *Macbeth*, with particular emphasis on influences by Italian translations of Shakespeare available in Verdi's time. The author conclusively demonstrates that Verdi based his original scenario for the opera on the translation by Carlo Rusconi. Piave later made use of a translation by Michele Leoni as he prepared the libretto.

766. Liebner, János. "Les deux Macbeth." *Atti 1* (item 224), 176–83.

Investigates the ways in which Verdi's approach to *Macbeth* departs from its Shakespearean model, particularly in the characterization of Lady Macbeth and Macbeth. The author asserts that Verdi reshaped the theme of the story to focus on the triumph of good over evil.

767. Noske, Frits. "Schiller e la genesi del *Macbeth* verdiano." *Nuova rivista musicale italiana* 10 (1976): 196–203.

Suggests that the libretto to *Macbeth* was influenced by Schiller's adaptation of Shakespeare's play for the theater in Weimar. Examines ways in which Shakespeare's play, Schiller's adaptation, and Verdi's opera differ in their portrayal of the witches.

768. Porter, Andrew. "Translating *Macbeth*." In *"Macbeth" Sourcebook* (item 762), 245–48.

Discusses representative problems encountered in preparing an English translation of *Macbeth*.

769. ———. "Verdi and the Italian Translations of Shakespeare's *Macbeth*." In *"Macbeth" Sourcebook* (item 762), 351–55.

Discusses differences in various Italian translations of *Macbeth* available in Verdi's era and their possible influence on the libretto for *Macbeth*.

770. Ruggiero, Matthew John. "Verdi's *Macbeth* Libretto and Its Literary Context."
      Ph.D. dissertation, Boston University, 1993. xiv, 226 p.

      The first portion of the dissertation contains a detailed discussion of
      Shakespeare reception in nineteenth-century Italy and an examination of pre-
      1847 Italian translations of Shakespeare. The second part of the study explores
      the genesis of the *Macbeth* libretto and how it related to Verdi's quest to
      transcend conventional operatic form. The author proposes that some of the
      negative reception accorded the opera at its premiere resulted from it being
      thrust into an ongoing debate about the relative merits of Shakespeare.

771. Vecchi, Giuseppe. "La polemica sul libretto di *Macbeth*." Il "vero" e il
      "fantastico": La "mescolanza dei generi." *Quadrivium: Studi di filologia e
      musicologia* 20 (1979): 77–128.
      Reprinted in *Studi e ricerche sui libretti delle opere di Giuseppe Verdi* (item 444)
      77–128.

      Suggests that while Verdi drew words, phrases, and ideas from Carlo Rusconi's
      translation of the play in his early sketches of passages for the libretto submitted
      to Piave, the librettist himself relied on many literary and linguistic ideas found
      in Giulio Carcano's translation of *Macbeth,* especially in the witches' dialogues.
      The author then examines the critical reception to some of the unusual features
      of the libretto at the opera's Florentine premiere in light of the aesthetic debate
      over issues of dramaturgy and the "fantastic genre" found in the writings of
      Giuseppe Mazzini and others. An appendix reproduces the full text of reviews
      by Luigi Casamorata and Alessandro Piazza published in the *Gazzetta musicale
      di Milano.*

772. Weaver, William. "The Shakespeare Verdi Knew." In *"Macbeth" Sourcebook*
      (item 762), 144–48.

      A short history of Italian translations of Shakespeare from the late eighteenth
      through the mid-nineteenth centuries and a discussion of their influence on
      Verdi's conception of *Macbeth.*

Studies of Compositional Process

773. Günther, Ursula. "The Verdi-Escudier Correspondence About *Macbeth*." In
      "Macbeth" Sourcebook (item 762) 174–81.

      Examines the history of Verdi's revision of *Macbeth* for Paris, including the
      negotiation of fees and author's rights, the translation of the libretto, the choice
      of singers, and the performance of the work in a five-act, rather than four-act
      version.

774. Lawton, David. "Observations on the Autograph of *Macbeth I.*" In *"Macbeth" Sourcebook* (item 762), 210–26.

    Suggests approximate dates for the composition and orchestration of the first version of *Macbeth* based on evidence from the autograph score, letters, and other documents. Analyzes some of the most significant revisions in the manuscript made at various stages in the compositional process.

775. Osthoff, Wolfgang. "Die beiden Fassungen von Verdis *Macbeth.*" *Archiv für Musikwissenschaft* 29 (1972): 17–44.

    An overview of the opera's history, focusing on revisions for the 1865 Paris production. Includes a detailed discussion of some passages in which the composer made significant revisions.

776. Powers, Harold S. "Making *Macbeth* Musicabile." In *Macbeth*. English National Opera Guides, 41 (item 756), 13–36.

    This interesting article delineates qualities Verdi considered essential for a stage play to be effective material for an operatic setting ("palpable ambience, striking characters, and strong situations") and the way in which Shakespeare's *Macbeth* meets these expectations. The author then demonstrates the way in which the composer would adopt and adapt generic forms and procedures to fashion a "sketch" for musical numbers, illustrating the process by reconstructing such a sketch for the murder sequence in Act I. The final section of the article examines the composer's characterization of the witches, Lady Macbeth, and Macbeth. Powers argues that while the 1865 revision brings the opera closer to Shakespeare's original play in some respects, the changes damage the sense of structural cohesion present in the original version of Acts III and IV. Table II, "Generic Expectations in Italian Romantic 'melodrama'," provides an exceptionally concise and easily understood encapsulation of formal and stylistic principles examined by the author in greater detail in other studies (see, in particular, item 496).

tylistic and Analytical Studies

777. Alper, Clifford. "Verdi's Use of the Minor Second Interval in *Macbeth.*" *The Opera Journal* 4 (Fall 1971): 11–14.

    Develops a thesis proposed by Francis Toye (item 144) that ascending or descending seconds are a principal identifying characteristic of the *Macbeth* score. The author suggests that the composer typically associated this figure with the murder, its anticipation, or feelings of guilt after its commission.

778. Antokoletz, Elliott. "Verdi's Dramatic Use of Harmony and Tonality in *Macbeth.*" *In Theory Only* 4 (Nov.–Dec. 1978): 17–28.

A technical examination of five major sections from the opera in which the dyad *c–db* is especially prominent, either in the foreground or as a background event. The author suggests that Verdi associated this particular dyad with the dramatic ideas of murder and guilt.

779. Budden, Julian. "*Macbeth*: Notes on the Instrumentation of the Two Versions." In "*Macbeth*" *Sourcebook* (item 762), 227–30.

Discusses the transitional role of the first version of *Macbeth*, which contains passages scored in the style of the early nineteenth century as well as other passages that show the more elaborate, coloristic orchestration typical of Verdi's later works. In addition, Verdi uses a unique combination of instruments to accompany several of the supernatural scenes. There were relatively few changes in orchestration in the later version of the work.

780. Chusid, Martin. "Evil, Guilt and the Supernatural in Verdi's *Macbeth*: Toward an Understanding of the Tonal Structure and Key Symbolism." In "*Macbeth*" *Sourcebook* (item 762), 249–60.

An examination of the tonal organization in both versions of *Macbeth* suggests that the keys of E and Bb represent two hierarchical levels of supernatural: Bb the most powerful realm, and E a lesser level. Other keys appear to be associated with the character of Macbeth (F/f), Scotland and its king or people (A), and the idea of murder and guilt (Db, C, and D).

781. Knowles, John. "The Banquet Scene from Verdi's *Macbeth*: An Experiment in Large-Scale Musical Form." In "*Macbeth*" *Sourcebook* (item 762), 284–92.

The banquet scene of *Macbeth* replaces the traditional Verdian finale structure with an exceptionally long and complex dramatic scene based on a *parlante* texture, followed by a static concertato in which the characters voice their emotions. The composer later reused this design in the opening scenes of *Rigoletto* and *La traviata*, the Act I finale of *Aroldo*, and the Act III finales of *Les vêpres siciliennes* and *Un ballo in maschera*.

782. Petrobelli, Pierluigi. "Verdi's Musical Thought: An Example from *Macbeth*." In *Music in the Theater: Essays on Verdi and Other Composers* (item 378), 141–52.

Asserts that the most important principle behind Verdi's musico-dramatic language by the time he wrote *Macbeth* was to establish inner coherence through the right balance among dramatic organization, poetic structure, musical form, and the elements comprising the *mise-en-scène*. The composer used simple gestures—pitch levels, rhythmic figures, and instrumental timbres—to unify the key dramatic points of the plot. Petrobelli illustrates these points by examining Verdi's use of a simple rhythmic/melodic motive (first associated with Macbeth's declaration "Tutto è finito!") and the distinctive timbre of the English horn to unify key dramatic moments in the duet between Macbeth and Lady Macbeth with parallel moments in the Act I finale.

* Powers, Harold S. "*Tempo di mezzo*: Three Ongoing Episodes in *Verdian Musical Dramaturgy.*" See item 497 above.

783. Sabbeth, Daniel. "On the Tonal Organization of *Macbeth II.*" In *"Macbeth" Sourcebook* (item 762), 261-69.

Verdi mixes major and minor modes to create unusual effects in *Macbeth*. Lowered sixth scale degrees are particularly prominent in both motivic and harmonic gestures. The overall tonal structure of the opera suggests that Verdi associated certain keys with particular characters, ideas, or events.

784. Tomlinson, Gary. "*Macbeth, Attila*, and Verdi's Self-Modeling." In *"Macbeth" Sourcebook* (item 762), 270–83.

Verdi used several musical-dramatic structures in his earlier operas, notably *Attila*, as models for similar structures in *Macbeth*. Specific examples discussed include the prelude, Macduff's aria "Ah, la paterna mano," the banquet scene of the original version of the opera, and the dagger scene and duet.

Performance Practice, Staging, Scenography

785. Somville, Marilyn Feller. "Vocal Gesture in *Macbeth*." In *"Macbeth" Sourcebook* (item 762), 239–244.

Investigates Verdi's intentions regarding vocal performance practice in *Macbeth* by examining the style of the vocal parts and the composer's expressive indications in the score.

786. Booth, Michael R. "*Macbeth* and the Nineteenth-Century Theatre." In *Macbeth*. English National Opera Guides, 41 (item 756 above), 37–43.

Discusses Verdi's conception of staging and scenography in *Macbeth* in light of production techniques used in melodramas and stagings of Shakespeare's plays in England.

787. Cohen, H. Robert. "*Macbeth* in Paris: New Iconographical Documents." In *"Macbeth" Sourcebook* (item 762) 182–98.

Presents evidence about the staging of the revised version of *Macbeth* in Paris based on drawings and engravings for set designs and costumes. Includes a list of reviews and articles dealing with the Paris premiere of *Macbeth*.

788. Conati, Marcello. "Aspetti della messinscena del *Macbeth* di Verdi." *Nuova rivista musicale italiana* 15 (1981): 374–404.

A shorter version of this article in English translation was published as "Aspects of the Production of *Macbeth*." In *"Macbeth" Sourcebook* (item 762), 231–38.

Examines the use of stage machinery in various scenes of *Macbeth* to create a supernatural effect: the appearances of Banquo's ghost, the three apparitions, the procession of the eight kings, and the ballet of the aerial spirits. Includes a discussion of the reaction of the audience at the premiere performances to these stage effects.

789. Varesi, Giulia Cora. "L'interpretazione del *Macbeth*, con lettere inedite di Giuseppe Verdi." *Nuova antologia* 364 (1932): 433–40.

The author gives a brief biographical summary of her father, Felice Varesi, who directed the first performances of *Macbeth*, and reproduces a group of letters written by Verdi, primarily concerning performance instructions for the opera. Item 40 restores some passages deleted in this publication and prints several additional letters.

Performance History; Reception

790. Chusid, Martin, and Thomas Kaufman. "More About the Performance History of *Macbeth*." *Verdi Newsletter* 13 (1985): 38–41.

Presents corrections and additions to the list of performances in the *Macbeth Sourcebook* (item 762). Evidence now suggests that very few performances of the revised *Macbeth* took place until after World War I.

791. Pinzauti, Leonardo. "Verdi's *Macbeth* and the Florentine Critics." In *"Macbeth" Sourcebook* (item 762), 137–43.

Examines nineteenth-century musical life in Florence and its influence on the reception of Verdi's opera.

I MASNADIERI

This opera has the distinction of being the only work Verdi wrote for a premiere in England. The most significant research on this opera has been done by Robert Montemorra Marvin, who is also preparing the score for the new critical edition.

Histories and General Studies

792. Marvin, Roberta Montemorra. "Censorship of *I masnadieri* in Italy." *Verdi Newsletter* 21 (1993): 5–15.

Differing issues that were of concern to the censors resulted in substantial alterations to *I masnadieri* as it was performed throughout the Italian peninsula. The most frequent change was to eliminate Moser, the priest. This not only radically altered one of the main premises of the story but also forced the deletion or modification of the impressive scene between Francesco and Moser in Act IV. Francesco's account of his dream of the final judgment at the beginning of Act IV was also often eliminated. The author includes examples from a number of Italian librettos, showing how they departed from the definitive London libretto of 1847.

793. ———. "Verdi's *I masnadieri*: Its Genesis and Early Reception." Ph.D. dissertation, Brandeis University, 1992. 2 vols. viii, 538; i, 402 p.

The most detailed historical study about this opera. The author examines the drafting of both libretto and music, revisions Verdi made at various stages in the music, tempo designations and metronome markings, and the work's reception (including the effect of governmental censorship on its reception in Italy). In light of evidence concerning the compositional chronology of the opera, Marvin suggests that many revisions made by the composer may have been influenced by his stylistic advances in *Macbeth*, written during a break in the composition of *I masnadieri*. The dissertation contains several items of particular interest, including: a reproduction in parallel columns (original language and English translation) of all known letters and documents, some previously unpublished, concerning the genesis and early history of the opera, a reconstruction of an early version of the libretto, a performance chronology from 1847 to 1852, a reprinting of several articles published in the *Gazzetta musicale di Milano* (1844–46) discussing the use of the metronome, and a reproduction of passages altered by censors in early performances. The dissertation includes a large bibliography.

Studies of Compositional Process

794. ———. "Artistic Concerns and Practical Considerations in the Composition of *I masnadieri*: A Newly Discovered Version of 'Tremate, o miseri!'." *Studi verdiani* 7 (1991): 79–110.

An abridged version appeared as "Verdi's Composition of *I masnadieri*: A Newly Discovered Early Setting of Francesco's Cabaletta, 'Tremate, o miseri!'." *The Opera Journal* 24 (March 1991): 19–43.

After reviewing the compositional history of *I masnadieri*, the author discusses a series of revisions made by the composer after his arrival in London and before the premiere of the opera, focusing on a new setting of the cabaletta "Tremate, o miseri!" composed for the Francesco's scene in Act I. The new cabaletta shows the composer responding to problems in harmonic movement, text declamation, and possibly tonal-dramatic associations. In addition to improving musical and dramatic weaknesses in the first version, Verdi's new conception of the cabaletta was undoubtedly influenced by the composer having had a chance to hear the voice of Filippo Coletti, who first created the role of Francesco. The article contains facsimile reproductions from the London *suggeritore* score, which transmits the first version of the cabaletta. For a more detailed analysis of some of the issues raised in this article, see the author's dissertation (item 793 above).

NABUCCO

Verdi himself deemed this opera to mark the true beginning of his career as a composer. The chorus "Va pensiero" has long been regarded as a prime example of Risorgimento sentiment, but several recent studies (see items 300 and 472) have shown that at the time of its premiere this chorus was not considered exceptional. The original printed libretto and Verdi's autograph score both use the title *Nabucodonosor*. As early as 1842, however, the composer began to use on occasion the shortened version, *Nabucco*; by the end of his life it had become standard.

Guides to the Work

795. *Nabucco. L'avant-scène opéra* 86 (April 1986). Paris: L'Avant-Scène, 1986. 130 p. ISSN 0764–2873. ML 5 .A9 v. 86.
      2nd ed. Paris: Société Premières Loges, 1991; revised 1994. 119 p. ISSN 0764–2873. ML 410 .V4 N3 1994.

A special issue on *Nabucco*, including a half-dozen articles dealing with the background to the story, the genesis of the opera, Verdi's musical style, the opera's reception, and its relation to the Risorgimento movement. The volume also includes a series of short essays about the performers who created the main roles in the opera. A detailed discography includes both complete recordings and individual arias or sections released since 1949; the bibliography of about 75 items lists major editions and librettos, studies of the work, and a substantial core of items relating to the historical background of the story. The libretto is reproduced in the original, with a parallel French translation by Georges Farret and descriptive analysis by Sylvaine Falcinelli. Tables list the earliest performances of the opera in major centers, as well as more detailed information about performances in major houses through the time of publication. The 1994 edition updates the performance history through that year but contains a substantially reduced bibliography of only the most significant items.

Dramaturgy; Studies of the Libretto

796. Cavicchi, Adriano. "Verdi e Solera: Considerazioni sulla collaborazione per *Nabucco*." *Atti 1* (item 224), 44–58.

Examines the details of Verdi's collaboration with Solera on *Nabucco*, emphasizing the background of Solera's literary and musical training.

797. Várnai, Péter Pál. "Dramma e musica nel *Nabucco*." *Atti 3* (item 226), 453–63.

Argues that *Nabucco* contains the germs of Verdi's mature ideas about dramaturgy and that it is the opera in which he marks out a definitive path distinct from his contemporaries. The author cites numerous passages from the opera to demonstrate the subtle use of related motivic ideas to underscore the unfolding of the dramatic action.

Stylistic and Analytical Studies

798. Petrobelli, Pierluigi. "*Nabucco*." In *Conferenze 1966–67*, 15–47. Milan: Associazione Amici della Scala, n.d.
    English translation by Roger Parker. "From Rossini's *Mosè* to Verdi's *Nabucco*." In *Music in the Theater: Essays on Verdi and Other Composers* (item 378), 8–33.

Proposes that Verdi drew on Rossini's *Mosè in Egitto* as a model for both dramatic characterization and musical approach. Resemblances in grandeur of musical tone and in structural organization are particularly notable between the opening scenes of the two operas. In the case of *Nabucco*'s most famous number, "Va pensiero," the composer used Rossini's *preghiera* only as a point of departure: Verdi radically departed from tradition by treating this section not as a chorus, but as an aria sung by the chorus. The English version of this article contains a postscript referring to the impact of recent research on some aspects of the original essay. The Italian version reproduces seven scene designs by Nicola Benois.

Performance History; Reception

799. Parker, Roger. "The Exodus of *Nabucco*." In *Studies in Early Verdi* (item 377), 111–41.

The earliest performances of *Nabucco* were clustered in northern Italy, primarily within a 50-mile radius of Milan. Cast lists suggest that certain singers specialized in the leading roles, performing it repeatedly in a number of places, and they often went on to create roles in other Verdi operas. The author surveys early reviews of the opera, which surprisingly do not single out any particular number as being especially popular. A table lists information regarding early performances of the opera through 1844, including casts.

Miscellaneous

* Parker, Roger. "The Critical Edition of *Nabucco*." See item 1036.

OBERTO

The origins of Verdi's first opera has been the subject of extensive debate. In 1939, Claudio Sartori (item 801) suggested that *Oberto* was closely related to an earlier composition, never performed, entitled *Rocester*. Frank Walker (item 152) took the opposite point of view, arguing that *Oberto* was a completely original work. More recently, Julian Budden (item 365), David Kimbell (item 800) and Roger Parker (item 803) have provided clear evidence of a connection between the two works, although any music from *Rocester* was likely thoroughly revised before it made its way into *Oberto*.

Histories and General Studies

800. Kimbell, David. "'Poi . . . diventò l'*Oberto*.'" *Music and Letters* 42 (1971): 1–7.

After surveying evidence regarding the young Verdi's earliest operatic attempts, the author concludes that *Oberto* was a refashioning of an earlier opera entitled *Rocester* based on a libretto by Antonio Piazza. Kimbell suggests that "Lord Hamilton," mentioned in some reminiscences of Verdi, was either the main character or an alternative title for the opera. The author then lists some of the major discrepancies between the autograph score of *Oberto* and the 1839 libretto, suggesting that these constitute some of the substantive changes in converting the old opera into a new one. Kimbell also responds to objections to this scenario by Walker (item 152). Many of the author's conclusions were later substantiated by Roger Parker's more thorough examination of the autograph manuscript (item 803).

801. Sartori, Claudio. "*Rocester*: La prima opera di Verdi." *Rivista musicale italiana* 43 (1939): 97–104.

One of the earliest studies dealing with the compositional history of *Oberto*. Sartori concludes that this opera, in essence, was a revision of an earlier work entitled *Rocester*. One of the most useful features of the article is the reproduction of six letters written by Verdi from the Pasini collection in Brescia. Five of them, dating from between 1836 to 1839, are addressed to Pietro Massini, director of the Società Filodrammatica del Teatro Filodrammatico in Milan. The remaining letter, dating from 1848, is addressed to Cammarano and relates to *La battaglia di Legnano*.

Dramaturgy; Studies of the Libretto

802. Giovanelli, Paola Daniela. "La storia e la favola dell'*Oberto*." *Studi verdiani* 2 (1983): 29–37.

After briefly reviewing the history of metrical conventions in Italian literature, the author demonstrates how the libretto of *Oberto* draws on two different stylistic traditions, both in treatment of versification and in approach to dramaturgy: the neoclassic style, as exemplified in the tragedies of Vittorio Alfieri and the librettos of Felice Romani, and a more modern, Romantic approach exemplified in the writings of Alessandro Manzoni and the librettos of Temistocle Solera. Giovanelli also examines the aesthetic position of Antonio Piazza, the librettist for *Oberto*, as seen in his *feuilletons* written for the *Gazzetta privilegiata di Milano*.

Studies of Compositional Process

803. Parker, Roger. "The Autograph Score of *Oberto, Conte di San Bonifacio*." In *Studies in Early Verdi* (item 377), 64–82.

The physical structure and composition of the autograph manuscript to *Oberto* suggests that most of the opera was written in a single, basic stage in which the names of all the characters were finalized. Extensive revisions in the music include a change in order in Act II, probably to accommodate the new quartet; one of the deleted numbers was placed in an appendix along with two other numbers composed sometime after the premiere. The textual revisions suggest that the libretto underwent substantial changes in plot, possibly including a change in locale and historical period. The study substantiates the view that *Oberto* was based on an earlier opera, *Rocester*, but that the material underwent such thorough rewriting that there is little, if any, trace of the earlier score.

Stylistic and Analytical Studies

* Dalmonte, Rossana. "Da *Oberto* a *Rigoletto*: Precisione di una formula." See item 465.

* Parker, Roger. "The Influence of the Singer in Early Verdi Opera." See item 490.

Performance Practice, Staging, Scenography

* Viale Ferrero, Mercedes. "Da *Norma* a *Attila*: Scene del Teatro Regio di Torino durante il regno di Carlo Alberto." See item 550.

Performance History; Reception

804. Conati, Marcello. "*L'Oberto, Conte di San Bonifacio* in due recensioni straniere poco note e in una lettera inedita di Verdi." *Atti 1* (item 224), 67–92.

Addresses the many contradictory statements in the secondary literature regarding the performance and reception of Verdi's first opera. Reviews in the

Allgemeine musikalische Zeitung and the *Révue et gazette musicale de Paris* provide previously unnoticed testimony that the early performances of *Oberto* were remarkably successful. Both reviews also recognize the young Verdi as a promising new talent. Conati also reproduces the text of a letter dated 11 January 1841 in which Verdi complains about the Genoese public's lack of refinement in connection with a performance of *Oberto*. In addition to its main topics, Conati's article offers useful assessments of full-length biographical studies of the composer. Inaccurate statements about *Oberto* are particularly rampant in early works by Eugenio Checchi and Gino Monaldi and from there found their way into later biographies.

805. Jensen, Luke. "The Early Publication History of *Oberto*: An Eye Toward *Nabucco.*" *Verdi Newsletter* 13 (1985): 6–20.

Investigates the early publication history of *Oberto* through information found in the *libroni* of Casa Ricordi. The large number of arrangements of pieces from the opera (including some revisions for particular singers or performers) and fantasies or other compositions based on themes from the opera attest to *Oberto*'s continuing popularity. Verdi increased his renumeration from the opera by doing some of the piano reductions himself, and his experiences during this period led to increasingly astute negotiations with his publishers. The article reproduces in facsimile a piano reduction of a chorus, "Sorge un canto e si difonde," written to replace the original chorus "Fidanzata avventurosa" for a set of performances in Genoa in January 1841.

OTELLO

The last tragic opera that Verdi would write, *Otello* marks perhaps the most dramatic single stylistic shift in Verdi's entire career. The rich source material about the genesis of the work available in letters and other documents, coupled with analytical examinations, has led to many remarkable studies about this extraordinary work.

Guides to the Work

806. Csampai, Attila and Dietmar Holland, eds. *Giuseppe Verdi, "Othello": Texte, Materialien, Kommentare.* Rororo Opernbücher. Reinbek bei Hamburg: Rowohlt Taschenbuch Verlag, 1981. 281 p. ISBN 3–499–17368–9. ML 410 .V4 G58 1981.

This guide contains a number of fine essays on the genesis of the opera and its place among Verdi's works, Boito's libretto and his and Verdi's relationship to Shakespeare, Verdi's dramaturgy, and the opera's reception history. The editors have also included a selection of about two dozen letters in German translation to and from Verdi concerning the opera. The libretto is reproduced in side-by-side format in Italian and a German translation by Karl Dietrich Gräwe. The volume concludes with a chronology, selective bibliography, and a discography of complete recordings.

807. Hepokoski, James A. *Giuseppe Verdi: "Otello"*. Cambridge Opera Handbooks. Cambridge: Cambridge University Press, 1987. xi, 209 p. ISBN 0–521–25885–5. ML 410 .V4 H48 1981.

An indispensable general study of the opera. After a detailed synopsis of the plot, subsequent chapters outline the genesis of the work, the preparation of the libretto, and the compositional history of the work. The latter includes an examination of the revisions Verdi made for subsequent productions after the work's premiere, with particular emphasis on changes and additions made for its performance at the Paris Opéra in 1894. Recently discovered primary source material allows Hepokoski to present a more complete discussion of the work's genesis and compositional history than is found in earlier studies. A chapter concerning Verdi's ideas about performance focuses on his conception of the major roles in the opera and his work with and comments about the singers who took part in the premiere. Hepokoski also includes an overview of the published *disposizione scenica* and assesses its usefulness for determining Verdi's intentions about the production of the opera. Illustrations include set designs for the first tour of the opera, based on those used in the premiere performances, and photographs of the leading characters in their costumes. The volume does not provide an analytical overview of the entire work. Instead, the analytical portion of the volume investigates the complex formal structure of Act II and its relationship to formal models from earlier ottocento opera. A concluding essay analyzes Verdi's and Boito's interpretation of Shakespeare's play against the background of translations available to them and of contemporary productions of the play in Italy. The volume also contains a brief history of the opera in performance contributed by William Ashbrook and a discography by Malcolm Walker (see item 1023).

808. *Otello*. L'avant-scène opéra 51 (May/June 1976). Paris: L'Avant-Scène, 1976. 129 p. ISSN 0395–0670.
2nd ed. Paris: Société Premières Loges, 1990. 144 p. ISSN 0764–2873. ML 410 .V4 O74 1991.

Seven articles focus on topics such as the relationship of Boito's libretto to Shakespeare's play, the compositional history of the opera, *Otello* as the end of the "old" style of nineteenth-century opera, vocal typology of the major roles, and essays on several of the main roles. The libretto is presented in the original Italian with a French translation by Pierre Malbos and a running descriptive analysis by Henry Barraud. The volume also includes a discography of complete recordings and individual arias or sections, accompanied by a prose essay, as well as tables listing the earliest performances of the opera in major centers with more detailed information about performances in major houses up to the present. This information is all updated in the later edition. In the original edition, the bibliography contains more than 120 items, including librettos, editions, general works about Verdi, and specialized literature about *Otello*. The bibliography in the new edition contains only 53 items, restricted to recent or very significant materials.

809. *Otello*. English National Opera Guides, 7. London: John Calder; New York: Riverrun, 1981. 80 p. ISBN 0–7145–3850–7. ML 50 .V58 O8 1988.

This guide contains a brief discussion of the opera's place in Verdi's career, a descriptive analysis of the work, and an essay on the reception of Shakespeare in nineteenth-century Italy, including a survey of operas by other composers based on Shakespeare. The volume presents the libretto in Italian, with a parallel English translation by Andrew Porter. A brief appendix shows a small revision Verdi made for the Parisian premiere of the work in 1894. The guide also contains a brief discography and a highly selective bibliography.

Histories and General Studies

810. Aldrich-Moore, James. "False Fidelity: *Othello*, *Otello*, and Their Critics." *Comparative Drama* 28 (1994): 324–47.

Examines the issue of fidelity to the original play in the reception of Verdi's and Rossini's *Othello* operas. While Rossini's opera has often been criticized for not being "faithful" to its source, Verdi has generally been praised for adopting a more reverent attitude toward his model as an "authoritative" source. The author proposes that Verdi may have been influenced in this thinking by the music and writings of Hector Berlioz. He also shows that this shift reflected a general change in attitude toward Shakespeare in the nineteenth century, paralleling a desire by composers, such as Verdi, to assert authorial autonomy over their own works.

  *   Busch, Hans, ed. and trans. *Verdi's "Otello" and "Simon Boccanegra" (revised version) in Letters and Documents*. See item 99 above.

811. Da Pozzo, Giovanni. "*Otello* tra Verdi e Boito." *Belfagor* 30 (1983): 129–54.

An interesting study of how Boito's and Verdi's collaboration on *Otello* fits into the general cultural and intellectual milieu of the nineteenth century. Among other topics, the author considers Shakespeare reception in Italy, including the fortunes of Rossini's *Otello*, differences between the libretto and Shakespeare's play, and influences on the language of the libretto.

812. Degrada, Francesco. "*Otello*: Da Boito a Verdi." In *Il palazzo incantato* (item 369), 2:155–66.

   Argues that *Otello*'s originality lies in both Boito's imaginative treatment of the text as well as Verdi's unprecedented rethinking of musical language and syntax. See item 822 for a critical reaction to some of Degrada's assertions.

813. Einsfelder, Stefan. *Zur musikalischen Dramaturgie von Giuseppe Verdis "Otello"*. Kölner Beiträge zur Musikforschung, 184. Kassel: Gustav Bosse, 1994. 203 p. ISBN 3–7649–2615–5. ML 410 .V4 E36 1994.

   A general study of the opera, including the work's genesis, the relation of the libretto to Shakespeare's play, formal design and musical style, and musical characterization of Iago, Desdemona, and Otello.

Dramaturgy; Studies of the Libretto

814. Balthazar, Scott. "Tectonic and Linear Form in the *Ottocento* Libretto: The Case of the Two *Otellos*." *The Opera Journal* 28 (March 1995): 2–14.

   Proposes that a fundamental difference between Francesco Maria Berio di Salza's libretto for Rossini's *Otello* and the libretto prepared by Boito for Verdi's opera on the same subject is that the former emphasizes atemporal "tectonic" elements, while Boito and Verdi stress a linear, progressing development of plot and characterization. The author suggests that this shift from atemporal structure to a more linear approach constitutes a general trend in Italian opera librettos during the course of the nineteenth century.

815. Del Seta, Stefano. "Desiderio e gelosia nell'*Otello* di Verdi." *Annali della Facoltà di Lettere e Filosofia (Università di Siena)* 11 (1990): 159–68.

   Contrasts Verdi's and Boito's treatment of the story with that of Shakespeare, noting that the operatic version focuses on the contrast between desire and jealousy as the central core of the drama. The author then notes similarities between Verdi's operatic treatment and some of the main ideas of the *scapigliatura* movement, as seen in Igino Ugo Tarchetti's unfinished novel *Fosca*, as well as some of Arthur Schopenhauer's beliefs as portrayed in Wagner's *Tristan und Isolde*.

816. Eösze, László. "*Otello*: Dramma di Shakespeare e opera di Verdi." *Atti 3* (item 226), 20–26.

   Analyzes reasons for Boito's and Verdi's parsimony in their recasting of Shakespeare's drama. The operatic version forgoes some of Shakespeare's complex characterization and tends to focus   on a single character trait for each individual. The simplification of the plot and the order of the scenes in the opera also masterfully creates a constantly increasing psychological tension.

817. Gradenwitz, Peter. "Otello, il Moro (?) di Venezia." In *Opern und Opernfiguren: Festschrift für Joachim Herz*, 187–200. Wort und Musik: Salzburger Akademische Beiträge, 2. Ed. by Ursula Müller and Ulrich Müller, with the assistance of Gerhard Heldt and Georg F. Mielke. Anif/Salzburg: Verlag Ursula Müller, 1989. ISBN 3–85145–002–7. ML 1720 .O64 1989.

Examines the significance of exoticism and ethnicity in Verdi's *Otello*, comparing it to his treatment of these issues in his earlier operas, in Shakespeare's play, and in Shakespeare's principal source, Cinthio Giraldi's "Moro di Venezia" from *Gli hecatommithi*. The author also points out fundamental differences between Verdi's approach and that by Rossini and Francesco Berio in their earlier Othello opera.

818. Hawes, Jane. *An Examination of Verdi's* Otello *and Its Faithfulness to Shakespeare*. Studies in the History and Interpretation of Music, 46. Lewiston, N.Y.: Edwin Mellen, 1994. xi, 137 p. ISBN 0–7734–9092–2. ML 410 .V4 H39.

Compares and contrasts the treatment of the story by Shakespeare and Verdi, concluding that the changes made by Verdi and Boito are effective in transferring it to the new medium of opera. Hawes does not take into account any of Hepokoski's important research on the opera, and her analysis of the topic is more facile than Hepokoski's (see items 807 and 819).

819. Hepokoski, James A. "Boito and F.-V. Hugo's 'Magnificent Translation': A Study in the Genesis of the *Otello* Libretto." In *Reading Opera*, 34–59. Ed. by Arthur Groos and Roger Parker. Princeton: Princeton University Press, 1988. ISBN 0–691–09132–3. ML 2110 .R4 1988.

After surveying the various editions of Shakespeare's play available to Boito, concludes that the most influential on Boito's conception of the libretto was a French translation made by François-Victor Hugo in 1860. Beyond the translation itself, Hugo's critical introduction and scholarly commentary also helped shape Boito's ideas: an English ballad that Hugo argued was the source of Desdemona's "Willow Song" clearly influenced Boito when he reworked the text in 1885, and Hugo's discussion of Iago's character appears to have inspired Boito to write Iago's "Credo." Other important influences on the libretto include August Wilhelm Schlegel's commentary on the play and the *Othello* acting tradition in Italy.

820. Marggraf, Wolfgang. "Desdemonas 'Canzon del salice'." In *Liedstudien: Wolfgang Osthoff zum 60. Geburtstag*, 371–82. Ed. by Martin Just and

Reinhard Wiesend. Tutzing: Hans Schneider, 1989. ISBN 3–7952–0613–8. ML 55 .O845 1989.

A detailed analysis of Desdemona's "Willow Song," emphasizing the unusual formal structure of Boito's text, its relationship to Shakespeare's play, and the relationship of the text to the music.

821. Martin, George. "*Otello*, Manzoni, and the Concept of 'La gloria.'" In *Aspects of Verdi* (item 244), 117–21.

Examines the ways in which Verdi and Boito used the nineteenth-century concept of "la gloria" in *Otello*. The author traces the concept itself back to the ideology of the Napoleonic era and discusses its embodiment in Manzoni's commemorative ode on the death of Napoleon, "Il cinque maggio."

822. Powers, Harold S. "Boito rimatore per musica." In *Arrigo Boito: Atti del Convegno Internazionale di Studi* (item 199), 355–94.

After reviewing some of the ways in which Boito's characterization of Iago and Desdemona differs from that of Shakespeare's play, the author examines the various ways in which Boito widened the contrast between *versi sciolti* (non-rhymed "recitative") and *versi lirici* (rhymed, metrical poetry) by introducing various subtle gradations in the level of lyric quality. Analyzing the three internal finales in *Otello*, Powers demonstrates how Boito carefully coordinated changes in the lyric quality of the language with the dramatic structure; these, in turn, influenced Verdi's choices about the level of tonal stability in each section. While the main focus of the article is on *Otello*, the author touches on other librettos by Boito showing, for instance, how his treatment of Paolo in *Simon Boccanegra* and Barnaba in Ponchielli's *La gioconda*—both characters with evil natures—foreshadows the broken, asymmetrical meter of Iago's "Credo." He also touches on some of the interesting metrical features of *Falstaff*, in which Boito completely abandons traditional *versi sciolti*.

823. Rozett, Martha Tuck. "*Othello, Otello*, and the Comic Tradition." *Bulletin of Research in the Humanities* 85 (Winter 1982): 386–411.

Compares Shakespeare's drama with operatic settings by Rossini and Verdi. While Shakespeare used elements of comedy to intensify the tragic effect in his play, Rossini and Berio emphasized the comic elements, although leading to a tragic ending built from misunderstanding and intrigue. By contrast, Boito's and Verdi's rewriting of the story shifts the emphasis from low comedy to high comedy, which is violently juxtaposed against elements of tragedy that emphasize a stronger sense of fatalism.

824. Schueller, Herbert M. "*Othello* Tranformed: Verdi's Interpretation of Shakespeare." In *Studies in Honor of John Wilcox*, 129–58. Ed. by A. Dayle Wallace and Woodburn O. Ross. Detroit: Wayne State University Press, 1958. PR 14 .W44.

A fairly detailed account of the differences between plot and characterization in Shakespeare's play and in Verdi's and Boito's opera. This article should be used in conjunction with later research on the sources for the *Otello* libretto, especially by Hepokoski (see items 807 and 819).

Studies of Compositional Process

825. Budden, Julian. "Time Stands Still in *Otello*." *Opera* 32 (1981): 888–93.

Verdi revised the Act III *concertato* for the French performance of *Otello* in 1894 in order to lessen the dramatic stasis and to set the character of Iago more strongly in relief. The author examines the history of the *concertato* in nineteenth-century Italian opera and Verdi's dissatisfaction with his original solution in *Otello*. He suggests that the revision in the French score ought to be considered more carefully as a definitive revision.

826. Fairtile, Linda B. "Verdi's First 'Willow Song': New Sketches and Drafts for *Otello*." *19th Century Music* 19 (1995–96): 213–30.

A newly discovered set of 19 photographs in the New York Public Library for the Performing Arts contains sketches and portions of a continuity draft for Act IV through the end of the "Ave Maria" in addition to sketches for the Brindisi from Act I. The article presents a detailed discussion of the material from Act IV, with particular attention given to the "Willow Song," in which the text and music differ completely from the final version of the work. Comparing this setting to Boito's original text in the holograph libretto, the author argues that difficulties associated with the original text's unorthodox formal structure and literary style probably led Verdi to abandon his initial musical setting and to request a new text from Boito.

827. Hepokoski, James A. "Verdi's Composition of *Otello*: The Act II Quartet." In *Analyzing Opera: Verdi and Wagner* (item 454), 125–49.

Discusses a one-page draft from the Act II quartet in which Verdi worked out musical material for additional lines of text he had requested from Boito on 9 December 1884 and the way in which this revision affected the structure and tone of the quartet as a whole. This draft confirms evidence in the autograph score that Verdi transposed a 61-bar passage from B to B♭ major during the final stages of composition, probably to suit the voice of Romilda Pantaleoni, who first sang the role of Desdemona. Despite this practical consideration, the author argues that the change also transforms, in a positive manner, some of the expressive implications of tonal associations within the opera.

Stylistic and Analytical Studies

828. Bergeron, Katherine. "How to Avoid Believing (While Reading Iago's 'Credo')." In *Reading Opera*, 184–99. Ed. by Arthur Groos and Roger Parker. Princeton: Princeton University Press, 1988. ISBN 0–691–09132–3. ML 2110 .R4 1988.

A textual and musical analysis of Iago's "Credo" from a semiotic point of view. "Signs" in text, music, and stage directions are unusually elusive and frustrate any attempt to arrive at a truly coherent reading.

829. Grace, Irwin. "An Analysis of the Dramatic Content of the Music of Verdi's *Otello*." Ed.D. dissertation, Teachers College, Columbia University, 1969. iii, 253 p.

Attempts to analyze how Verdi's music illuminates and depicts the drama in this opera. Devotes special attention to the dramatic role of music (focusing on the brindisi in Act I) the respective functions of recitative and aria (focusing on the opening of Act II), and the way in which the composer approached tonality in the opera (focusing on the storm scene in Act I). The author proposes that, at times, the music carries the entire weight of expression, rendering the words superfluous to understanding its meaning.

830. Lawton, David. "On the 'Bacio' Theme in *Otello*." *19th Century Music* 1 (1977–78): 211–20.

Analyzes the "bacio" theme, heard first at the end of the love duet in Act I from the standpoint of Schenkerian voice leading as a prolongation of an E_4^6 chord, which immediately before its resolution, gives prominent emphasis to a C_4^6 sonority. Lawton proposes that juxtaposition of the tonal areas of E, C, and Db in this theme and the surrounding passage portrays, in microcosm, the dramatic conflict among the various sides of Otello's personality: C Major is associated throughout the opera with his downfall, E Major with his greatness, and Db with his tender side. See item 495 for a somewhat different perspective on some of Lawton's ideas.

831. Noske, Frits. "*Otello*: Drama through Structure." In *The Signifier and the Signified* (item 488), 133–70.
Also published in *Essays on Music for Charles Warren Fox*, 14–47. Ed. by Jerald C. Graue. Rochester, N.Y.: Eastman School of Music, 1979. ISBN 0–9603186–0–7. ML 55 .F7 1979.

Argues that Verdi's opera is tightly woven together through a series of structural repetitions of musical material, primarily short motives. The second part of the article focuses on Verdi's musical characterizations of Iago, Desdemona, and Otello. The author proposes that while Iago is the central character of the plot, Otello is the central character in the drama.

832. Parker, Roger, and Matthew Brown. "'Ancora un bacio': Three Scenes from Verdi's *Otello*." *19th Century Music* 9 (1985–86): 50–61.

After a brief survey of recent analytical approaches to Verdi's music by authors such as Julian Budden, Frits Noske, and David Lawton, the authors present their own analytical commentary on three scenes from the opera. In the storm scene from Act I, the authors describe Verdi's use of diminished-seventh chords to create tonal ambiguity and his use of a Db diminished-seventh chord to lead toward tonal resolutions in E major. The love scene, while bearing a superficial resemblance to a *tempo d'attacco*, adagio, and *tempo di mezzo*, ultimately achieves coherence through a complex web of recurring harmonic and melodic gestures. Finally, the reminiscence of the "bacio" theme at the end of the final scene of Act IV achieves great dramatic force because it serves as a grand culmination to many layers of thematic and harmonic relationships carefully traversed throughout the opera. See also Harold Power's expansion of some of the authors' ideas in item 495.

833. Várnai, Péter P. "'. . . è sempre ugual . . .'" *Nuova rivista musicale italiana* 9 (1975): 205–18.

The second portion of this article offers an analysis of Iago's "Credo," focusing on ways in which Verdi creates a "negative" impression with his music.

834. Youens, Susan Lee. "The Quartet in Act II of Verdi's *Otello*." *The Opera Journal* 16/1 (1983): 2–15.

A detailed discussion of the quartet, emphasizing the ever-increasing intrusion of musical ideas previously associated with Iago as an ironic foil to the feelings of Otello and Desdemona.

Performance Practice, Staging, Scenography

835. Coe, Doug. "The Original Production Book for *Otello*: An Introduction." *19th Century Music* 2 (1978–79): 148–58.

A brief overview of the published *disposizione scenica* for *Otello*. The author points how an assessment of Verdi's intentions regarding the blocking of characters on stage and other stage directions can be extremely useful to modern producers.

836. Gualerzi, Giorgio. "*Otello*: The Legacy of Tamagno." *Opera* 38 (1987): 122–27.

Examines the performance history of *Otello* with respect to the title role. Verdi's music for the character of Otello, originally conceived for the voice of Francesco Tamagno, places unusual demands on the singers with its wide range and expressive demands. The author assesses the performance of some of the more significant interpreters of the role since the work's premiere.

837. Hepokoski, James A., and Mercedes Viale Ferrero. "*Otello*" *di Giuseppe Verdi. Musica e spettacolo.* Milan: Ricordi, 1990. 324 p. ISBN 88–7592–085–0. ML 410 .V4 H48 1990.

Hepokoski contributes a long and authoritative essay analyzing the history and significance of the *disposizione scenica* for the premiere performance (Milan, 1887), while Viale Ferrero's article investigates the scenography and costumes for the premiere at La Scala and for later performances at the Teatro Costanzi (Rome, 1887) and the Théâtre de l'Opéra (Paris, 1894). The volume contains complete facsimile reprintings of the original libretto and of the *disposizione scenica*. In addition, the book includes color reproductions of scenery sketches and costumes from these three early productions, as well as diagrams and engravings published in contemporary periodicals.

838. Maurel, Victor. *A propos de la mise en scène du drame lyrique "Otello": Étude précédée d'aperçus sur le théâtre chanté en 1887.* Rome: Imprimerie Editrice Romana, 1888. 183 p. ML 410 .V48 M450.

A fascinating study prepared by the singer who created the role of Iago. The author includes a short essay on the state of contemporary opera, short characterizations of each of the leading characters in the opera, and a description of the *mise-en-scène* for the original production.

   * Viale Ferrero, Mercedes. "Boito inventore di immagini sceniche: Rapporti significativi tra immagine poetica e immagine scenica." See item 713.

Performance History; Reception

839. "*Otello*," *dramma lirico in quattro atti, versi di Arrigo Boito, musica di Giuseppe Verdi: Giudizi della stampa italiana e straniera.* Milan: Ricordi, n.d. 199 p.

A conveniently anthologized set of reviews and articles issued after the premiere performance of the work. The small volume unfortunately lacks an index or table of contents, so individual reviews must be found by browsing.

RIGOLETTO

One of Verdi's most popular operas and an important turning point in his career, *Rigoletto* has also received much attention from scholars, particularly in the area of analysis. The published continuity draft (item 878) is Verdi's only complete draft for an opera that has been generally available to scholars until very recently.

Guides to the Work

840. Conati, Marcello. *"Rigoletto": Un'analisi drammatico-musicale*. Saggi Marsilio. Venice: Marsilio, 1992. x, 331 p. ISBN 88–317–5642–7. MT 100 .V52 C6 1992.

This volume, directed primarily to the non-Verdi specialist, provides a detailed history of the opera, an overview of its dramatic and musical organization, and a scene-by-scene descriptive analysis. The published libretto for the first performance is reproduced in its entirety; a useful synoptic table compares the plot and characters of *Rigoletto* to the original source of the story, Victor Hugo's *Le roi s'amuse*. Other useful features include the reproduction of twelve early reviews (1851–53) from contemporary periodicals, and a specialized bibliography about *Rigoletto*. The volume updates the author's earlier *"Rigoletto" di Giuseppe Verdi: Guida all'opera* (Milan: Mondadori, 1983); it lacks, however, the earlier volume's discography prepared by Mario Vicentini.

841. Csampai, Attila, and Dietmar Holland, eds. *Giuseppe Verdi, "Rigoletto": Texte, Materialien, Kommentare*. Rororo Opernbücher. Reinbek bei Hamburg: Rowohlt Taschenbuch Verlag, 1982. 267 p. ISBN 3–499–17487–1. ML 50 .V484 .R54 1982.

This illustrated guide includes a number of fine essays on the genesis of the opera and its relationship to Hugo's play, its place in Verdi's stylistic development, and its reception history. The libretto is reproduced in both Italian and a German translation by Christoph Schwandt. The volume concludes with a chronology, selective bibliography, and a discography of complete recordings.

842. Osborne, Charles. *"Rigoletto": A Guide to the Opera*. London: Barrie & Jenkins, 1979. 160 p. ISBN 0–214–20654–5.

In addition to a bilingual libretto (the English translation by the author), this volume contains a historical introduction to the opera, a synopsis of the plot and music, and a survey of performances and recordings. Written for the Verdi novice; does not incorporate recent scholarly research about the opera.

843. *Rigoletto. L'avant-scène opéra* 112/113 (September–October 1988). Paris: L'Avant-Scène, 192 p. ISSN 0764–2873. ML 5 .A9 v. 112–113.

Includes about a dozen essays examining the opera from historical and analytical points of view. Two items of particular interest are an article by Maria Teresa Muraro about Giuseppe Bertoja's scenography for the opera's premiere performance at La Fenice and an essay by Martin Chusid (item 1026) about his edition of *Rigoletto*, the first to be published in the new complete critical edition of Verdi's works. The libretto is presented in the original Italian with a modern French translation by Gilles De Van. The volume also includes a discography of complete recordings and individual arias or sections as well as tables listing the earliest performances of the opera in major centers, with more detailed information about performances in major houses up to the present. This information is updated in the second edition. The bibliography includes 125 items relating to the opera, Victor Hugo, and *Le roi s'amuse.*

344. *Rigoletto.* English National Opera Guides, 15. London: John Calder; New York: Riverrun, 1982. 80 p. ISBN 0–7145–3939–2. ML 50 .V484 R52 1982.

This guide contains a short history of the work, an essay on the "Timelessness of *Rigoletto*," an extensive descriptive analysis, and a selective discography and bibliography. The libretto is presented in Italian and an English translation by James Fenton.

345. Roccatagliati, Alessandro. *Invito all'opera "Rigoletto" di Giuseppe Verdi.* Milan: Mursia, 1991. 158 p. ML 410 .V4 R62 1991.

This opera guide provides a discussion of the history of the work, the genesis of the libretto, musical conventions, and reception. Also includes a full libretto and index of names.

Histories and General Studies

346. Chusid, Martin. "Notes on the Performance of *Rigoletto*." *Verdi Newsletter* 8 (November 1980): 3–6.

Discusses three examples of situations in which Verdi's manuscript clarifies performance issues relating to the opera. The Duke's first words as he enters the tavern at the beginning of Act III were originally "Tua sorella e del vino," but censors demanded a change to "Una stanza e del vino." Before the coda to "Caro nome," Verdi rewrote the cadence so that the melodic line does not resolve as Gilda sings twice "Gualtier Maldè," forging a stronger link to the beginning of the scene. Finally, Verdi clearly intended three on-stage orchestras to play dance music during the *Introduzione* to Act I; a note in the manuscript indicating that "these violins were removed" is not in Verdi's hand.

847. *Giuseppe Verdi nella casa di Rigoletto.* Issued by the Museo Teatrale alla Sca
     [Verona]: Cassa di Risparmio di Verona, Vicenza, e Belluno, [1977]. 46
     ML 141 .M237 V43.

     An exhibition catalogue containing significant iconographic material relati
     to early performances of the work. The catalog gives special attention to seve
     scenographic descriptions that correspond to actual sites in Mantua.

848. Lavagetto, Mario. *Un caso di censura: il "Rigoletto".* Contraddizioni. Mila
     Edizioni il Formichiere, 1979. 141 p. ML 410 .V4 L32.

     A fascinating study of how censorship affected both the genesis a
     performance history of *Rigoletto.* The author includes a scene-by-sce
     summary of changes made in the libretto during the formative stages of t
     opera, comparing Victor Hugo's original play, *Le roi s'amuse,* to the final versi
     of *Rigoletto* as well as to two intermediate versions, "La maledizione" and
     duca di Vendome" (the author hypothetically reconstructs the contents of t
     former). A later chapter provides a scene-by-scene comparison of *Rigoletto* wi
     three censored versions that were performed in Italy: *Viscardello, Clara di Per
     and *Lionello.*

849. Marchesi, Gustavo. "Gli anni del *Rigoletto.*" *Verdi: Bollettino dell'Istituto
     Studi Verdiani* 3 [No. 7, 8 and 9] (1969–82): 1–26, 849–75, 1517–4
     English and German translations of the article are found on pp. 367–41
     1151–95, 1914–40 (the final section is English only).

     A history of the genesis of *Rigoletto* organized around a collation of lette
     (mostly already published) from Verdi to various correspondents. Particu
     attention is given to the life of Charles III, Duke of Parma, which may ha
     contributed to Verdi's characterization of the Duke of Mantua.

850. Schmid, Patric. "Maddalena's Aria." *AIVS Newsletter* 5 (June 1978): 4–7.

     Discusses an aria for Maddalena that appears in a French edition of the vo
     score published by Escudier in late 1857 or early 1858. The music is identi
     to Verdi's song "Il poveretto," transposed from F to E major. The origins
     the aria remain uncertain, although it postdates the first French-langua
     performance in 1863. The author reproduces the music for the aria in
     entirety.

851. *Verdi: Bollettino dell'Istituto di Studi Verdiani,* 3. Parma: Istituto di Stu
     Verdiani, 1969–82. lxxxvii, 2113 p. ML 410 .V4 A5.

     Most articles in the this volume of the *Bollettino* concern *Rigoletto.* Topi
     include the history and genesis of the opera, its reception, and an extensi
     descriptive analysis by Guido Pannain. Articles are printed in Italian, Englis

and German; several of the most significant items concerning *Rigoletto* are listed separately as numbers 849, 854, 857, 864–66, 869, 872, 874, and 875. A final fascicle published in 1982 (111 p.) contains a catalogue of libretti and a bibliography compiled by Marcello Conati, a discography by Mario Vicentini, and an index for the entire vol. 3 of the *Bollettino*.

Dramaturgy; Studies of the Libretto

852. Donatelli, Bruna. "Les drames de Victor Hugo et les livrets d'opera italiens." In *Le rayonnement international de Victor Hugo*, 27–35. Ed. by Francis Claudon. New York: Peter Lang, 1989. ISBN 0–8204–0790–9. PQ 2300 .I58 1989.

Examines Verdi's and Piave's adaptation of *Le roi s'amuse* for *Rigoletto* in the context of Hugo's dramaturgy and linguistic style.

853. Edelman, Susanne Popper. "Rigoletto's Cryptic Aside: 'Marullo—Signore.'" *The Opera Journal* 18/2 (1985): 8–12.

Argues that Rigoletto's appeal to the "kind heart and soul" of Marullo, one of his daughter's abductors, has its roots in Hugo's play. There the character of Marot is based on the historical Clèment Marot (1496–1544), a poet and "man of the people," although he aspired to join ranks of nobility by currying favor with the king.

854. Guichard, Léon. "Victor Hugo e *Le roi s'amuse.*" *Verdi: Bollettino dell'Istituto di Studi Verdiani* 3 [No. 7] (1969): 57–88. English and German translations of the article are printed on pp. 412–65.

Examines the genesis of Hugo's play and assesses its significance within his *oeuvre* as a whole. A comparison of Hugo's play with Piave's adaptation for libretto of *Rigoletto* shows that the librettist removed all historical and geographical allusions and excised or reduced the epic or lyrical digressions. The faster-paced action of the opera has made it more popular, over time, than the original play.

855. Iotti, Gianni. "Le metamorfosi di Triboulet." In *Il sense del nonsenso: Scritti in memoria di Lynn Salkin Sbiroli*, 295–312. Ed. by Monique Streiff Moretti, Mireille Revol Cappelletti, and Odile Martinez. Collana di letterature moderne e contemporanee dell'Università di Perugia. Naples: Edizioni Scientifiche Italiane, 1994. ISBN 88–7104–976–4. PC 2026 .S3 S467 1995.

Compares ways in which Hugo and Verdi/Piave characterize the multi-faceted personality of Rigoletto (Triboulet in Hugo's original drama).

856. Lavagetto, Mario. "Quella porta, assassini, m'aprite." In *Opera & Libretto I*, 299–313. Studi di musica veneta. Florence: Olschki, 1990. ISBN 88–222–3825–7. ML 1700 .O655 1990.

A discussion of archetypal symbols in opera librettos, focusing on doors and their significance in *Rigoletto*.

*   Roccatagliati, Alessandro. "Drammaturgia romantica verdiana: *Luisa Miller* e *Rigoletto*." See item 436.

857. Vecchi, Giuseppe. "Il libretto." *Verdi: Bollettino dell'Istituto di Studi Verdiani* 3 [No. 8] (1973): 876–911. English and German translations are found on pp. 1196–1247.
      Reprinted in *Studi e ricerche sui libretti delle opere di Giuseppe Verdi* (item 444), 41–76.

A detailed study of the genesis of the libretto for *Rigoletto* and a descriptive summary of the story. The narrative includes many citations from Verdi's correspondence.

858. Wentzlaff-Eggebrecht, Harald. "*Le roi s'amuse* and *Rigoletto*: Zum Verhältnis zwischen romantischem Drama und dramatischer Oper." In *Romanische Literaturbeziehungen im 19. und 20. Jahrhundert: Festschrift für Franz Rauhut zum 85. Geburtstag*, 335–49. Ed. by Angel San Miguel, Richard Schwaderer, and Manfred Tietz. Tübingen: Gunter Narr Verlag, 1985. ISBN 3–87808–705–5. PN 813 .R66 1985.

Presents a detailed comparison of the dramaturgical organization of *Le roi s'amuse* and *Rigoletto* based, in part, on Victor Hugo's dramatic theories expressed in his *Preface to Cromwell*.

Studies of Compositional Process

*   Lawton, David. "Tonality and Drama in Verdi's Early Operas." See item 480.

859. Martin, George. "The Curse in *Rigoletto*." In *Aspects of Verdi* (item 244), 157–79.

Discusses Verdi's revisions of the "curse theme" in the continuity draft of *Rigoletto* and its function, in various guises, as a unifying feature of the opera. Includes a set of musical examples showing occurrences of the theme in both the continuity draft and the completed score.

*   Petrobelli, Pierluigi. "Osservazioni sul processo compositivo in Verdi." See item 452.

    *   Powers, Harold S. "One Halfstep at a Time: Tonal Transposition and 'Split Association' in Italian Opera." See item 453.

860.   Roncaglia, Gino. "L'abbozzo del *Rigoletto* di Verdi." *Rivista musicale italiana* 48 (1946): 112–29.

    A description of the sketches and continuity draft for *Rigoletto* (see item 878 for a description of the published facsimile edition) and a survey of some of the more notable changes made by the composer during the work's gestation. For a more systematic discussion of the sketches and continuity draft, see Martin Chusid's edition of the work in *The Works of Giuseppe Verdi*.

Stylistic and Analytical Studies

861.   Chusid, Martin. "The Tonality of *Rigoletto*." *Analyzing Opera: Verdi and Wagner* (item 454), 241–61.

    An earlier version of the article was published in *Report of the Eleventh Congress [of the International Musicological Society], Copenhagen 1972*, 1:325–36. Ed. by Henrik Glahn, Søren Sørensen, and Peter Ryom. Copenhagen: Wilhelm Hansen, 1974. 2 vols. ISBN 87–7455–026–8. ML 36 .I67 1972.

    The early version was later reprinted in *Verdi: Bollettino dell'Istituto di Studi Verdiani* 3 [No. 9] (1982): 1544–81.

    Proposes that Db major, the key of Monterone's curse and its fulfillment, is the central key of the entire opera. Acts I and II also emphasize Ab major and keys related to it. The more distant keys of D, B, and E major gradually become more important during the course of Act II and are significant in the tonal structure of Act III. In particular, Verdi uses specific tonalities to connect dramatic situations across the span of the entire opera and to underscore irony in the development of the plot.

    *   Della Seta, Fabrizio. "Il tempo della festa: Su due scene della *Traviata* e su altri luoghi verdiani." See item 934.

862.   Gallico, Claudio. "Ricognizione di *Rigoletto*." *Nuova rivista musicale italiana* 3 (1969): 855–901.

    Offers a scene-by-scene descriptive analysis of the music, emphasizing its dramatic division into two main parts with "Caro nome" as the center point. While the first part meticulously characterizes the main figures in the story, the second part relentlessly pursues the dramatic thread of the tragedy itself.

863.   Hudson, Elizabeth. "Gilda Seduced: A Tale Untold." *Cambridge Opera Journal* 4 (1992–93): 229–51.

Proposes that Verdi and Piave used the three narrative episodes in Act II to substitute, in a veiled manner, for the lack of an actual seduction scene between the Duke and Gilda, a scene that would have never been allowed by the censors. The author suggests that Gilda's Act I duets with her father, Rigoletto, and the Duke demonstrate her immaturity and powerlessness to act independently of the men. "Tutte le feste" marks a turning point, in which Gilda's expressive power deepens, suggesting something substantial has changed within her. The Duke's solo aria from the beginning of Act II ("Ella mi fu rapita") may be viewed as a key passage: as a replacement for the actual seduction scene, it presents his lyrical, suave "voice of seduction" which Gilda found irresistible, while the ensuing banal cabaletta ("Possente amor") shows his true colors as a shallow libertine.

864. Lawton, David. "Tonal Structure and Dramatic Action in *Rigoletto*." *Verdi: Bollettino dell'Istituto di Studi Verdiani* 3 [No. 9] (1982): 1559–81.

Proposes that in *Rigoletto,* Verdi achieved the most secure connection to date between tonal structure and drama. Two contrasting tonal areas, Db and D, are established during the curse scene in the *Introduzione;* these two tonal areas and their respective cycles of related keys dominate the tonal structure of the entire rest of the opera. The author shows that many significant structural articulations in the opera cut across the nominal division of the work into set pieces, establishing an unusually high degree of musical and dramatic continuity.

865. Leibowitz, René. "L'orchestration de *Rigoletto*." *Verdi: Bollettino dell'Istituto di Studi Verdiani* 3 [No. 8] (1973): 912–930. An Italian translation of this article is published on pp. 931–49; English and German translations are on pp. 1248–74.

Examines Verdi's orchestration in selected passages from the opera. The author establishes that Verdi effectively uses a large number of imaginative orchestral effects, in conjunction with other aspects of musical style, to create particular moods for dramatic situations.

866. Osthoff, Wolfgang. "Musikalische Züge der Gilda in Verdis *Rigoletto*." *Verdi: Bollettino dell'Istituto di Studi Verdiani* 3 [No. 8] (1973): 950–79. English and Italian translations are printed on pp. 1275–1314.

Verdi shows the changing character of Gilda by utilizing different musical means to portray her in each act of *Rigoletto*. The choice of E major and the use of two flutes in "Caro nome," drawing on traditions that go back to Mozart, evoke a pastoral aura with an individual at peace with surrounding nature. In "Tutte le feste al tempio," Verdi switches to E minor and introduces the plaintive sound of the oboe to establish Gilda's maturation, through suffering, into a more subtle and real human individual. In Act III, the exotic keys of Db major and minor and ethereal orchestral effects underscore Gilda's self-sacrifice and subsequent transfiguration, foreshadowing later passages in the *Requiem* and the *Pezzi sacri.*

867. ———. "Verdis musikalische Vorstellung in der Szene III,4 des *Rigoletto*." *Nuove prospettive nella ricerca verdiana* (item 231), 57–73.

Proposes that Verdi uses the effect of organ-grinder music in part of this scene to invoke images of beggarly existence, withdrawal from society, and melancholy monotony.

868. Petrobelli, Pierluigi. "Verdi e il *Don Giovanni*: Osservazioni sulla scena iniziale del *Rigoletto*." *Atti 1* (item 224), 232–46.
English translation by Roger Parker. "Verdi and *Don Giovanni*: On the Opening Scene of *Rigoletto*." In *Music in the Theater: Essays on Verdi and Other Composers* (item 378), 34–37.

Demonstrates how Verdi's reference to the ballroom scene in Mozart's *Don Giovanni* at the beginning of *Rigoletto* establishes the moral atmosphere of the plot and the promiscuous character of the Duke. In addition to the structural resemblance between the two scenes, two of Verdi's dances refer to Mozart's music, particularly the Minuetto, which he notated in unusual detail in the continuity draft.

869. Zecchi, Adone. "Cori e corifei nel *Rigoletto*." *Verdi: Bollettino dell'Istituto di Studi Verdiani* 3 [No. 7] (1969): 124–46. English and German translations are provided on pp. 510–44.

A descriptive analysis of choral scenes in *Rigoletto*, including those merged with solo numbers. The vocalises of the male chorus during the tempest scene of Act III emerge as an unprecedented and particularly effective dramatic/musical device.

Performance Practice, Staging, Scenography

870. Mauceri, John. "*Rigoletto* for the 21st Century." *Opera* 36 (1985): 1135–44.

Discusses various ways in which late nineteenth- and early twentieth-century traditions in areas of dynamics, articulation, and tempo have departed from Verdi's original intentions. The author presents a particularly interesting analysis of metronome markings in *Rigoletto*. Although they do not appear in the autograph manuscript, metronome markings were probably inserted by the composer in early published sources or at least approved by him. Mauceri argues that the tempo marking of 66 beats per minute (although linked to different descriptive tempo indications) is an important structural element that recurs at key moments in the opera. Several other specific metronome markings also occur in parallel fashion. The article includes a synoptic chart showing metronome markings for the entire opera.

871. Venius, Abraham, and John Clarke Adams. "*Rigoletto as Drama*." *Atti 3* (item 226), 464–94.

Offers suggestions for performing *Rigoletto* based on the composer's ideas for the original performance and on the author's analysis of the drama and the musical score. One of the most interesting aspects of this article is its survey of performance tradition for this opera from its premiere through modern times.

872. Muraro, Maria Teresa. "Giuseppe Bertoja e le scene per la prima di *Rigoletto* alla Fenice." *Verdi: Bollettino dell'Istituto di Studi Verdiani* 3 [No. 9] (1982): 1582–87. An English translation of the article appears on pp. 1982–87.

Describes the influence of Verdi's unconventional ideas about staging and iconography on Giuseppe Bertoja's stage designs for the premiere performance of *Rigoletto*. The article includes eight illustrations, including some sketches by Bertoja and reproductions of contemporary engravings.

Editions

*   Chusid, Martin. "Editing Rigoletto." See item 1026.

Performance History; Reception

873. Conati, Marcello. "Saggio di cronologia delle prime rappresentazioni di *Rigoletto*." *Verdi: Bollettino dell'Istituto di Studi Verdiani* 3 [No. 9] (1982): 1853–1912.

Provides information about locations, dates, and casts for "first" performances of *Rigoletto* throughout the world for a period of ten years, starting with its premiere in March 1851. For the years from March 1861 through 1977, the author has included a more selective list of performances. The article includes a useful index of locations.

874. Della Corte, Andrea. "Saggio di bibliografia delle critiche al *Rigoletto*." Ed. and completed by Marcello Conati. *Verdi: Bollettino dell'Istituto di Studi Verdiani* 3 [No. 9] (1982): 1634–1772.

A selection of citations from periodicals and books, ranging from Verdi's times to the present, assessing *Rigoletto*. Most entries contain short quotations from the original sources.

875. Gualerzi, Giorgio. "Il cammino dell'opera." *Verdi: Bollettino dell'Istituto di Studi Verdiani* 3 [No. 7, 8, and 9] (1969–82): 147–76, 980–1014, 1588–1633. English and German translations of the article are printed on pp. 545–98, 1315–77, 1988–2034 (the final section is in English only).

A comprehensive study of the work's reception from its first performances through the mid-twentieth century. The author focuses his commentary on performers who realized the principal roles in the opera, drawing on letters and reviews published in contemporary periodicals.

876. Günther, Ursula. "*Rigoletto* à Paris." In *L'opera tra Venezia e Parigi*, 269–314. Ed. by Maria Teresa Muraro. Studi di musica veneta, 14. Florence: Olschki, 1988. ISBN 88–222–3600–9. ML 1720 .O63 1988.

Examines reasons why *Rigoletto* was not performed in Paris until 1857, nearly six years after its premiere. In part, the delay can be attributed to the severe criticism directed at Hugo's play *Le roi s'amuse* in Paris. More importantly, Verdi attempted to hinder performances of his works at the Théâtre-Italien because Torribio Calzado, the director from 1855 to 1860, had violated conditions of a contract stipulating the use of specific performers for a production of *Il trovatore*. The article provides documentation regarding Verdi's attempt to obtain legal redress and offers much interesting information about the issue of international copyright during the mid-nineteenth century. The author concludes by examining the reception of *Rigoletto* at its early performances in Paris (Théâtre-Italien, 1857; Théâtre-Lyrique, 1863; Théâtre de l'Opéra, 1885). The article includes a dozen illustrations, showing primarily costumes and scenery from these early productions and an appendix, which reproduces a number of contracts and other legal documents.

Miscellaneous

877. Porter, Andrew. "Translating *Rigoletto*." *Verdi Newsletter* 8 (November 1980): 6–11.

The author discusses the methodology behind his singing translation of *Rigoletto* and defends the practice of performing opera in translation.

878. *L'abbozzo del "Rigoletto" di Giuseppe Verdi.* Introduction by Carlo Gatti. Edizione fuori commercio a cura del Ministero della Cultura Popolare, 1951. 60 p.
 Republished as *"Rigoletto": Ristampa anastatica dell'abbozzo autografo.* Bologna: Forni, 1978. 56 p.

Presents a facsimile reproduction of Verdi's continuity draft for *Rigoletto*. Until very recently, this was the only complete continuity draft of any of Verdi's operas that had been commercially published; other composing manuscripts have not even been available for systematic study, with the recent exceptions of *Stiffelio* and *La traviata* (see items 910 and 940).

SIMON BOCCANEGRA

Verdi's large-scale revision of the work late in his life, made after a period of more than two decades, has led to a large number of interesting comparative studies between the early and late versions. Although conventional wisdom tends to regard the later version as superior, several studies have argued that the first version contained some unusual and forward-looking characteristics.

Guides to the Work

879. *Simon Boccanegra. L'avant-scène opéra* 19 (January/February 1979). Paris: L'Avant-Scène, 1979. 137 p. ISSN 0395–0670. MT 95 .A94 no. 9.
2nd ed. Paris: Société Premières Loges, 1994. 124 p. ISSN 0764–2873.

Two essays consider the relationship of Verdi's revision of the work to the contemporary political situation in Italy and the relation of fathers and daughters in Verdi's dramaturgy. The libretto for the revised version is presented in the original Italian with a modern French translation by Gilles De Van. The volume includes a discography of complete recordings and individual arias or sections accompanied by a prose essay. It also features tables listing the earliest performances of the opera in major centers, with more detailed information about performances in major houses up to the present (this information is updated in the second edition). The bibliography includes complete editions and arrangements of individual numbers from the opera, librettos, and secondary literature dealing with *Simon Boccanegra*.

880. *Simon Boccanegra.* English National Opera Guides, 32. London: John Calder; New York: Riverrun, 1985. 96 p. ISBN 0–7145–4064–1. ML 50 .V484 S5.

This guide contains an introductory essay evaluating the opera's place in Verdi's career, a descriptive analysis of the opera, and an essay describing the work's genesis. The volume reproduces the 1881 version of the libretto in Italian with a performing English translation by James Fenton; in addition, passages from the 1857 version that were altered or deleted are presented in footnotes and an appendix, with literal English translations by Sylvia Mulcahy.

Histories and General Studies

881. Bogianckino, Massimo. "*Simon Boccanegra*: Il testo in prosa, i libretti, le prime esecuzioni delle due versioni al Teatro alla Scala e la critica milanese del tempo." *Annali della Facoltà di Lettere e Filosofia della Università degli Studi di Perugia* 16 (1976–77): 295–359.

Describes differences between Piave's prose draft of *Simon Boccanegra* and the two versions of the libretto, concluding that the conciseness and poetic language required by both librettos mar some of the subtleties of the original story. While most critics agree that Verdi's 1881 revision is superior to the original version, the author discusses several passages that he feels were more effective in the early version. The final portion of the article describes the mixed reception of both versions of the opera as seen in the Milanese press. An appendix provides a transcription of Piave's prose draft (albeit with a few errors).

* Busch, Hans, ed. and trans. *Verdi's "Otello" and "Simon Boccanegra" (revised version) in Letters and Documents.* See item 99 above.

882. Conati, Marcello. *Il "Simon Boccanegra" di Verdi a Reggio Emilia (1857): Storia documentata; Alcune varianti alla prima edizione dell'opera.* Reggio Emilia: Teatro Municipale "Romolo Valli," 1984. 129 p. ML 410 .V48 C743 S6 1984.

An examination, based on letters and other documents, of the events leading to the performance of *Simon* in Reggio Emilia and its reception there. This performance, which followed shortly after its premiere in Venice, is particularly significant because the composer made substantial revisions for it. The author examines these in some detail. Appendices reproduce some previously unpublished correspondence of Verdi.

883. Detels, Claire Janice. "Giuseppe Verdi's *Simon Boccanegra*: A Comparison of the 1857 and 1881 Versions." Ph.D. dissertation, University of Washington, 1982. vi, 221 p.
Parts of the dissertation emphasizing the history of the opera were published in abridged form in two short articles. "*Simon Boccanegra*: Notes on the 1857 Version." *The Opera Journal* 18/4 (1985): 12–20 and "*Simon Boccanegra*: The Making of the 1881 Revision." *The Opera Journal* 19/1 (1986): 16–28.

Following a brief historical introduction, the author compares and contrasts the two versions of the opera in the areas of libretto, form, vocal style, and orchestral accompaniment. While Boito and Verdi sought to develop striking new situations and characterizations in the revision, the author concludes that they did not strive for consistency within the plot nor faithfulness to the original play by García Gutiérrez. With respect to the music, the author argues that the revision shows greater subtlety of approach, with greater attention to unification through tonal areas, melodic ideas, and textures.

884. Noske, Frits R. "*Simon Boccanegra*: One Plot, Two Dramas." In *The Signifier and the Signified* (item 488), 215–40.

Begins by examining the principal differences between the two versions of *Simon Boccanegra*. The author argues that while they share the same plot (or course of events), Verdi's substantial revision in characterization (primarily due to individuals' interaction with other characters) engenders an entirely different drama (interrelationship of action and emotion) in the revised version. The essay includes a useful tabular comparison of the two versions. An appendix provides English translations by Harold Lindberg of correspondence between Verdi and Boito concerning the revision of *Simon Boccanegra*, although many readers will prefer to turn to the recently published complete correspondence of Verdi and Boito (item 46), available in both Italian and English. This correspondence is also available in less reliable form in item 99.

885.   Osthoff, Wolfgang. "Die beiden *Boccanegra*-Fassungen und der Beginn von Verdis Spätwerk." *Analecta musicologica* 1 (1963): 70–89.

Proposes that the stylistic changes in Verdi's reworking of *Simon Boccanegra* mark the true beginning of his late style. An examination of specific musical examples reveals significant changes in the composer's approach to phrase construction, melody, rhythm, harmony, and a tightening of musical and dramatic interconnections. The author proposes that the revised work leaves the realm of conventional tragic opera and approaches a dramatic chronicle somewhat similar to Musorgsky's *Boris Godunov*.

Dramaturgy and Studies of the Libretto

886.   Gerhartz, Leo Karl. "Spiele, die Träumen vom Menschen nachhängen . . . : Das dramaturgische Vokabular des Verdischen Operntyps, entschlüsselt am 'Prologo' des *Simon Boccanegra*." In *Giuseppe Verdi: Musik-Konzepte* 10 (item 423): 27–37.

Discusses the prologue to *Simon Boccanegra* as a concise distillation of the composer's aesthetic principles. Proposes that Verdi's primary concern was the immediate establishment of a *tinta* that permeates all subsequent material in the opera.

887.   Goldin, Daniela. "Il *Simon Boccanegra* da Piave a Boito e la drammaturgia verdiana." In *La vera Fenice*, 283–334. Turin: Einaudi, 1985. ISBN 88–06–57398–5. ML 2110 .G64 1985.

A detailed and important study of dramaturgical principles underlying the libretto for both versions of *Simon Boccanegra*. The author suggests that many of the literary qualities of García Gutiérrez's play—particularly images and metaphors—provided a strong sense of "parola scenica" for the composer and forcefully influenced his conception of the original libretto for the work. Piave, in turn, reacted to the composer's suggestions by adopting a parsimony of metrical forms that differed sharply from his earlier work. The author argues that Verdi's elimination of the character of Lorenzo Buchetto substantially weakens the political overtones of the play and also removes the character who provides the most comic relief. She further suggests that Verdi was prompted to revise the work in later life by reading Petrarch's portrayal of the Genoese doge in the then recently republished *Lettere familiari* and asserts that the composer, not Boito, exerted the strongest influence on the shape of the revised libretto. For a closely related study dealing with Petrarch's influence on Verdi, see Leonardo Pinzauti's article cross-listed immediately below.

* Pinzauti, Leonardo. "Le due 'stupende lettere' del Petrarca e il romanticismo di Giuseppe Verdi." See item 431.

888. Puccini, Dario. "Il *Simon Boccanegra* di Antonio García Gutiérrez e l'opera di Giuseppe Verdi." *Studi verdiani* 3 (1985): 120–30.

Describes the main differences in plot and mood between the original play *Simón Boccanegra* by García Gutiérrez and Piave's adaptation of it as a libretto, including subsequent alterations by Arrigo Boito for the revised version of the opera. Piave eliminated the character of Lorenzino Buchetto, a significant character who also represented the rich aristocracy as a class type, as well as several particularly felicitous scenes from the original play. Boito's revisions tend to clarify key situations and the general plot of the drama.

889. Walker, Frank. "Verdi, Giuseppe Montanelli and the Libretto of *Simon Boccanegra*." *Verdi: Bollettino dell'Istituto di Studi Verdiani* 1 [No. 3] (1960): 1373–90. Italian and German translations are published on pp. 1767–89.

Correspondence between Verdi and Giuseppe Montanelli, a writer and political activist living in exile in Paris, shows that Montanelli revised parts of the libretto to the original version of *Simon Boccanegra* during the winter of 1856–57. The article reproduces several letters written by Montanelli (misattributed to Antonio Somma in Abbiati's biography), passages from the libretto showing revisions, as well as an extensive reply to the first letter from Verdi. These letters clarify comments by the composer to Piave in an undated letter referring to "necessary changes" in the *Boccanegra* libretto. The article concludes with a transcription of a letter from Verdi to Clara Maffei (cited with many errors in the *Copialettere*) that contains the only other known reference by Verdi to Montanelli.

890. Schweikert, Uwe. "'Das Wahre erfinden': Musikalische Dramaturgie in Verdis *Simon Boccanegra*." In *Oper und Operntext*, 81–93. Ed. by Jens Malte Fischer. Reihe Siegen: Beiträge zur Literatur- und Sprachwissenschaft, 60.

Heidelberg: Carl Winter Universitätsverlag, 1985. ISBN 3–533–03665–0 (cloth); 3–533–03664–2 (paper). ML 2110 .O645 1985.

Discusses Verdi's concentrated use of musical gestures and symbols, focusing on the way in which he uses them to underscore the dramaturgy of the opera.

891. Vecchi, Giuseppe. "Sulla travagliata genesi del libretto del *Simon Boccanegra*." *Quadrivium: Studi di filologia e musicologia* 20 (1979): 179–92.
Reprinted in *Studi e ricerche sui libretti delle opere di Giuseppe Verdi* (item 444), 179–92.

Suggests that the libretto to *Simon Boccanegra* shows several different levels of linguistic style due to its long and relatively troubled gestation. In particular Vecchi argues that the revisions made by Giuseppe Montanelli tend toward a more archaic style that at times mars the smooth flow of the text.

Studies of Compositional Process

* Powers, Harold S. "One Halfstep at a Time: Tonal Transposition and 'Split Association' in Italian Opera." See item 453.

Stylistic and Analytical Studies

892. Basevi, Abramo. "*Simon Boccanegra*" (chapter 19 of *Studio sulle opere di G. Verdi* [item 460]). Trans. by Walter Grauberg. Intro. by Ian Bent. In *Music Analysis in the Nineteenth Century*. Vol. 2: *Hermeneutic Approaches*, 195–212. Ed. by Ian Bent. Cambridge Readings in the Literature of Music. Cambridge: Cambridge University Press, 1994. ISBN 0–521–46183–9. MT 90 .M88 1994.

While Verdi enthusiasts await the publication of Basevi's entire volume in English translation (see item 460), this chapter on *Simon Boccanegra* will provide English-speaking readers with a good example of his style and approach. This chapter is particularly interesting, since the original version of *Simon* was the penultimate opera that Basevi examined in his *Studio*. He is critical of the composer's relaxation of traditional formal structure in parts of the opera and the increasing dominance of *parlante* texture. Basevei suggested that both of these trends betrayed the influence of Wagner's aesthetic ideas.

* Bates, Carol N. "Verdi's *Les vêpres siciliennes* (1855) and *Simon Boccanegra* (1857)." See item 970.

893. Budden, Julian. "The Vocal and Dramatic Characterization of Jacopo Fiesco." *Studi verdiani* 10 (1994–95): 67–75.

Begins by examining Verdi's conception of the role of Fiesco in light of the treatment of the "basso cantante" in earlier Italian operatic tradition and in Verdi's prior works. While the vocal writing for Fiesco and Simone shares many characteristics, Verdi introduces some subtle distinctions between bass (Fiesco) and baritone (Simone) that underscores the dramatic development of the two characters. In the second section of the article, Budden examines the way in which Verdi altered Fiesco's part when he revised the opera. He suggests that the musical changes makes the characterization even stronger than in the original version.

894. Cone, Edward T. "On the Road to *Otello*: Tonality and Structure in *Simon Boccanegra*." *Studi verdiani* 1 (1982): 72–98.

Proposes that clarification and reinforcement of tonal unification around a circle of keys a third apart (E–C–Ab) was one of Verdi's chief concerns in the revision of *Simon Boccanegra*. The author's analytical comments focus on the way in which harmonic movement in the revised version underscores dramatic development.

895. Kerman, Joseph. "Lyric Form and Flexibility in *Simon Boccanegra*." *Studi verdiani* 1 (1982): 47–62.

In *Simon Boccanegra*, Verdi largely abandoned the four-phrase, sixteen-bar lyric prototype commonly found in his earlier operas in favor of a broader, more extended construction typically based on lyric units of three phrases and a large ABA form. The composer had begun to experiment with this more flexible approach in *Les vêpres siciliennes* and his ideas reached full fruition in *Un ballo in maschera*. The melodic style in these operas is less lyrical, focusing greater attention on other musical elements. Kerman also suggests that Verdi was searching for a musical style in *Simon* that would be appropriate for his intended composition of *Re Lear* and that his dissatisfaction with the earlier opera may have contributed to his decision not to compose the latter.

896. Powers, Harold. "*Simon Boccanegra* I.10–12: A Generic-Genetic Analysis of the Council Chamber Scene." *19th Century Music* 13 (1989–90): 101–28. Earlier version published in *Atti del XIV Congresso della Società Internazionale di Musicologia: Trasmissione e recezione delle forme di cultura musicale*, 3: 407–41. Ed. by Angelo Pompilio, Donatella Restani, Lorenzo Bianconi, and F. Alberto Gallo. Turin: Edizioni di Torino, 1990. 3 vols. ISBN 88–7063–070–6.

When he revised *Simon Boccanegra*, Verdi modified the prototypical formal structure of the Council Chamber scene for a new Act I by eliminating the final stretta, an approach he had used in five other operas ranging from *Luisa Miller* to *Falstaff*. The author describes the relationship of the revised scene to these parallel structures, pointing out that its shape most closely resembles the Act III finale to *Otello*, composed just prior to it. The main portion of the study makes a generic comparison of the 1857 Act I finale with its replacement and considers in detail the "genetic" process of revision leading from the original version to the definitive form of the new finale. Appendices provide a side by side outline of the two finales, a chronological summary of correspondence and other documents relating to the composition of the Council Chamber scene, and an informative summary of Verdi's use of the term "parola scenica" in his correspondence.

897.   Sopart, Andreas. *Giuseppe Verdis "Simon Boccanegra" (1857 und 1881): Eine musikalisch-dramaturgische Analyse.* Analecta musicologica, 26. Laaber: Laaber-Verlag, 1988. xiv, 213 p. ISBN 3–89007–138–4. MT 100 .V525 S6 1988.

This substantial study, a revision of the author's doctoral dissertation, provides a detailed comparison of the opera's two versions. The author considers the prologue and each act individually, then discusses issues relating to the dramaturgy of the entire work. The volume contains a bibliography of 63 items.

898.   Tanenbaum, Faun Stacy. "Tonal Identity in *Simon Boccanegra.*" *Verdi Newsletter* 13 (1985): 20–29.

Argues from a Schenkerian perspective that Verdi's revision of *Simon* shows an emphasis on F$\sharp$ as a tonality, a consonant tone within a harmony, and an enharmonic entity.

899.   Várnai, Péter Pál. "Paolo Albiani: Il cammino di un personaggio." *Studi verdiani* 1 (1982): 63–71.

Examines Verdi's musical characterization of Paolo Albiani as a "mascalzone dei meno mascalzoni" ("scoundrel among lesser scoundrels.")

Performance Practice, Staging, Scenography

900.   Cordell, Albert O. "The Orchestration of Verdi: A Study of the Growth of Verdi's Orchestral Technique as Reflected in the Two Versions of *Simon Boccanegra.*" Ph.D. dissertation, Catholic University of America, 1991. xxii, 291 p.

Examines the development of Verdi's orchestration through a section-by-section comparison of the two versions of *Simon Boccanegra*. In addition, the dissertation contains much information regarding Verdi's orchestration in his other operas. The introductory chapter, entitled "Instruments, Orchestras, and Orchestration in Nineteenth-Century Italy," provides an especially useful overview; a later chapter discusses orchestral devices used in *Simon Boccanegra* that occur in other operas. The volume also contains helpful appendices. One lists for each opera the type of instrumental introduction ("Overture," "Prelude," "Introduction," etc.); another provides the orchestration for each of Verdi's operas.

901. Conati, Marcello, and Natalia Grilli. *"Simon Boccanegra" di Giuseppe Verdi. Musica e spettacolo.* Milan: Ricordi, 1993. 263 p. ISBN 88–7592–359–0. ML 410 .V4 C675 1993.

Major essays by each of the authors provide the most detailed and authoritative analyses available regarding the staging, scenography, and costumes for the premiere and important later performances of both versions of the opera. The volume contains facsimile reprintings of the original librettos for the first performances (Venice, 1857; Milan, 1881) and the extremely rare *disposizione scenica* for the premiere of the revised version. In addition, the book contains color reproductions of scenery sketches and costumes from many important early productions as well as engravings published in contemporary periodicals.

STIFFELIO / AROLDO

Scholars have devoted considerable attention to these operas, primarily because Verdi's thorough revision of the earlier *Stiffelio* affords a rich opportunity to examine ideas about compositional process. Very recently, all extant compositional documents for this work have been made available to scholars (see items 910 and 911), the first time all such materials for any of Verdi's operas have been available for study.

Histories and General Studies

902. Medici, Mario and Marcello Pavarani, eds. *Stiffelio.* Quaderni dell'Istituto di Studi Verdiani, 3. Parma: [Istituto di Studi Verdiani], 1968. 157 p. + 5 p. plates. ML 410 .V4 A48 vol. 3.

A commemorative booklet, issued in connection with a performance of the opera at the Teatro Regio in Parma on 26 December 1968. More than any other volume in this series, the format of this Quaderno resembles that of the Institute's *Bollettini*, although less expansive. Individual essays are listed below as numbers 905, 906, 913, 916, 920, and 921.

* *Tornando a "Stiffelio": Popolarità, rifacimenti, messinscena, effettismo e altre "cure" nella drammaturgia del Verdi romantico.* See item 234.

903. Shrader, Steven W. "Verdi, *Aroldo*, and Music Drama." *Verdi Newsletter* 12 (1984): 8–18.

The manuscript libretto of *Aroldo* contains elaborate annotations and entire inserted pages in the composer's hand. Particularly in Act I, Verdi's own text provides the special background for the unusually fluid musical mixture of recitative, arioso, and chorus that effectively conveys the dramatic development. In this way, Verdi arrived at an ideal of music drama that was similar to ideas formulated during the same period by Richard Wagner.

Dramaturgy; Studies of the Libretto

904. Ascari, Diano Dionisi. "Da *Stiffelio* a *Guglielmo Wellingrode*: Gli inverventi della censura." In *Tornando a "Stiffelio"* a "Stiffelio" (item 234), 129–39.

Describes several layers of censorship in the libretto for *Stiffelio*. Piave, who carefully avoided or diluted potentially questionable passages in preparing the libretto, worked from an expurgated Italian translation of Souvestre's *Le pasteur* by Gaetano Vestri rather than the original play. The police at Trieste demanded changes before the premiere of the work; divergent librettos printed for the premiere show that last-minute changes were demanded even after the preliminary approval. An anonymous librettist substantially rewrote much of the drama under the title *Guglielmo Wellingrode* in order to satisfy censors for an 1851 performance at the Teatro Apollo in Rome.

905. Ludwig, Hellmut. "La fonte letteraria: *Le pasteur, ou L'evangile et le Foyer*." In *Stiffelio* (item 902), 9–20.

Discusses the history of the play by Souvestre and Bourgeois, which appears to have had much greater success on Italian stages than on French ones. The author concludes that the play's protagonist was probably modelled after Michael Stifel, a preacher active at the time of Martin Luther.

906. Marchesi, Gustavo. "Il libretto." In *Stiffelio* (item 902), 21–36.

A detailed discussion of the libretto's organization, emphasizing the development of each of the main characters.

907. Natoli, Salvatore. "A proposito di *Stiffelio*; su Verdi e l'idea di teatro: Digressioni d'amatore." In *Tornando a "Stiffelio"* (item 234), 69–88.

Argues that *Stiffelio* was an important turning point in Verdi's conception of dramaturgy, particularly in his complex and sophisticated characterization of the protagonists. In turn, the composer's reevaluation of dramatic approach during this period led him to alter aspects of his musical style.

908. Sala, Emilio. "Tra *mélodrame* e dramma borghese: Dal *Pasteur* di Souvestre-Bourgeois allo *Stiffelio* di Verdi-Piave." In *Tornando a "Stiffelio"* (item 234), 97–106.

An important historical study of the literary sources for *Stiffelio* including the little-circulated romance by Emile Souvestre; its adaptation for the stage by the author and Eugène Bourgeois, in which the story acquired attributes of the popular *mélodrame*; and Piave's and Verdi's reformulation of the latter part of the play as a libretto.

Studies of Compositional Process

909. Chusid, Martin. "Apropos *Aroldo*, *Stiffelio*, and *Le pasteur*, with a List of 19th-Century Performances of *Aroldo*." In *Tornando a "Stiffelio"* (item 234), 281–303.

    The article is reprinted (with one minor addition to an appendix) in the *Verdi Newsletter* 14 (1986): 15–28.

    Argues that many dramatic weaknesses in the story of *Stiffelio* come directly from its model, *Le pasteur*. Contrariwise, a complete draft of the libretto for *Aroldo* in Piave's hand, with notes and additions by Verdi, suggests that none of the changes for which Verdi was responsible come from the original play. The author's main focus is Mina's *scena ed aria* at the beginning of Act II. Comparing the libretto sketch to both the original version in *Stiffelio* and the final version of *Aroldo* demonstrates the composer's interest in improving dramatic consistency. Consideration of all known nineteenth-century stagings of *Stiffelio* (including several missing in item 920) and *Aroldo* contradicts the often-repeated notion that performances of the works were few and unsuccessful. Appendices to the article provide important documentation regarding the performance history of *Aroldo*. Appendix A lists librettos in the AIVS Archive for nineteenth-century performances. Appendix B lists other nineteenth-century performances of *Aroldo*. Both include publication and cast information if known. Appendix C provides a chronological summary of all 88 performances.

910. Gossett, Philip. "New Sources for *Stiffelio*: A Preliminary Report." *Cambridge Opera Journal* 5 (1993): 199–222.

    Reprinted in *Verdi's Middle Period, 1849–1859: Source Studies, Analysis, and Performance Practice* (item 235), 19–43.

    It has been difficult to study Verdi's compositional process in *Stiffelio* because the composer cannibalized his original score when he reworked the material into *Aroldo*. Autograph musical materials at Sant'Agata relating to *Stiffelio* were released to scholars for the first time in 1992. The author, who studied the materials with Pierluigi Petrobelli, found most of the pages that Verdi removed from the autograph score of *Stiffelio*. In addition, they were able to examine the composer's continuity draft and sketch fragments for *Stiffelio* and the newly composed sections of *Aroldo*. The author briefly discusses two issues raised by these newly available sketches. First, Verdi sketched a number of pieces a whole or half-step higher than their final version in the full score, suggesting that vocal ranges of performers played a key role in the composer's decisions about tonal structure. Second, the composer frequently sketched multiple versions of cabaletta themes, suggesting that these sections posed particular difficulties in establishing a satisfactory dramatic design. Two or three sketches are related to Verdi's next opera, *Rigoletto*, showing that he was already thinking about it while he was composing *Stiffelio*. One, an alternative cabaletta theme for Lina's aria, "Dunque perdere volete," contains the essence of what would become Gilda's famous "Caro nome" in *Rigoletto*. Gossett provides tables detailing the structure of the *Aroldo* autograph and its relationship to the original manuscript for *Stiffelio*; the reconstructed autograph of *Stiffelio*, including the material found at Sant'Agata; and a description of the sketch material for *Stiffelio*. The article also contains a brief overview of known sketch material by Verdi in other locations.

911. Hansell, Kathleen Kuzmick. "Compositional Techniques in *Stiffelio*: Reading the Autograph Sources." In *Verdi's Middle Period, 1849–1859: Source Studies, Analysis, and Performance Practice* (item 235), 45–97.

After surveying *Stiffelio*'s progressive features and the reactions of Verdi's contemporaries to them, the author describes the physical format of the newly available continuity draft and sketches for *Stiffelio* and what this material reveals about the composer's basic working method. The main portion of the article examines in detail Verdi's compositional process in Lina's *Scena e Preghiera* (No. 3), in which the composer made substantial revisions after trying out ideas in two early drafts; Lina and Stankar's *Scena e Duetto* (No. 4), in which the continuity draft provides insights into the opening passage, which Verdi later excised from the autograph manuscript when making revisions for *Aroldo*; and the *Preghiera e Finale Ultimo* (No. 10), for which the continuity draft makes available for the first time the original uncensored version of the controversial text and in which Verdi worked out organizational problems in at least three drafts before attempting to write the skeleton score. Hansell provides parallel transcriptions of significant passages, lining up successive versions to facilitate comparison by the reader. Among other things, the author demonstrates that Verdi revised the opening and closing sections of a number more frequently than the middle section, most often to change their relative weight in the piece and to make the phrase structure less regular.

Stylistic and Analytical Studies

912. Budden, Julian. "Differences in Musical Language Between *Stiffelio* and *Aroldo*." In *Tornando a "Stiffelio"* (item 234), 273–280.

Most of the new music composed for *Aroldo* has a specific dramatic purpose. Although *Stiffelio* shows greater musical and dramatic consistency than *Aroldo*, Verdi's use of a more straightforward plot in *Aroldo* allowed him to utilize a more complex degree of musical development and to provide greater psychological insight into the development of individual characters.

913. Celletti, Rodolfo. "La vocalità dello *Stiffelio*." In *Stiffelio* (item 902), 74–87.

A study of the vocal writing for each of the major characters in the opera and its relationship to the singers who first created the roles.

914. Conati, Marcello. "'E quasi si direbbe prosa strumentata' (L'aria 'a due' nello *Stiffelio*)." In *Tornando a "Stiffelio"* (item 234), 243–63.

A close examination Verdi's departure unconventional treatment of Stiffelio's aria, or "quasi-duet," beginning "Vidi dovunque gemere" (Act I) and, to a lesser extent, the scena e duetto of Lina and Stiffelio at the dramatic climax of the opera in Act III. In both cases, Verdi abandons traditional formal expectations and includes textures that have been described as "orchestrated prose" ("prosa strumentata"). The author lauds this treatment, also found in the contemporarily composed *Rigoletto*, as a major stylistic advance for the composer. The introductory portion of the article surveys the "aria a due" or "quasi-duet" tradition in the works of Rossini, Bellini, and other early nineteenth-century opera composers as background for the main discussion. See item 917 below for a closely related article focusing on the changes in these two pieces when Verdi reworked the opera as *Aroldo*.

915. Girardi, Michele. "Un aspetto del realismo nella drammaturgia di *Stiffelio*: La musica da fuori scena." In *Tornando a "Stiffelio"* (item 234), 223–41.

The opening section of this article provides an important survey of Verdi's use of off-stage music in his operas in the context of nineteenth-century opera in general, with particular attention on the use of an organ. Afterwards, the author examines in greater detail the use of off-stage music in *Stiffelio* to heighten the sense of realism in several scenes. The author concludes by arguing that off-stage music in *Aroldo* does not serve this dramatic function as effectively as in the earlier opera.

916. Gotti, Tito. "L'opera: Appunti per un'analisi." In *Stiffelio* (item 902), 37–73.

Offers an analytical assessment of *Stiffelio*, focusing on both the story and the music. The author includes a discussion of several passages from *Aroldo* that differ substantially from the earlier opera.

917. Powers, Harold S. "Aria sfasciata, duetto senza l'insieme: Le scene di confronto tenore-soprano nello *Stiffelio/Aroldo* di Giuseppe Verdi." In *Tornando a "Stiffelio"* (item 234), 141–88.

The battle between two opposing dramatic forces—jealousy and Christian forgiveness—within the heart of the title character rather than between two different characters leads Verdi to adopt an unusual formal approach in several of the extended pieces from *Stiffelio*. The author provides a detailed formal analysis of two of these: the cavatina of the lost ring (Act I) and the divorce duet (Act III), focusing on changes made in reworking the material for *Aroldo*. In both cases, Verdi reworked the musical material even more than the change of text would have required, retreating from his earlier, more experimental shapes and adopting a more conventional musical approach. The author published an abridged version of this article in English that focuses on the Act I aria (see item 497 above). See also item 914 above for a closely related article by Marcello Conati examining these two pieces in *Stiffelio*.

Performance Practice, Staging, Scenography

918. Martin, George. "Verdi's *Stiffelio*: Lost, Found, and Misunderstood." *Opera Quarterly* 13 (Fall 1996): 11–19.

After briefly surveying the history of the opera and its plot, the author suggests that the effect of recent stagings by the Royal Opera Company (1993), the New York Metropolitan Opera (1994), and the Los Angeles Opera Company (1995) has been seriously marred by deviating from Verdi's stage directions at the conclusion of the work.

919. Surian, Elvidio. "Aspetti espliciti e impliciti di regìa teatrale (didascalie musicali) presenti nella partitura di un'opera verdiana dell'età di mezzo." In *Tornando a "Stiffelio"* (item 234), 189–201.

Presents a catalogue of stage directions explicitly or implicitly indicated in the piano-vocal score of *Stiffelio* and discusses the significance of these directions in reconstructing Verdi's ideas about staging in operas before he began using formal *disposizioni sceniche*.

Performance History; Reception

* Chusid, Martin. "Apropos *Aroldo, Stiffelio,* and *Le pasteur,* with a List of 19th-Century Performances of *Aroldo*." See item 909 above.

920. Conati, Marcello. "Cronologia—critica—bibliografia." In *Stiffelio* (item 902), 97–137.

Provides a selective list of early performances, republications of reviews for nearly two dozen performances from contemporary journals and newspapers, evaluations of the work excerpted from fourteen books, and a bibliography of books and articles relating to *Stiffelio*. See item 909 above for additions and corrections to the list of performances.

921. Gualerzi, Giorgio. "Il cammino dell'opera." In *Stiffelio* (item 902), 88–96.

A concise overview of *Stiffelio*'s early performances (through the early 1860s) and their reception, focusing on the performance of specific singers. Marcello Conati supplements this essay with other documentary material; see item 920.

LA TRAVIATA

Verdi wrote this opera in great haste, revising it somewhat after the disappointing reception accorded its first performances. It has the distinction of being the only one of his operas to be based on a contemporary subject, the life of Marie Duplessis.

Guides to the Work

922. Csampai, Attila, and Dietmar Holland, eds. *Giuseppe Verdi, "La traviata": Texte, Materialien, Kommentare.* Rororo Opernbücher. Reinbek bei Hamburg: Rowohlt Taschenbuch Verlag, 1983. 252 p. ISBN 3–499–17690–4. ML 50 .V484 T63 1983.

923. *La traviata. L'avant-scène opéra* 51 (April 1983). Paris: L'Avant-Scène, 1983. 178 p. ISSN 0395–0670. MT 100 .V53 A97.
2nd ed. Paris: Société Premières Loges, 1993. 177 p. ISSN 0764–2873. ML 410 .V4 T7 1993.

Nearly a dozen articles focus on topics such as the background to the story (including the life of Marie Duplessis), the main characters of the opera as archetypes, the genesis of the work and its early reception, some of the principal singers who have sung the role of Violetta, and a historical-iconographical study of the 1955 production at La Scala. The libretto is presented in the original Italian with a modern French translation by Michel Orcel. The volume also includes a discography of partial and complete recordings, accompanied by a prose essay, tables listing the earliest performances of the opera in major centers as well as more detailed information about performances in major houses up to the present. In addition to principal editions, librettos, and musical studies relating to *La traviata* (nearly 100 items), the bibliography in this issue also includes a large listing of nearly 500 general items pertaining to Verdi's life and works. The second edition features a substantially updated discography, but a smaller bibliography than the first edition, focusing on recently published materials.

924. *La traviata.* English National Opera Guides, 5. London: John Calder; New
York: Riverrun, 1981. 80 p. ISBN 0–7145–3848–5. ML 50 .V484 T62
1981.

This guide contains essays on the history of Alexandre Dumas fils' play, *La
dame aux camélias,* which formed the basis for the opera's libretto, the genesis
of the opera, and the singers for the premiere performance. The libretto is
reproduced in Italian and English translation; the volume also contains a
selective discography and a short bibliography.

Histories and General Studies

925. D'Amico, Fedele. "Il *coup de foudre* di Verdi." In *Fedele d'Amico: Un ragazzino
all'Augusteo. Scritti musicali,* 59–74. Ed. by Franco Serpa. Turin: Giulio
Einaudi, 1991. ISBN 88–06–12385–8. ML 160 .D195 1991.

After briefly tracing the history of the opera's conception, the author examines
various ways in which it departed from tradition. These include the use of
contemporary dress, the dramatic function of the apparently "ambient"
instrumental music in the opening portion of the opera, and the unusually
complex characterization of Violetta.

926. Gerhartz, Leo Karl. "Die Wirklichkeit als Märchenspiel: Zum Problem des
Realismus in Verdis *La traviata.*" In *Zwischen Aufklärung & Kulturindustrie:
Festschrift für Georg Knepler zum 85. Geburtstag,* 2: 85–93. Ed. by Hanns-
Werner Heister, Karin Heister-Grech, and Gerhard Scheit. Hamburg: von
Bockel Verlag, 1993. 3 vols. ISBN 3–928770–11–X (set); 3–928770–13–6
(vol. 2). ML 3845 .Z95 1993.

Examines the duality in Verdi's conception of *La traviata.* On the one hand,
La traviata is Verdi's most "realistic" opera, based on the story of a
contemporary heroine which has some resonance to the blossoming of the
composer's own relationship with Giuseppina Strepponi. On the other hand,
a fairy-tale aura, created in part by the dance music and glittering vocal writing,
comprises an important part of the opera, reflecting Violetta's (and
Giuseppina's?) search for a utopian existence. The author also points out the
tension between the dramatic and musical treatment of Alfredo's father, who
represents established convention and propriety, and that of Alfredo and
Violetta, who seek to move beyond established social mores.

927. Issartel, Christiane. *Les dames aux camelias de l'histoire à la légende.* Paris:
Chêne Hachette, 1981. 165 + x p. ISBN 2–85108–274–4. NX 652 .D86 I8.

This richly illustrated volume examines the life of Marie Duplessis (Alphonsine
Plessis) and the literary, artistic, and musical works it inspired. The book is

more valuable for historical background and iconography than for historical and musical commentary on Verdi's opera.

928. Stuppner, Hubert. "*La traviata* oder: die sinnliche Aufdringlichkeit von Musik." In *Giuseppe Verdi: Musik-Konzepte* 10 (item 423): 38–45.

Discusses the aesthetic position of *La traviata* in the history of Italian opera and its unique status among Verdi's compositions as his only work with a contemporary bourgeois setting.

Dramaturgy; Studies of the Libretto

929. Buia, Anna. *Un così eroico amore: Genesi e diffusione censurata del libretto de "La traviata" di F.M. Piave.* Musica e teatro, 10. Quaderni degli Amici della Scala. Milan: Associazione Amici della Scala, 1990. 79 p. ISBN 88–85843–11–5.

After a brief discussion of the genesis of the opera, the author explores Dumas' dramatic adaptation of his early novel *La dame aux camélias* and the way in which Verdi and Piave transformed it into the libretto for *La traviata*. Later chapters consider the unfavorable early reception of the opera, subsequent alterations by the composer, and changes demanded by the censors in areas outside of Lombardy-Venetia. An appendix reproduces the libretto, showing variants imposed by censors in Bologna (1853), Florence (1854), Rome (1854–55), and Naples (1855). The study contains a substantial bibliography.

Studies of Compositional Process

930. Budden, Julian. "The Two Traviatas." *Proceedings of the Royal Musical Association* 99 (1972–73): 43–66.

Examines reasons for the poor reception of the opera at its Venetian premiere in 1853 and chronicles the composer's subsequent revisions for a new production the following year. The author then surveys the musical changes in five numbers from the last two acts. For an expansion of many of the ideas brought out in this article, see the more recent study by Wolfgang Osthoff (item 932).

931. Della Seta, Fabrizio. "Varianti (d'autore e non) ne *La traviata*." In *Napoli e il teatro musicale in Europa tra sette e ottocento: Studi in onore di Friedrich Lippmann*, 417–35. Ed. by Bianca Maria Antolini and Wolfgang Witzenmann. Quaderni della Rivista italiana di musicologia/Società Italiana di Musicologia, 28. Florence: Olschki, 1993. ISBN 88–222–4026–X. ML 1720 .N36 1993.

Discusses some of the more interesting problems and variants that have come
to light in the process of preparing the new critical edition of *La traviata*.
Passages discussed include, among others, the opening choral scene, "Addio,
del passato," and "Parigi, o cara."

932. Osthoff, Wolfgang. "Aspetti strutturali e psicologici della drammaturgia
verdiana nei ritocchi della *Traviata*." In *Opera & Libretto I*, 315–60. Studi
di musica veneta. Florence: Olschki, 1990. ISBN 88–222–3825–7. ML 1700
.O655 1990.

Argues that many of Verdi's revisions in the initial version of *La traviata* show
a tightening of dramatic structure and an increase in psychological intensity.
The article includes musical examples for most of the passages discussed. Much
of the article uses Julian Budden's earlier article (item 930) as a foundation for
further discussion and elaboration.

Stylistic and Analytical Studies

933. Chusid, Martin. "Drama and the Key of F Major in *La traviata*." *Atti 3* (item
226), 89–121.

Earlier studies have proposed that Verdi used a recurring thematic idea ("Di
quell'amor, quell'amor, ch'è palpito") to represent the deeply felt emotion of love
that Alfredo kindles in Violetta. This study suggests two additional unifying
features. One is that Verdi used the key of F major to symbolize the short-lived
romance between Violetta and Alfredo. The second is an orchestral motive,
heard three times in the first part of Act II, associated with Alfredo's and
Violetta's pain at parting and taking their own individual paths. The
concluding portion of this study examines Verdi's use of F major throughout
his operas. While the composer associates this key with a happy love scene in
only two of operas before the *Traviata* period, this association recurs fairly
frequently in his later works.

934. Della Seta, Fabrizio. "Il tempo della festa: Su due scene della *Traviata* e su altri
luoghi verdiani." *Studi verdiani* 2 (1983): 108–46.

An analysis of Verdi's use of dance music in the opening scene, focusing on
tonal and formal structure, leads to an appraisal of the entire first act based on
the logic of sonata form. The author then draws parallels to the second act
finale of *Traviata*, the opening scene of *Rigoletto*, and the finale of *Ballo in
maschera*.

935. Groos, Arthur. "'TB Sheets': Love and Disease in *La traviata*." *Cambridge
Opera Journal* 7 (1995): 233–60.

Examines how nineteenth-century medical literature and fiction—especially Dumas's *La dame aux camélias*—dealt with consumption (tuberculosis) and how Verdi and Piave employed contemporary ideas about the disease in the libretto and music of *La traviata*. While the author analyzes references to the disease throughout the opera, he draws particular attention to how Violetta's death scene differs from similar scenes in other Verdi operas, interpreting it as a musical representation of *spes phthisica*, the false illusion of recovery that often immediately preceded the death of a consumptive.

936. Hepokoski, James A. "Genre and Content in Mid-Century Verdi: 'Addio, del passato' (*La traviata*, Act III)." *Cambridge Opera Journal* 1 (1989): 249–76.

Verdi's insistent use of conventional structures in his mid-century works poses obstacles for critics who identify him as a progressive composer who championed the modification or abandonment of traditional operatic conventions. The author proposes that this dilemma might be addressed by focusing on Verdi's conception of the dramatic function of these conventions in his early and middle works. He then illustrates his proposed methodology in Violetta's aria "Addio, del passato" by analyzing the affective content embodied in such features as text structure, poetic-metrical conventions, instrumental timbres, and melodic *topos*. Alterations in the autograph score suggest that the composer refined his earlier conception of the piece from a need to make the vocal part less taxing for the performer. Verdi's solution—interpolating short melodic phrases for the oboe—connects the aria to a melodic *topos* traditionally associated with psychological estrangement and at the same time suggests the faltering breath of the tuberculosis-stricken heroine. The author proposes, in conclusion, that Verdi's mid-century aesthetics feature the use of economic means to achieve maximum effect and that apparent simplicity or facileness should not be disparaged as shallow. Instead, listeners and scholars should try to discover how the affective responses Verdi was attempting to evoke support the drama as a whole.

937. Martin, George. "The Orchestration of *La traviata*." In *Aspects of Verdi* (item 244), 195–210.

Argues that Verdi's orchestration in *La traviata* is highly sophisticated, imaginative, and often delicate, refuting George Bernard Shaw's remark (probably based on a comment by Wagner) that the composer used the orchestra "like a big guitar."

* Rosen, David. "Meter, Character, and *Tinta* in Verdi's Operas." See item 501.

Performance History; Reception

938. Morelli, Giovanni. "'Le situazioni riescono quasi tutte d'un colore, mancan di varietà': Cinque glosse ad una lettera di Felice Varesi." In *Musica e immagine tra iconografia e mondo dell'opera: Studi in onore di Massimo Bogianckino*, 209–19. Ed. by Biancamaria Brumana and Galliano Ciliberti. Historiae Musicae Cultores Biblioteca, 70. Florence: Olschki, 1993. ISBN 88–222–4110–X. ML 85 .M972 1993.

Analyzes the assertions made by baritone Felice Varese, who created the role of the first Germont, that the scenario for *La traviata* was defective because it lacked distinctive contrasts. Unfortunately, the article contains no references notes, nor does it reproduce the letter containing Varese's remarks written to Guglielmo Brenna, secretary of La Fenice, on 24 November 1852.

939. Zheng, Sue. "*La traviata* in China." *Verdi Newsletter* 16 (1988): 29–30.

La traviata's popularity in China stems, in part, from the success of *Cha Hua Nü*, a translation of Dumas' *La dame aux camélias* made early in this century. *La traviata* was not only one of the first Western operas to be heard in China (during the 1950s), but also one of the most performed works by the Central Opera Theater after the demise of the Mao's anti-Western "Cultural Revolution."

Miscellaneous

940. Della Seta, Fabrizio, ed. *Gli abbozzi della "Traviata."* Parma: Istituto Nazionale di Studi Verdiani, forthcoming.

A critical edition of Verdi's complete continuity draft for the opera, together with a historical introduction, a description and inventory, critical-analytical commentary, and a facsimile reproduction of the manuscript.

IL TROVATORE

Il trovatore was written during the same period as *Rigoletto* and *La traviata*. It shares a close association with both operas in its conception: the idea of an "outcast" female character, as well the tension between the opposing passions of love and revenge. While critics have long considered this opera to be the most "traditional" and least "progressive" among the famous middle-period trilogy, *Il trovatore* has recently acquired persuasive advocates who argue that it is not the "backwater" opera that many have labeled it.

Guides to the Work

941. Csampai, Attila, and Dietmar Holland, eds. *Giuseppe Verdi, "Der Troubadour": Texte, Materialien, Kommentare*. Rororo Opernbücher. Reinbek bei

Hamburg: Rowohlt Taschenbuch Verlag, 1986. 220 p. ISBN 3–499–17996–2. ML 50 .V484 T84 1986.

This guide contains a series of essays dealing with the compositional history of the opera and its libretto (including a German translation of Cammarano's *programma* for the opera); Antonio García Gutiérrez's play, *El trovador*, and the historical milieu that it depicts; and the reception of the opera in the twentieth century. The libretto is reproduced in side-by-side format in Italian and a German translation by Reinhard Müller. The volume concludes with a selective bibliography, a discography of complete recordings with accompanying essay, and a videography (with only a single entry).

942. *Le trouvère*. *L'avant-scène opéra* 60 (February 1984). Paris: L'Avant-Scène, 1984. 161 p. ISSN 0395–0670.

    2nd ed. Paris: Société Premières Loges, 1990. 145 p. ISSN 0764–2873. ML 410 .V4 V364 1990.

The bulk of this issue is devoted to *Il trovatore*. More than half a dozen articles focus on topics such as the genesis of the libretto and the music, Verdi and the chivalric ideal, the composer's recasting of the work as *Le trouvère* for performances in Paris, and several character studies of Azucena. The libretto is presented in the original Italian with a modern French translation by Michel Orcel. The volume also includes a discography of complete and partial recordings, accompanied by a prose essay, tables listing the earliest performances of the opera in major centers, as well as more detailed information about performances in major houses up to the present. In addition to entries relating to principal editions, librettos, and musical studies relating to *Il trovatore* (nearly 100 items), the bibliography in this issue also includes a large listing of nearly 500 general items pertaining to Verdi's life and works. The second edition contains very few changes from the first.

943. *Il trovatore*. English National Opera Guides, 20. London: John Calder; New York: Riverrun, 1983. 80 p. ISBN 0–7145–3877–9. ML 50 .V484 T82 1983.

The guide contains a short essay tracing the history of the work's conception and an assessment of its place among Verdi's works, a detailed descriptive analysis of the opera, and an article that examines Antonio García Gutiérrez's play, *El trovador*, which provided the raw material for the libretto. The volume includes the libretto in Italian and an English translation by Tom Hammond, a concise discography, and a brief bibliographical note.

Histories and General Studies

944. Lawton, David. "*Le trouvère*: Verdi's Revision of *Il trovatore* for Paris." *Studi verdiani* 3 (1985): 79–119.

Describes how Verdi's decision to mount a performance of *Le trouvère* at the Opéra was intimately connected with the threat of unauthorized performances of his works at the Théâtre Italien and the composer's concern for solidifying legal and financial rights for his earlier work in France as well as Italy. The second part of the article describes revisions Verdi made for the Paris production and assesses their effect on the composition. The author concludes by considering the question of whether any of these revisions might be incorporated in modern performances. Appendices reproduce the contract between Verdi and Alphonse Royer for *Le trouvère* and two previously unpublished letters of introduction written by Verdi for Halévy, one to Tito Ricordi, and the other to Alberto Mazzucato.

Dramaturgy; Studies of the Libretto

945. Black, John N. "Salvadore Cammarano's *Programma* for *Il trovatore* and the Problems of the Finale." *Studi verdiani* 2 (1983): 78–107.

Discusses Cammarano's *programma* for *Il trovatore* and Verdi's response to it in a letter dated 9 April 1851. The article focuses on the evolution of the finale at the end of Part II. Cammarano first wrote a conventional finale, but Verdi wanted a more concise ending that would bring the act to a quicker close. This version, however, was too abrupt. When Cammarano died, the composer requested that Leone Emanuele Bardare revise Cammarano's original, longer ending. Verdi remained dissatisfied with the finale, even in its third form, and eventually decided to eliminate the stretta and adjust the bridge passage to serve as the conclusion. Appendices reproduce Cammarano's original *programma*, the three versions of the finale in manuscript form, and the text for the finale as printed in the original libretto.

946. Canessa, Francesco. "Salvatore Cammarano e il 'libretto ideale' del *Trovatore*." *Atti 3* (item 226), 14–19.

This article defends Gabriele Baldini's assertion (see item 155) that *Il Trovatore* owes its success to the fact that, for the first time, Verdi worked with an ideal libretto. After briefly tracing Cammarano's career as a librettist, the author suggests that the libretto for *Trovatore* was particularly successful due to the extensive outline supplied by Verdi to the librettist in a letter dated 9 April 1851.

947. Gerhard, Anselm. "Dalla fatalità all'ossessione: *Il trovatore* fra 'mélodrame' parigino e opera moderna." *Studi verdiani* 10 (1994–95): 61–66.

Proposes that one of the major differences between the place of García Gutiérrez and Verdi's opera is the composer's decision to eliminate the notion of fatality associated with Manrico's incubus in the original play and instead focus attention on the gypsy's vengeance as the primary motivating factor in the drama. The author argues that Verdi ensconced as the dramatic and musical nucleus of the opera the "past" narrative about the burning of Azucena's child, encapsulated in the highly original and evocative ballatas of Ferrando and Azucena, followed by Manrico's stunning solo number that culminates in "Di quella pira."

948. Kimbell, David R.B. "*Il trovatore*: Cammarano and García Gutiérrez." *Atti 3* (item 226), 34–44.

The dramatic motivations of the main characters in the libretto, particularly the Count of Luna, often seem weak or unintelligible because Cammarano eliminated much of the political and social background found in the original play by García Gutiérrez. Kimbell suggests that Verdi's conception of the main characters and their development came primarily from the play itself and not from Cammarano's libretto.

949. Mossa, Carlo Matteo. "La genesi del libretto del *Trovatore*." *Studi verdiani* 8 (1992): 52–103.

The most sophisticated study to date of the history of *Trovatore*'s libretto, based on a number of important primary sources including: the letter exchange between Verdi and Cammarano (quoted from the soon to be published *Carteggio Verdi-Cammarano*, item 48), early drafts for the libretto, and the autograph libretto itself. Verdi encouraged his librettist to preserve the force and originality resulting from the unusual features of the original Spanish play. The characterization of Azucena and her role in the opera's dramaturgy became a central point of controversy between composer and librettist. Cammarano's untimely death allowed Verdi free reign to develop his own conception of the role, particularly in her *canzona* and the subsequent finale in Part II.

950. Todde, Felice. "Cenni sul rapporto fra *El trovador* di García Gutiérrez ed *Il trovatore* di Verdi." *Nuova rivista musicale italiana* 20 (1986): 400–15.

A scene-by-scene comparison of the Spanish drama with its refashioning by Verdi and Cammarano as the libretto for *Il trovatore*. The author notes that while the opera follows the general outline of the drama and even some of its linguistic expressions, the libretto differs most from its model in the way in which many of the characters are introduced and developed.

Studies of Compositional Process

951. Rosenberg, Jesse. "A Sketch Fragment for *Il trovatore*." *Verdi Newsletter* 14 (1986): 29–35.

Discusses an early sketch fragment for the *finale ultima* of Part IV, evidently torn from the complete continuity draft. The author examines differences between the early version of this passage and the definitive version, focusing on a change in tonal structure: the sketch moves from E minor to E major, while the definitive version modulates from C minor to E♭ major.

Stylistic and Analytical Studies

952. Chusid, Martin. "A New Source for *El trovador* and Its Implications for the Tonal Organization of *Il trovatore*." In *Verdi's Middle Period, 1849–1859: Source Studies, Analysis, and Performance Practice* (item 235), 207–25.

The play *Macías* by Mariano Jose de Larra, with its plot about courtly lovers, has long been considered García Gutiérrez's main source for *El trovador*. It lacks, however, the idea of vengeance and the plot element of a stolen child. Chusid proposes that García Gutiérrez may have appropriated these ideas from Jacques Halévy's and Eugène Scribe's opera *La Juive*. He shows that the playwright developed these two main strands of the plot relatively independently until the end of the play, an organization Cammarano also followed in the libretto for *Il trovatore*. In the final part of the paper, the author proposes that Verdi continued the distinction between the two main dramatic threads through tonal means: E major and minor, A minor, G major and minor, and C major for the story of the gypsies and the stolen child and E♭ major and minor for the courtly lovers, Leonora and Manrico, and Manrico's death. The character of Manrico belongs to both strands of the plot, and his music moves in both tonal areas according to the particular strand that is emphasized at any one moment. Appendices chart in tabular form the keys and sonorities associated with each strand of the story.

953. Drabkin, William. "Characters, Key Relations, and Tonal Structure in *Il trovatore*." *Music Analysis* 1 (1982): 143–53.

Develops Petrobelli's analytical commentary about Verdi's use of tonal structure in *Trovatore* (see item 959). Proposes that Verdi builds a dual polarity around E minor (representing Azucena's love *amor filiale* for her adopted son, Manrico), moving in one direction to G major (representing Azucena's *amor materna* for her own mother, who was burned at the stake) and in the other direction to C major (representing gypsy courage and Manrico's heroism). E major becomes an important structural key, related both to E minor and, through an enharmonic pivot tone (*G♯/A♭*), to the flat keys of A♭ major and F minor (associated in general with the aristocratic Leonora and Count di

Luna and specifically with Leonora's heroism and despair). For a critique of some of the author's conclusions, see item 955.

954. Friedheim, Philip. "Formal Patterns in Verdi's *Il trovatore.*" *Studies in Romanticism* 12 (1973): 406–25.

Argues that the musical structure of the opera shows strong symmetry and balance as a foil to the libretto, which presents a deliberately disordered plot and avoids depicting any social norm.

955. Greenwood, Joanna. "Musical and Dramatic Motion in Verdi's *Il trovatore.*" *Jahrbuch für Opernforschung* 2 (1986): 59–73.

The main portion of the article examines the tonal structure of Part III, Scene 2, focusing on the harmonic and tonal roles of the sonority *e′* throughout the traditional four formal sections of the number. While the kinetic sections (*tempo d'attacco* and *tempo di mezzo*) initiate an ascent to a structural pitch (*eb* or *f′*), they never complete the ascent, while the more static sections (adagio and cabaletta) feature prominent vocal sonorities and structural points of arrival. Much of the analysis is based on Schenkerian principles. The author also considers the overall juxtaposition of sharp-sided keys and flat-sided keys throughout the opera and critiques William Drabkin's article (item 953), arguing against the semantic association of specific words or ideas with particular pitches. Greenwood demonstrates that while the composer repeatedly employs chromatic opposition between the sonorities of *eb* and *e* to highlight important dramatic moments, each individual passage features different tonal, harmonic, and dramatic contexts. The introductory portion of the article offers a useful summary of the debate over tonal analysis in Verdi's operas.

956. Hepokoski, James. "*Ottocento* Opera as Cultural Drama: Generic Mixtures in *Il trovatore.*" In *Verdi's Middle Period, 1849–1859: Source Studies, Analysis, and Performance Practice* (item 235), 147–96.

The opening portion of the article examines the history and cultural implications of strophic song in Italian opera, noting a close relationship to the French tradition of *opéra comique* and to the notions of simplicity, naturalness, and even modernity. The author suggests that the mixing of strophic song with traditional Italian lyric form was a central issue that occupied Verdi during the late 1840s and early 1850s. The concluding portion of the article illustrates this process of hybridization in three passages from *Il trovatore*: Ferrando's "Di due figli vivea padre beato"/"Abbietta zingara, fosca vegliarda!" (Act I), with its ties to the French operatic ballade; Leonora's "Tacea la notte placida" (Act I), which has a close connection to the strophic romance; and the "Anvil Chorus" with Azucena's canzone "Stride la vampa! — la folla indomita" (Act II), influenced by the tradition of the strophic-text demotic chorus. The author suggests that in general, analyses of Verdi's opera might seek to locate and explain not only features of unity and inner coherence, but heterogeneity and inner tension as well.

957. Martin, George. "The Essence of *Il trovatore*." In *Aspects of Verdi* (item 244), 181–93.

Argues that *Il trovatore* holds an unusual place among Verdi's operas for several reasons. The composer created a strong sense of propulsion from one scene to the next, in part by modifying traditional structures for dramatic reasons. The opera's *tinta*, centered in repeated notes and rhythmic figures associated with the music of Azucena and Manrico, is also unusually strong. The author characterizes Abramo Basevi's term *insistenza* as a particularly apt description of this opera's special qualities.

958. Parker, Roger. "The Dramatic Structure of *Il trovatore*." In *Studies in Early Verdi* (item 377), 201–19.
Republished in *Music Analysis* 1 (1982): 155–67.

Through an examination the structure of Act I, Scene 2, the author proposes that the symmetries and connecting links noted throughout the opera by Baldini (item 155) and Petrobelli (item 959) also exist within smaller units and that these provide both unification and clarification of dramatic intent.

959. Petrobelli, Pierluigi. "Per un'esegesi della struttura drammatica del *Trovatore*." *Atti 3* (item 226), 387–407.
English translation by William Drabkin. *Music Analysis* 1 (1982): 129–41; slightly revised in *Music in the Theater: Essays on Verdi and Other Composers* (item 378), 100–112.

Il trovatore, in contrast to *Rigoletto* and *La traviata*, which were composed during the same time period, contains very little character development. Instead, the composer adopted a complex system of musical devices and symmetries that rigorously and systematically underscore the dramatic structure of the work. The author focuses on Verdi's use of sonority ("a specific pitch prolonged by various means of articulation and considered independently of any harmonic function it may imply as a result of being heard in a particular context"), rhythmic motives, and figuration to unify and accentuate dramatic development. See items 953 and 955 for further development of Petrobelli's ideas.

*   Rosen, David. "Meter, Character, and *Tinta* in Verdi's Operas." See item 501.

Performance Practice, Staging, Scenography

960. Fairtile, Linda B. "The Violin Director in *Il trovatore* and *Le trouvère*: Some Nineteenth-Century Evidence." *Verdi Newsletter* 21 (1993): 16–26.

Examines parts for the violin director in a set of parts for *Il trovatore* and in another set for *Le trouvère* in light of the explanation of the violin director's job by Giuseppe Scaramelli in his *Saggio sopra i doveri d'un primo violino direttore d'orchestra* (Trieste, 1911). The *Trovatore* violin director's part contains up to four staves of cues above the violin part. Lightly scored recitative passages often contain only the first violin line and the unpitched vocal text, suggesting that the singers controlled the rhythmic flow in these passages. Vocal cues generally occur only in places where it would be difficult to coordinate the ensemble, such as beginnings of phrases, or bars with tempo changes or fluctuations. The part for the violin director in *Le trouvère* is much more detailed, resembling a "short score." The vocal line is continuous and fully texted, and separate lines are devoted to cues for the woodwinds, the brass, and the cellos and basses. The author speculates that a director using this score may have functioned more nearly like a modern director, routinely cuing players rather than serving primarily as a backup when omissions or errors occurred. See item 527 above for a broader examination by this author of the violin director tradition during the 1840s and 50s.

Performance History; Reception

961. Chusid, Martin, and Thomas Kaufman. "The First Three Years of *Trovatore*: A List of Stagings from 19 January 1853 to 18 January 1856." *Verdi Newsletter* 15 (1987): 30–49.

Il trovatore was one of the most immediately successful of Verdi's operas, with 229 stagings during the period covered by this article. A brief essay on the early reception of the opera, focusing on important centers such as Naples, Milan, Genoa, Venice, and Florence, introduces the list of performances. Performance information includes, as available, cast and directors, as well as sources referring to the performance.

LES VÊPRES SICILIENNES

Vêpres was Verdi's first entirely new work written for the Paris Opéra. It was an important precursor of his later operas written for the venerable Parisian institution, marking a new, more international stage in Verdi's musical development after the popular trilogy.

Guides to the Work

962. *Les vêpres siciliennes. L'avant-scène opéra* 75 (May 1985). Paris: L'Avant-Scène, 1985. 150 p. ISSN 0395–0670. ML 410 .V4 V35 1985.

The bulk of this issue (121 p.) is devoted to *Les vêpres siciliennes*, including a half-dozen articles dealing with the background to the story, the genesis of the opera, and Verdi's relationship to Meyerbeer, Paris, and the tradition of French *grand opéra*. A substantial discography includes both complete recordings and individual arias or sections; the bibliography of nearly 150 items covers major editions and librettos, studies of the work and of representative performances, and general historical background to the story of the opera. The volume includes the Italian libretto for *I vespri siciliani*, with a parallel French translation by Michel Orcel (not the original French libretto for *Vêpres*). Charts list the earliest performances of the opera in major centers and provide more detailed information about performances in major houses through the present.

Histories and General Studies

963. Budden, Julian. "Verdi and Meyerbeer in Relation to *Les vêpres siciliennes*." *Studi verdiani* 1 (1982): 11–20.

Assesses the influence of Meyerbeer on Verdi's style in *Vêpres*, particularly in several passages from Act I. As a point of reference, the author compares Donizetti's treatment of the same libretto in his uncompleted opera *Le Duc d'Albe*. The strongest stylistic influences from Meyerbeer seem to come from *Les huguenots* rather than *L'etoile du nord*, which Verdi heard while composing *Vêpres*.

964. Conati, Marcello. "Ballabili nei *Vespri*: Con alcune osservazioni su Verdi e la musica popolare." *Studi verdiani* 1 (1982): 21–46.

An analytical and historical study of the Act III dance suite, *Le quattro stagioni*, against the background of dance music in Verdi's operas generally. Rhythmic and melodic gestures in the dances show strong ties to folk music, and Verdi often endows them with dramatic significance. The article includes a discussion of choreographic aspects of *Le quattro stagioni*.

*   Gerhard, Anselm. *Die Verstädterung der Oper*. See item 265.

965. Marchesi, Gustavo. "L'ambiente culturale e artistico parigino al tempo dei *Vespri*: Appunti per una definizione." *Quadrivium: Studi di filologia e musicologia* 27 (1986): 21–68. This volume of *Quadrivium* is listed in some indexes as a monograph: *Universalità della musica, prestigio dell'Italia, attualità di Verdi: Studi in onore di Mario Medici*, Vol. 2. Ed. by Giuseppe Vecchi. Bologna: Antiquae Musicae Italicae Studiosi, 1986.

Provides an excellent overview of the cultural milieu of the Second Empire, touching on trends in philosophy, literature, theater, and drama; the Exposition universelle of 1855; and the reception of Verdi's works prior to the composition of *Vêpres*, as well as reactions to the opera itself. The article contains a wealth of citations from primary sources, including the full texts of eleven letters from Verdi to Cesare De Sanctis and Clara Maffei.

* Porter, Andrew. "*Les vêpres siciliennes:* New Letters from Verdi to Scribe." See item 101.

* "*I vespri siciliani.*" *Convegno di Studi Verdiani, Torino, 7–10 aprile 1973: Sunte delle relazioni.* See item 236.

966. Viale Ferrero, Mercedes. "'È l'insolenza è la vendetta': Tra Vesperi e *Vêpres.*" In *Musica senza aggettivi: Studi per Fedele d'Amico,* 1:323–44. Ed. by Agostino Ziino. Quaderni della Rivista italiana di musicologia, 25. Florence: Olschki, 1991. 2 vols. ISBN 88–222–3903–2. ML 55 .D22 1991.

Examines the transmission of the story of the Sicilian Vespers during the first half of the nineteenth century in art, history, literature, and drama and its influence on Verdi and Scribe. The author argues that reviews of Verdi's opera in Italy—at least in the Kingdom of Sardinia-Piedmont—criticized the change of locale to Portugal in the version known as *Giovanna de Guzman* as a betrayal of the Italians' patriotic cause. An appendix traces citations in Sardinian-Piedmontese periodicals to the Sicilian Vespers and the reception of Verdi's opera from February 1855 through January 1866. It includes extensive quotations from many of the reviews.

Dramaturgy; Studies of the Libretto

967. Gerhard, Anselm. "'Ce cinquième act sans intérêt': Preoccupazioni di Scribe e di Verdi per la drammaturgia de *Les vêpres siciliennes.*" Trans. by Luca Tutino. *Studi verdiani* 4 (1986–87): 65–86.

The dramatic difficulties in Scribe's original version of Act V largely stem from the fact that it was an expansion of the earlier four-act *Le duc d'Albe.* Scribe began the act with a choral number that was irrelevant to the action, and the remaining numbers emphasized traditional arias for Hélène and Henri, who had already passed the dramatic climax of their relationship. Although Verdi and Scribe collaborated on revisions for the act, they were never able to resolve the difficulties posed by the passive dramatic quality of the final act in its initial version. An appendix reproduces Act V from Scribe's original libretto, now conserved at the Bibliothèque Nationale in Paris.

968. Vecchi, Giuseppe. "Momenti e vicende del libretto italiano dei *Vespri*: Polemiche e giudizi." *Quadrivium: Studi di filologia e musicologia* 20 (1979): 157–77.

    Reprinted in *Studi e ricerche sui libretti delle opere di Giuseppe Verdi* (item 444), 157–77.

    Through an examination of selected passages from the libretto and the largely negative contemporary reviews of the opera, the author discusses the difficulties in transferring the original French libretto into Italian (for both *Vespri* and *Giovanna de Guzman*) while minimizing changes in the music itself.

Studies of Compositional Process

969. Budden, Julian. "Varianti nei *Vespri siciliani*." *Nuova rivista musicale italiana* 6 (1972): 155–81.

    Discusses several revisions made by Verdi in *Vêpres*: a reworking of a passage in the lament of Hélène at the beginning of Act I, the excision of a passage from the opera's final scene (based on text published in the libretto for the first performance but since dropped), and the addition of a romance, "O toi qu j'ai chérie," to the beginning of Act IV, composed especially to feature the voice of tenor M. Villaret at a revival of the work in 1863. Budden also discusses the historical position of the work in relationship to the tradition of Meyerbeer and French *grand opéra* and reasons for the increasingly unfavorable reception accorded the work beginning the decade after its premiere.

Stylistic and Analytical Studies

970. Bates, Carol N. "Verdi's *Les vêpres siciliennes* (1855) and *Simon Boccanegra* (1857)." Ph.D. dissertation, Yale University, 1970. 2 vols. xi, 352; 118 p.

    Proposes that these two operas contain many forward-looking stylistic features that become fully synthesized into a new style in Verdi's next opera, *Un ballo in maschera*. Some of these include: increased prominence and sophistication in handling the orchestration and choral scenes, treatment of the cavatina/cabaletta structure, and handling of fast-moving dramatic sequences. Appendices provide information about the compositional genesis of *Vêpres* and significant revisions in that opera; similarities between the librettos of *Vêpres* and Meyerbeer's *Les Huguenots*, and Verdi's revisions to *Simon* for the 1857 performance at Reggio nell'Emilia.

971. Langford, Jeffrey. "Poetic Prosody and Melodic Rhythm in *Les vêpres siciliennes*." *Verdi Newsletter* 23 (1996): 8–18.

    After a brief review of principles of Italian prosody, the author examines Verdi's approach to the considerably greater variety of accent patterns in his first newly composed French opera. He shows that composer utilized several ways to make the more irregular French patterns fit into regular melodic patterns, often symmetrical in some way, with minimal distortion of the natural word stresses. The melodic rhythms in this opera therefore differ little from his Italian operas. The latter portion of the article compares Verdi's approach to prosody with that of Meyerbeer in *Le prophète*, showing that French composer often went in the opposite direction of Verdi by increasing the effect of metrical irregularities in the text. For a related examinations of Verdi's approach to French prosody, see items 479 and 645.

972. Noske, Frits. "Melodia e struttura in *Les vêpres siciliennes* di Verdi." *Ricerche musicali* 4 (1980): 3–8.

Discusses several passages from the opera in which the sequence of chords cannot be easily explained according to traditional rules of tonality. In each case, however, an "explanation" of the passage can be given by taking into consideration the interaction of the chords in question with other elements of music at those points, particularly melody.

973. Smart, Mary Ann. "'Proud, Indomitable, Irascible': Allegories of Nation in *Attila* and *Les vêpres siciliennes*." In *Verdi's Middle Period, 1849–1859: Source Studies, Analysis, and Performance Practice* (item 235), 227–56.

Examines Verdi's representation of the "Liberty" archetype in Hélène's entrance aria from *Vêpres* against the background of Balzac's 1837 novella *Massimila Doni*, Delacroix's 1831 painting "Liberty Leading the People," Odabella's first aria in *Attila*, and Hélène's final aria in *Vêpres*. Both Odabella's aria and Hélène's initial aria portray the heroine as a "rabble-rouser" with respect to the chorus. Hélène's final aria shows an extremely sophisticated approach loosely based on a double-aria framework, for which the author suggests several possible interpretations.

974. Várnai, Péter Pál. "La struttura ritmica come mezzo di caratterizzazione ne *I vespri siciliani*." *Studi verdiani* 10 (1994–95): 93–103.

Describes Verdi's use of the anapestic "rhythm of death" as a semiotic sign that permeates the entire score of *Vespri*, the use of certain rhythmic formulas as "positive" and "negative" signs, and the association of some of the "positive" rhythmic ideas with local color in the context of compound meters ($\frac{6}{8}$ and $\frac{12}{8}$) associated with popular Sicilian dances.

975. Vlad, Roman. "Unità strutturale dei *Vespri siciliani*." In *Il melodramma italiano dell'ottocento: Studi e ricerche per Massimo Mila*, 45–89. Ed. by Giorgio Pestelli. Saggi, 575. Turin: Einaudi, 1977. ML 1733.4 .M5.

Describes an unusually complex series of thematic relationships that provide a powerful sense of unity throughout the work. The most pervasive idea is a short rhythmic motive, presented initially in the opening bars of the overture. The melodic theme associated with the singing of the "De profundis" in Act IV acts as another central reference. The author also discusses Verdi's use of irregular phrase structure and striking harmonic effects in the opera.

Staging; Scenography

* Conati, Marcello. "Ballabili nei *Vespri*: Con alcune osservazioni su Verdi e la musica popolare." See item 964.

Performance History; Reception

976. Gartious, Hervé, ed. *Giuseppe Verdi, "Les vêpres siciliennes": Dossier de presse parisienne (1855)*. Critiques de l'opéra français du XIXème siècle, 6. N.p.: Musik-Edition Lucie Galland, 1995. 146 p. ISBN 3–925934–23–5.

The main body of the volume reproduces nearly 24 reviews of the opera from contemporary newspapers and journals. An introductory section surveys the history of the opera, its relationship to the tradition of French *grand opéra*, and the state of the French press under the Second Empire. The volume includes a brief bibliography and an index of composers and their works.

CHAPTER 13

Never Realized Operatic Plans

This chapter includes studies about operas that Verdi planned to write, but were never completed.

L'ASSEDIO DI FIRENZE

977. Mossa, Carlo Matteo. "A Monk and At Least Some New Things: Verdi, Cammarano, and *L'Assedio di Firenze.*" In *Verdi's Middle Period, 1849–1859: Source Studies, Analysis, and Performance Practice* (item 235), 99–126.

Traces Verdi's interest in Francesco Domenico Guerrazzi's novel *L'assedio di Firenze* as a potential subject for an opera during the latter half of 1848 and the early months of 1849, largely through correspondence with Cammarano and Piave, some previously unpublished. Mossa argues that in addition to its patriotic theme, Verdi was drawn to the idea of utilizing striking scenic tableaus. One, which he envisioned for the opening scene, featured the reconciliation of the Buondelmonte brothers during a sermon preached by the monk Benedetto da Foiano, an idea that was rejected by the censors. The author also describes Cammarano's scenario for the opera, sent to the composer in March 1849, with a transcription for part of the intended fourth act and Verdi's subsequent revision of the passage. Appendices list principal characters and provide a summary of chapters in Guerrazzi's novel.

LORENZINO DE'MEDICI

978. Vecchi, Giuseppe. "Alcune osservazioni su un libretto approntato e mai realizzato: *Lorenzino de'Medici.*" *Quadrivium: Studi di filologia e musicologia* 20 (1979): 129–56.

Reprinted in *Studi e ricerche sui libretti delle opere di Giuseppe Verdi* (item 444), 129–56.

Although Verdi showed an interest in Piave's libretto to *Lorenzino de'Medici*, he sensed that the project would provoke an ongoing battle with the censors at Venice and went on to compose *I due Foscari* instead. The author summarizes the striking similarities between the two librettos and compares the critical reaction of Alberto Mazzucato to *I due Foscari* to Luigi Casamorata's review of the *Lorenzino* story as set by Giovanni Pacini (both reviews are reprinted in full). The author also reproduces the original scenario for the *Lorenzino* opera.

RE LEAR

979. Gerhartz, Leo Karl. "Il *Re Lear* di Antonio Somma ed il modello melodrammatico dell'opera verdiana: Principi per una definizione del libretto verdiano." *Atti 1* (item 224), 110–15.

The libretto for *Re Lear* differs from other librettos that Verdi set to music in that it retains the character of a spoken drama. The text focuses on the thoughts and psychological feelings of the characters rather than theatrical gestures or actions. Verdi's correspondence shows that while he appreciated the novelty of approach, he had serious doubts that the text could be set to music effectively.

* Guandalini, Gina. "I due *Macbeth* e i molti *Lear* di Verdi." See item 759.

* Luzio, Alessandro. "Il *Re Lear* di Verdi." See item 85.

980. Martin, George. "Verdi, *King Lear*, and Maria Piccolomini." *Columbia Library Columns* 21 (1971): 12–20.

Describes the background of a letter dated 22 August 1856 from Verdi to Vincenzo Torelli, Secretary of the Teatro San Carlo in Naples, and presents an English translation of the entire letter. The document contains the composer's suggestions for a contractual offer to Maria Piccolomini, whom he wished to create the role of Cordelia in his projected opera. Verdi ultimately stopped work on *Re Lear*, in part, because Piccolomini turned down the role and because Torelli's proposed substitute was unacceptable to him.

* Medici, Mario. "Lettere sul *Re Lear*." See item 100.

* Pascolato, Alessandro. *Re Lear e Ballo in maschera: Lettere di Giuseppe Verdi ad Antonio Somma.* See item 86.

981. Schmidgall, Gary. "Verdi's *King Lear* Project." *19th Century Music* 9 (1985–86): 83–101.

Reviews the history and development of the aborted *Re Lear* project based on both previously published material (correspondence and a scenario sent by Verdi to Cammarano) and on material from Sant'Agata recently made available to scholars on microfilm at the AIVS archives. New materials include two manuscript librettos in the hand of Antonio Somma, with a copy of the preliminary libretto in Verdi's hand, and over a dozen letters from Somma to Verdi. The author concludes that despite the composer's desire to treat the material in a "completely new way, on a grand scale, without any regard for convention," the opera was beginning to take shape as a typical number opera that may have closely resembled his general approach in *Macbeth*. While it is clear that Verdi halted work on the opera in part because he could not find a suitable cast, Schmidgall suggests that Verdi may have been unable to reconcile his expressed desire for unconventional treatment with the more conventional pattern that had begun to emerge in the libretto. The author describes in detail the second, and apparently final, version of the Somma's libretto, interspersed with commentary about significant changes from the earlier version and Verdi's reactions as seen in the correspondence.

CHAPTER 14

Non-Operatic Works

This chapter contains citations regarding Verdi's compositions outside the realm of opera, including juvenilia.

MESSA DA REQUIEM

Guides to the Work

982. Prosperi, Virgilio. *La Messa da Requiem di Giuseppe Verdi: Guida all'ascolto.* Introduction by Paolo Isotta. Preface by Claudio Sartori. Cortona: Calosci, 1994. 204 p. ISBN 88–7785–091–4. MT 115 .V48 P7 1994.

A sophisticated guide to the work, which includes essays on Verdi's sense of religion, religion in his *Requiem*, the history of the composition, the work's reception, and the place of the *Requiem* in the history of nineteenth-century religious music. The analytical portion of the volume considers the *Requiem*'s structure and musical style as a whole and offers comments about each individual section. In an appendix, the author presents a transcription of Verdi's original version of the "Liber scriptus," written as part of the composite Mass for Rossini. The volume also contains a bibliography and discography.

983. Rosen, David. *Verdi: Requiem.* Cambridge Music Handbooks. Cambridge: Cambridge University Press, 1995. ix, 115 p. ISBN 0–521–39448–1 (cloth); 0–521–39767–7 (paper). ML 410 .V4 R73.

This guide to the *Requiem* provides a useful distillation of the author's dissertation (item 985) and other writings about the composition. Sections of the handbook consider the history of the work (including its relationship to the Mass for Rossini); its premiere, subsequent performance history, and performing practices; concise analyses of each of the movements; the process of revision in the "Liber scriptus" and "Lacrymosa," which had their origins in earlier compositions; the issue of musical coherence in the work as a whole; and the relationship of the work to the genres of church music and opera. In the analytical sections of the book, readers will find it useful to have on hand a copy of the critical edition of the work, edited by Rosen. The volume includes a selective bibliography and a useful detailed index.

Histories and General Studies

984. Martin, George. "Verdi, Manzoni, and the *Requiem*." In *Aspects of Verdi* (item 244), 31–58.

Argues that the effectiveness of the *Requiem* is diminished if the listeners do not understand its connection to Alessandro Manzoni and the philosophical views that he represents. The author reviews the major literary works of Alessandro Manzoni, including the Ode "Il cinque maggio," the verse dramas, *Il conte di Carmagnola* and *Adelchi*, and his novel, *I promessi sposi*, suggesting ways in which their themes must have appealed to Verdi. Verdi's own religious beliefs, however, seem to have been at odds with Manzoni's idea that trust in God could ameliorate life's troubles. Martin argues that Verdi's treatment of the Requiem text emphasizes his own religious position—the nonbeliever's not knowing of God or the believer's failure to find a response in God, a theme that he also finds in several other works, particularly *Luisa Miller* and the Te Deum. Appendices to the article include the text of Manzoni's "Il cinque maggio," set to music by the young Verdi but apparently later lost or destroyed, and a comparison between the version of the Requiem text used by Verdi to that used by Mozart.

Studies of Compositional Process

985. Rosen, David. "The Genesis of Verdi's *Requiem*." Ph.D. dissertation, University of California, Berkeley, 1976. vi, 240 p.

A study of the *Requiem*'s origins, including motivation for the work, and compositional chronology and process. The major portion of the dissertation analyzes three movements that involved substantial revisions. Verdi's music for the "Libera me" was a revision of a movement originally written several years earlier as his contribution to a composite Mass honoring Rossini. The "Lacrymosa" borrows material from a duet he had withdrawn from *Don Carlos*, while the "Liber scriptus" section was originally composed as a fugue for chorus and orchestra. Verdi later changed it to a solo for mezzo-soprano, probably for reasons of greater musical contrast. Parts of this dissertation have been published in expanded form in items 983, 987, and 988.

986. ———. "La *Messa* a Rossini e il *Requiem* per Manzoni." *Rivista italiana di musicologia* 4 (1969): 127–37; 5 (1970): 216–33.

Republished in *Messa per Rossini: La storia, il testo, la musica* (item 993), 119–49.

Evidence shows that as early as 1871, Verdi conceived of using material from his "Libera me" in a Mass setting and that some of the music from this movement would be incorporated cyclically into other movements. The author concludes, however, that Verdi did not begin to write any other movements for the Manzoni *Requiem* until the spring of 1873, one month before the death of Manzoni. The second section of the article discusses significant changes made by Verdi when he adopted the previously composed "Libera me" as the final movement of his *Requiem* for Manzoni.

987. ———. "The Operatic Origins of Verdi's 'Lacrymosa.'" *Studi verdiani* 5 (1988–89): 65–84.

An expansion of part of the author's dissertation (item 985 above). Verdi modelled the "Lacrymosa" melody on a tune he had previously written for *Don Carlos*. The original melody, sung by Philippe, belongs to a duet, "Qui me rendra ce mort," that he cut from Act IV of the opera before its premiere. The composer's revision of the melody for the *Requiem* can be explained, in part, by the different text. Some aspects of the revision, however, show that Verdi went on to substantially improve his original idea, particularly in terms of rhythmic and harmonic shape.

988. ———. "Verdi's 'Liber scriptus' Rewritten." *Musical Quarterly* 55 (1969): 151–69.

An expansion of part of the author's dissertation (item 985 above). The author suggests that Verdi replaced his original choral-orchestral fugue for "Liber scriptus" with an alto solo about a year after the premiere performance because the original setting did not integrate well with the preceding "Mors stupebit" and the following reprise of the "Dies irae." The article includes a reproduction of the original version from the published piano-vocal score and a short appendix, showing that while Maria Waldmann (for whom the new solo was written) was generally regarded as a mezzo-soprano, Verdi thought of her as a contralto.

Stylistic and Analytical Studies

*   Cantoni, Angelo. "Verdi e Stravinskij." See item 351.

989. Pizzetti, Ildebrando. "Introduzione alla *Messa da Requiem*." In *La musica italiana dell'ottocento*, 279–90. Turin: Edizioni Palatine di R. Pezzani & C., 1947. Reprint, with introductory essays by Marzio Pieri, Gian Paolo Minardi and Evelina Schatz. Parma: Battei, 1988. ML 290.4 .P69 1988.

A brief survey of the composition and a consideration of what grants the work its tremendous power to move listeners.

990. Roeder, John. "Pitch and Rhythmic Dramaturgy in Verdi's 'Lux aeterna'." *19th Century Music* 14 (1990–91): 169–85.

Explores the roles of hypermeter and scale-degree function in "Lux aeterna." The author points out a series of ways that hypermeter and harmony together underscore the dramatic essence of the "Lux aeterna" text. This harmonic and metric symbolism also significantly bolsters the effect of the recapitulatory passages of the final movement, "Libera me." See item 991 for additional commentary and a critique of some of Roeder's ideas.

991. Rosen, David. "Reprise as Resolution in Verdi's *Messa da Requiem*." *Theory and Practice* 19 (1994): 83–104.

Discusses the issue of coherence in the work by examining five passages in which Verdi presents a musical idea one or more times in an "unresolved" state and later "resolves" it through an altered repetition of the passage. Rosen offers some elaboration and critique of John Roeder's analysis of the "Lux aeterna" movement (item 990).

Performance History; Reception

992. Schlitzer, Franco. "Il *Requiem* a Londra (1875)." In *Giuseppe Verdi: Scritti raccolti in occasione delle "Celebrazioni Verdiane" dell'VIII Settimana Musicale* (item 243), 81–85.

Discusses the performances of Verdi's *Requiem* in London during 1875 as part of a grand tour that originated in Paris. Reviews show that the performances were so successful that several additional concerts were added to the schedule.

MASS FOR ROSSINI

993. Girardi, Michele, and Petrobelli, Pierluigi, eds. *"Messa per Rossini": La storia, il testo, la musica.* Quaderni dell'Istituto di Studi Verdiani, 5. Parma, Istituto di Studi Verdiani: Milan: Ricordi, 1988. 166 p. ISBN 88–85065–08–2. ML 410 .V4 A48 vol. 5.

A commemorative volume issued in connection with the first performance in September 1988 of the work proposed by Verdi and composed by him and twelve other composers. Individual essays discuss the history of the work and the difficulties that led to the termination of plans for its performance, the Mass's musical style, the orchestra required by the work, and the Mass's relationship to the Manzoni *Requiem.* A concluding essay summarizes biographical information about each of the other composers who wrote music for the Mass. In addition to the essays, the volume contains important illustrative material, including pictures of the individual composers and a facsimile reproduction of the original libretto.

994. *"Libera me Domine": Messa per Rossini.* Facsimile reproduction of the autograph manuscript. Preface by Pierluigi Petrobelli. Parma: Istituto di Studi Verdiani, 1988. [xii, 40] p. in 5 fascicles. ISBN 88–85065–07–4. ML 96.5 V463 no. 2.

A beautiful, full-size reproduction of the manuscript for "Libera me," issued in a limited commemorative edition of 1000 copies. Verdi intended the movement to be part of the composite Mass honoring Rossini. When the performance of the Mass fell through, Verdi revised the movement as part of his *Requiem* for Manzoni (see item 993 above). The original manuscript is part of the collection of Verdi's heirs at Sant'Agata.

QUATTRO PEZZI SACRI

Histories and General Studies

* Dunning, Albert. "Verdi e lo storicismo musicale." Cited above as item 264.

995. Osthoff, Wolfgang. "Dante beim späten Verdi." *Studi verdiani* 5 (1988–89): 35–64.

Dante's influence on Verdi can first be seen in Act IV of *Aida*, where the composer requested the use of *terzina* for the chorus of the priests. Verdi's regard for Dante is clearest, however, in the *Quattro pezzi sacri*, written during a period in which the composer was increasingly interested in earlier Italian music, particularly that of Palestrina, and in which he experienced a degree of rapprochement with Catholicism. Of these four pieces, only the *Laudi alla Vergine Maria* is based on a text by Dante; the other three works, however, boast many points of philosophical resonance with Dante's writings.

* Zanetti, Emilia. "La corrispondenza di Verdi conservata a 'S. Cecilia': Contributi all'epistolario." See item 42.

Studies of Compositional Process

996. Conati, Marcello. "Le *Ave Maria su scala enigmatica* di Verdi dalla prima alla seconda stesura (1889–1897)." *Rivista italiana di musicologia* 13 (1978): 280–311.

The most definitive study to date of the genesis and compositional history of *Ave Maria*. Conati shows that the author of the "scale-rebus" that stimulated the composition of Verdi's piece was Adolfo Crescentini. An early version of the work, previously unknown, was premiered at a small, private performance in Parma directed by Giuseppe Gallini in 1895 (this version appears in facsimile at the end of the article). The author traces attempts by various individuals over the next year to persuade Verdi to publish the work, finally resulting in his grudging consent to allow its anonymous publication in the *Gazzetta musicale di Milano* in 1897. A letter to Giulio Ricordi shows, however, that Verdi had misplaced the original autograph and therefore reconstituted it from memory, during which he introduced several minor alterations from the first version. The remainder of the article traces the early performance and publication history of all four of the *Pezzi sacri*.

STRING QUARTET

Histories and General Studies

997. Guglielmi, Edoardo. "Il quartetto di Verdi e la rinascita della musica strumentale in Italia." *Atti 1* (item 224), 126–31.

   Provides general historical background to the piece and offers an assessment of its place among Verdi's works.

* Martinotti, Sergio. "Verdi e lo strumentalismo italiano." Cited as item 273.

MISCELLANEOUS COMPOSITIONS

998. Berger, Rupert. "Osservazioni sul *Pater noster* di Verdi." *Atti 1* (item 224), 22–26.

   Discusses the genesis of *Pater noster* against the background of a revival of Renaissance polyphonic music in Italy during the nineteenth century and evaluates Verdi's attempt to recreate the spirit of Renaissance musical style.

999. Martin, George. "Two Unpublished Early Works: *La madre e la patria* and *Marcia funebre*." In *Aspects of Verdi* (item 244), 139–56.

   Describes two short continuity drafts in the author's private collection that appear to be early works by Verdi. One is a patriotic song, the other a funeral march that seems to have been part of a larger composition. The author places these pieces in context of other juvenilia, most of which the composer destroyed, and presents evidence pointing to their authenticity. The music for both works is reproduced in facsimile and in transcription.

1000. ———. "Verdi's Second *Ave Maria*, 1880." In *Aspects of Verdi* (item 244), 211–25.

   Examines the composition, publication, and reception of Verdi's settings of *Ave Maria* and *Pater noster*, set to texts taken from *La professione di fede* by Antonio de' Beccari da Ferrara but credited in the nineteenth century to Dante. The author compares the *Ave Maria* to the composer's other settings of the text in *I Lombardi* and *Otello* and rebuts the notion that the 1880 setting was merely a preliminary study for the setting in *Otello*. He proposes that its lack of popularity is due to the fact that the string parts have never been published but only a piano-vocal score. Furthermore, Pope Pius X's *Motu proprio* of 1903 discouraged performances of church music written in a theatrical style.

1001. Marvin, Roberta Montemorra. "A Verdi Autograph and the Problem of Authenticity." *Studi verdiani* 9 (1993): 36–61.

Discusses an instrumental *sinfonia* in D major written in Verdi's hand in a manuscript in the Biblioteca Livia Simoni at the Museo Teatrale alla Scala in Milan. The author describes the physical features of the manuscript and the musical content of the piece, noting affinities both to the general plan and style of Rossini's overtures and to several unpublished *sinfonie* by his teacher Ferdinando Provesi, particularly a work in E-flat Major subtitled "Fricandò." Marvin then attempts to place the work into the context of Verdi's "student" years, discussing several possible occasions for its composition and performance. The article includes a facsimile reproduction of fourteen pages from the manuscript.

1002. Mingardi, Corrado. "Composizioni giovanili di Giuseppe Verdi in quattro programmi inediti della Filarmonica bussetana del 1838." *Biblioteca '70* 1 (1970): 39–44.

These programs show performances of several early compositions by Verdi: one or more *sinfonie*, an aria, a recitative and aria, a Capriccio for horn, an Introduction, Variations, and Coda for bassoon, and a comic duet. One of the programs is reproduced in facsimile.

1003. Ortombina, Fortunato. "'Sgombra, o gentil': Un dono di Verdi all'amico Delfico." *Studi verdiani* 8 (1992): 104–17.

Discusses a newly discovered album leaf in which Verdi set a short verse from Alessandro Manzoni's *Adelchi* for voice and piano as a gift to Melchiorre Delfico upon the composer's departure from Naples in 1858. The article reproduces the song in facsimile and in transcription and presents a concise analysis of the music. Ortombina also examines Verdi's attitude toward Manzoni and discusses the composer's unrealized plans to compose music based on texts by Manzoni.

* Parker, Roger. "Verdi and the *Gazzetta privilegiata di Milano*." See item 176.

1004. Rizzo, Dino. "'Con eletta musica del Sig. Verdi da Busseto, fu celebrata la
       messa solenne.'" *Studi verdiani* 9 (1993): 62–96.

       Discusses a *Messa di Gloria*, consisting of a Kyrie and Gloria, begun by
       Ferdinando Provesi and finished by Verdi. The author describes in detail an
       incomplete autograph manuscript of the work, preserved in the collection of the
       Società Filarmonica di Busseto, focusing on details of graphology that
       distinguish the hands of the young Verdi from his teacher. Rizzo provides
       evidence that this work is the same mentioned by Verdi's earliest biographer,
       Giuseppe Demaldè (see item 127), and that Verdi revised it two years after its
       initial completion for a performance at the Chiesa di S. Anna on 15 September
       1835, the Feast of the Madonna Addolorata. The performers on this occasion
       included twelve singers and fifteen instrumentalists (including Verdi as the
       continuo player). One other documented performance of the work took place
       on 8 October 1837 at a church of Croce Santo Spirito (a village near
       Castelvetro Piacentino), which received an enthusiastic report in the *Gazzetta
       privilegiata di Milano*. The article includes facsimile reproductions of six pages
       from the manuscript.

1005. Stivender, David. "The Composer of *Gesù morì*." *AIVS Newsletter* 2 (December
       1976): 6–7.

       Demonstrates that the four duet settings of texts for a Good Friday Service and
       part of a fifth (collectively entitled *Gesù morì*) that had been attributed to Verdi
       by Hans F. Redlich and Frank Walker in their article "*Gesù morì*: An
       Unknown Early Verdi Manuscript" (*Music Review* 20 [1959]: 232–43) was
       actually composed by Vincenzo Bellini. While it remains possible that Verdi
       himself may have copied Bellini's manuscript, the author concludes that the
       signature "G Verdi" at the bottom of the page containing the end of the fourth
       duet is a forgery.

1006. Walker, Frank. "*L'abandonnée*: A Forgotten Song." *Verdi: Bollettino
       dell'Istituto di Studi Verdiani* 1 [No. 2] (1960): 785–89. Italian and German
       translations are printed on pp. 1069–76.

       This little-known song was originally published in 1849 by Escudier as a
       musical supplement to *La France Musicale* and was later reprinted in a limited
       edition of 25 copies by Heugel & Fils in 1882. During the same year as its
       original publication, Schott issued two editions of 700 each (one in French and
       one in Italian and German); the woman on the title page of the German edition
       bears a striking resemblance to Giuseppina Strepponi. The author reproduces
       the title page and text of the German/English edition, as well as the text of the
       Heugel edition.

1007. ———. "Goethe's *Erster Verlust* Set to Music by Verdi: An Unknown Composition." *Music Review* 9 (1948): 13–17.

German translation by Willi Reich. "Ein unbekanntes Goethe-Lied von Giuseppe Verdi." *Schweizerische Musikzeitung/Revue musicale suisse* 91 (1951): 9–13.

Discusses the genesis and style of Verdi's song, *Chi i bei di m'adduce ancora*, based on a translation of Goethe's *Erster Verlust* probably made by Luigi Balestra. The author points to differences from the composer's earlier songs as well as similarities to passages in his later operas. The article reproduces the song in its entirety.

CHAPTER 15
Discographies & Videographies

Ongoing discographies prepared by M. Vicentini (vol. 1 only) and C. Marinelli can be found in each issue of *Studi verdiani* as listed in the following table. Beginning with vol. 8, the lists include video material as well.

Vol.	Date	Years Covered by Discography/Videography
1	1982	1977–80
2	1983	1981–82
3	1985	1983–84
4	1986–87	1985–86
5	1988–89	1987–88
6	1990	1989
7	1991	1990
8	1992	1991–92
9	1993	1993
10	1994–95	1994–95

1008. Ardoin, John. "Verdi on Record: The Early Years." *Opera Quarterly* 5/2–3 (Summer/Autumn 1987): 48–58.

Reviews thirteen early recordings, with extensive comments about performance practice. The three earliest (*Le trouvère, La traviata,* and *Rigoletto*) are French performances released by Pathé in 1912 and recently reissued by Bourg. The remainder of the recordings (two each of *Rigoletto, La traviata, Il trovatore,* and *Aida* and one recording each of *Otello* and *Falstaff*) were issued by the rival Italian HMV and Italian Columbia labels between 1927 and 1931.

* Bragaglia, Leonardo. *Verdi e i suoi interpreti (1839–1978).* See item 518.

* Cabourg, Jean, ed. *Guide des opéras de Verdi.* See item 366.

1009. Cipriani, Nicola, and Mario Stefanoni. *Verdi dal vivo: Antologia di edizioni discografiche.* N.p.: Azzali, [1989]. 229 p. ML 156.5 .V37 C5 1989.

Covers live recordings of Verdi's operas and the *Requiem* (excluding most recordings originating as radio broadcasts). The authors provide detailed discussions of one to four pages for about 50 significant recordings, focusing mainly on the period from 1950–70. Over 100 additional recordings are listed with only cast and publication information. A useful introductory section provides a summary statement or two about series and companies with recordings represented in the discography.

* Crutchfield, Will. "Vocal Ornamentation in Verdi: The Phonographic Evidence." See item 526.

* "'Dal labbro il canto estasiato vola . . .'. " See item 21.

1010. Davis, Peter G. "Le incisioni complete del *Don Carlo.*" *Atti 2* (item 225), 484–93.

A comparative description of five recordings of the complete opera issued between 1951 and 1965.

1011. De Schauensee, Max. *The Collector's Verdi and Puccini.* Keystone Books in Music, 46. Philadelphia and New York: J.B. Lippincott, 1962. Reprint. Westport, Conn.: Greenwood, 1978. 156 p. ISBN 0–313–20241–9. ML 410 .V4 D28 1978.

Lists LP recordings of each opera available at the time of publication and presents a discussion of each recording's relative strengths and weaknesses.

1012. Faw, Marc Taylor. *A Verdi Discography.* Norman, Okla.: Pilgrim Books, 1982. xi, 214 p. ISBN 0–937664–63–4.

A listing of complete performances of Verdi's works issued through 1981 with timings, casts, and publication information. The recordings are primarily commercial, but some privately issued are also included. The volume includes an excellent index of performers.

1013. Green, London. "*Otello* on Records: A Tragic Vision." *Opera Quarterly* 4 (Summer 1986): 49–56.

Discusses performances of the leading roles in seven complete recordings and two partial ones made between 1902 and 1978.

1014. ———. "*Rigoletto* on Records: Singers in Search of a Character." *The Opera Journal* 16/1 (1983): 16–29.

Examines the performance of the leading roles in seven complete recordings and one partial recording made between 1930 and 1963.

1015. Levine, Robert. "Videos." *Opera Quarterly* 5 (Summer/Autumn 1987): 142–63.

A bibliographic listing of 22 video recordings of thirteen different operas, followed by a prose review. The commentary offers interesting insights, particularly into operas for which multiple recordings exist (*Ernani, Il trovatore, Don Carlo, Aida, Otello,* and *Falstaff*).

* Marchesi, Gustavo. *Verdi.* See item 165.

* Metzger, Heinz-Klaus, and Rainer Riehn, eds. *Giuseppe Verdi.* See item 423.

1016. Modugno, Maurizio. "La discografia dell'*Ernani* 1899–1985." In *"Ernani" ieri e oggi* (item 228), 273–323.

A complete discography of full and partial recordings of the opera, preceded by a substantial historical essay discussing major performers and recordings.

1017. Pugliese, Giuseppe. "La discografia." *Verdi: Bollettino dell'Istituto di Studi Verdiani* 1 [No. 1–3] (1960): 157–208, 732–50, 1198–1250. English and German versions of this article may be found on pp. 494–592, 977–1012, 1572–1662.

A comparative analysis of eight complete recordings issued between 1943–61 of *Un ballo in maschera.*

1018. ———. "La discografia." *Verdi: Bollettino dell'Istituto di Studi Verdiani* 2 [No. 4–6] (1961–66): 177–254, 904–948, 1907–93. English and German versions of this article may be found on pp. 541–670, 1347–1428, 2471–2617.

A comparative analysis of six complete recordings issued between 1941–1960 of *La forza del destino.*

* ———. "Verdi: Da *Nabucco* ai *Vespri siciliani.*" See item 182.

1019. Pugliese, Giuseppe, and Rodolfo Celletti. "La discografia." *Verdi: Bollettino dell'Istituto di Studi Verdiani* 3 [No. 7–9] (1969–82): 177–245, 1015–37, 1773–1852. English and German translations are printed on pp. 599–717, 1378–1408, 2033–2113 (the last is in English only).

A general discussion of problems in Verdi discography, focusing on the issue of "privately issued" recordings, followed by a detailed analytical commentary about more than 20 complete recordings of *Rigoletto,* dating from 1916–1980.

1020. Quattrocchi, Arrigo. "Guida essenziale all'ascolto di Verdi." *Musica e dossier* 2 (December 1986), special insert, 64–66.

A listing of more than 80 recordings (primarily made during the last 20 years) judged by the author to be exceptional in quality. Includes short evaluative and comparative comments about some of the recordings.

1021. "Recordings." *Opera Quarterly* 5 (Summer/Autumn 1987): 165–259.

Reviews 80 recordings of Verdi's operas organized chronologically by opera. Commentary for each individual opera is provided by a different author. Its sheer size and detail makes this one of the most important general discographies available.

    *   Stinchelli, Enrico. *Verdi: La vita e l'opera.* See item 186.

    *   Tintori, Giampiero. *Invito all'ascolto di Giuseppe Verdi.* See item 384.

1022. Walker, Malcolm. "Discography." In *Giuseppe Verdi: "Falstaff"* (item 695), 176–77.

A comprehensive list of complete recordings of *Falstaff* dating from 1930 through 1982. Also includes one recording of excerpts and two early recordings made by Antonio Pini-Corsi and Victor Maurel, who sang in the original production.

1023. ———. "Discography." In *Giuseppe Verdi: "Otello"* (item 807), 203–05.

A comprehensive list of complete recordings of *Otello* dating from 1931 through 1985. Also includes several recordings of excerpts.

CHAPTER 16
Libretto Collections

While this *Guide* makes no attempt to catalogue the many different librettos for Verdi's operas, these two publications are particularly significant collections that might be considered major reference sources.

1024. Baldacci, Luigi, ed. *Tutti i libretti di Verdi*. 4th ed. Milan: Garzanti, 1992. xiv, 610 p. ML 49 .V45 B3 1992.

Presents, in chronological order, the librettos of all Verdi's operas except *Stiffelio*, accompanied by historical illustrations and photographs of contemporary productions. Unfortunately, the format of this edition does not always show details about the verse structure and forms. An appendix provides concise background information for each opera, including information about the genesis of the libretto. A second appendix provides biographical information about each of Verdi's librettists and collaborators.

1025. Weaver, William, ed. and trans. *Verdi Librettos in New English Translations with the Original Italian*. Garden City, N.Y.: Anchor Books, 1961. xi, 417 p.
Enlarged republication as *Seven Verdi Librettos with the Original Italian*. New York: Norton, 1975. x, 533 p. ISBN 0–393–00852–5. ML 49 .V45 O62.

The original publication offers excellent, relatively literal translations of the librettos to *Rigoletto, Il trovatore, La traviata, Aida,* and *Otello*, placed in parallel columns with the original Italian text. The Norton edition adds *Un ballo in maschera* and *Falstaff*.

CHAPTER 17

Editions & Editing Practices

This chapter contains articles dealing with some of the complex issues in editing Verdi's music. Most of these studies originated in research and planning for *The Works of Giuseppe Verdi*.

026. Chusid, Martin. "Editing Rigoletto." *Nuove prospettive nella ricerca verdiana* (item 231), 49–56.

Expanded version, translated into French by Dennis Collins. "La nouvelle édition de *Rigoletto*." In *Rigoletto*. *L'avant-scène opéra* 112/113 (item 843): 106–112.

Illustrates principles of editorial practice in the *New Verdi Edition* using examples from *Rigoletto*. In general, the composer's last thoughts about a passage should be considered definitive. Exceptions to this rule mainly involve external constraints, such as changes imposed by the censors.

027. Della Seta, Fabrizio. "Varianti nel testo della *Traviata*." In *L'edizione critica tra testo musicale e testo letterario: Atti del Convegno Internazionale, Cremona, 4–8 ottobre 1992*, 443–47. Ed. by Renato Borghi and Pietro Zappalà. Lucca: Libreria Musicale Italiana, 1995. ISBN 88–70961–21–4. ML 3849 .E35 1995.

As part of a conference round-table discussion, the author surveys some of the complex problems in establishing an accurate source-critical text for the libretto to *La traviata*.

* Gallico, Claudio. "Verso l'edizione critica di *Ernani* di Verdi." See item 682.

028. Gavazzeni, Gianandrea. "Problemi di tradizione dinamico-fraseologica e critica testuale, in Verdi e in Puccini." *Rassegna musicale* 29 (1959): 27–41, 106–22; 30 (1960): 60–67.

Republished as a monograph. N.p.: Ricordi, 1961. 153 p. ML 410 .V4 G3.

This article has historical significance as one of the earliest systematic attempts to consider problems associated with the preparation of a critical edition of Verdi's music. The author offers a detailed response to Denis Vaughan's article "Discordanze fra gli autografi verdiani e la loro stampa" (*La Scala*, July 1958, pp. 11–15 and 71–72), shorter essays and letters by Vaughan published in various periodicals, and reactions to these by several music critics, including Massimo Mila. Gavazzeni regards as grossly exaggerated and sensationalist Vaughan's charge that there are about 8,000 differences between the autograph and published score of the *Requiem* and about 27,000 in *Falstaff*. He discusses some of the specific examples noted by Vaughan, pointing out that many of Vaughan's "discrepancies" are results of Verdi expecting that phrasing and dynamic markings would be extrapolated from one part to parallel parts. He further argues that it is frequently difficult or impossible to arrive at an indisputable assessment of the composer's precise intentions. At the end of the main article (vol. 30 in *Rassegna musicale*) is a response by Vaughan and a reply to it by Gavazzeni. The monograph presents Gavazzeni's essay in three languages: Italian (pp. 5–51), an English translation by Gwin Morris (pp. 53–99), and a German translation by Joachim Popelka (pp. 101–153).

1029.   Gossett, Philip. "Censorship and Self-Censorship: Problems in Editing the Operas of Giuseppe Verdi." In *Essays in Musicology: A Tribute to Alvin Johnson*, 247–57. Ed. by Lewis Lockwood and Edward Roesner. N.p.: American Musicological Society, 1990. ISBN 1–878528–00–9. ML 55 .L217.

German translation by Birgit Gotzes. "Zenzur und Selbstzensur: Probleme bei der Edition von Giuseppe Verdis Opern." In *Über Musiktheater: Eine Festschrift gewidmet Arthur Scherle anläßlich seines 65. Geburtstages*, 103–15. Ed. by Stefan G. Harpner and Birgit Gotzes. Munich: Ricordi, 1992. ISBN 3–980–3090–0–2. ML 1700 .U24 1992.

Several problems peculiar to editing nineteenth-century opera pose special challenges: composers did not envision the publication of full orchestral scores for their works, nor did they usually supervise the preparation of piano reductions or circulating scores and parts. Some of the most intriguing problems faced by editors concern external censorship, which the author illustrates with examples from *Rigoletto* and *Ernani*. The chorus "Immenso Jeovha" in *Nabucco* contains changes in text and music that may have resulted from merely the fear of intervention by the censors. This and other similar cases present particularly difficult problems for editors and may have no simple solution.

1030. ———. "*The Works of Giuseppe Verdi.*" *Nuove prospettive nella ricerca verdiana* (item 231), 3–9.

For an earlier version of this paper see "L'edizione critica delle opere di Verdi" in *Per un "progetto Verdi" anni '80* (item 232), 35–44.

Reviews recent advances in Verdi research that made possible the preparation of a critical edition and provides an overview of editorial policy for the new complete edition.

1031. ———. "Toward a Critical Edition of *Macbeth.*" In "*Macbeth*" *Sourcebook* (item 762), 199–209.

A discussion of the guidelines established by the editorial board of the critical edition of the works of Verdi using examples from *Macbeth.*

1032. Hepokoski, James A. "Overriding the Autograph Score: The Problem of Textual Authority in Verdi's *Falstaff.*" *Studi verdiani* 8 (1992): 13–51.

The author asserts that the process of preparing the final "definitive" text for *Falstaff* (as well as other late operas) differed considerably from earlier operas, since the composer was personally involved in the preparation of printed instrumental parts after the "completion" of the autograph full score. Hepokoski proposes that the first printed orchestral score prepared for rental purposes, which also incorporated revisions made for Roman performances in early 1893, should be considered the primary source for a critical edition of the opera. The article presents important evidence and conclusions regarding the respective roles of Verdi, Boito, and Ricordi in the publication process. The article contains an important discussion of editing principles for Verdi's later works.

1033. Lawton, David. "The Autograph of *Aida* and the New Verdi Edition." *Verdi Newsletter* 14 (1986): 4–14.

Argues that because the publication and performance history of *Aida* is more complex than other operas, the autograph full score cannot always be considered the definitive source for a critical edition in the *Works of Giuseppe Verdi.* The author illustrates this point with several passages in the Prelude in which the reading of the autograph was apparently superseded by revisions in later, non-autograph sources. He also discusses discrepancies from several other passages in the opera that seem to have no satisfactory explanation based on currently available sources.

1034. ———. "Critical Performers and Critical Editions." *Nuove prospettive nella ricerca verdiana* (item 231), 10–19.

Discusses, using an example from the opening bars of *Macbeth*, characteristic problems in accurately interpreting Verdi's autograph scores. Specific issues raised here focus on ambiguities in dynamics and articulation.

1035. ———. "Why Bother with the New Verdi Edition?" *Opera Quarterly* 2 (Winter 1984–85): 43–54.

Lists reasons why a critical edition of Verdi's works is necessary for scholars, performers, and Verdi enthusiasts: 1) there has never been a complete edition of Verdi's works (full orchestral score of some operas have never even been printed); 2) recent Verdi research has disclosed a wealth of previously unknown material, including substitute arias and non-definitive revisions for some of the early operas; and 3) existing scores inadequately represent the composer's intentions. The author concludes by illustrating some of the problems that the critical edition will resolve, or at least present as alternative choices, involving discrepancies between Verdi's autographs and existing scores. The author argues that the critical edition will not limit performers' roles as interpreters, but will, in many cases, make available to them more interpretative options.

1036. Parker, Roger. "The Critical Edition of *Nabucco*." *Opera Quarterly* 5 (Summer/Autumn 1987): 91–98.

Illustrates differences between the approach of the new critical edition and earlier editions using "Va pensiero" as an example.

Catalogue of Verdi's Compositions

OPERAS[1]

1. *Oberto, Conte di San Bonifacio.* Dramma in due atti (1839).
2. *Un giorno di regno.* Melodramma giocoso in due atti (1840).
3. *Nabucodonosor.* Dramma lirico in quattro parti (1842).
4. *I lombardi alla prima crociata.* Dramma lirico (1843).
5. *Ernani.* Dramma lirico in quattro parti (1844).
6. *I due Foscari.* Tragedia lirica (1844).
7. *Giovanna d'Arco.* Dramma lirico (1845).
8. *Alzira.* Tragedia lirica, divisa in prologo e due atti[2] (1845).
9. *Attila.* Dramma lirico in un prologo e tre atti (1846).
10. *Macbeth* (1847).
11. *I masnadieri.* A tragic opera in four parts (1847).
12. *Jérusalem.* Opéra en quatre actes (1847).
13. *Il corsaro* (1848).
14. *La battaglia di Legnano.* Tragedia lirica in quattro atti (1849).
15. *Luisa Miller.* Melodramma tragico in tre atti (1849).
16. *Stiffelio* (1850).
17. *Rigoletto.* Melodramma. (1851).
18. *Il trovatore.* Dramma in quattro parti (1853).
19. *La traviata* (1853).
20. *Les vêpres siciliennes.* Opéra en cinq actes (1855).
21. *Simon Boccanegra.* In tre atti e un prologo (1857).
22. *Aroldo.* In quattro atti (1857).

---

[1]Titles and descriptions are taken from the librettos for the premiere performances as listed in Martin Chusid, *A Catalog of Verdi's Operas* (item 1).

[2]The autograph manuscript is divided into three acts. See Chusid, *A Catalog of Verdi's Operas*, p. 14.

23. *Un ballo in maschera.* Melodramma in tre atti (1859).
24. *La forza del destino.* Opera in quattro atti (1862).
25. *Macbeth* (revised). Opéra in quatre actes (1865).
26. *Don Carlos.* Opéra en cinq actes (1867).
27. *La forza del destino* (revised). Opera in quattro atti (1869).
28. *Aida.* Opera in 4 atti e 7 quadri (1871).
29. *Simon Boccanegra* (revised). Melodramma in un prologo e tre atti (1881).
30. *Don Carlo* (revised). Opera (1884).
31. *Otello.* Dramma lirico in quattro atti (1887).
32. *Falstaff.* Commedia lirica in tre atti (1893).

SACRED CHORAL COMPOSITIONS[1]

1. *Messa di Gloria* (Kyrie and Gloria) for chorus and orchestra (ca. 1833).[2]
2. *Tantum ergo* for tenor and orchestra, with alternative organ accompaniment (1836).
3. *Libera me* for soprano, chorus, and orchestra. Contribution to a composite Mass in honor of Rossini (1868–69).
4. *Messa da Requiem* for soloists, chorus, and orchestra (1874).
5. *Pater noster* for five-part chorus, *a cappella* (1880).
6. *Ave Maria* for soprano and strings (1880). Text: attributed to Dante.
7. *Quattro pezzi sacri*
   6a. *Ave Maria su scala enigmatica* for four-part chorus (1889).
   6b. *Stabat mater* for four-part chorus and orchestra (1897). Text: Jacopone da Todi.
   6c. *Laudi alla Vergine Maria* for women's chorus, *a cappella* (1886). Text: attributed to Dante.
   6d. *Te Deum* for double chorus and orchestra (1895).

SONGS

1. *Sei romanze* (published 1838).
   1a. *Non t'accostare all'urna.* Text: Jacopo Vittorelli.
   1b. *More, Elisa, lo stanco poeta.* Text: Tommaso Bianchi.
   1c. *In solitaria stanza.* Text: Jacopo Vittorelli.
   1d. *Nell'orror di notte oscura.* Text: Carlo Angiolini.
   1e. *Perduta ho la pace.* Text: Wolfgang Goethe, trans. Luigi Balestra.
   1f. *Deh, pietosa, oh addolorata.* Text: Wolfgang Goethe, trans. Luigi Balestra.
2. *L'esule* (published ca. 1839). Text: Temistocle Solera.

---

[1]Dates refer to the date of composition.

[2]The Mass was begun by Ferdinando Provesi and completed by Verdi. See item 1004.

3. *La seduzione* (published 1839). Text: Luigi Balestra.
4. *Chi i bei di m'adduce ancora* (composed 1842). Text: Wolfgang Goethe, trans. Luigi Balestra?
5. *Sei romanze* (published ca. 1845).
    5a. *Il tramonto.* Text: Andrea Maffei.
    5b. *La zingara.* Text: S.M. Maggioni.
    5c. *Ad una stella.* Text: Andrea Maffei.
    5d. *Lo spazzacamino.* Text: S.M. Maggioni.
    5e. *Il mistero.* Text: Felice Romani.
    5f. *Brindisi.*[1] Text: Andrea Maffei.
6. *Il poveretto* (published 1847). Text: Manfredo Maggioni.
7. *La patria: Inno nazionale a Ferdinando II* (composed 1848?). Text: Michele Cucciniello.
8. *L'abandonnée* (publication 1849). Text: Marie and Léon Escudier.
9. *Barcarola: Fiorellin che sorge appena* (composed ca. 1850). Text: Francesco Maria Piave.
10. *Fiorara* (composed 1853). Text: Buvoli.
11. *La preghiera del poeta* (composed ca. 1858). Text: Nicola Sole.
12. *Sgombra, o gentil* (composed in 1858). Text: Alessandro Manzoni.
13. *Il brigidin* (composed ca. 1869). Text: Francesco Dall'Ongaro.
14. *Stornello* (composed ca. 1869). Text: Anonymous.
15. *Cupa e il sepolcre mutolo* (composed before 1873). Text: Unknown.
16. *Pietà, Signor* (published 1894). Text: Arrigo Boito.
17. *Due lagrime* (date unknown; unpublished).
18. *Elisa* (date unknown).
19. *Non t'accostare all'urna more* (date unknown).

OTHER WORKS (Provisional List)[2]

1. Adagio (date uncertain; only survives in fragmentary form)
2. Sinfonia in D Major (date uncertain)
3. *Introduzione, variazioni, e coda* for bassoon (date uncertain)
4. Overture (substitute overture for Rossini's *Il barbiere di Siviglia*; composed 1828).†
5. *I deliri di Saul*: Cantata for baritone and orchestra (1828).†
6. *Le lamentazioni di Geremia* for chorus (1829).†
7. Aria: *Io la vidi* for voice and orchestra (date unknown, possibly 1833–35). Text: Calisto Bassi.

---

[1]This song exists in two versions; the one published as part of this set is the later version.

[2]The symbol † indicates that the work appears to be lost.

8. *Il cinque maggio* for voice and piano (composed 1836). Text: Alessandro Manzoni.†
9. *Capriccio* for horn (composed 1838?).†
10. *Divertimento* for trumpet (composed 1838).†
11. Notturno: *Guarda che bianca luna* for soprano, tenor, and bass with flute obbligato (published 1839). Text: Jacopo Vittorelli.
12. *Inno popolare: Suoni la tromba* for male chorus and piano (composed 1848). Text: Goffredo Mameli.
13. *Inno delle nazioni* for soprano solo, five-part chorus, and orchestra (composed 1862). Text: Arrigo Boito.
14. *Romanza senza parole* for piano (published 1865).
15. String Quartet, E Minor (composed 1873).
16. La madre e la patria (date unknown).
17. Marcia funebre (date unknown).

Contents of *The Works of Giuseppe Verdi / Le Opere di Giuseppe Verdi*

(Critical Edition of the Complete Works published by
the University of Chicago Press and Casa Ricordi)[1]

SERIES I: OPERAS

1. *Oberto, Conte di San Bonifacio*
2. *Un giorno di regno*
3. *Nabucodonosor*, ed. by Roger Parker (1988)
4. *I lombardi alla prima crociata*
5. *Ernani*, ed. by Claudio Gallico (1985)
6. *I due Foscari*, ed. by Luca Tutino
7. *Giovanna d'Arco*
8. *Alzira*, ed. by Stefano Castelvecchi with the collaboration of Jonathan Cheskin (1994)
9. *Attila*, ed. by Frank Traficante
10. *Macbeth* (first version), ed. by David Lawton
11. *I masnadieri*, ed. by Roberta Montemorra Marvin (1999)
12. *Jérusalem*
13. *Il corsaro*, ed. by G. Elizabeth Hudson (1998)
14. *La battaglia di Legnano*
15. *Luisa Miller*, ed. by Jeffrey Kallberg (1991)
16. *Stiffelio*, ed. by Kathleen Kuzmick Hansell (1998)
17. *Rigoletto*, ed. by Martin Chusid (1983)
18a. *Il trovatore*, ed. by David Lawton (1993)

---

[1]I am grateful to Kathleen K. Hansell, Managing Editor of the series at the University of Chicago Press, for supplying the information for this table.

SERIES II: SONGS

SERIES III: SACRED MUSIC

SERIES IV: CANTATAS AND HYMNS

SERIES V: CHAMBER MUSIC

SERIES VI: JUVENILIA

Volumes and content to be determined

Locations of Premiere Performances of Verdi's Operas

Cairo, Opera	*Aida* (1871)
Milan, Teatro alla Scala	*Oberto* (1839)
	Un giorno di regno (1840)
	Nabucodonosor (1842)
	I lombardi alla prima crociata (1843)
	Giovanna d'Arco (1845)
	Don Carlo (Italian version, 1867)
	La forza del destino (revision, 1869)
	Simon Boccanegra (revision, 1881)
	Otello (1887)
	Falstaff (1893)
Florence, Teatro La Pergola	*Macbeth* (1847)
London, Her Majesty's Theatre	*I masnadieri* (1849)
Naples, Teatro San Carlo	*Alzira* (1845)
	Luisa Miller (1849)
Paris, Opéra	*Jérusalem* (1847)
	Les vêpres siciliennes (1855)
	Don Carlos (1867)
Paris, Théâtre-Lyrique	*Macbeth* (revision, 1865)
Rimini, Teatro Nuovo	*Aroldo* (1857)

Rome, Teatro Apollo   *Il trovatore* (1853)
                                        Un ballo in maschera (1859)

Rome, Teatro Argentina   *I due Foscari* (1844)
                                      La battaglia di Legnano (1848)

St. Petersburg, Imperial Theater   *La forza del destino* (1862)

Trieste, Teatro Grande   *Il corsaro* (1848)
                                                Stiffelio (1850)

Venice, Teatro La Fenice   *Ernani* (1844)
                                                 Attila (1846)
                                              Rigoletto (1851)
                                             La traviata (1853)
                                        Simon Boccanegra (1857)

Verdi's Librettists & Other Collaborators

Bardare, Leone Emanuele (1820 – after 1874)
Il trovatore (additions to main libretto)

Beaumont, Alexandre (1827–1909)
Macbeth (revised version)

Boito, Arrigo (1842–1918)
Simon Boccanegra (revised version)
Otello
Falstaff

Cammarano, Salvatore (1801–52)
Alzira
La battaglia di Legnano
Luisa Miller
Il trovatore

De Lauzières, Achille
Don Carlo (Italian version)

Du Locle, Camille (1832–1903)
Don Carlos (also collaborated on Italian version)
Aida (expanded Mariette's scenario)

Duveyrier, Charles (1803–66)
Les vêpres siciliennes

Ghislanzoni, Antonio (1824–93)
La forza del destino (revised version)
Aida

Maffei, Andrea (1798–1885)
Macbeth
I masnadieri

Mariette, Auguste (1821–81)
Aida (prepared original scenario)

Méry, Joseph (1797–1865)
Don Carlos

Montanelli, Giuseppe
Simon Boccanegra (additions to main libretto)

Nuitter, Charles-Louis-Etienne (1828–99)
Macbeth (revised version)

Piave, Francesco Maria (1810–76)
Ernani
I due Foscari
Attila (completed libretto)
Macbeth
Il corsaro
Stiffelio
Rigoletto
La traviata
Simon Boccanegra
Aroldo
La forza del destino

Piazza, Antonio
Oberto

Romani, Felice (1788–1865)
Un giorno di regno

Royer, Alphonse (1803–73)
Jérusalem (translation & revision of *I lombardi*)

Scribe, Eugène (1791–1861)
　　Les vêpres siciliennes

Solera, Temistocle (1815–78)
　　Oberto (revised Piazza's libretto)
　　Nabucodonosor
　　I lombardi alla prima
　　Giovanna d'Arco
　　Attila

Somma, Antonio (1809–65)
　　Un ballo in maschera

Vaëz, Gustave (1812–62)
　　Jérusalem (trans. & revised *I lombardi*)

Zanardini, Angelo
　　Don Carlo (Italian version)

Literary Sources for Verdi's Operas Including Some Considered by Verdi for Prospective Operas[1]

This table shows both the literary sources that Verdi and his librettists used for his operas, as well as some additional sources that Verdi was known to have considered for operas that were never realized. The list of prospective sources is not intended to be comprehensive, but illustrative. It does not include some plays or other materials simply sent to Verdi by his librettists and others.

DRAMAS AND NOVELS

Anicet-Bourgeois, Auguste (1806–71) and **Francis Cornue** (dates unknown)
Nabuchodonosor (1836) . . . . *Nabucco* (1842)

Byron, George Gordon, 6th Baron (1788–1824)
The Bride of Abydos (1813)
Cain (1821)
The Corsair (1814) . . . . *Il corsaro* (1848)
The Two Foscari (1821) . . . . *I due Foscari* (1833)

---

[1]References to potential operatic subjects are scattered throughout Verdi's correspondence but are particularly rich in the letter exchange with Cammarano. The American Institute for Verdi studies has microfilm copies from the Sant'Agata collection of some scenarios and librettos that the composer was considering (see item 19). Verdi made several lists of potential opera subjects in his copialettere; the published edition (item 28) includes a poor quality facsimile of the larger list as table XI (facing p. 422). For a recent discussion of these lists and other materials relating to prospective opera subjects, see Martin Chusid's "Toward an Understanding of Verdi's Middle Period" (item 367).

Calderón de la Barca, Pedro (1600–81)
A secreto agravio secreta venganza (1635)

Chateaubriand, François-Auguste-René, Viscount (1786–1848)
Atala (1801)

Dall'Ongaro, Francesco (1808–73)
Usca

Dennery, Adolphe Philippe (1811–99)
Marie Jean, ou Le femme du peuple (1845)

Dumas, Alexandre, pére (1802–70)
Acté et Néron
Caterina Howard (1834)
Kean, ou Désordre et génie (1836)

Dumas, Alexandre, fils (1824–95)
La dame aux camélias (1852) . . . . *La traviata* (1853)

García Gutiérrez, Antonio (1813–84)
Simón Bocanegra (1843) . . . . *Simon Boccanegra* (1857)
El trobador (1836) . . . . *Il trovatore* (1853)
La vengeance catalane (1857)

Grillparzer, Franz (1791–1872)
Die Ahnfrau (1817)

Grossi, Tommaso (1790–1853)
I lombardi alla prima crociata (1826) . . . . *I lombardi alla prima crociata* (1843)

Guerrazzi, Francesco (1804–73)
L'assedio di Firenze (1836)
   (early working titles: *Ferruccio* and *Maria dei Ricci*)

Hugo, Victor (1802–85)
Cromwell (1827)
Hernani (1830) . . . . *Ernani* (1844)
Le roi s'amuse (1832) . . . . *Rigoletto* (1851)
Marion Delorme (1829)
Ruy Blas (1838)

López de Ayala y Herrera, Adelardo (1829–79)
El tanto por ciento (1861)

Lytton, Edward George Earle Bulwer-Lytton, Baron
Rienzi: The Last of the Tribunes (1835)
    (early working title: *Cola di Rienzi*)

Méry, Joseph (1797–1865)
La bataille de Toulouse (1828) . . . . *La battaglia di Legnano* (1849)

Molière (1622–73)
Tartuffe (1664–69)

Pineau-Duval, Alexandre Vincent
Le faux Stanislas (1808) . . . . *Un giorno di regno* (1840)

Prévost d'Exiles, Antoine François, Abbé (1697–1763)
Manon Lescaut (1731)

Racine (1639–99)
Phèdre (1677)

Rivas, Ángel De Saavedra, Duke of (1791–1865)
Don Álvaro: o, La fuerza del sino (1835) . . . . *La forza del destino* (1862)

Sardou, Victorien (1831–1908)
Patrie (1869)

Schiller, Friedrich (1759–1805)
Don Carlos (1787) . . . . *Don Carlos* (1867)
Die Jungfrau von Orleans (1801) . . . . *Giovanna d'Arco* (1845)
Kabale und Liebe (1784) . . . . *Luisa Miller* (1849)
Die Räuber (1781) . . . . *I masnadieri* (1847)
Wallensteins Lager (1799) . . . . *La forza del destino* (1862)

Scott, Sir Walter (1771–1832)
Kenilworth (1821)
Woodstock, or The Cavalier (1826)
    (early working title: *Allan Cameron*)

Shakespeare, William (1564–1616)
Hamlet (1601–02)
King Henry IV (1597–98) . . . . *Falstaff* (1893)

Shakespeare, William (continued)
King Lear (1605–06)
Macbeth (1606) .... *Macbeth* (1847
The Merry Wives of Windsor (1599–1600) .... *Falstaff* (1893
Othello, or The Moor of Venice (1604) .... *Otello* (1887
Romeo and Juliet (1595)
The Tempest (1611)

Souvestre, Emile (1806–54) and **Eugène Bourgeois**
Le pasteur .... *Stiffelio* (1850

Voltaire, François-Marie Arouet (1694–1778)
Alzire, ou Les américans (1736) .... *Alzira* (1845

Werner, Zacharias (1768–1823)
Attila, König der Hunnen (1808) .... *Attila* (1846

Zorilla y Moral, José (1817–93)
El zapatero y el rey (1840–42)

ORIGINAL SCENARIO

Mariette, Auguste (1821–81)
Aida .... *Aida* (1871

LIBRETTOS NOT ORIGINALLY WRITTEN FOR VERDI

Cammarano, Salvatore (1801–52)
Buondelmonte (set by Giovanni Pacini, 1845)
Ines de Castro (set by Giuseppe Persiani, 1835)

Piave, Francesco Maria (1810–76)
Lorenzino de' Medici (set by Giovanni Pacini, 1845)

Piazza, Antonio
Lord Hamilton/Rocester .... *Oberto, Conte di San Bonifacio* (1839
(revised by Temistocle Solera for Verdi's use)

Romani, Felice (1788–1865)
Medea in Corinto (set by Simon Mayr, 1813)

Scribe, Eugène (1791–1861)
Gustave III, ou Le bal masqué (1833) .... *Un ballo in maschera* (1859
(set by Daniel-François-Esprit Auber, 1833)

Scribe, Eugène and Charles Duveyrier (1803–66)
Le duc d'Albe (1839) . . . . *Les vêpres siciliennes* (1855)
(partially set by Gaetano Donizetti, 1839)

TOPICS WITH UNKNOWN SOURCES

Anna Erizzo

Baldassare

Beatrice Cenci

Caduta dei Longobardi
Possibly from *Adelchi* (1822) by Alessandro Manzoni (1785–1873)

Cleopatra

Elfrida di Provenza
Based on a prospective, though never completed, revision of *La battaglia di Legnano*

Elvida d'Arles
Based on a prospective, though never completed, revision of *La battaglia di Legnano*

Guzmán el Bueno
Probably the drama by the same title by either **Nicolás Fernández de Moratín** (1737–80) or **Antonio Gil y Zárate** (1793–1861)

I pompeiani

Rowena
Possibly based on a Shakespeare forgery by **William Henry Ireland** (1770-1835)

Sordello

Il tesoriere del Re Don Pedro

Some Alternate Titles Associated With Verdi's Operas[1]

Attila	*Gli unni e i romani*
Un ballo in maschera	*Adelia degli Adimari* ‡ *Amelia* *Il Duca Ermanno* † *Gustavo III* *Una vendetta in Domino* † *Der Verhängnisvolle Maskenball*
La battaglia di Legnano	*L'assedio di Arlem* *Das heilige Feur* *Lida* † *Patria* *Pour la patrie* *La sconfitta degli Austriaci*
I due Foscari	*Aachan*
Ernani	*Il bandito* ‡ *Don Gomez de Silva* ‡ *Elvira d'Aragona*

---

[1] †=early working title; ‡=title proposed by censors; most others are titles of performed censored versions. Source for the censored titles is Martin Chusid, *A Catalog of Verdi's Operas* (item 1), 175–83. It contains details of performances and locations of librettos. See also Cecil Hopkinson's *A Bibliography of the Works of Giuseppe Verdi* (item 2), 2:189.

Ernani (continued)	*Ester* *L'onore castigliano* ‡ *Le proscrit, ou Le corsaire de Venise* (*Il proscrito, ossia Il corsaro di Venezia*)
La forza del destino	*Don Alvaro*
Un giorno di regno	*Il finto Stanislao*
Giovanna d'Arco	*Orietta di Lesbo*
Jérusalem	*Giselda*
Macbeth	*Saul. Azione sacra.* *Sivardo il Sassone*
I masnadieri	*Adele di Cosenza*
Nabucodonosor	*Anato* *Nabucco* *Nino* *Sennacherib*
Otello	*Iago* †
Rigoletto	*Clara di Pert* *Lionello* *La maledizione (di Vallier)* † *Triboulet*
Stiffelio	*Guglielmo Wellingrode*
La traviata	*Amore e morte* † *Violetta*
Il trovatore	*The Gypsy's Vengeance*
Les vêpres siciliennes	*Batilde di Turenna* *Giovanna de Guzman* *Giovanna di Sicilia* *Il vespro siciliano*

Chronology of Verdi's Life

1813 Born on October 9 to Carlo Verdi and Luigia Uttini at Le Roncole near Busseto in the Duchy of Parma. Baptized on October 11 at the Church of San Michele Arcangelo. Because the Duchy of Parma was under French rule, the child's name was recorded in French: Joseph Fortunin François Verdi.

1817 Begins formal schooling (and first music lessons?) with Don Pietro Baistrocchi, the local teacher and organist at Le Roncole.

1820 Substitute organist for Don Pietro Baistrocchi at the village church.

1822 Officially succeeds Baistrocchi as organist and "maestrino" at the church.

1823 Moves to Busseto, where he enters the local *ginnasio*; continues to play for Sunday and holiday services in Le Roncole.

1825 Begins to study music theory and composition with Ferdinando Provesi, *maestro di cappella* at the collegiate church of San Bartolomeo and director of its affiliated music school, as well as the town's Società Filarmonica.

1828 Composes a substitute overture for a performance of Rossini's *Barber of Seville* at Busseto and a cantata for baritone and orchestra, *I deliri di Saul*.

1829 Composes several sacred pieces for the Easter season. Beginning in the fall, becomes Provesi's assistant; unsuccessfully applies for a job as organist in the town of Soragna.

1831 Moves into the home of Antonio Barezzi, a merchant and music-lover who later becomes Verdi's benefactor, father-in-law, and a father figure. Gives singing and keyboard lessons to Margherita Barezzi, his future wife.

1832   The Monte di Pietà e d'Abbondanza of Busseto provides Verdi a four-year scholarship (beginning November 1833) to continue his musical studies in Milan. During the summer, he travels with his father and Provesi to Milan, where he applies to enter the Conservatory. His application is rejected on the grounds that he is over age, not a citizen of Lombardy-Venetia, and his poor performance on the keyboard examination. He takes up lodging with Barezzi's son Giovanni at the home of Giuseppe Seletti and by the end of summer has arranged for private lessons with Vincenzo Lavigna, former *maestro al cembalo* at La Scala and professor of composition at the Conservatory.

1833   Ferdinando Provesi dies.

1834   Serves as *maestro di cembalo* at a performance of Haydn's *Creation* by the Società Filarmonica in Milan. In June, makes an abrupt return to Busseto with his father in order to apply formally for Provesi's position. While in Busseto, he conducts concerts of the local Società Filarmonica.

1835   Returns to Milan in early January with Luigi Martelli, a former student of Barezzi, who supports them both financially. He gives lessons to Martelli, while resuming his own studies with Lavigna and continuing to rehearse and conduct performances with the Milanese Società Filarmonica. Verdi also begins work on his first opera, *Rocester*. By mid-summer, receives a formal certificate of completion of his studies by Lavigna, who unsuccessfully recommends him for a position as *maestro di cappella* and organist at Monza.

1836   Verdi's scholarship is suspended in January, due to his early completion of studies. An official competition for Provesi's position is announced. Verdi applies, undergoes an examination by court organist Giuseppe Alinovi in Parma, and is officially appointed to the position of *maestro di musica* at Busseto. Marries Margherita Barezzi on 4 May. Finishes first operatic attempt, *Rocester*, by September. Also composes a setting of Manzoni's *Il cinque maggio* and much instrumental and vocal music, including a *Tantum ergo* for voice and orchestra.

1837   Giuseppe and Margherita's first child is born, a daughter named Virginia after the title character of the tragedy by Vittorio Alfieri. In October, travels to Parma in hopes of persuading an impresario to stage his opera. When this is unsuccessful, he tries to stir up interest in the work at La Scala in Milan.

1838   Composes more instrumental music, as well as *Sei romanze* for solo voice and piano. The Verdis' second child is born in July, a son named Icilio after a character in Alfieri's *Virginia*; their daughter Virginia dies the following month. After a trip to Milan in the early fall, Verdi returns to Busseto and submits a letter of resignation, giving as the main reason his meager salary.

1839   Verdi and his family leave Busseto in February and settle in Milan. In April, the Milanese publisher Giovanni Canti issues three works by the composer: two songs and a *Notturno* for three voices with flute obbligato. La Scala commits to producing *Oberto, Conte di San Bonifacio* (a radical reworking of *Rocester*) for its annual benefit concert on behalf of the Pio Istituto Filarmonico. The performance on 17 November was modestly successful, and the impresario Bartolomeo Merelli offers Verdi a contract for three more operas at eight-month intervals.

1840   Begins composing *Un giorno di regno* in early March. In June, Margherita dies of encephalitis. *Un giorno di regno* premieres at La Scala on 5 September but is not well received. The theater administration immediately replaces it with a revival of *Oberto*, which goes well.

1841   *Oberto* performed, with some revisions, in Genoa during the first part of January; Verdi supervises rehearsals. Merelli convinces him to write music for *Nabucco*, which is completed by October. In December, Verdi enlists the support of Giuseppina Strepponi to convince the impresario to produce the work during the upcoming season.

1842   *Nabucco* premieres at La Scala on 9 March and is very successful; Verdi immediately chooses and begins to work on *I lombardi*. In May composes a song for voice and piano, "Chi i bei dì m'adduce ancora." During the summer, travels to Bologna to visit Rossini.

1843   *I lombardi alla prima crociata* premieres at La Scala on 11 February. During the rest of this year, the composer travels to several locations for productions of his operas: *Nabucco* in Vienna and Parma (both in April) and in Bologna (October); *I lombardi* in Senigallia (July) and Venice (December). Continues negotiations begun the previous year with La Fenice in Venice for a new opera; considers a number of topics, including *Re Lear* and *I due Foscari*, but eventually decides on Victor Hugo's *Ernani*. This becomes his first collaboration with Francesco Maria Piave and his first new work written for Venice's Teatro La Fenice. In December, he accepts a commission for *Giovanna d'Arco* for La Scala's 1844–45 season.

1844   Completes work on *Ernani* in February; its successful premiere at La Fenice takes place on 9 March. In late February, accepts commission for *I due Foscari* at the Teatro Argentina in Rome; less than a month later accepts commission for *Alzira* at the Teatro San Carlo in Naples. In addition, he has Piave examine the prospects for a libretto about *Attila*. Supervises the production of *I due Foscari*, which premieres on 3 November, then returns to Milan, where he begins work on *Giovanna d'Arco*. Supervises a revival of *I lombardi* at La

Scala during the last days of December. During this year, Verdi begins formal tutoring of Emanuele Muzio, who becomes a close friend of the composer, sometimes serving as his executive secretary.

1845   Supervises the premieres of *Giovanna d'Arco* at La Scala (15 February) and *Alzira* at San Carlo in Naples (12 August), as well as productions of *Ernani* and *I due Foscari* in Venice (March); later in the fall, La Fenice successfully stages a production of *Un giorno di regno* as *Il finto Stanislao*. A fight with Bartolomeo Merelli, the impresario at La Scala, escalates during the production of *Giovanna d'Arco* and Verdi vows not to return to La Scala. During March and April, composes the *Sei romanze* for voice and piano, which was published by Lucca. In October, Verdi contracts with Lucca to write a new opera, which will become *Il corsaro,* and grants the Escudier firm in Paris rights to his works in France.

1846   Directs the premiere of *Attila* at La Fenice on 17 March but becomes sick and exhausted from overwork. Not much progress is made on *Il corsaro,* but Verdi begins to consider subjects for an opera at Florence, soon settling on *Macbeth*. By the end of the year, Acts I and II of *Macbeth* are completed.

1847   Completes Act III and the scoring of *Macbeth* by mid-February. Leaves immediately for Florence, where he carefully supervises the rehearsals and the premiere of the work on 14 March. After returning to Milan, begins work on *I masnadieri,* a new work for London. Finishing all but the scoring in mid-May, he travels to London, passing through Switzerland, Germany, Belgium, and France. On 1 June, he attends the Paris Opéra for the first time. Supervises rehearsals and the premiere of *I masnadieri* (22 July) at Her Majesty's Theatre in London. Upon his return to Paris, signs a contract with the Opéra to produce *Jérusalem,* a French version of *I lombardi,* which premieres on 26 November, and renews his acquaintance with Giuseppina Strepponi.

1848   By February completes *Il corsaro* which, upon payment of his fee, becomes the property of the publisher Lucca. Lucca arranges for a premiere at the Teatro Grande in Trieste on 25 October, but the composer does not participate in the rehearsals or the performance. In May, Verdi purchases an estate at Sant'Agata, which will become his home for the remainder of his life. Composes *La battaglia di Legnano* from summer through mid-December. Also dating from this year, in which revolutions broke out throughout Europe, is a setting of Goffredo Mameli's patriotic hymn "Suoni la tromba" for three-part male chorus.

1849   Verdi assists with rehearsals and the premiere performance of *La battaglia di Legnano* in Rome (27 January). Begins collaboration with Cammarano on

Luisa Miller; the work premieres at San Carlo in Naples on 8 December under Verdi's direction. A short song, "L'abandonnée," dedicated to Giuseppina Strepponi, appears as a supplement to *La France musicale.*

1850   Considers many possibilities for new operas, including the dramas that eventually became *Il trovatore, Stiffelio,* and *Rigoletto;* also returns to the idea of an opera based on *King Lear* and begins some correspondence with Cammarano about the project. In March, accepts a contract for a new opera at La Fenice. Begins work on *Rigoletto* (in earlier versions called *La maledizione* then *Il duca di Vendôme*) for the Venice commission as well as *Stiffelio* for the Teatro Grande in Trieste. In early October, the composer directs a performance of *Macbeth* in Bologna. *Stiffelio* premieres under Verdi's direction on 16 November in Trieste, while the composer continues to encounter difficulties with the Venetian censors about *Rigoletto.* On 26 December, La Scala presents the premiere of *Gerusalemme,* an Italian version of *Jérusalem.*

1851   The impasse with the Venetian censors is finally broken, and *Rigoletto* premieres at La Fenice under Verdi's direction on 11 March. Later that spring the composer sends an outline for *Il trovatore* to Cammarano, and he and Giuseppina formally relocate to a farmhouse on the Sant'Agata estate. In October, Verdi returns to Bologna to supervise performances of *Macbeth* and *Luisa Miller.* In November, composes a song for tenor and piano, "Fiorellin che sorge appena." On 10 December, Verdi and Giuseppina leave Sant'Agata for Paris, where they will spend the holidays and the first months of the new year.

1852   While in Paris during February, signs a contract with the Opéra for *Les vêpres sicilennes* and attends a performance of Dumas's play *La dame aux camélias,* which will soon become the basis for *La traviata.* Verdi returns to Sant'Agata in March; two months later he signs a contract with La Fenice for *La traviata.* Forward momentum on *Il trovatore* is stopped by Cammarano's continuing illness; he dies on 17 July. In late September, Verdi enlists the help of Leone Emanuele Bardare to complete the libretto and a month later signs a contract with the Teatro Apollo in Rome for the new opera. *Il trovatore* is completed in mid-December and Verdi leaves for Rome for rehearsals.

1853   *Il trovatore* premieres under Verdi's direction on 19 January. He returns immediately to Sant'Agata, rushing to complete *La traviata.* By mid-February he has finished the new opera except for the orchestration and travels to Venice for rehearsals. The premiere takes place on 6 March. He again considers taking up *Re Lear,* this time in collaboration with Antonio Somma.

Problems getting the libretto for *Vêpres* and other information from Paris lead Verdi to consider cancelling his contract with the Opéra. In October Verdi and Strepponi leave for Paris, where he receives the libretto from Scribe and works out other details with the management of the Opéra.

1854   Much of the year, starting in about March, is devoted to composing *Vêpres* and to working through difficulties with Scribe and the Paris Opéra. Rehearsals for the new opera begin in October, but after little more than a week, Sofia Cruvelli, the lead soprano, disappears for a month. On 26 December, the composer conducts *Il trovatore* at the Théâtre-Italien.

1855   *Vêpres* finally premieres at the Opéra on 13 June. In the fall, Verdi supervises an Italian translation of *Vêpres* by Arnoldo Fusinato and a French translation of *Il trovatore* by Emilien Pacini. On 26 December, *Vêpres* premieres in Italy at the Teatro Ducale in Parma and the Teatro Regio in Turin under the title of *Giovanna di Guzman*.

1856   In mid-March, supervises a revival of *La traviata* in Venice. Throughout much of the spring, he and Piave work on revising *Stiffelio* into *Aroldo*. In May, signs a contract with La Fenice for a new opera the following season (*Simon Boccanegra*); also begins negotiations lasting almost a year with San Carlo in Naples for a new opera (Verdi at first thinks of writing *Re Lear*, but eventually decides upon *Un ballo in maschera*). During the summer, Verdi and Strepponi travel to Paris, where he negotiates with the Opéra about producing *Il trovatore* in French translation and tries to press legal injunctions against the impresario Calzado. In September, work begins on *Simon Boccanegra*.

1857   The premiere of *Le trouvère* takes place at the Opéra on 12 January under the composer's direction. On 12 March conducts the premiere of *Simon Boccanegra* at La Fenice; he makes some changes for a production of the work in Reggio Emilia in May, at which he supervises rehearsals. The end of July and first of August are devoted to preparing *Aroldo* for its premiere in Rimini on 16 August. Upon his return to Sant'Agata in September, Verdi begins work with Somma on the new opera for Naples, based on Scribe's *Gustavo III di Svezia*. Due to difficulties with the censors, the libretto is revised several times, changing its name from *Gustavo III* to *Una vendetta in domino*.

1858   Verdi completes scoring for *Una vendetta* on his trip to Naples. In mid-February, however, the censors demand radical changes in the libretto, including a change of title to *Adelia degli Adimari*. The composer refuses to have the work performed in Naples and enters into negotiations for its premiere at the Teatro Apollo in Rome. To fulfill his contract with San Carlo, Verdi agrees to stage *Simon Boccanegra* in the fall. Much of the late summer and fall is occupied with revising *Una vendetta* to satisfy the Roman censors; its title now becomes *Un ballo in maschera*.

1859 *Ballo* premieres on 17 February. During the summer, Verdi and Strepponi marry at Collognes-sous-Salève (near Geneva). In September, the people of Busseto elect Verdi to represent them at an assembly in Parma. Together with other delegates from Parma, Verdi travels to Turin where they request annexation to the Kingdom of Piedmont.

1860 Verdi and Strepponi spend most of the winter in Genoa and most of the remainder of the year at Sant'Agata. In mid-December, he receives a commission for a new opera for the Imperial Theater in St. Petersburg.

1861 Elected a deputy in the first Italian parliament and spends much of the spring in Turin carrying out political duties. During much of the second part of the year, the composer completes *La forza del destino* (except scoring) for the St. Petersburg commission. In late November, Verdi and Giuseppina leave for Russia via Paris. After arriving in St. Petersburg, however, the prima donna Emma Lagrua falls ill, and the production is postponed for a year.

1862 On his return trip through Paris (late February–March), composes the cantata *Inno delle nazioni* for the forthcoming International Exposition in London. Verdi meets Arrigo Boito, who wrote the cantata text, for the first time. In late April and May, witnesses the premiere of the cantata at Her Majesty's Theatre, then travels to Turin for a session of Parliament in June. During August, completes the scoring of *Forza* and begins another trip to Russia, again passing through Paris. The opera premieres on 10 November under the composer's direction, and by early December the couple start their return trip to Paris, where they arrive in mid-December.

1863 The Verdis travel from Paris to Madrid, where he directs a performance of *Forza* at the Teatro Real on 21 February. After traveling through Spain in late February and early March, Verdi returns to Paris to supervise a new production of *Vêpres* at the Opéra on 20 July. The following day, he leaves for Turin and Busseto. In December composes a song "Il bridigin" for soprano Isabella Gianoli.

1864 During this year Verdi and Giuseppina travel to Turin several times for sessions of the Parliament and also visit Genoa several times during the first half of the year. During the summer, Émile Perrin broaches the subject of a new opera for Paris, but with no immediate result. In late October, Léon Escudier asks Verdi to prepare a French version of *Macbeth* for performance at the Théâtre-Lyrique. Charles-Louis-Etienne Nuttier and Alexandre

Beaumont prepare the translation; Verdi begins work on revisions in the music.

1865   Completes the revision of *Macbeth* by 3 February. Much of the rest of spring is spent at Parliament; Verdi decides not to run for another term. The revised *Macbeth* premieres on 21 April, but the composer does not attend. By the end of summer, Verdi agrees to revise *Forza* for the Paris Opéra as well as writing a new work for them; he considers again the possibility of taking up *Re Lear* but eventually becomes more interested in *Don Carlos*. Work on the new opera begins in earnest by the end of the year, and the Verdis spend December through mid-March in Paris.

1866   Before leaving Paris, Verdi has completed Act I of *Don Carlos*. The draft of Act IV is finished by early July and the first four acts orchestrated by the end of the month. He returns to Paris and begins work on the final act; it is completed during a month-long stay at Cauterets, a resort in the Pyrenees. Rehearsals with singers begin on 11 August and full-scale rehearsals start in late September. Scoring of the final act is finished in early December.

1867   *Don Carlos* premieres on 11 March. Verdi and Giuseppina leave the next day for Genoa, where they outfit an apartment that they rented the previous fall. This will become a second home for the two until the end of 1874; on 24 April, Verdi is granted honorary citizenship from the city. In late May, Verdi and Giuseppina adopt seven-year-old Filomena (Maria), a relative of Verdi's father. In October, they travel to Bologna, where Verdi supervises preparations for the first performance of *Don Carlo* (in Italian translation by Achille de Lauzières). Angelo Mariani conducts the premiere on 27 October. Two significant deaths occur this year: Carlo Verdi on 14 January and Antonio Barezzi on 21 July. Piave also suffers a stroke in December and remains incapacitated for the rest of his life.

1868   On 30 June meets the national literary hero Alessandro Manzoni in Milan; it is their only personal encounter. When Rossini dies on 13 November, Verdi conceives the idea of a Requiem Mass, individual movements of which would be written by prominent composers. Begins a cautious rapprochement with La Scala, providing advice for a production of *Don Carlos* and agreeing to supervise the production of a revised *Forza* the following year.

1869   Supervises the production of *Forza*, which opens on 27 February. During the summer Verdi completes a setting of *Libera me*, his contribution toward the Requiem for Rossini, but a performance of the hybrid work does not materialize. Receives an invitation to compose a hymn for the celebration of the opening of the Suez Canal but declines. Late in the year, both Camille Du

Locle and Muzio inform Verdi that there would be a favorable opportunity for him to compose a new grand opera for the Cairo opera house.

1870 Plans slowly materialize for *Aida*. By mid-May, receives a synopsis of the libretto by Auguste Mariette and by the end of the month agrees to undertake the project. Composition begins in August and is finished (except for scoring) by mid-November. The work's premiere, planned for January 1871, as well as the European premiere at La Scala, must be postponed as a result of the Franco-Prussian War, which impedes the shipping of scenery and costumes from Paris. At the turn of the year Verdi is offered the directorship of the Naples Conservatory, but declines.

1871 Completes the scoring of *Aida* by mid-January. Much of the late winter and early spring is occupied as a member of a commission to reform Italian conservatories. In November, Verdi travels to Bologna to hear the Italian premiere of *Lohengrin*. During late November and December, principal singers for La Scala's production of *Aida* rehearse with the composer in Genoa. The Cairo premiere takes place on 24 December under the direction of Giovanni Bottesini.

1872 Supervises preparations for La Scala's production of *Aida*, which premieres on 8 February under the baton of Franco Faccio; also supervises the production of the work at Parma in April and of a revised *Don Carlo* in Naples in November. Plans are made during the spring for French productions of *Aida* and *Forza*, and Camille Du Locle begins to prepare translations of both works.

1873 Supervises and directs the Neapolitan premiere of *Aida*, which takes place on 30 March. The following evening attends a private performance of his string quartet, composed during a lull in rehearsals the previous weeks. During the spring, resolves to undertake a long considered project of expanding his *Libera me* movement into a full Requiem Mass. When Manzoni dies in May, Verdi decides to dedicate the work to him, planning the premiere performance on the first anniversary of his death. He begins the composition in Paris, where he and Giuseppina spend much of the summer.

1874 The *Requiem* is completed by 10 April, and Verdi travels to Milan to conduct rehearsals in early May. The work premieres at the Church of San Marco on 22 May followed by a performance at La Scala three days later, both under Verdi's direction. He then travels to Paris for rehearsals of the work there and conducts seven performances at the Opéra-Comique. In late June the composer travels to London to explore the possibility for a performance of the work there. Later in the year, Verdi is appointed senator of the Kingdom of

Italy. The Verdis also relinquish their old apartment in Genoa and set up new accommodations at the Palazzo Doria.

1875   Plans begin to materialize for a European tour featuring the *Requiem*. Verdi rehearses the soloists during early April in Milan before presenting performances in Paris at the Opéra-Comique, in London at Albert Hall, and in Vienna at the Hofoperntheater. Verdi conducts *Aida* twice at the Hofoperntheater with the soloists from the Requiem performance.

1876   Verdi and Giuseppina spend most of the winter in Genoa. In late March, they leave for Paris to supervise performances of *Aida* and the *Requiem* at the Théâtre-Italien in April, May, and June. While in Paris consults with Nuitter and Du Locle about the translation of *Aida* into French.

1877   In May, the composer conducts the *Requiem* at the Lower Rhine Music Festival in Cologne. During the trip home, he and Giuseppina visit Holland, Belgium, and Paris.

1878   Makes several short trips to Paris, Monte Carlo, and Genoa. On 11 October their adopted daughter Maria marries Alberto Carrara.

1879   Conducts a benefit performance of the *Requiem* at La Scala on 30 June for the victims of floods that spring in the Po River Valley. Giulio Ricordi attempts to bring Boito and Verdi together for an operatic project. After seeing a brief sketch for a libretto on *Otello*, Verdi provides mild encouragement, and Boito sets to work on a more extensive draft for a libretto, which is finished in mid-September and sent to Verdi two months later. On 20 November, Verdi arrives in Milan, where he discusses the *Otello* project with Boito and Ricordi and formally acquires the rights to the libretto.

1880   In February travels to Paris to supervise rehearsals of *Aida* (in French translation) at the Paris Opéra; Verdi conducts the performance, which premieres on 22 March. On April 18, Faccio presents a performance of the composer's *Pater noster* and *Ave Maria* at La Scala; Verdi is in attendance. By late summer, Boito forwards a revised libretto and, in response to Verdi's suggestions, a new version of the Act III finale in mid-October. The composer postpones work on the new opera to begin revising *Simon Boccanegra*, scheduled for performance at La Scala early the next year.

1881   Musical revisions for *Boccanegra* begin early this year, while Boito completes revisions in the libretto by early February. In late February, Verdi has completed work on *Simon* and travels to Milan, where he directs the premiere on 24 March. In July Giulio Ricordi and Boito visit Sant'Agata to discuss *Otello*; later that month, Boito forwards revisions for the Act III finale. Léon

Escudier dies, leaving his firm in bankruptcy and raising the question of ownership for Verdi's scores in France.

1882   Muzio encourages the composer to consider making a shorter version of *Don Carlo* that would be more appealing to theaters and the public. In a trip to Paris during May, Verdi attempts to settle legal matters relating to the Escudier bankruptcy and consults with Charles Nuitter and Camille Du Locle regarding the revision of *Don Carlo* and the translation of *Forza* and *Simon Boccanegra* into French. Revising *Don Carlo* occupies Verdi most of fall and winter.

1883   The revision of *Don Carlo* is completed by mid-March. At the end of the year, travels to Milan to supervise the production of the opera at La Scala.

1884   The revised *Don Carlo* premieres at La Scala on 10 January. The composer slowly begins to work on *Otello*.

1885   Work continues on *Otello*, particularly in the fall. Boito and Ricordi visit Sant'Agata in October to discuss performers and staging.

1886   Makes a brief trip to Paris in March to hear Victor Maurel perform; he begins negotiations for Maurel to take the part of Iago. Plans are laid to initiate a French translation of the new opera. *Otello* is completed by 1 November.

1887   Supervises rehearsals of *Otello* during much of January; the work premieres on 5 February. During the remainder of the year there are many trips to Busseto, Genoa, and Milan.

1888   Anonymously endows and builds a hospital in Villanova; more publicly arranges for the building and endowment of a Casa di Riposo per Musicisti (rest home for musicians) in Milan.

1889   In June, discusses the prospects of an opera on *Falstaff* with Boito. Only a few days after Boito sends him a draft for a libretto, Verdi decides to undertake the project. Boito comes to Sant'Agata in November with the libretto for Acts I and II.

1890   Boito sends the libretto for Act III in early March; about the same time, Verdi has completed composing Act I. Emanuele Muzio dies on 27 November.

1891   Most of *Falstaff* is completed by mid-September, and Verdi begins orchestrating the work. Franco Faccio dies on 21 July.

1892   To celebrate the centenary of Rossini's birth, Verdi conducts the "Preghiera" from *Mosè* at La Scala on 8 April. Details about the premiere of *Falstaff* are worked out with Boito and Ricordi at the end of July and again in October. By late September, the composer has finished the orchestration except for the opening part of Act II.

1893   Rehearsals for *Falstaff* begin during the first days of January; Verdi directs the premiere on 9 February. Verdi and Giuseppina travel with Boito for productions of the opera in Genoa (early April) and Rome (14 April), where they share the royal box with King Umberto and Queen Margherita. In September, Boito visits Sant'Agata to discuss a French translation of *Falstaff*.

1894   In early April the Verdis travel to Paris for the Parisian premiere of *Falstaff*, which contains some revisions in both text and music. Later in the year, Verdi returns to Paris to supervise the premiere of *Othello* at the Opéra, for which he composes new ballet music. At the end of the year, the composer writes a short setting of *Pietà Signor* for the benefit of victims of an earthquake in southern Italy.

1895   Composes a setting of the *Te Deum* in April.

1896   Makes several trips to Milan to oversee the construction of the Casa di Riposo.

1897   More trips to Milan about the Casa di Riposo. In late October, sends the *Quattro pezzi sacri* to Ricordi for publication. Giuseppina dies on 14 November.

1898   The *Stabat mater, Laudi alla Vergine,* and *Te Deum* are performed for the first time at the Paris Opéra on 7 April but, on the advice of his physician, Verdi does not attend.

1899   Formally completes the endowment of the Casa di Riposo.

1900   Visits Milan in May to finalize his will and again in mid-December, where he celebrates the arrival of the New Year with Ricordi, Boito, Teresa Stolz, and other acquaintances. Asks Maria Carrara to destroy his early compositions.

1901   Suffers a fatal stroke in his hotel room on 21 January. Dies at 2:50 a.m. on 27 January and is buried next to Giuseppina in the Cimitero Monumentale on 30 January. The coffins are moved to a crypt in the Casa di Riposo on 26 February, accompanied by a massive public ceremony.

A Short Biographical Dictionary of People Associated With Verdi

Appiani, Giuseppina (ca. 1797 – ?). Born Countess Strigelli. In her salon outside of Milan, the young Verdi mingled with some of the most influential figures in Milanese society.

Arditi, Luigi (1822–1903). Violinist, conductor, and composer. Directed the premiere of Verdi's *Inno delle nazioni* at Her Majesty's Theatre in London in 1862, as well as British and American premieres of many other Verdi works.

Arrivabene, Count Opprandino (1805–87). Italian patriot and literary figure, editor of the *Gazzetta di Torino* during the early days of the Italian Republic. Became a close friend of Verdi; item 43 provides a published edition of their correspondence.

Balestra, Luigi (1808–63). Lawyer and poet from Busseto. Translator of two Goethe poems set by Verdi in his *Sei romanze* (1838); also wrote the text for a duet Verdi planned to add to *Oberto* for an 1841 revival in Genoa.

Barbieri-Nini, Marianna (1818–1887). Italian soprano, whose relatively short career spanned the years 1840–56. Verdi created the role of Lady Macbeth for her in 1847, although his initial choice for the role had been Sofia Loewe.

Bardare, Leone Emanuele (1820 – ca. 1874). Neapolitan librettist, who completed *Il trovatore* after the death of Cammarano. Also prepared an altered version of *Rigoletto* entitled *Clara di Perth* under the direction of Neapolitan censors for a performance in December 1857.

Barezzi, Antonio (1798–1867). The young Verdi's patron and eventual father-in-law, a merchant and amateur musician from Busseto. His financial assistance enabled the composer to obtain advanced musical training in Milan and later helped to establish his career. The composer considered him to be a "second father," to whom he felt closer emotionally than to his real father.

Barezzi, Margherita (1814–40). Verdi's first wife. She bore him two children, Virginia (1837–38) and Icilio (1838–40).

Basevi, Abramo (1818–95). Florentine music critic and composer. Today he is best known for his *Studio sulle opere di Giuseppe Verdi* (see item 460), considered the first serious analytical study of Verdi's works and an important monument that has provided a theoretical foundation for modern scholars. See item 491 for a recent assessment of the significance of Basevi's work for modern Verdi scholarship.

Boito, Arrigo (1842–1918). Poet, composer, and librettist for Verdi's last two operas, *Otello* and *Falstaff.* He also wrote the text for *Inno delle nazioni* and revised the libretto of *Simon Boccanegra.* Became a close friend of Verdi in his later years. See item 46 for a critical edition of their correspondence, as well as the items listed under Boito in Chapter 5.

Bottesini, Giovanni (1821–1889).   Italian double bass virtuoso, composer, and conductor. Conducted the premiere of *Aida* in Cairo in 1871; Verdi later formally nominated him to be director of the Parma Conservatory.

Brenna, Guglielmo (1806 or 1807 – after 1882). Executive secretary to the presidency at La Fenice from 1843–82, with a break between 1859–67, when the theater was closed during a period of Austrian rule. Brenna was incarcerated for a while in Bohemia for revolutionary activities; after his release, he remained in exile in Florence until Venice was formally united with Italy in 1866. Brenna carried on much correspondence with Verdi on behalf of the presidency at La Fenice (which regularly rotated), negotiating details about the production of *Ernani, Rigoletto, Simon Boccanegra,* and *La traviata.*

Cammarano, Salvatore (1801–1852). Librettist and playwright (although his original training was in painting and sculpture). Wrote many librettos for nineteenth-century opera composers, including four for Verdi: *Alzira, La battaglia di Legnano, Luisa Miller* and *Il trovatore.* Verdi also considered collaborating with Cammarano on *Re Lear.* See item 204 for a recent biography. A critical edition of his important correspondence with Verdi will soon be published; see item 48.

Canti, Giovanni. Milanese music publisher who issued Verdi's first published compositions, the *Sei romanze,* in 1838 and well as several additional works the following year.

Carrara, Alberto (1854–1925). Lawyer and husband of the Verdis' adopted daughter and legal heir, Filomena Maria Verdi.

Carvalho, Léon (1825–1897). Director of the Parisian Théâtre-Lyrique during several periods starting in 1856; under his direction the theater presented significant productions of *Rigoletto* and *La traviata*, as well as the revised *Macbeth* in 1865. During the years 1868–72, Carvalho managed the Cairo Opera, which hosted the premiere of *Aida* in 1871.

Corticelli, Mauro. A theatrical agent working for Alessandro Lanari at the Teatro Comunale in Bologna for 15 years, he later managed the theatrical company of Adelaide Ristori. From 1867–79 Corticelli served as an administrator for Verdi at his Sant'Agata estate, where he assisted the composer in a variety of business and personal affairs.

De Amicis, Giuseppe. Genoese engineer, and the Verdis' business agent in Genoa. Item 50 reproduces their correspondence.

De Sanctis, Cesare (? – 1881). Neapolitan businessman and close personal friend of the Verdis and Cammarano. See item 51 for his correspondence with the Verdis.

Delfico, Melchiorre (1825–95). Neapolitan artist, composer, and poet who became a good friend of Verdi. His caricatures of Verdi have been widely reproduced (see item 113).

Draneht, Paul Bey (born Pavlos Pavlidis) (1815–94. Greek Cypriot who settled in Egypt and became superintendant of railways and intendant of the Cairo Opera house. Commissioned *Aida*.

Du Locle, Camille (1832–93). French librettist and impresario; son-in-law and secretary to Emile Perrin, director of the Paris Opéra from 1862–70 and afterward the Opéra-Comique. At the end of his tenure there, he sponsored important performances of Verdi's *Requiem* conducted by the composer. Du Locle completed the libretto of *Don Carlos* after the death of Joseph Méry; he later condensed the libretto from five to four acts at Verdi's request. Du Locle was also a key figure in persuading Verdi to undertake the composition of *Aida* and assisted in the preparation of its libretto by versifying Mariette's original scenario. He prepared French translations of the librettos for *Aida, La forza del destino* and *Simon Boccanegra*. For important published correspondence with the composer, see the citations and cross-references under "Du Locle" in Chapter 2.

Duveyrier, Charles (1803–66). Author and librettist. Co-authored *Il duca d'Alba* for Donizetti, later revised for Verdi as *Les vêpres siciliennes*.

Escudier, Léon (1815–81). Publisher, author, and impresario, who published most of Verdi's works in France, both at the Bureau Central de Musique and later at his own firm. Founded, with his brother Marie, the important Parisian music journal *La*

France musicale. Assumed directorship of the Théâtre Italien in 1875, but the enormous expenses associated with the French premiere of *Aida* led him to declare bankruptcy and a subsequent complete falling out with Verdi during the final years of his life. See item 354 for his sketch of Verdi's career and references under "Escudier" in Chapter 2 for some of his correspondence with Verdi.

Escudier, Marie (1809–80). Worked closely with his brother, Léon, in music publishing.

Faccio, Franco (1840–91). Conductor and composer. A close friend of Boito during student days. From 1871 to 1889, Faccio served as orchestral director at La Scala. Directed the Italian premiere of *Aida* at La Scala and the premieres of the revised *Simon Boccanegra* and *Otello*. Item 58 includes a biography and excerpts from Faccio's correspondence with Verdi.

Ferrario, Carlo (1833–1907). Stage designer and scene painter, who designed the sets for some important productions of Verdi's operas, including the premieres of *Otello* and *Falstaff.*

Florimo, Francesco (1800–88). Author and librarian at the Naples conservatory, where he had earlier studied during the same time period as Vincenzo Bellini. Became a close friend of the Verdis. See Chapter 2 under "Florimo" for some of their published correspondence.

Gemito, Vincenzo (1852–1929). Sculptor who made busts of Giuseppe and Giuseppina in return for money to buy his exemption from military service.

Ghislanzoni, Antonio (1824–93). Librettist, music critic, writer, and singer (he sang Carlo in an 1851 Parisian production of *Ernani!*). He collaborated with Verdi on the revision of *Don Carlos* and *La forza del destino*, and he prepared the libretto for *Aida.* Item 205 offers a recent conference report dealing with Ghislanzoni; see the entries and cross-references under his name in Chapter 2 for published correspondence.

Ivanoff, Nicola (1810–77). Russian tenor and friend of Rossini, who commissioned Verdi to write substitute arias for him in *Ernani* and *Attila.*

Jacovacci, Vincenzo (1811–81). Italian impresario, associated primarily with the Teatro Apollo in Rome. He mounted the premiere productions of *Il trovatore* and *Un ballo in maschera* at that theater, as well as the first Italian performance of *La forza del destino.*

Lanari, Alessandro (1790–1862). Italian impresario, associated primarily with the Teatro alla Pergola in Florence. Lanari mounted the premiere production of Verdi's *Macbeth*; he also managed the career of Giuseppina Strepponi for some years.

Lavigna, Vincenzo (1776–1836). Composer, long-time *maestro di cembalo* at La Scala, and instructor at the Milan Conservatory. He gave Verdi private instruction for several years after he had been refused admission at the Conservatory.

Lucca, Francesco (1802–72). Owned—with his wife, Giovannina Strazza Lucca (1814–94)—an important music publishing firm. He contracted with Verdi to publish two operas, *I masnadieri* and *Il corsaro*, and had previously acquired rights to *Attila*. Eventually, he ran into difficulties with the composer, who refused to continue dealing with the firm. In later years, Lucca specialized in acquiring the Italian rights to operas by foreign composers, including Wagner.

Lucca, Giovannina Strazza (1814–94). Wife of Francesco Lucca and his business partner in the music publishing business. Her forceful personality and keen business sense was largely responsibile for the firm's growth and success through the late 1880s, when she sold out to Ricordi.

Lumley, Benjamin (1811–75). Impresario at Her Majesty's Theatre in London at various times between 1841–59. Commissioned *I masnadieri* and arranged for Verdi to oversee the premiere production.

Maffei, Andrea (1798–1885). Milanese poet and translator who became close friends with Verdi near the beginning of his career. Author of several poem set as songs by Verdi; librettist for *I masnadieri*; collaborated in the preparation of the libretto for *Macbeth*. Verdi also used his translation of Schiller's *Wallensteins Lager* as the basis for Fra Melitone's sermon in *Forza*.

Maffei, Countess Clara (1814–86). Born Clara Carrara-Spinelli. Important intellectual figure in Milan, where her salon became an important meeting place for artists, writers, and Italian patriots, including Verdi. In 1868, introduced Verdi to Alessandro Manzoni. Married for some time to the writer Andrea Maffei; after their legal separation, became the partner of Carlo Tenca. See Chapter 2 under "Clara Maffei" for several publications of her correspondence.

Manzoni, Alessandro (1785–1873). Generally considered the foremost Italian literary figure of the nineteenth century. Verdi revered him and his work, although they met only once, in 1868. Verdi wrote his *Requiem* to commemorate the first anniversary of Manzoni's death.

Mariani, Angelo (1821–73). Conductor and composer. Directed *I due Foscari* and *I lombardi* in Milan (1846); Verdi was so impressed that he attempted to engage him to direct the premiere of *Macbeth*, but his fees were too high. From 1852 to the end of his life, Mariani was the orchestral director at the Teatro Carlo Felice in Genoa, which he turned into one of the outstanding opera orchestras on the Italian peninsula. He became a close personal friend of Verdi while working on a production of *Aroldo* at Rimini in 1857. Verdi wanted him to direct the Cairo premiere of *Aida*, but illness prevented it. Mariani and Verdi had a falling out in the 1870s over Teresa Stolz (Mariani's former mistress) and Wagner. See items 68 and 69 for some of Mariani's correspondence and item 218 for a recent publication of Mariani's autobiography.

Mariette, August-Édouard (1821–81). French Egyptologist and archeologist who wrote the original scenario for *Aida*. Received honorary title of Bey in 1858 and Pasha in 1879.

Martinelli, Aldo. Family lawyer for the Verdis; drafted Giuseppina's will. Published some of their correspondence in *Verdi: Raggi e penombre* (item 32).

Mascheroni, Edoardo (1852–1941). Conductor and composer. Mascheroni made his conducting debut in Brescia with two works by Verdi, *Macbeth* and *Un ballo in maschera*, and from that time continued to be an important proponent of his works. Between 1891–94, he was the chief conductor at La Scala, where he conducted, at Verdi's request, the premiere performances of *Falstaff*. Later in the decade, he conducted productions of *Falstaff* throughout continental Europe.

Maurel, Victor (1848–1923). French baritone selected by Verdi to create the roles of *Simon Boccanegra* in its revised version, Iago in *Otello*, and the title role in *Falstaff*. He also sang the role of Amonasro in the American premiere of *Aida* (New York Academy of Music, 1873).

Mazzucato, Alberto (1813–77). Conductor, composer, and instructor of singing at the Milan Conservatory; writer and eventually editor for the *Gazzetta musicale di Milano*. Mazzucato was *maestro concertatore* and *direttore d'orchestra* at La Scala between 1859–68. There he conducted the Milanese premiere of *Don Carlo*; item 70 reproduces some especially interesting instructions by Verdi to Mazzucato regarding this performance.

Merelli, Bartolomeo (1794–1879). Impresario and librettist. Merelli was the impresario at La Scala from 1829–50 and 1861–63, where he oversaw the production of Verdi's first four operas. Verdi had a falling out with Merelli after the 1845 production of *Giovanna d'Arco*, vowing not to return to La Scala; his absence there lasted two and a half decades.

Méry, Joseph (1797–1865). Pseudonym of Joseph Pierre Agnes. Librettist and writer. Wrote most of the libretto for *Don Carlos*, but died before its completion.

Mocenigo, Count Alvise. President of La Fenice in Venice during the period that saw the premieres of *Ernani* and *Attila.*

Morelli, Domenico (1826–1901). Neapolitan painter. Painted a portrait of Verdi and exchanged letters with the composer about scenography and costumes for *Otello* (see item 71).

Muzio, Emanuele (1825–90). Verdi's only long-time student, who later became a composer and conductor. Traveled with Verdi during part of his early career, serving at times as his personal secretary; later in life, conducted several U.S. Verdi premieres in New York City. Items 72 and 73 reproduce some of Muzio's important correspondence; see also item 220 for a recent biography.

Nuitter, Charles-Louis-Etienne (1828–99). Librettist and translator who collaborated in the French translation of *Macbeth* (with Alexandre Beaumont), *Aida* (with Camille Du Locle), *Forza* (with Du Locle), and *Simon Boccanegra.* Held the important position of archivist at the Paris Opéra; served for several years as director of the Opéra-Comique. Item 96 reproduces some of Nuitter's correspondence with Verdi.

Perosio, Giuseppe (1844–1922). Genoese music critic and librettist. Author of two books about Verdi, *Cenni biografici su Giuseppe Verdi* (item 130) and *Ricordi verdiani* (item 141). Item 74 reproduces some of Verdi's correspondence with Perosio.

Perrin, Emile-César-Victor (1814–85). Director, at various times, of the Opéra-Comique, the Opéra-Lyrique, the Théâtre-Français, and the Paris Opéra. As director of the Opéra, commissioned Verdi to write *Don Carlos.*

Piave, Francesco Maria (1810–76). Verdi's most frequent collaborator as librettist, working on ten operas from *Ernani* in 1844 to *La forza del destino* in 1862 in addition to completing Solera's work on *Attila.* A stroke in 1867 largely incapacitated him. Items 33, 75, 76, and 344 present some of the letters exchanged between Verdi and Piave; see also 206 for a biographical study.

Piazza, Antonio. Milanese journalist and author of the libretto for *Oberto* (at first called *Lord Hamilton* or *Rocester*), later substantially revised by Solera.

Piccolomini, Maria (1834–99). Soprano who rang roles in many Verdi operas. Verdi particularly admired her performance in *La traviata*; he intended to create the role of Cordelia for her in his aborted *Re Lear* opera.

Piroli, Giuseppe (1815–1900). Childhood friend of Verdi who became a lawyer and important statesman and Senator. Item 77 reproduces some of their voluminous correspondence.

Provesi, Ferdinando (ca. 1770–1833). Verdi's first important music teacher. Provesi was maestro di cappella and organist at the Church of San Bartolomeo in Busseto, director of the Società Filarmonica, and composer of several comic operas that were performed locally. Verdi eventually became his assistant and after Provesi's death assumed his teacher's positions for a short time. Item 221 provides the most substantial available biography of Provesi.

Ricordi, Giovanni. (1785 – 1853). Founder of Casa Ricordi in 1808, the publishing house with which Verdi had the strongest ties. Giovanni built the firm from a small enterprise to being most important publishing house on the Italian peninsula. Later founded the *Gazzetta musicale di Milano*.

Ricordi, Giulio (1840–1912). Son of Tito, and the firm's main liaison with Verdi from the 1870s. Became the real artistic administrator of the firm during the mid-1860s, while Tito dealt primarily with the business end. Giulio's encouragement was a significant factor that led to Verdi's final operas and revisions of several earlier ones. Composed music under the pen name of J. Burgmein; also wrote and painted. Editor of the *Gazzetta musicale di Milano* from 1866. See the entries listed under "Ricordi" in Chapter 2 for a publication of some of the important correspondence between Verdi and the Ricordi firm.

Ricordi, Tito (1811–88). Son of Giovanni. Not so closely linked to Verdi artistically as was his son, Giulio, but rather saw him as a profitable source of revenue. Responsible for adoption of new printing methods and expansion of the Ricordi firm, partly by absorption of other companies.

Royer, Alphonse (1803–75). Librettist and co-director, with Gustave Vaez, of the Paris Opéra. Co-author, with Vaez, of the libretto of *Jérusalem*.

Scribe, Augustin Eugène (1791–1861). Librettist and author; closely associated with the Paris Opéra from the time of its rise to new stature during the 1820s and 30s. Somma based the libretto for *Un ballo in maschera* on Scribe's earlier libretto, *Gustave III*, written for Auber; revised a previously completed libretto, *Le duc d'Albe*, for Verdi's use as *Les vêpres siciliennes*.

Seletti, Pietro (1770–1853). Priest and teacher of Verdi at the Ginnasio in Busseto.

Solera, Antonio (1815–78). Librettist and composer. Revised a libretto by Antonio Piazza that would become *Oberto*, Verdi's first opera; also prepared librettos for *Nabucco*, *I lombardi*, *Giovanna d'Arco*, and *Attila*. He left to assume a job as director in Spain before completing *Attila*, however, and Verdi entrusted its completion to Piave.

Somma, Antonio (1809–64). Librettist, poet, playwright, and lawyer; for some years, director of the Teatro Grande in Trieste. Prepared the libretto for *Un ballo in maschera*; worked with Verdi on the libretto for *Re Lear*, although the opera never materialized. The section devoted to Somma in Chapter 2 lists three significant collections of letters exchanged between him and the composer.

Stolz, Teresa (1834–1902). Soprano of Bohemian birth, who specialized in the performance of Verdi's music. Her career spanned the years between 1857–77. She sang in the Italian premiere of *Don Carlos* and *Aida*, the revised *Forza del destino* (La Scala, 1869), as well as the first performances of the *Requiem*. Verdi devoted considerable attention to Stolz during the 1870s; although their exact relationship is unclear, it spawned jealousy and bitterness on the part of both Giuseppina and Mariani.

Strepponi, Giuseppina (1815–97). Soprano; partner and eventually second wife of Verdi. After graduating from the Milan Conservatory in 1834, she began a successful concert career. She created the role of Abigaille in *Nabucco* at its premiere at La Scala in 1842. By this time, however, her career was already in decline due to health problems and several pregnancies; she retired from the stage in 1846. In October of 1846, Giuseppina moved to Paris, where she taught singing lessons and became reacquainted with Verdi. They seem to have become partners by 1847, but were not officially married until 1859. Giuseppina became a most important figure in Verdi's life, providing not only companionship, but moral and creative support, professional advice, and the ability to act as a skillful intermediary, advocate, and mouthpiece for Verdi in all kinds of situations. While Giuseppe and Giuseppina had no children of their own, in 1867 they adopted a distant relative who had been orphaned, Filomena Maria Verdi. Item 87 presents a highly edited version of Giuseppina's *Copialettere*; see also the entries under Giuseppina Strepponi in Chapter 5 for additional biographical and evaluative studies.

Tamagno, Francesco (1850–1905). Tenor selected by Verdi to create the title role of *Otello*. He had previously sung Gabriele Adorno in the premiere of the revised *Simon Boccanegra* and sang significant roles in other Verdi operas.

Tamberlick, Enrico (1820–89). Tenor who created the role of Don Alvaro in *La forza del destino* and who was largely responsible for both arranging the commission of the work and convincing Verdi to write it. Tamberlick sang roles in many of Verdi's operas. See item 88 for correspondence with the composer about *Forza*.

Tenca, Carlo. (1813–83). Political insurgent, journalist and critic, Clara Maffei's partner after her separation from Andrea, and a close friend of Verdi. Worked, among other places, for *La fama*, *Il cosmorama pittorico*, *Il corriere delle dame*, *Rivista europea* and the house periodical of Francesco Lucca, *L'Italia musicale*. See item 38 for some of his correspondence.

Torelli, Achille (ca. 1844–1922). Neapolitan dramatist; at times, served as manager of the Teatro San Carlo.

Torelli, Vincenzo (ca. 1806–84). Neapolitan journalist and music critic, editor of l'*Omnibus*; father of Achille. Served at various times as secretary of the Teatro San Carlo. A close confidant of Verdi. Items 28 and 89 reproduce some of his important correspondence with Verdi.

Tornaghi, Eugenio (ca. 1844–1915). Served as Ricordi's agent in Milan and therefore conducted much correspondence with Verdi on behalf of the Ricordi firm, particularly concerning contractual details.

Varese, Felice (1813–89). Baritone who created title role of *Macbeth* and *Rigoletto*, as well as the first Germont in *La traviata*.

Vigna, Cesare (1814–1912). Important leader in Italian psychiatry; a close friend of Verdi, with whom he exchanged much correspondence (see item 90); item 223 offers a recent biography of Vigna.

Waldmann, Maria (1842–1920). Austrian mezzo-soprano who sang Amneris in the Italian premiere of *Aida*. Verdi also entrusted her with the mezzo-soprano solo part in his *Requiem*. She became a close friend of the Verdis. Item 91 contains some of Verdi's letters to Waldmann.

Index of Authors, Editors & Translators

Numbers in this index refer to items in the bibliography, not page numbers.

Subject Indexes

The subject indexes are designed to help the reader find items that are not apparent from the category headings in the bibliography; they do not list some items that can be easily found from headings themselves. Numbers refer to items in the bibliography, not pages.

GENERAL ITEMS ABOUT VERDI

VERDI'S CORRESPONDENCE WITH SPECIFIC INDIVIDUALS

VERDI'S MUSIC (GENERAL TOPICS)

VERDI'S MUSIC (INDIVIDUAL COMPOSITIONS)

GENERAL INDEX

Composer Resource Manuals
Guy A. Marco, *General Editor*